GIVING AID EFFECTIVELY

Giving Aid Effectively

THE POLITICS OF ENVIRONMENTAL PERFORMANCE AND SELECTIVITY AT MULTILATERAL DEVELOPMENT BANKS

Mark T. Buntaine

OXFORD
UNIVERSITY PRESS

OXFORD
UNIVERSITY PRESS

Oxford University Press is a department of the University of Oxford. It furthers
the University's objective of excellence in research, scholarship, and education
by publishing worldwide.Oxford is a registered trade mark of Oxford University
Press in the UK and certain other countries.

Published in the United States of America by Oxford University Press
198 Madison Avenue, New York, NY 10016, United States of America.

Library of Congress Cataloging-in-Publication Data
Names: Buntaine, Mark T., author.
Title: Giving aid effectively : the politics of environmental performance and selectivity at multilateral
development banks / Mark T. Buntaine.
Description: Oxford ; New York : Oxford University Press, [2016] | Includes bibliographical references
and index.
Identifiers: LCCN 2015034920 | ISBN 978-0-19-046745-6 (hardcover : alk. paper)
Subjects: LCSH: Economic development projects—Environmental aspects—Developing countries. |
Economic assistance—Environmental aspects—Developing countries. | Environmental policy—
Economic aspects—Developing countries.
Classification: LCC HC59.72.E44 B86 2016 | DDC 332.1/53—dc23 LC record available at http://lccn.
loc.gov/2015034920

9 8 7 6 5 4 3 2 1
Printed by Sheridan, USA

Contents

Preface

THIS PROJECT BEGAN with a rather simple observation: very little evidence was available to assess whether investments in evaluation and learning make international organizations more effective. This book is an attempt to understand how project evaluation, strategic planning, citizen complaint mechanisms, and administrative procedures can be used to steer international organizations toward decisions that more effectively achieve their mandates. I focus specifically on the environmental performance of the multilateral development banks, since activities related to preventing environmental harm and promoting good environmental management have faced intense scrutiny over the past three decades. My purpose is not to retell a history about performance diverging from mandate; I seek instead to understand when and why environmental performance can be improved by producing better information about the outcomes of the development and environmental activities of the multilateral development banks.

The other purpose of this book is to propose a better way to give development assistance. Researchers and the development community have converged around the idea that development assistance is most effective when it is provided to recipient countries that have the capacity and incentives to use it well. Most scholarly and practical effort has focused on identifying capacity and aligned incentives at the level of countries, often through indices of the quality of governance or policy. The challenge with this approach is that it tends to shift development assistance toward the middle-income countries that have the least need for it. I argue that by producing better information about the outcomes of development and environmental assistance, organizations that allocate development assistance can be more focused and move toward the projects that have a successful record and away from projects that have an unsuccessful record for individual countries. This book demonstrates that a focused approach can work.

I could not have completed this project without the assistance and support of numerous people. Over the several years that it took to complete this project, our research team poured through hundreds of thousands of pages of more than 1,000 evaluations and compiled primary documentation for a number of case studies that appear in this book. More than 50 staff members and managers at the multilateral development banks provided me interviews. I also received invaluable advice and support from mentors and colleagues as I pulled together the evidence in this book. I gratefully acknowledge these various contributions.

I have benefited greatly from the research assistance of Sarah Freitas, Susan Carter, Selim Selimi, Jacob Wolff, Hannah Freedman, and Varun Kumar. Coding hundreds of documents that are each hundreds of pages long is an arduous and unseen task. This book would not have been possible without their diligent work. I am also grateful to Rahul Madhusudanan, who helped compile the primary documentation for many of the case studies that appear in this book. His keen eye for relevant evidence has been a valuable asset.

I benefited from the time of numerous staff members at the World Bank, Asian Development Bank, African Development Bank, and Inter-American Development Bank, who for reasons of confidentiality must remain anonymous. The interviews that these staff provided assisted me in understanding the incentives at multilateral development banks to use information about performance. The interviewees greatly influenced many of the conclusions reported in this book and I hope will bring to life many of the findings from the statistical analyses.

Many people have offered guidance and suggestion in the design of this research and writing this book. Like many books, the seed of this book was a dissertation. Erika Weinthal was an excellent dissertation supervisor, even when I was not sure of my direction. She has been a steadfast advocate and has always encouraged me to think broadly about the implications of this research. Judith Kelley, through her consistent engagement with the core theoretical issues of this project and her constructive approach to the research process, has shaped my intellectual journey in lasting ways. Chris Gelpi and Meg McKean provided important comments about this research at various points, and this book is surely better for their efforts. I received other important support for this project while I was completing doctoral studies at Duke University, including comments from seminar participants and several travel and fellowship grants. A National Science Foundation Decision, Risk, and Management Sciences Doctoral Research Grant (#0962436) supported this work, without which it would have been impossible to collect the evaluation and interview data that I use as the basis of this book.

I expanded and began refining the dissertation into a book while I was a faculty member in the Department of Government at the College of William & Mary. I owe a special debt to Mike Tierney, who has been one of my greatest advocates as I turned this project into a book. He organized an extremely helpful book workshop, where I received exhaustive comments from Tamar Gutner, Joe Jupille, Christopher Kilby, Paula Manna, Amy Oakes, Brad Parks, Sue Peterson, and Maurits van der Veen. These comments shaped the development of this book greatly and assisted me in honing the arguments and presentation of evidence. I also received excellent and helpful comments on the penultimate version of this book from Sarah Bush and Ron Mitchell. The reviewers for this manuscript took their jobs very seriously and offered insightful comments that have shaped the final product, particularly regarding the presentation of qualitative evidence.

Finally, the long road that is a book project would not have been nearly as enjoyable without the support of friends and family. I would like to extend a special thanks to my parents, Robbie and Jim Buntaine, for always supporting my education and to my wife, Ryoko Oono, who has endured many years of living separately and countless late evenings so that I could complete this project. To them, and a large number of supportive friends, I am forever grateful.

GIVING AID EFFECTIVELY

1

The Problem of Performance

CONTROLLING PERFORMANCE AT INTERNATIONAL ORGANIZATIONS

International organizations are involved in managing and responding to almost all problems that cross national borders. They facilitate international bargaining, coordinate the activities of different countries, provide technical expertise, develop transboundary programs, and implement international agreements. International organizations are so important for global governance because they do many of these tasks better than individual countries acting alone.

Yet relying on international organizations can have a number of downsides. The management and staff of international organizations might not have the same goals as their member countries. It can be difficult for member countries to coordinate the management of international organizations when they want different outcomes. International organizations are not always accountable to the local people affected by their activities, since they are not subject to democratic feedback. Like many large organizations, international organizations can be slow to change and adapt to new circumstances and demands from their member countries. This book addresses the challenge of managing international organizations to take advantage of their useful capabilities while limiting their downsides.

The benefits and challenges of relying on international organizations come into particular focus for development assistance. Large bodies of research show that development assistance is not always allocated and managed to achieve the best results. The empirical focus of this book is the allocation of development and environmental projects by the multilateral development banks, which for a number of reasons offer an excellent platform to investigate the more general challenge of controlling international organizations. More practically, allocation decisions are also vitally important for international development and environmental management. Member countries rely on the multilateral development banks to allocate development and environmental projects because the development banks concentrate expertise, have advantages in managing programs, and help coordinate the development goals of various countries.

However, the multilateral development banks have been severely criticized, often by member countries themselves, for failing to meet their mandated environmental and social objectives. In response to significant and public failures, member countries set up or strengthened administrative procedures, complaint mechanisms, project evaluation, and strategic planning at the multilateral development banks. Research about international organizations has focused on blunt tools like restricting discretion (Cortell and Peterson 2006), reforming international organizations (Nielson and Tierney 2003), and reducing appropriations for international organizations (Lavelle 2011). I investigate when and why finer and more practical control mechanisms have been effective at aligning the allocation of aid with results.

The main outcome of interest in this book is whether these control mechanisms have increased the allocation of projects with a successful record and decreased the allocation of projects with an unsuccessful record—a practice called *selectivity*. Practically speaking, selectivity is critical for increasing the positive impact of scarce development and environmental financing. I argue and demonstrate that member countries can promote selectivity and thereby give aid more effectively when they generate information about the outcomes of the decisions made by international organizations and use that information to modify how easy new projects are to approve. Neither of these two steps alone is sufficient.

Information to promote selectivity can be generated by independent evaluators or external parties. In turn, this information can be used to modify the incentives of staff by making it harder to approve projects with a poor record or easier to approve projects with a good record in a particular country. This can happen either because information helps staff make decisions about which projects will be difficult to steer through preparation procedures or because it decreases uncertainty for borrowing countries about projects that are likely to be successful. In the context of this study, that means aid can be given more effectively. By linking information about outcomes with decision-making processes that include real barriers to approval, member countries take advantage of the benefits international organizations offer while limiting many of the downsides. Before proceeding to my specific argument, it is useful to consider the point in history that brought the challenge of controlling the multilateral development banks to the fore.

The World Bank entered the 1990s at odds with both environmental advocates and the countries that contributed the bulk of its funds. These tensions went on display during the planning of a dam project in the Narmada Valley, India. The $3 billion project to build the Sardar Sarovar Dam, partially financed by the World Bank, was expected to displace up to a quarter million residents and inundate more than 130,000 hectares of forest that was important for local livelihoods. Environmental advocacy groups in India argued that beyond these immediate impacts, millions of poor villagers would be affected by the degradation of forest and freshwater resources downstream.[1] According to advocacy groups, the Indian government had a poor record compensating the people harmed by large development projects. They cited examples of multiyear delays in compensating local residents for the deadly and widespread toxic releases of the World Bank–funded Union Carbide chemical plant in Bhopal. In October 1989, the *New York Times* reported the reaction of one Narmada Valley resident who would lose land because of the Sardar Sarovar dam: "They [the Indian government] will never find us land like this" (Crossette 1989).

These concerns echoed around the world. Environmental groups based in the United States, such as the Environmental Defense Fund, lobbied the World Bank to withdraw support for the project (Crossette 1989). Lawmakers in the United States took note. In October 1989, the US House of Representatives Subcommittee on Natural Resources, Agricultural Research and Environment held a hearing about the Sardar Sarovar dam, during which a range of lawmakers expressed concerns that the new World Bank president, Barber Conable, was not following through on earlier commitments to limit environmental harms in World Bank projects. A number of lawmakers called for greater oversight of the World Bank. As chairman of the committee James Scheuer commented about the Sardar Sarovar project specifically, "The American taxpayer and the American Government and certainly the American Congress does not want to pour money down the drain into capital-intensive, labor-saving projects that are misguided and—and badly designed to meet the needs of those [Indian] people" (Sardar Sarovar Dam Project 1989, 4). Lori Udall of the Environmental Defense Fund testified that "we have seen that the environmental reforms [at the World Bank] have had few positive tangible results in ongoing projects in developing countries which we've been monitoring" (Sardar Sarovar Dam Project 1989, 5).

Concerns about the *performance* of the World Bank—its achievement of established policies, mandates, and objectives—were not exclusive to the United States. Other donor countries raised concerns that the World Bank was not living up to established policies and mandates. In 1990, for example, the United Kingdom led the charge to eliminate World Bank financing for extractive forestry projects, recognizing that these projects often failed to live up to established environmental policies (Palmer 1990). Facing this pressure, the World Bank adopted a moratorium on extractive forestry projects in September 1990. In early 1991, the World Bank adopted a new forestry policy that excluded financing for the extraction of timber from primary forests and required infrastructure projects located in or near primary forests to undergo strict environmental assessments (*Globe and Mail* 1991). Reacting to the shortcomings with the Sardar Sarovar Dam, the Japanese International Cooperation Agency withdrew its own financing for the project in May 1990, which the *Tokyo Shimbun* newspaper attributed to "the carelessness of environmental and cultural impact assessment conducted prior to the project's start" (as reported in Pearce 1990). Donor countries united behind the position that World Bank actions had fallen short of established policies. In other words, the World Bank had a performance problem.

Calls for improved supervision of the World Bank grew. Buoyed by international support, residents of the Narmada Valley participated in protests that reached tens of thousands of people, often clashing with police near construction sites. Protests became a regular occurrence outside the World Bank in Washington, D.C. Elected representatives to the US Congress, the most important veto power at the World Bank, began to talk about withholding funds from the World Bank unless the World Bank further reformed its environmental and social policies and implemented them diligently. In a March 22, 1990, hearing of the Foreign Operations Subcommittee of the Senate Appropriations Committee, Senator Patrick Leahy was very clear about how badly lawmakers in the United States thought the World Bank had deviated from expectations:

> I'm going to be very reluctant to support any contribution to the World Bank next year if their environmental image doesn't improve and if their environmental sensitivity doesn't dramatically improve.... I hope the World Bank is listening carefully. If they don't get their act together on the environment, they may get other votes in the Senate, but they won't get my vote for any contribution whatsoever. (World Bank Fiscal Year 1991 Appropriations 1990)

Activist groups even persuaded the United States to vote against other dam projects that the World Bank was considering, a major departure from past practice (Crossette 1992). After sustained pressure from activist groups and US lawmakers, the World Bank withdrew from the Sardar Sarovar project in 1993.

This is not where the story ends. Member states realized that they needed more effective ways to supervise the multilateral development banks and manage the discretion they granted to them. An independent commission was appointed to review the Sardar Sarovar project and to generate lessons about improving the performance of the World Bank. The Morse Commission, as it was called in shorthand, found systematic flaws in planning, design, and implementation of the Sardar Sarovar project (Morse and Berger 1992). In an effort to have the project approved quickly, the World Bank had not ensured that displaced people would be properly compensated or that the environmental consequences of the dam would be properly managed. As the Morse report noted, "There developed an eagerness on the part of the Bank and India to get on with the job. Both, it seems, were prepared to ease, or even disregard, Bank policy and India's regulations and procedures dealing with resettlement and environmental protection" (Morse and Berger 1992, ch. 17). The report highlighted a number of grave risks posed to local people by the project, such as the spread of malaria by irrigation canals. Such risks were not assessed according to established environmental policies.

Concerns grew that the World Bank had a more general problem. The Morse Commission report was part of a growing body of evidence that the World Bank was not using the authority and discretion it had been granted to design and implement projects in the interest of donor countries. For example, significant alarm was raised also about the Polonoroeste road project in Brazil, which caused rapid and widespread deforestation (Rich 1994). With external concerns growing, World Bank president Lewis Preston commissioned a systematic, internal review of performance across the entire lending portfolio. This portfolio review described a system of incentives within the World Bank that favored rapid approval of loans over careful appraisal and supervision (Wapenhans 1992). Donor countries, and especially the United States, began to realize that the World Bank was in need of better oversight if it was to simultaneously manage large amounts of development assistance and protect local people from negative environmental and social consequences of development projects. As Barney Frank, chairman of the US House Subcommittee on International Development, Finance, and Trade said during a June 21, 1994, hearing, "[Reforms] are important if we are to maintain within the country and the Congress representing the country support for continued appropriations to the Bank."[2]

This episode raises important questions about how the World Bank had come to be so out of step with its largest and most influential member countries. Although the United States had instigated changes to environmental policies at the World Bank beginning in 1987, including the creation of a dedicated environmental office to implement environmental policies and operating guidelines, the World Bank did not live up to expectations. Within scholarship on international relations, this type of problem has become a major concern, prompting a large body of research about when and why international organizations act in ways that are misaligned with the interests of their member countries (Abbott and Snidal 1998; Pollack 1997; Barnett and Finnemore 1999; Nielson and Tierney 2003; Gutner 2005; Martens 2005; Weaver 2010; Frey 2006). Such concerns also appear in the popular media, where international organizations are criticized for being unaccountable to the states that set them up, especially among the publics of powerful states that have other options for conducting their foreign relations. For example, criticisms of the "unaccountable" United Nations are common in the mass media and think tanks in the United States.[3] If international organizations so commonly and routinely act counter to the interests of their member countries, then their wide participation in international affairs is both puzzling and problematic. I argue that member states can and do find ways to control international organizations without losing the benefits of granting them resources and decision-making authority.

States turn to international organizations like the World Bank because of their organizational, technical, and coordinating advantages. To take advantage of these capabilities, international organizations must be granted some *discretion*, which is the authority to make decisions without explicit approval. If the member states had to approve every operational, design, and management decision made by the multilateral development banks, the resulting transactions costs would surely outstrip any benefits offered by these international organizations. A lack of discretion would also prevent member states from taking advantage of technical expertise. However, discretion can lead to problems, as with the Sardar Sarovar project. Management and staff might use their discretion to make decisions that are not aligned with achieving the mandates given to them by member countries.

Member countries have attempted to control and manage the discretion they grant to international organizations. Returning to the aftermath of the Narmada episode, we find that the threat to withhold funding from the World Bank turned out not to be a bluff. In 1994, the US Senate voted to withhold replenishment funds from the arm of the World Bank that lends to the poorest countries, the International Development Association. Soon, reforms at the World Bank that intended to root out the projects that had generated so much negative attention were afoot, with a particular emphasis on preventing projects from harming local people.

New environmental and social safeguard policies were established to prevent projects from being approved without due consideration of risks for local people. A complaint mechanism was established to receive and process claims from local people who alleged that they experienced material harm because of World Bank projects. The evaluation office at the World Bank was reinvigorated, and its staff grew considerably to produce better information about the outcomes of projects. New multi-year country evaluations were completed to ensure that country assistance strategies would be informed by results of previous projects. Little is known about whether such mechanisms can be used to control international organizations by managing discretion.

Understanding how international organizations can be controlled to ensure that they use discretion to achieve goals has many practical applications, most significantly for our understanding about the promise and limits of foreign aid. Ensuring that the multilateral development banks make allocation decisions that are responsive to past performance is critical for development effectiveness. Many policymakers and researchers have been skeptical that development assistance can do much good, since donor organizations are not often responsive to past performance. At the project level, international donors have often overlooked the failure of recipients to meet covenants or conditions, because doing so would imperil the disbursement of large loans. At the sector level, past staffing decisions can solidify tendencies to do things in certain ways and at certain levels of effort, regardless of updated information about performance. At the country level, donors continue to engage with recipients that have poor governance and policy performance for political reasons. In combination, these impediments to more selective allocation raise valid concerns about the effectiveness of aid.

I investigate whether information about performance can be used to make decisions about the allocation of aid more selective. To complete this investigation, I created a comprehensive data set of environmental outcomes, both positive and negative, from thousands of multilateral development bank projects from 1994 to 2009, using every publicly available evaluation document. This data set thus represents the first attempt to measure an element of performance that is applicable to projects across disparate sectors of development financing in a consistent way across organizations and time. This unique data set allows me to move beyond previous studies that have dealt with the macro-level causes of reform and policy changes at international organizations (e.g., Nielson and Tierney 2003) and instead to examine the effects of control mechanisms. This shift in focus recognizes that not all macro-level reforms on paper are implemented well and asks what control mechanisms make them more successful.

I also spent one month conducting interviews at each of the World Bank, Asian Development Bank, Inter-American Development Bank, and African Development Bank. I use these interviews to evaluate the logic of my causal claims and to extend the results of quantitative models when data are sparse or suggestive. Together, my analysis of these two streams of data moves the study of international organizations forward by showing how they can be controlled for better performance. This research demonstrates more generally how the allocation of aid can be aligned with results.

DISCRETION, THE PROBLEM OF CONTROL,
AND ENVIRONMENTAL OUTCOMES

Discretion is risky, but necessary to take advantage of the benefits that bureaucracies and international organizations offer. International organizations must have some discretion; otherwise their ability to use expertise and reduce coordination costs will be limited. However, when states grant discretion to international organizations, the possibility arises that the management and staff of international organizations will choose actions that lead to poor performance. This might come about because the management and staff of international organizations have uncertainty about how to achieve mandates or have different interests than member states. Member states in international organizations have an interest in managing discretion when it results in *agency slack*—the condition when there is a discrepancy between the collective preferences of member states and the actions of the international organization. Member states have a number of ways to manage discretion, including banning certain actions, requiring *ex ante* procedures before decisions, or evaluating the performance of international organizations.

Scholars have expressed skepticism that member states can find effective mechanisms of control, even when they are able to deliver collective mandates to international organizations (Vaubel 2006). Much less attention has focused on the consequences of control mechanisms, which is unfortunate for understanding how international organizations might contribute to global governance. States are not helpless after they grant discretion to international organizations. They can put in place institutions that generate information about performance and change the incentives of staff and management on the basis of this information.

Finding the optimal trade-off between discretion and control when mandates have been assigned is a complicated endeavor that has the potential to shed light on many fields of study. For scholars of international relations, the problem of controlling international organizations has figured prominently in debates about the merits of multilateralism and the challenges of collective responses to international problems. To the extent that performance can be optimized by trading off technical benefits for political control in low-cost ways, international organizations might be able to play more important roles in global governance. For scholars of organizational sociology and management, the challenge of shaping individual incentives to promote collective goals is a core problem. In the case of multilateral development banks, incentivizing strong preparation and implementation of projects when individual rewards accrue for getting projects approved is a major concern. For scholars of program evaluation and information management, the question about how to produce information that is useful for managers is a critical question. Bringing core problems in these different areas of study, I argue that there are a number of low-cost ways to increase political control without decreasing the benefits of discretion.

Before proceeding to questions about control mechanisms, it is worth exploring two particular problems that can arise when discretion is granted. First, the management or the staff of international organizations may not have strong interests in implementing directives from member states. This is the problem of divergent preferences, which can range from incentives of individual staff to divert international resources for private gain, to the incentives that management has to resist costly reforms and changes to organizational practices. The worst cases of divergent preferences are easy to observe. For example, in 2005, news broke that the United Nations office tasked with monitoring the Oil-for-Food Program in Iraq had not ensured that revenues were spent only on humanitarian and development needs, resulting in billions of dollars of funds that were overpaid or lost (Miller 2005). Staff at the United Nations were accused of receiving private kickbacks for awarding contracts to favored vendors, among other crimes.

In other cases, states hand down conflicting or underresourced mandates that require international organizations to balance competing demands. For example, the UN security forces have been severely criticized for standing by during the 1994 genocide of the Tutsi people in Rwanda despite their mandate to secure the peace, inaction that occurred in part because of bureaucratic incentives to resist action and in part because members of the Security Council did not authorize the forceful actions that were required to prevent the genocide (Kenna 1999; Carlsson, Han, and Kupolati 1999). At the multilateral development banks, member states have prioritized both industrial development and environmental protection, two mandates that are often at odds with each other (Gutner 2002). Because of private interests, organizational incentives of management, or conflicting mandates, international organizations can fail to meet the goals set by member states.

Second, international organizations may not effectively collect information about outcomes or performance, and they may not update their decisions in light of new information that helps them overcome uncertainty. States often turn to international organizations to manage technically complex operations in situations where expertise is an important asset. It can be difficult for states to understand whether expertise is being used effectively to achieve goals and to monitor whether decisions account for new information. For example, the multilateral development banks can choose an innumerable variety of programs and lending modalities to achieve environmental and development goals in borrowing countries. This makes it difficult to know whether decisions are taking past lessons into account. As former World

Bank president Robert McNamara argued, this is one of the central challenges facing the multilateral development banks:

> Certainly the Bank has had its failures . . . it has learned and is continuing to learn from its failures. . . . Taking account of these lessons will, I believe, increase the Bank's rate of success for the future. (Grasso, Wasty, and Weaving 2003, ix)

Member states are not helpless in the face of divergent preferences or uncertainty, however. They can insist on monitoring and evaluation practices that help them hold international organizations accountable for outcomes and generate information that reduces uncertainty about future decisions. Member states can also insist that the staff and management at international organizations consider, process, and use new information in decision-making, through administrative procedures. In the aftermath of the Narmada project at the World Bank, for example, a number of policies were put in place to improve oversight and accountability for environmental and social outcomes by generating and processing information about performance. These policies included the adoption of stronger internal processes for assessing the environmental impacts of projects, the establishment of a permanent accountability mechanism that civil society groups can use to file complaints about poor performance, increased staffing and resources for an evaluation department, and a greater emphasis on strategic planning at the country level.

More generally, information and control mechanisms might help member states and other stakeholders manage discretion at international organizations. At the multilateral development banks, the outcome of better control would be more careful selection of projects. Over time, if officials in these international organizations and their counterparts in borrowing governments were able to more effectively select projects that are likely to succeed over projects that are likely to fail, the overall effectiveness and impact of development finance would increase. This outcome is called *selectivity* and will be the primary outcome of focus in this book. Selectivity is the practice of decreasing investment in the types of projects that have poor records and increasing investments in the types of projects with good records.

To this point, research has considered the intersection of allocation and effectiveness at the level of countries and focused mostly on blunt tools of control. Researchers, practitioners, and borrowing governments have debated whether more funds should be allocated to the countries that use funds effectively or to the countries that have the greatest need for development (Dollar and Levin 2006; Nunnenkamp and Thiele 2006; Easterly 2007; Hout 2007; Feeny and McGillivray 2009; Hoeffler and Outram 2011). In practice, the proponents of selectivity have won the day and shifted the allocation of development finance at least formally. Countries that have more successful records at implementing aid projects or that are recognized for better governance receive more aid, especially from multilateral donors, though there exist significant differences between donors (Dollar and Levin 2006; Clist, Isopi, and Morrissey 2012). For example, in 1993 the International Development Association, the arm of the World Bank that provides concessional loans to poor countries, began factoring the performance ratings of previous projects into the formula that determines allocations to countries (Operations Evaluation Department 2001c). This practice continues to the present day. The US Millennium Challenge Corporation has eligibility criteria that depend on recipient countries meeting governance standards (Chhotray and Hulme 2009). At the heart of these programs is the notion that aid can have the most impact when it is allocated to the countries that have shown the ability to use it well.

But this approach has downsides. By allocating aid exclusively or primarily to countries with good overall records, aid may be diverted from the neediest people who happen to live in poorly governed countries. Alongside research that investigates whether the allocation of aid is driven by the implementation record or governance levels of recipient governments, concerned observers have asked whether focus on selectivity and other political incentives have diverted aid away from the neediest recipients. For example, a 2012 report commissioned by the UK House of Commons on patterns of official development assistance channeled through the European Commission and noted this concern directly:

> It is unacceptable that only 46% of aid disbursed through European institutions goes to low income countries. It devalues the concept of aid. . . . The UK must continue to press for funding to be diverted from those higher middle income countries, who have their own resources to provide for their people, to give greater help to the poorest people in the world. (2012, para. 45)

Since middle-income countries also tend to be better governed and have better records implementing projects, selectivity applied at the country level, taken to its furthest logical conclusion, would result in aid being diverted in ways that are problematic to officials in donor countries. This particular report notes that such a situation would not be providing "value for money" on aid disbursements.

In many cases, international aid donors have sought out other ways to reach the neediest people who happen to live in poorly governed countries, by channeling aid differently, limiting their geographic focus, or engaging recipient countries through pockets of functionality in governments. For example, political scientist Simone Dietrich (2013) argues that donor agencies can be effective in implementing programs by finding pockets of functionality within recipient governments or bypassing government agencies and instead partnering with local civic organizations. Matt Winters (2014) argues that many of the risks associated with the local capture of foreign aid for nondevelopment purposes can be averted by clearly specifying outcomes, responsibilities, and geographic scope during the design of aid projects.

These options offer pathways to *selectivity* that are not so blunt as increasing or decreasing aid flows at the level of countries. Yet research about selectivity in the allocation of aid is mostly considered at the country level. This book examines when and why the multilateral development banks are selective about certain types of environmentally risky and environment-improving projects *within* the portfolio of individual recipient countries. In particular, are countries less likely to receive additional projects of a certain type when they fail to implement them well, or are they more likely to receive additional projects of a certain type when they succeed? If member states in the multilateral development banks are able to prompt this type of selectivity, the allocation of aid will become more effective over time while avoiding the downsides of selectivity at the level of countries. In addition, this pattern of allocation is precisely what would be observed if the administrative policies, complaint mechanisms, evaluation procedures, and planning processes were able to promote more effective management of the discretion that member states grant to the multilateral development banks.

This book focuses specifically on the ability of the multilateral development banks to respond to past environmental performance when making decisions about lending. Performance is understood as the achievement of objectives and adherence to policies set out by member states. The focus on environmental outcomes is important for theoretical, empirical, and practical reasons. The environmental components of multilateral development bank lending created the impetus for new policies and procedures aimed at managing discretion and the allocation of projects. The environmental aspects of multilateral lending have also generated mixed and controversial performance records. This mixed record offers an ideal setting to investigate when and why the changes to allocation practices instigated in the early 1990s have actually prompted selectivity.

The multilateral development banks have been credited with causing alarming deforestation because of poorly designed road projects, while at the same time they have helped borrowing countries to adopt national-level environmental regulatory frameworks (Rich 1994; Independent Evaluation Group 2008). The multilateral development banks have funded some of the largest, high-polluting, fossil fuel energy projects in the world, while also becoming the largest donor-assisted financers of clean-energy projects globally (Bretton Woods Project 2010; Independent Evaluation Group 2010a). They have financed large dam projects that displaced thousands of people and inundated vast tracks of natural areas, but they have also supported innovative, community-driven natural resource management projects that successfully addressed the connection between poverty and environmental degradation in rural areas (Khagram 2004; Kumar et al. 2000). Many activists regard the multilateral development banks as harbingers of environmental destruction, whereas government leaders have turned to them to manage international financing efforts on climate change, forest conservation, and pollution prevention.

This mixed performance record has provided the multilateral development banks the chance to change their practices in response to past outcomes, whether through new information available from evaluations, citizen complaints, or environmental planning. Fortunately from a research standpoint, it is possible to observe both the environmental outcomes of thousands of projects across the multilateral development banks and the subsequent pattern of allocation. These data allow me to explore when information about performance influences decisions about allocation. Many pages have been written about the mixed environmental records of the multilateral development banks; I seek to explain when monitoring and evaluation has helped the multilateral development banks move beyond their mixed records. It is important to note from the outset that I am not seeking to directly measure environmental outcomes in a consistent way, but instead measure whether allocation decisions change in response to information about environmental performance. Given the wide range of environmental performance measures, it is not possible to speak directly to the aggregate quality of environmental management in projects allocated by the multilateral development banks.

MOTIVATING EXAMPLES OF OPPORTUNITIES TO RESPOND TO PERFORMANCE

Consider some of the real opportunities the multilateral development banks had to respond to performance. In some instances, information from past operations was available to help select more effective operations in the future. For example, in 1984, the Asian Development Bank approved the Fisheries Infrastructure Sector Project in Indonesia (Asian Development Bank 1997a). This project supported increased fishing effort in underutilized coastal areas and aimed to promote economic development in fishing communities. The project produced poor results, especially for environmental conditions. The independent evaluation completed for this project described degradation of the environment and fishery:

> The landing area has become polluted from uncontrolled discharge of wastes . . . contributing to a deterioration in fish quality . . . the rapid growth in the number of small boats, many of which use the Project facilities, is contributing to overfishing in many coastal areas. (Asian Development Bank 1997a, iv)

The evaluation concluded that the project was poorly designed and that Indonesia's fisheries agency was poorly capable of carrying out similar projects. It recommended future operations "should incorporate measures to limit fishing effort in coastal waters or focus on aspects that do not encourage increased fishing," which would represent a shift in the portfolio composition (Asian Development Bank 1997a, iv). That same year, the ADB board approved the Coastal Community Development and Fisheries Resources Management Project. This new project directly followed the recommendations of the independent evaluation, having primary goals to "conserve coastal fisheries resources" and to "rehabilitate the physical fisheries facilities . . . to improve environmental and sanitation conditions" (Asian Development Bank 1997b, ii–iii). The sequence of events in this case suggests that the Asian Development Bank responded to Indonesia's poor performance at mitigating environmental damages by redesigning the lending portfolio in that sector. Is this type of response common and systematic across the multilateral development banks, or are such instances only incidental? Did the adoption of administrative procedures that require environmental impact assessments make it easier for member states and the environmental offices that they created to steer project staff away from high-risk projects without eliminating flexibility to take on high-risk projects where they are useful and can be implemented well?

Consider alternatively the controversy surrounding the Chad-Cameroon Oil Pipeline and the outcry by civil society groups about its negative environmental consequences. Despite being portrayed as a state-of-the-art, environmentally friendly oil project, the pipeline has left the World Bank embroiled in controversy ever since it approved financing for the project. In 2001, more than 100 residents across three areas in Chad filed a formal complaint with the World Bank's Inspection Panel alleging that the environmental assessments and management plans for the project were insufficient to protect them from negative environmental impacts. In particular, the complaint alleged that the pumping of oil across Chad had the potential to destroy important medicinal plants, pollute surface waters used by local communities, and negatively impact agricultural production. Similar concerns were echoed by other environmental groups (e.g., Horta, Nguiffo, and Djiraibe 1999). These were the kinds of outcomes the member states in the World Bank wanted to avoid in crafting environmental policies and creating the Inspection Panel to gather information.

Under great scrutiny, the World Bank Inspection Panel investigated these allegations. The investigation report found that while the implementing department made a "substantial effort" to mitigate negative environmental impacts, shortcomings were evident in the environmental assessment process, the environmental management plan, and the implementation arrangements for the environmental management plan (Inspection Panel 2002, xii). The Inspection Panel report called for improved environmental assessments and management plans before the project proceeded. The World Bank management agreed to prepare a regional development and environmental assessment plan, convene an expert advisory panel to oversee compliance with environmental safeguard policies, and collect further baseline data on the health of local populations to allow for more effective monitoring of environmental impacts (International Bank for Reconstruction and Development and International Development Association 2002, 17–19).

This case demonstrated that civil society groups can push the multilateral development banks for better environmental practices by using their voice and access to complaint mechanisms. Since civil society groups provide monitoring of environmental outcomes independently, they might provide states with information that they need to credibly threaten management with decreased appropriations for acting outside of environmental rules. Can monitoring provided by civil society groups prompt allocation patterns that are more careful about these negative outcomes by solving information problems for member states and their management? Do the multilateral development banks systematically respond to complaints about actions that fall outside policies and mandates? Does this type of monitoring cause the multilateral development banks to move away from projects that local people oppose?

The opportunities to manage discretion extend beyond mitigating environmental damages. Using information from evaluations, staff at multilateral development banks might identify opportunities where they are most able to meet member state demands for results with the considerable discretion that they are granted. In 1993, for example, the World Bank approved the $76 million Environmental Technical Assistance Project in China. This project was designed to upgrade the institutional capacity of the State Environmental Protection Agency and the Chinese Academy of Science, and thereby address China's rapidly deteriorating environmental conditions. An independent evaluation found the project to be "highly successful" and noted substantial achievements, including the establishment of national environmental legislation (Independent Evaluation Group 2007). The conclusion of the evaluation recommended a "continuing role for the Bank in strengthening monitoring and enforcement at the provincial level" and identified "a strong desire for a second technical assistance project targeted to provincial Environmental Protection Bureaus" (17). Because the project was deemed so successful, all parties showed a desire to pursue similar projects in the future. According to the World Bank project database, China borrowed more than $3 billion of environmental financing in the three years following this evaluation, one of the largest environmental portfolios at the World Bank.[4]

In this case, the successful implementation of an environment-improving project generated information about future programs that could be pursued with broad support. More broadly, can evaluation enable the multilateral development banks to identify opportunities to build an effective record? Can evaluations help the multilateral development banks overcome technical uncertainty that prevents them from being more effective in the complex and technical decisions about what types of projects to pursue? Is this type of updating limited to high-performing countries, or have all countries received more environment-improving projects?

Each of the above examples showed a positive response to measured environmental performance, but counterexamples also exist. In 2004, for instance, the Asian Development Bank evaluation department completed an evaluation of the Cambodia lending portfolio during the previous decade (Asian Development Bank 2004). This evaluation paid particular attention to environmental management activities in the Tonle Sap region, which covers 38% of Cambodia's area and whose fisheries "provide for up to 80% of the protein intake for Cambodian people, 50% of whom depend on the lake's resources, directly or indirectly" (Asian Development Bank 2004, 17). The country program evaluation chronicled a series of technical assistance and investment projects that achieved less than satisfactory results, owing to the fact that the programs did not properly account for Cambodia's poor institutional capacity (Asian Development Bank 2004, 16–18). The evaluation recommended that future programs should be "modest" in nature. In the years that followed, however, additional technical assistance projects were approved, eventually leading to the $40 million Tonle Sap Poverty Reduction and Smallholder Development Project in 2009.[5]

In this case, poor performance at meeting environmental goals did not decrease investment in future Tonle Sap natural resource management and development programs. This raises a number of questions about when and why high-level, thematic evaluations can set the stage for strategies that prioritize sectors with strong records. These high-level evaluation and strategic planning processes might offer an opportunity for discretion that does not lead to poor performance because of miscommunication or lack of information about performance at the multilateral development banks. But can planning processes promote selectivity in the types of projects that are chosen?

These examples are only a small subset that illustrate how procedures, policies, and oversight practices might be used to manage discretion at international organizations and overcome principal-agent problems without resorting to the blunt tools that populate so much of the literature on international organizations. Building a greater appreciation for these kinds of control mechanisms is an important step toward understanding when international organizations can be relied on to carry out the intentions of states and achieve collective goals in international affairs.

THE APPROVAL IMPERATIVE

At the multilateral development banks, many problems of performance are based on the strong incentives that staff have to secure the approval of new loans. I call this the *approval imperative*. The multilateral development banks are among the largest international organizations, and they all have one core function—to allocate and manage development financing delegated to them by member states. Between 1994 and 2009, the years that are part of the empirical analysis in this book, the multilateral development banks collectively approved nearly $1 trillion in development financing, according to the AidData database.

The process of allocating and managing development financing to achieve mandated results, like reducing poverty, generating economic growth, or improving environmental conditions, has not always been smooth. As described above, the multilateral development banks entered the 1990s at odds with member states. The review that was commissioned by World Bank president Lewis Preston, and subsequently the reviews commissioned at other multilateral development banks, found that differences between expectations and results were not limited to a single project or country. As noted above, the 1992 World Bank Portfolio Management Task Force report, also known as the "Wapenhans report," chronicled a significant deterioration in the performance and effectiveness of World Bank programs, with 20% of active projects in 1991 having "major problems" (Wapenhans 1992, ii). The report cited an entrenched "approval culture" as one of the main reasons for this decline:

> There are also aspects of Bank practice that either may contribute to portfolio management problems or are insufficiently effective in resolving them. Underlying many of these aspects is the Bank's pervasive preoccupation with new lending. In the eyes of Borrowers and co-lenders as well as staff, the emphasis on timely loan approval (described by some assistance agencies as the "approval culture") and the often active Bank role in preparation, may connote a promotional—rather than objective—approach to appraisal. (Wapenhans 1992, iii)

Additionally, the report indicated that the career and promotion prospects of Bank staff were dependent on planning new operations, rather than successfully managing existing projects (17–18). The report stated that this incentive structure was derived from "a predominant Board interest in new lending," which makes "the task of engineering cultural change in support of portfolio performance management considerably more difficult" (18). Thus, while the characteristics of borrowing countries certainly influenced the performance of individual projects, the fundamental problem of performance for the World Bank was an inability to put supervision, careful project design, and selectivity ahead of the organizational necessity to approve new projects quickly.

Indeed, one of the primary recommendations that came out of the Wapenhans report was that "if the Bank is to remain effective, portfolio performance must be taken into account in the Bank's country assistance strategies, business processes, and personnel policies" (Wapenhans 1992, ii). Under an incentive structure that rewarded the approval of new projects, it was not in the interest of staff to be selective about projects or take into account information about past performance.

The attention created by the Wapenhans report soon rippled out to the other multilateral development banks. In the following two years, the Asian Development Bank, African Development Bank, and Inter-American Development Bank all completed portfolio performance reviews. Each one reported performance problems associated with the same type of approval culture (Inter-American Development Bank 1993; Knox 1994; Asian Development Bank 1994). For example, the Asian Development Bank Task Force produced the following findings:

> An important issue that has emerged from the analyses of the Task Force is the need for the Bank to reconcile its resource transfer and development objectives. Its resource transfer role is to transfer programmed amounts of financial resources annually to its developing member countries. This sometimes translates into an emphasis on obtaining loan approvals as per the annual program. Related pressures are created during the project preparation and implementation processes, sometimes leading to compromises on project quality and on potential development impact. This phenomenon has been termed the "approval culture" in the Bank. (1994, 5)

The member states of the multilateral development banks expect a certain amount of financial resources to be transferred, which causes staff at these development banks to take shortcuts in preparation and supervision to meet targets. Indeed, one of the main findings of the ADB review was that "feedback on the lessons of past experiences is not fully utilized in programming and project design, and in implementation activities" (Asian Development Bank 1994, iii).

These findings have been echoed in scholarly work on performance problems at the multilateral development banks (Weaver 2007; Nielson and Tierney 2003;

Weaver and Leteritz 2005; Svensson 2003; Weaver 2008). As Weaver writes about the approval culture:

> There is equal skepticism regarding the extent to which [the evaluation department's] findings are taken into consideration by project managers within the organizational culture, which rewards project approval but until recently made little visible effort to hold managers accountable for the outcomes of projects. (2008, 67)

Like other types of bureaucratic agencies, entrenched incentives have developed at the multilateral development banks based on their need to transfer resources. These incentives clash with the interests of donor states for certain social and environmental outcomes, which are supposed to be achieved alongside lending targets. This clash of external mandates and internal incentives has been discussed as a major and general problem for controlling international organizations (Abbott and Snidal 1998; Pollack 1997; Barnett and Finnemore 1999; Nielson and Tierney 2003; Gutner 2005; Martens 2005; Weaver 2010). In particular, international organizations can develop interests in increasing their budgetary resources, maintaining internal practices that benefit top decision-makers, and adhering to professional or technical norms (Barnett and Finnemore 1999; Weaver 2008). The approval imperative at the multilateral development banks is a clear example. At the multilateral development banks, an entrenched set of practices developed around using technical expertise to secure new lending (Weaver 2008, 26–31). In many cases, states funding the multilateral development banks reinforce the approval imperative, since their official function is to approve projects sent to them by the management. Member states want the multilateral development banks to transfer target amounts of resources, while also achieving good environmental outcomes.

Operational departments are primarily responsible for ensuring that concessional financing is spent, in order to justify future replenishments by donor countries, and that commercial lending is expanded, since it represents the main source of operating revenue for the multilateral development banks (Vaubel 1996; Weaver 2007). As a consequence, career advancement for operational staff and management is largely dependent on the volume of lending that is approved and disbursed, rather than the outcomes and impacts of projects. Given that many projects are implemented over multiyear time horizons and that staff rotation within multilateral development banks is extremely high, there are neither strong lines of accountability for project performance nor significant incentives for management to prioritize project implementation and supervision (Wapenhans 1992; Asian Development Bank 1994).

Under these circumstances, it remains an open question whether better monitoring and evaluation can enhance oversight and promote selectivity. As long as member states task the multilateral development banks with meeting lending targets as their primary mandate, the approval imperative will be difficult to dislodge, despite member states' interests in other concurrent goals. The portfolio performance reviews of the early 1990s recommended that the multilateral development banks redouble efforts on monitoring and evaluation to address the "approval culture." As the Asian Development Bank review stated, for example, "A major feedback activity, post-evaluation, has provided limited feedback into Bank operations until recently. Monitoring of implementation has rarely extended beyond routine aspects of physical and financing progress" (Asian Development Bank 1994, para. 113). One of the primary recommendations of the ADB report was to reorient evaluation to focus on performance during implementation and the impact of projects on development (Asian Development Bank 1994, iv). In this way, staff would have better information about effective project design, and donor states would have the information they needed to provide better oversight. It remains unclear, however, whether the monitoring and evaluation mechanisms put in place by member states are sufficient to cause this response.

Although strategies to control the approval imperative have been put in place, the core incentives involved with the approval imperative have remained remarkably steady over time. For example, in 2010 the evaluation unit at the African Development Bank released an independent evaluation about the current state of project management, and the conclusions did not look all that different from those that were reached nearly a decade and a half earlier: "The fundamental factors that continue to affect supervision performance at the Bank include a persistent approval culture and incentives stacked towards that end, while the overall accountability for results remains low" (Operations Evaluation Department 2010, iii). The evaluation reported that 70% of staff viewed project supervision as less than satisfactory, with "too much emphasis on portfolio building compared to portfolio implementation" (13).

The emphasis on building portfolios and disbursing funds can mean that new information is not taken into account when designing new operations. The multilateral development banks hire staff with a certain mix of specialties, which can make it difficult to move away from existing types of projects, even if results do not meet expectations in certain areas, according to one country director whom I interviewed for this project. Furthermore, inertia exists in development practice based on professional norms and accumulated wisdom about "best practices." Staff are not always motivated to consider new information and review evaluation results among their many other tasks, having only limited attention and capacity to process complex streams of information. These barriers contribute to difficulties in getting decision-makers to update practices.

The multilateral development banks have incentives to approve projects quickly, potentially at the expense of donor state preferences for certain social and environmental outcomes. Donor states lack the ability to perfectly monitor whether the multilateral development banks are acting in accordance with their wishes for certain environmental outcomes because they cannot observe day-to-day decisions and they cannot determine whether decisions about the design of projects are based on divergent preferences, since they are cloaked in technical uncertainty.

STRATEGIES FOR CONTROLLING DISCRETION

The problems of performance created by diverging preferences and uncertainty are not impossible to address. And problems of performance are not unique to multilateral development banks, although they will be the focus of this book. Organizations fail every day. Corporations go bankrupt. Bureaucracies provide poor services. Schools do not meet performance criteria. International organizations miss their mandates. Sometimes these failures come about because managers of organizations do not respond to the directives of their principals to move in new directions, reorganize, or modify practices. Sometimes these failures come about because the managers of organizations simply do not know how to achieve their goals. Sometimes failure results from a combination of these factors, when organizations fail to update their practices to take into account new information.

The inability of organizations to update their practices in light of new information is a common source of failure. Organizations have many sources of information about performance, and the challenge is to adopt process, procedures, and methods of incorporating this information into future decisions. In this book, I examine four specific control mechanisms that member states have used to address problems of performance at the multilateral development banks.

The first mechanism is administrative procedures that require operational staff at the multilateral development banks to assess environmental impacts and to create environmental management plans before a project is eligible for approval. These procedures provide donor countries an easier way to monitor whether MDB staff are acting on their preferences while designing projects. The procedures also provide a set of performance criteria against which to measure results at the completion of a project. To support the creation of both types of information, specialized environment offices have been established in the multilateral development banks that have a primary mandate to support the design, monitoring, and evaluation of these environmental safeguard procedures. Because these environment offices have the ability to slow down the approval of projects, I argue that operational staff will be responsive to information about the past environmental performance of projects. In countries where results have been poor, operational staff know that approval is likely to be delayed because donor states will require more extensive environmental planning during the design of projects. If this argument is correct, safeguard procedures will align allocation decisions with performance.

Second, I examine whether external accountability mechanisms that allow civil society groups to lodge complaints about poor environmental performance have enhanced oversight and thus created more selectivity. These accountability mechanisms provide members states with "fire alarm" monitoring from external groups, alleviating much of the challenge member states face in monitoring on-the-ground performance themselves. Member states can use notable instances of poor performance to insist on policy reforms and to highlight the types of projects that are more likely to have problems during implementation. Thus, external accountability mechanisms should help to overcome the information problems that give rise to the problem of performance.

Third, I examine whether evaluation itself has prompted selectivity at the multilateral development banks for environment-improving projects. In contrast to environmental safeguard policies, there are no special policies or offices that slow the approval of environment-improving projects. This means that environment-improving projects offer a test case to examine whether evaluation alone can make the multilateral development banks more responsive to the results of previous projects when making decisions about allocation. I show that evaluation alone does not constrain the approval imperative at the multilateral development banks. Most importantly, the states that donate to the multilateral development banks have pushed for drastically increased levels of environmental lending. This mandate has taken priority over selecting projects based on past performance. Since donors have shown little interest in oversight that would decrease the amount of lending, information from evaluations does not make projects harder to approve. Learning alone does not appear to result from evaluation in areas where donor states push for lending. I show that, as a consequence, environmental projects with global targets are not at all responsive to past performance contained in evaluations. In contrast, environmental projects that address local needs are sometimes responsive to past performance, but only because evaluations solve information problems of borrowing countries.

Finally, I examine the potential for strategic planning to prompt selectivity. One way that donor states might control the multilateral development banks is to require them to draw up strategic plans for lending every few years and to consider past results as part of their deliberations. Thus, strategic planning offers donor states the opportunity to mandate that information about performance be considered in allocation decisions. Again, I show that without incentives to slow down the approval of environment-improving projects, strategic planning offers little potential for making the multilateral development banks practice selectivity. These findings show that planning alone will not result in better performance; it must be coupled with a strong external commitment to oversight and selectivity.

Together, these results represent a systematic analysis of the tools available to the member states of international organizations. Like research on bureaucratic oversight, these results underscore the importance of establishing either external or internal mechanisms for controlling international organizations that change the costs of decision-making. The primary challenge is to get information about performance to parties that have preferences to manage international organizations according to performance. Information alone is not sufficient to promote more selective allocation practices.

OUTLINE OF THE BOOK

To this point, research examining allocation decisions at multilateral development banks has focused primarily on aggregate financing, rather than responses to performance in particular types of projects.[6] The allocation of financing among environmentally risky and environment-improving projects is a unique area in which to make progress on understanding how international organizations can be overseen for performance, for three reasons. First, data on the allocation of funds to different programs and projects in a portfolio, including environmentally risky and environment-improving projects, are complete over many years. Second, evaluations about project outcomes, including environmental results, are available across multilateral development banks over many years. And third, the political factors that frame allocation decisions at development banks have been well theorized, as reviewed in the next chapter.

The rest of the book proceeds as follows. In chapter 2, I introduce the empirical setting and practical implications of this book in greater detail. In particular, I review how this book advances research on the allocation and effectiveness of aid in general and of environmentally relevant aid in particular. In chapter 3, I review the theoretical literature on the oversight of international organizations and apply its lessons to aid allocation and development lending. By doing so, I lay a common foundation for the empirical chapters that follow, since the outcome of interest throughout this book is decision-making about allocation. The next chapters sequentially evaluate different monitoring and evaluation mechanisms that might enhance oversight and promote selectivity: administrative procedures (chapter 4), citizen accountability mechanisms (chapter 5), project evaluation (chapter 6), and strategic planning (chapter 7). In chapter 8, I summarize the contributions that this research has made to understanding the performance of international organizations and the ways allocation of aid can align with effectiveness.

At a time when donor states are planning to drastically scale up the financing of climate change mitigation and adaptation projects by channeling such funds through the multilateral development banks, the findings here point to the need to ensure that the process of allocating funds constrains the notorious "approval imperative" at the multilateral development banks, especially by empowering internal and external actors with better information about performance that can change incentives affecting the allocation of aid.

2

The Politics of Aid Effectiveness

RESPONDING TO PERFORMANCE WHEN DELIVERING AID

Research about how international donors allocate aid has a long history. Aid is an integral part of statecraft and international cooperation, as well as a tool for poverty reduction and economic development. Enormous bodies of research investigate both the strategic and development implications of aid, each following somewhat independent traditions. Research on aid as a tool of statecraft has attempted to understand why states supply it and what role it plays in shaping international politics. Debate focuses on the ability of aid to achieve foreign policy goals. In early work, Schelling (1955, 606) argued that American foreign assistance became "a main—sometimes the main—vehicle of American diplomacy and military cooperation" following World War II. Research on the effectiveness of aid has asked whether aid can successfully promote development and reduce poverty. Early work was divided between those who saw evidence that aid could have large economic, social, and political benefits (Wurfel 1959) and those who found such claims to be oversold (Wood 1959). Even after several decades and a large number of pages written, these debates continue.

This chapter reviews these two threads of research to show that the strategic priorities of donors often prevent the allocation of aid to countries that can achieve the best development results. Development organizations, including the multilateral development banks, often do not condition future allocations on past performance at the country level. Even if they did, it might be problematic, since less aid would reach the people in greatest need. Donors have been sensitive to ethical considerations about moving out of low-performing but high-need recipient countries.

I suggest a different way forward. By managing discretion at the multilateral development banks, selectivity can be pursued *within* the portfolios of individual recipient countries. Because different countries have different capacities and interests, significant development and environmental gains can be made by selecting the types of projects that have a good record and avoiding the types of projects that have a poor record within the portfolios of individual countries. This focused approach to selectivity requires more information and greater attention to steering the incentives of staff about allocation, but it addresses persistent tensions between allocating aid according to strategic considerations, need, and effectiveness.

Existing research about the strategic and development implications of aid has progressed along somewhat distinctive paths, but tensions between the goals of statecraft and development weave them together. It is clear, for example, that bilateral donors sometimes allocate aid to secure military cooperation or favorable trade policies from foreign countries (e.g., Alesina and Dollar 2000). By doing so, however, they may be less able to withdraw aid following poor outcomes. Likewise, multilateral donors allocate more development lending to countries that have stronger relations with major donor countries and are less likely to enforce the conditions in aid contracts for these recipients (Neumayer 2003; Andersen, Hansen, and Markussen 2006; Schneider and Tobin 2013). By doing so, multilateral donors may overlook the countries that are able to produce the best development results with scarce resources.

Aid is more likely to achieve development goals when it is allocated to recipient agencies that have both the interest and the capacity to use it effectively. To the extent that political goals of donors steer aid toward other recipients, the chances of meeting development goals decline. For example, the United States has always had a strong strategic interest in maintaining stability in Haiti, given its proximity. During the Cold War, many policymakers in the United States considered aid to Haiti necessary to repel communism from the Western Hemisphere, even though the country was under the military rule of François Duvalier. Evaluations of the development impacts of US aid to Haiti during Duvalier's rule from 1957 to 1971 largely concluded that aid was ineffective and did little to lift people out of poverty. Instead, foreign aid primarily benefited Duvalier and his close associates (Buss 2008). Despite being ineffective for development purposes, strategic considerations won the day.

When strategic considerations take precedence over development goals, donors are unlikely to allocate aid in ways that create incentives for good implementation of projects and programs. As was the case with Duvalier, recipients of aid often have incentives to use foreign resources for their own private or political gain. If the political leaders in recipient countries know that they will continue receiving aid regardless of what they do with it, they will have little incentive to use it for anything other than private gain. To curb this problem, donors can reward good performance with additional aid or punish poor performance with reductions in aid at the level of countries (Pietrobelli and Scarpa 1992; Svensson 2000; Drezner 2003; Easterly 2003). If donors credibly commit to being selective about allocation, then even the most corrupt and ineffective leaders will have some incentives to implement development programs well. While allocating resources according to performance is widely thought to be desirable for achieving development goals, allocating resources in this way is often at odds with strategic or organizational goals of donors. This is the core tension between the political and the development goals of aid and is unlikely to change fundamentally in the foreseeable future.

Allocating aid according to performance at the national level raises other issues for achieving development goals. Recipient countries are not singular entities. They are compositions of agencies and branches of government with different interests and capabilities. Consider a recipient country with a poor record of implementing aid projects. Perhaps a particular minister or governor within this country has performed well at providing public services and promoting development in her jurisdiction. For example, the United Nations Environment Programme has published designated "Champions of the Earth" each year since 2005.[1] Included on the list are a number of environment ministers and other public officials, including some from countries that are generally regarded as poorly governed. If donors were to practice selectivity at the level of countries, opportunities in subnational regions or specific sectors might be overlooked.

If aid is withdrawn completely from the poorest and poorest-governed countries, then these countries are also likely to have a harder time escaping the vicious cycle of weak institutions and poverty. From a purely operational perspective, donor agencies are unlikely to develop the relationships and local knowledge necessary to design and finance successful programs without some continuing presence in a country. For these reasons, observers and researchers are often uncomfortable with selectivity achieved by large and fast reductions in aid for whole countries, branding them "unjust" or finding that such shocks can lead to instability and conflict (Pronk 2001; Hout 2002; Farmer, Fawzi, and Nevil 2003; Nielsen et al. 2011). Selectivity at the national level might not be the ideal way to promote development. Given that selectivity at the national level is frequently unrealistic because of the political considerations of donors, other types of selectivity might be needed to resolve the tension between the political and the development goals of aid.

Practicing selectivity at the national level is not the only way to accomplish the primary goals of selectivity, which are to create positive incentives for good implementation and not to waste resources on unsuccessful programs. Within countries, donor agencies might select sectors, projects, or ministries that offer opportunities for success. Indeed, recent research suggests that even the most poorly governed countries often have pockets of functionality where aid can be used well (Dietrich 2011). Being more selective about allocation within countries is more difficult and requires better information. But if donors are able to systematically find these opportunities and move away from programs that have proven ineffective, they might achieve the benefits of selectivity without the downsides. This type of allocation might also decrease tensions with strategic goals, since donors can maintain relationships with countries that have poor overall records.

Examining how the allocation of aid by multilateral development banks responds to the performance of specific projects is an opportunity to assess when this type of selectivity is possible. Assessing what information and procedures make selectivity within countries more likely also contributes to theoretical concerns about managing discretion at international organizations. Multilateral development banks have performance problems caused by incentives to approve resources without necessarily prioritizing development goals. Misaligned incentives to pursue quick approval are often cited as the reason why aid fails to achieve development goals (Easterly 2003; Rich 2013). Understanding when and why evaluation and other procedures can promote selectivity *within* country portfolios can thus answer questions about the practices that lead to the effective management of international organizations.

Data on allocation at multilateral development banks are complete across many years. In few other areas of organizational studies is it possible to observe the actions of an agent so clearly and completely. Furthermore, the multilateral development banks have all invested considerable resources in monitoring and evaluation, and this information is available publicly, but not in a compiled format. The same is not true of many bilateral donor agencies. Thus, after compiling large amounts of performance data, we can examine when and why the multilateral development banks are responsive to past performance at the project level within individual recipient countries. I specifically examine environmental performance because it has been an area of more intensive oversight efforts by states and because environmental performance is consistently relevant to projects across many sectors, which generates the density of data necessary to test hypotheses about the control of these international organizations. While other types of performance might also be the basis of selectivity for development agencies, none are as easy to systematically measure across the portfolios of the development banks considered in this book.

Bilateral Donors and the Beginning of Aid Allocation Research

Research on the allocation practices of bilateral donors has offered the clearest picture of the tension between allocating aid for strategic purposes and achieving good development outcomes. Indeed, early research focused on the efficacy of foreign assistance for achieving foreign policy goals rather than development results. For example, Morgenthau described six types of aid: "humanitarian foreign aid, subsistence foreign aid, military foreign aid, bribery, prestige foreign aid, and foreign aid for economic development" (1962, 301). According to Morgenthau, each type of aid influences recipient countries in unique ways, which explains why donor states choose them to achieve different kinds of foreign policy goals. Interestingly, Morgenthau questioned whether aid for economic development could be an effective component of foreign policy, given that its benefits "are likely to appear only in the more distant future" (1962, 308). Donor countries with more immediate goals are not likely to prioritize programs that yield benefits in the distant future.

The research that followed supported this possibility, showing that the development aid of bilateral donors is conditioned on their strategic interests. Dudley and Montmarquette (1976) developed a model of bilateral aid supply based on the benefits to donor countries. They found that preexisting political links with recipients are highly predictive of bilateral aid flows, rather than the need of recipient countries. McKinley and Little (1979) put forward two competing models of allocating aid—based on either interests of donors or needs of recipients—and found that the geopolitical interests of the United States during the Cold War offered a much better explanation for US aid allocation patterns than the economic characteristics of the recipient country. These early findings prompted examination of a broader array of strategic reasons why bilateral donors would allocate aid, including security arrangements, military cooperation, economic potential, cultural similarity, recipient need, proximity, and governance characteristics (Schraeder, Hook, and Taylor 1998; Dowling and Hiemenz 1985; Turmbull and Wall 1994). This line of research suggests that aid for economic development can be broadly understood as a way for bilateral donors to cement strategic and economic ties with recipient countries, with development goals being subservient to these objectives.

Even when allocating aid to promote development, bilateral donor countries often use "tied aid," which requires the recipient country to contract with firms in the donor country for implementation. Previous research has also shown that bilateral donors decrease aid to countries from which they have high levels of imports (Lundsgaarde, Breunig, and Prakash 2007). Taken together, past research shows that bilateral donors primarily allocate aid based on their foreign policy interests, calling into question whether the allocation of aid can align with development goals.

Importantly, a great deal of research has shown that because bilateral donors allocate aid for strategic reasons, they are not selective about directing aid to recipients that have the governance characteristics and policy environment to support the successful achievement of development goals. Although aid is most successful in promoting economic growth in countries with good governance, research found little evidence that bilateral donors select for these conditions (Burnside and Dollar 2000). Alesina and Dollar (2000), for example, find that strategic relationships between donor and recipient countries better predict aid flows than the quality of governance in the recipient country. Alesina and Weder (2002) do not find evidence that bilateral donors favor recipient countries with less corruption, suggesting that a great deal of aid is wasted. Other research echoes the finding that bilateral donors are not often responsive to corruption, poor policy environments, and low institutional quality, even since the end of the Cold War (Birdsall, Claessens, and Diwan 2003; Easterly 2007).[2]

Since bilateral donors tend to allocate aid according to strategic factors, they also tend to be less concerned with monitoring and evaluating their performance at achieving development goals, at least in transparent ways. For example, only in 2011 did the US Agency for International Development (USAID) adopt a policy to publicly release evaluations of its development performance.[3] Easterly and Pfutze (2008) chronicle with dismay the lack of transparency in aid flows from bilateral donors. This lack of transparency, combined with the strong evidence that political and strategic factors shape bilateral aid allocation, does not suggest that bilateral aid agencies respond systematically to their measured performance. Since this type of learning has been highlighted as key for the effective allocation of foreign aid (Svensson 2000), I turn to multilateral donors that might not have these problems.

Allocation at Multilateral Development Organizations

Multilateral organizations, such as the multilateral development banks and UN agencies, might be better than bilateral donors at allocating aid in ways that lead to effective outcomes. Some researchers have argued that this is why states rely on multilateral organizations to handle development financing in many instances (Balogh 1967; Easterly and Pfutze 2008; Martens et al. 2002). Multilateral donor agencies might have three advantages.

First, it has been argued that multilateral development banks, as specialized agencies and collective actors, are better able than national governments to collect and process information about the types of programs and projects that are likely to be successful. As Milner recounts in her review of delegation, because "information about recipients is a collective good, it will tend to be underprovided by individual donors. Multilateral agencies are supposedly better at providing information, especially that necessary to monitor the recipient" (2006, 109).[4] When bilateral donor agencies independently gather information, appraise projects, and monitor outcomes, there is risk of duplicated effort and fragmented information. It may be in the interests of donor states to forfeit some control to multilateral organizations in order to utilize their ability to collect and process information (Martens 2005). The multilateral development banks have more staff than most bilateral aid agencies and they tend to work in more sectors and have more projects, reinforcing the advantages of coordinated information gathering.

Second, the coordination of aid portfolios across sectors can improve effectiveness, in contrast to aid programs that are fragmented across bilateral donors with smaller portfolios (Acharya, de Lima, and Moore 2006; Martens 2005; Knack and Rahman 2007). Aid activities can have synergistic development effects when planned together and sequenced correctly, a reason why many donors have moved toward sector-based and policy-based program loans (Operations Evaluation Department 2007f). When different donor countries are interested in the same outcomes from development assistance, it can be in their interest to find mechanisms to lower the costs of coordination. Delegating resources to multilateral development banks is one way to address coordination problems. The multilateral development banks have attempted to improve coordination in recent years, recognizing that coordination gives them a comparative advantage in allocating and managing development assistance for results (Eriksson 2001).

Finally, the multilateral development banks may be insulated from political pressures to allocate aid in certain ways. As reviewed above, bilateral donors have the tendency to allocate aid to strengthen military cooperation, cement colonial relations, extend political influence, and push for favorable trade ties. By comparison, it is not clear that multilateral donors have any of these interests, at least directly. Indeed, empirical research has shown that multilateral donors are less likely to allocate aid and development lending to corrupt and poorly governed recipient countries than bilateral donors (Easterly and Pfutze 2008). Since multilateral donor agencies act under the direction of collective principals, they might be less susceptible to pursuing political ends that are unique to individual donor countries. The independence of international organizations and their insulation can help explain their effectiveness at achieving certain policy aims (Haftel and Thompson 2006). Domestic constituencies in donor countries demand aid effectiveness, which is one reason political leaders delegate resources to multilateral organizations, rather than manage and allocate those resources themselves (Milner 2006; Milner and Tingley 2013).

If these advantages are correct, then monitoring, evaluation, and feedback mechanisms at the multilateral development banks might be used to improve allocation, promote selectivity, and enhance effectiveness at meeting development goals. Multilateral development banks are thought to have advantages in information, so they should be better able to collect the information necessary to adjust lending decisions for particular borrowing countries. They have a greater ability to coordinate their efforts across sectors and regions within countries, which might provide opportunities to shift financing away from underperforming projects toward projects that can achieve development results. These organizations are insulated from some political pressures, so they may have an easier time shifting toward opportunities with the greatest promise, rather than the most politically expedient opportunities. If selectivity through evaluation were to happen at any development organization, it would likely happen at the multilateral development banks. If this is the case, it would suggest key advantages of multilateral development finance. Since multilateral organizations are active in many areas of international affairs where performance matters—such as global health, financial management, peacekeeping operations—a better understanding of the ability of multilateral organizations to collect and respond to information offers insights into the benefits of multilateralism more generally.

Past research offers glimpses into the advantages of development finance managed by multilateral organizations. For example, some authors have suggested that multilateral development banks are better than bilateral donors at tracking and allocating development assistance to borrowing countries with strong macroeconomic institutions and good policy performance (Cline and Sargen 1975; Dollar and Levin 2006; Alesina and Dollar 2000; Neumayer 2003; Hicks et al. 2008; Dollar and Levin 2005). In turn, these recipient countries are more likely to use aid to achieve development goals (Burnside and Dollar 2000). Many of the development banks now produce broad indices of policy performance and use these indices as part of a formulaic framework to determine lending amounts to borrowing countries (Asian Development Bank 2008a). Thus, the multilateral development banks are not only subject to fewer direct political pressures to allocate aid to poorly governed countries, they have also adopted allocation procedures that commit them to avoid doing so.

Earlier research also suggests that the multilateral development banks are more responsive to poverty in borrowing countries than are bilateral donors. Maizels and Nissanke (1984) show that multilateral aid is more likely to go to low-income recipients than is bilateral aid, since development banks do not have direct geopolitical concerns. Frey (1985) also reports that development banks direct more aid to recipients with lower per capita income than do bilateral donors, although low-income recipients with a better track record of repayment receive more aid than do low-income recipients with a history of default. Dowling and Hiemenz (1985) also find that multilateral development aid tends to go to recipients with lower per capita income.

Despite the finding that political pressures are less acute for multilateral development banks, they are not completely insulated from political pressures. Some research suggests that multilateral development banks respond to the interests of their dominant shareholders, which often treat the multilateral development banks as their agents and seek to influence lending practices (Schraeder, Hook, and Taylor 1998; Stone 2011; Fleck and Kilby 2006; Harrigan, Wang, and El-Said 2006). Kilby (2009) finds, for example, that borrowing countries that are aligned with the United States face less conditionality as part of structural adjustment loans from the World Bank. Kilby (2011) also finds that disbursement rates increase for borrowing countries that have close relations with either the United States or Japan at the Asian Development Bank, indicating that donor countries find ways to shield their allies from conditionality. To the extent that top bank shareholders influence the allocation of development bank lending, we may see more loans and grants going to borrowers that have special relations with large shareholders, regardless of their economic need or performance at achieving development (Fleck and Kilby 2006; Andersen, Hansen, and Markussen 2006). In addition, the management at multilateral development banks can be responsive to pressures that they face from even small shareholding states. Kaja and Werker (2010) find that when a borrowing member at the World Bank rotates on as an executive director at the Bank's board, it tends to receive more market rate loans from the International Bank for Reconstruction and Development (IBRD).[5] If these kinds of pressures are strong and selectivity becomes less likely as a result, then the development benefits of multilateral aid are likely to weaker than many scholars have suggested.

Compounding these challenges, incentives at the multilateral development banks often favor fast allocation and disbursement of loans over careful appraisal and supervision. Too often, development outcomes have been conflated with disbursement targets at the multilateral development banks (Easterly and Pfutze 2008). Combined with complex organizational structures, these incentives can make it difficult for the multilateral development banks to respond to performance information gained about past projects (Easterly 2002). Other operational pressures may push the multilateral banks away from allocating projects according to performance. Morrison (2011) found that countries with higher outstanding IBRD balances tend to receive more concessional lending from the International Development Association (IDA) of the World Bank group. This finding indicates that the World Bank group manages financial flows to prevent default on its market-rate commitments, which might not be the best way to achieve good results.

Taken together, existing accounts of multilateral development banks see some potential for improved development results from selectivity, but also a number of challenges arising from political and organizational incentives. Existing research has not focused on when and why these tensions can be resolved by examining how different types of information flows promote selectivity within the portfolios of individual recipient countries.

Toward Performance-Based Allocation

The substantial majority of the research reviewed in this chapter deals with decisions about aggregate, country-level allocation at the multilateral development banks, rather than what projects to fund within the portfolios of individual countries. By focusing on decisions about the total funds to be allocated to countries, rather than to individual projects within countries, research to date has overlooked ways that the multilateral development banks might practice selectivity, and the mechanisms that promote selectivity. The multilateral development banks have discretion to use a number of different methods of financing and to direct financing to a variety of sectors within a particular country.

The information needed to be selective about the composition of a country's portfolio is fundamentally different from the information that is often used to determine a country's overall eligibility for borrowing. Surprisingly, existing research has not made this distinction, and findings to date do not examine how lenders choose among projects, particularly in light of variation in the performance of different sectors. Instead, research has considered whether the sectoral allocation of aid portfolios is aligned with broad policy goals (e.g., Thiele, Nunnenkamp, and Dreher 2007; Brech and Potrafke 2014) or whether the allocation to specific sectors is aligned with indicators of need or performance in those sectors (e.g., Wilson 2011; Nielsen 2013; Miller, Agrawal, and Roberts 2013). There are certain conditions that are likely to render all development assistance ineffective, such as violent political instability or poor macroeconomic policy. These conditions aside, selectivity at the level of designing a portfolio of projects for a country remains a distinct possibility for almost all remaining countries.

While there are important results showing that multilateral donors have become more selective about their total lending to different recipients in recent years (Dollar and Levin 2006), it is unclear whether donors have grown more selective about the types of projects they will pursue with a particular recipient country. To gain a better understanding of performance-based allocation, future research must disaggregate aid by project type and sector (Wright and Winters 2010).

Just because a country has better bureaucratic capacity and macroeconomic policies than others, for instance, does not necessarily imply that it will have more stringent or more effective environmental policies. While it might make sense to base aggregate, country-level allocation decisions on factors related to bureaucratic capacity or macroeconomic policies, these types of indicators provide little guidance about the most important choices facing MDB staff—the choice between a new expressway or an upgraded metro system; the choice between a new hospital or a sewage project; the choice between a solar power plant or a large hydropower project. The most important decisions facing development staff involve assembling portfolios of projects that are likely to be successful in particular borrowing countries.

The goal of *selectivity* is to assess outcomes and adjust allocation decisions accordingly (Gilbert, Powell, and Vines 1999), as opposed to conditionality that requires certain procedures during implementation but is not directly concerned with outcomes. In general, conditionality is found to be ineffective at changing the practices and policies of borrowing countries because the multilateral development banks have ignored their own terms and given out funds anyway (Collier et al. 1997; Killick 1997; Svensson 2000, 2003; Guillaumont and Chauvet 2001; Easterly 2003; Gibson et al. 2005; Burnside and Dollar 2000, 2004; Hansen and Tarp 2000).[6] As Easterly (2003, 38) argues, the problem for donors is that "the success of past aid to follow conditions and the failure of past aid to follow conditions are both taken as justification for future aid." Weak institutions and poor policies are precisely the issues that development assistance attempts to address.

With selectivity, borrowing countries have flexibility in implementation, but are responsible for results. Later allocations are made conditional on results, at least within particular sectors. Researchers have focused on the importance of accountability for results, mutually agreeable standards of performance, and allocation that directs financing to the places where it will most likely achieve successful outcomes, particularly for environmentally targeted financing (Ghosh and Woods 2009; Werksman 2009; Davis and Dadush 2009). Thus, attention within the development community has shifted toward allowing more flexible arrangements for implementation, but increasing accountability of borrowers for results.

In practice, donor organizations have mixed incentives about both selectivity and conditionality (Rowat and Seabright 2006). The problem for donors is that assistance is intended to address the lack of development, which often includes poor institutional capacity or performance in the borrowing country. Thus, if donors were to approve financing only for high-performing countries, they would be giving assistance to those who may not need it, and they would not be contributing to any development where it is most needed. This would prevent the multilateral development banks from fulfilling their broader mandate to generate development. In particular, the multilateral development banks often justify their lending activities, especially for the least-developed countries, by pointing out that private markets do not offer financing to such countries (Hostland 2009). This problem has been dubbed the "Samaritan's Dilemma" and is the source of significant debate within the development community about how donors should work in the poorest and worst-governed countries (see Gibson et al. 2005; Easterly 2003).

Since multilateral donors are often prone to make allocation decisions based in part on recipient need, it has often proved difficult to be selective at the level of countries despite the promise of doing so (Svensson 2000, 2003). International development organizations face the "budget-pressure problem," which requires them to fully disburse all funds regardless of performance to maintain future budget levels (Svensson 2003). By pursuing selectivity within the portfolios of individual countries, the tensions between allocating aid according to need and allocating aid according to effectiveness can be resolved.

The Promise of Project-Level Performance Data

I look beyond the standard measures of performance that have been used in past research on the allocation of aid, like indices of government capacity, effectiveness, or macroeconomic performance. Instead, I compile and code project-level information available to the staff and member states that decide what projects to pursue. I use these data to examine when the multilateral development banks adjust their decisions about the allocation of projects in light of new information that is produced in different kinds of evaluations and feedback mechanisms.

By collecting project-level data on performance at the multilateral development banks, I also seek to understand the effect of information on the management of organizations that are not firms more generally. Evaluating performance when there is no profit motive is more difficult, and responding to evaluations is likely to be conditional on the characteristics of the organization and the political context. To this point, the majority of studies that examine how organizations respond to evaluations are based on self-reported assessments of decision-makers or evaluators, rather than observable impacts on decision-making (Forss, Cracknell, and Samset 1994; Vanlandingham 2011; Cousins et al. 2014). A review cast doubt on the validity of such research and its ability to advance our knowledge about how evaluations and other information devices affect decisions (Leviton 2003). Because decision-makers have strong incentives to portray themselves as responsive to evaluations, self-reported data on the use of evaluations are likely to be predictably biased.

In other cases, only a trail of citations is available to investigate the impact of evaluations on decision-making. For example, a recent study of performance-based budgeting by government ministries in the Netherlands investigates whether evaluations are referenced in budgeting documents (van der Knaap 2007). While this may be an indication that evaluations are considered when making decisions, it might not mean that evaluations affected decisions. In other research, data have not been available to link the results of evaluations to decisions by agencies. For example, in a study about the use of evaluations by agencies charged with serving victims of domestic violence in the United States, Riger and Staggs (2011) found that staff in state agencies reported that funding was conditional on the results of evaluations. However, no data were available to verify respondent reports of conditional funding. Across many settings, it is not clear that self-reported impacts of evaluations are actually realized. I advance this research frontier by combining two methods: building a rich account of decision-making processes based on staff interviews at the multilateral development banks and collecting data that can verify the impact of information on thousands of decisions about allocation.

Moving forward with a focus on environmentally relevant projects has two primary advantages for assessing the information flows and procedures that can promote selectivity. First, these projects offer an empirical setting that permits a robust research design. Unlike many areas of lending by development donors, environmentally relevant projects at the multilateral development banks have a relatively stable and consistent set of performance criteria both across projects and across multilateral organizations. Because these criteria offer a way to measure performance consistently, as will be discussed in greater detail in the empirical chapters, they allow for comparisons between organizations, time periods, and types of projects.

Although environmental aid is important in its own right, I expect the findings to generalize to other sectors and types of projects. For example, consider that donor countries have been interested in rapidly increasing environment-improving lending. This allows for an examination of whether donor pressures to approve a certain type of project decreases selectivity. It is rather easy to find parallel situations in other sectors, where donors, for example, have a stronger interest in civil society building and democracy promotion projects than recipient countries (Goldsmith 2008). Likewise, multilateral donors have worked hard to avoid environmental harms in infrastructure projects for nearby residents. These efforts parallel attempts by donors to limit irregularities with procurement that often result in lost or wasted funds (Kalbe 2001; Pallas and Wood 2009). In addition to pointing out the relevance of selectivity for environmental goals, an area of direct concern for other organizations like the Global Environment Facility or the Green Climate Fund, I also point to parallels with other sectors and programs in each of the empirical chapters that follow.

THE ALLOCATION DECISION PROCESS AT THE MULTILATERAL
DEVELOPMENT BANKS

Since the purpose of this research is to understand when and why the multilateral development banks are responsive to their environmental performance within the portfolios of individual countries, it is first necessary to look inside the "black box" of decision-making about allocation (Bourguignon and Sundberg 2007). To this point, the vast majority of research on aid allocation has ignored the rules and procedures that shape the allocation of specific projects. While research that addresses how different donors select among recipients is important for both the research traditions on statecraft and development effectiveness, this type of analysis is particularly weak at understanding how aid portfolios within countries can be managed to improve performance.

Over the last decade, practitioners and researchers have recognized that one-size-fits-all approaches to development assistance are less effective than designing portfolios that best suit the needs and capacities of particular recipient countries (World Bank 2009a). Thus, the connection between allocation decisions and performance is most fruitfully addressed by examining *portfolio composition*. That is, do donor organizations approve the projects that are likely to succeed within specific recipient countries? The decision-making process used to set overall assistance levels for a particular recipient country is distinct from the process that is used to make decisions about portfolio composition.

To make portfolio composition decisions in ways that promote effectiveness, donor organizations must assess which types of projects will succeed in a particular recipient country and then select those projects. Donor organizations might use information about past project performance, recipient demand, and recipient governance capacity. Indeed, most country assistance strategies at the multilateral development banks assess all of these factors (Operations Evaluation Department 2005a).

Each of the multilateral development banks considered in this book follow a similar, hierarchical decision process to ultimately determine the portfolio composition for individual borrowing countries (figure 2.1). The first major component of this process is the adoption of organization-wide assistance strategies. These assistance strategies reflect the development priorities for a particular sector or region over the next decade and are usually approved by the board of executive directors. These broad assistance strategies are adopted by the member states, but often reflect the interests of donor states, who shape these strategies through their control over concessional fund replenishments and capital increases.

Organization-wide strategies set the lending preferences for the bank as a whole. For example, in 2008 the Asian Development Bank adopted Strategy 2020, which

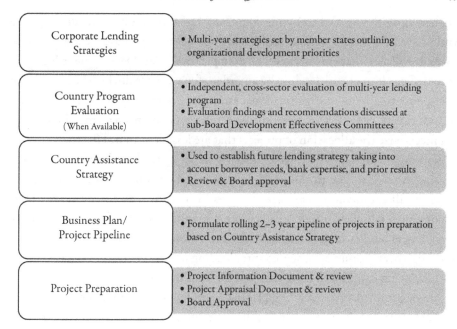

Corporate Lending Strategies	• Multi-year strategies set by member states outlining organizational development priorities
Country Program Evaluation (When Available)	• Independent, cross-sector evaluation of multi-year lending program • Evaluation findings and recommendations discussed at sub-Board Development Effectiveness Committees
Country Assistance Strategy	• Used to establish future lending strategy taking into account borrower needs, bank expertise, and prior results • Review & Board approval
Business Plan/ Project Pipeline	• Formulate rolling 2–3 year pipeline of projects in preparation based on Country Assistance Strategy
Project Preparation	• Project Information Document & review • Project Appraisal Document & review • Board Approval

FIGURE 2.1 Allocation process for projects at the multilateral development banks

laid out prioritized areas for investment over the next decade (Asian Development Bank 2008b). These areas included clean energy, infrastructure, and regional cooperation. Likewise, in 2002, the African Development Bank adopted a strategic plan that prioritized water supply, primary education, and basic health, while calling for more limited investments in other areas (African Development Bank 2002). Instead of developing a bank-wide lending strategy, the World Bank develops strategies for specific sectors. For example, in 2003, the World Bank approved a strategy for the water sector that prioritized reengagement with hydropower and large-scale water supply (World Bank 2003b). In each of these cases, member states approved organization-wide strategies and expected allocation decisions by staff to reflect those strategies.

When finance and treasury ministers come together to assess overall lending performance of the multilateral development banks at annual meetings, they consider whether the portfolio being financed aligns with these assistance strategies. For example, Naoto Kan, Japan's governor to the Asian Development Bank, highlighted a number of development challenges facing Asia in his speech to the 2010 annual meeting. However, in concluding he emphasized the role that high-level strategy plays in guiding investment: "We strongly hope that the ADB keeps playing a leading role in addressing such challenges as I have touched upon today, under its long-term Strategy 2020."[7] Thus, at a general level, when designing lending portfolios in partnership with specific borrowing countries, staff at the multilateral development banks have incentives to pursue projects aligned with organization-wide strategies. There is evidence that this occurs. For example, the Asian Development Bank has increased its clean-energy lending by an order of magnitude during the past decade in response to a series of organizational strategies prioritizing new energy production.[8] It may be the case that by requiring certain types of investments, these strategies incentivize the allocation of projects that are less likely to be effective.

Working within bank-wide strategies that are set by the board, specific processes are also in place to design the portfolios for specific countries over several years, which I will call *country assistance strategies*.[9] Every three to five years, the team responsible for implementing projects in a particular country from a multilateral development bank, which is usually a mix of in-country staff and headquarters staff, come together to formulate a new country lending strategy with representatives from the borrowing country. During this process, lending priorities for a specific country are determined. These lending priorities are intended to guide decisions about the composition of a country's portfolio. The country assistance strategy must fit within organization-wide lending priorities and borrowing country demands, and is intended to be responsive to past performance. Unlike with individual projects, donor states are significantly engaged in steering the country assistance strategy.

Prior to the formulation of a country assistance strategy, the evaluation departments at the various multilateral development banks sometimes produce a *country program evaluation*. This evaluation assesses the performance of the previous country strategy and lending program to help the country team design and choose more effective projects in the next period. Unlike other types of evaluations, operational staff are required to respond to the findings of country program evaluations during meetings with board committees that deal with development effectiveness. These committees ensure that board members are properly apprised of performance issues that come up in country program evaluations. During the meeting with this committee, operational staff must also specify the actions that they will take to address performance issues in future operations. Thus, the recommendations and findings of country program evaluations formally feed into the process of determining country assistance strategies, and thus the sectors and types of projects that will be emphasized during the following several years.

After a country assistance strategy is in place, it is the responsibility of the project team to negotiate with the particular borrowing country about the projects that will be part of the actual lending portfolio. During this process, the operational staff have a great deal of discretion in generating a project pipeline, together with the borrowing country. The negotiation process to transform a country strategy into a project pipeline is informal and does not follow any prescribed process. There is no way for the board to enforce strict compliance with the country assistance strategy. However, when the board meets to discuss and approve particular projects, donor states will often question the extent to which they address the major development concerns outlined in the country assistance strategy. At some of the banks, such as the Asian Development Bank, the country assistance strategy is followed closely when planning projects. At others, like the Inter-American Development Bank, the "improvisation rate"—the proportion of projects that deviate from the assistance strategy—is substantially higher (for example, Office of Evaluation and Oversight 2009). Across all the multilateral development banks, however, there is no formal way for board members, evaluators, or civil society groups to influence how the country assistance strategy becomes a portfolio of projects for a particular country. Thus, specific projects are determined by the preferences and expertise of staff at the multilateral banks and the borrowing country.

A number of different factors influence how MDB staff determine portfolio composition. Most importantly, staff choose a project portfolio that they will be able to design and send for approval quickly. Alignment with country assistance strategies can help. Additionally, borrowing countries often have either general guidance on the projects that they would like to pursue, or in the case of middle-income countries, fully developed proposals for projects. Since borrowing countries are more committed to projects they propose and this commitment is likely to speed approval, staff at the multilateral banks often benefit from pursuing these proposals. In addition, staff representing different technical sectors often vie for projects, since incentives at both the individual and unit level revolve around securing new lending.

The country directors that I spoke with about the process of determining a project portfolio were skeptical that evaluation information played a significant role in decisions as compared to other streams of information. In general, they indicated that the country team considered a variety of information sources and their own operational experience to determine which projects are likely to be problematic. According to interviews with country directors, evaluation information has a more direct role in formulating the country assistance strategy and at best an indirect role in revealing the types of projects that are likely to be problematic when designing a portfolio. I return to these hypotheses in the later chapters.

Once the project pipeline is determined, staff and their counterparts in borrowing countries design projects. At this point, the composition of the portfolio for a particular borrowing country is basically set. While evaluation and monitoring information might help MDB staff to make better *design choices* within individual projects, the vast majority of projects that make it to the design stage are eventually approved by the board. For example, of the 2,930 operations for which an initial project information document was prepared by the World Bank between 2000 and

2008, 2,584 were eventually approved by the board of executive directors.[10] Thus, while decisions made at the project preparation stage are important for the effectiveness of individual projects, they are less pertinent to decisions about the composition of lending portfolios that are the core outcome of this research.

To shepherd a project to approval, staff at the multilateral banks prepare an initial project information document and submit it to interdepartmental comment, and then prepare a full project appraisal and submit it to interdepartmental comment. During this process, various design and administrative requirements must also be met, which include the completion of an environmental impact assessment for environmentally risky operations, consultations with civil society groups, and the formulation of a loan agreement and implementation plan with the borrowing country. Evaluation staff often use interdepartmental comment periods to disseminate the lessons from evaluations and ask operational staff to account for lessons in design decisions.

Since this research examines portfolio composition outcomes over time, decisions that occur when designing a country assistance strategy and determining the project pipeline are most important. It is only at the former stage that evaluations play a direct and institutionalize role in decision-making. Once a country assistance strategy is set, evaluations only have the ability to indicate to operational staff the projects that are likely to be difficult to design and implement.

Environmental Agenda and MDB Lending

This book will focus on environmental performance and lending, because this area offers some of the clearest and most consistent measures of performance across the multilateral development banks. It is also an area where the problem of performance for member states is most acute. Before proceeding, we will look at how environmental considerations became a focus for the multilateral development banks specifically and development assistance more generally.

The 1992 Rio Earth Summit set the tone for environmental and development assistance for years to come. The Rio Declaration on Environment and Development, which was agreed to by more than 150 heads of state, declared that "in order to achieve sustainable development, environmental protection shall constitute an integral part of the development process and cannot be considered in isolation from it."[11] In the years that followed, international donors adopted new policies and practices that put this intention into practice. Bilateral and multilateral donors funded a surge of projects that aimed to improve environmental conditions. In his speech to the Rio Earth Summit, World Bank president Lewis Preston proposed that donor states delegate an additional $5 billion to the World Bank's concessional lending organization, the International Development Association (IDA), for environmental programs (Lewis 1992). At the same time, donor countries pushed the multilateral development banks to move away from the types of projects that had the largest negative environmental impacts (Khagram 2004; Hicks et al. 2008).[12] Between 1992 and 1994, for example, the US Congress held 21 hearings that focused on the World Bank, several of them directly related to achieving environmental objectives.[13]

The multilateral development banks responded to this growing focus on the environment with organizational reforms, the development of environmental strategies, and the implementation of new policies designed to reduce environmental harms from development projects. In 1987, the World Bank established the Environment Department, which was tasked with ensuring that environmental assessments were completed before a project could proceed to approval at the board (Operations Evaluation Department 2001a). The new Environment Assessment Sourcebook was adopted in 1991, and it significantly changed the way that development projects were assessed for negative environmental impacts.[14] At the Asian Development Bank, a new Environment Division was created between 1987 and 1989 and upgraded to the Office of Environment and Social Development in 1995, reporting directly to the president, largely because it needed greater resources to oversee implementation of the newly required safeguard policies (Environment Division 1995; Asian Development Bank 2001). At the African Development Bank, an environmental policy that provided operational guidance on mitigating environmental risks in projects was adopted in 1990 (African Development Bank and African Development Fund 2004). In 1994, as a direct response to the Rio meetings, the Inter-American Development Bank adopted an organizational strategy that "declared the Environment, together with poverty reduction and social equality, as priority areas for Bank support" (Inter-American Development Bank 2006). In 1994, the Sustainable Development Department was also established to meet Rio commitments and was charged with aligning bank practices with the global recognition of environmental priorities (Sustainable Development Department 2002). This included establishing an interdepartmental Committee on Environment and Social Impacts to review projects for compliance with safeguard policies.

In this book, I examine the decisions about the allocation of three types of projects that came into being as a result of these changes. *Environmentally risky projects* came under much greater scrutiny by both donor states and civil society groups beginning in the early 1990s. The list of environmental "disaster projects" at the multilateral development banks grew sufficiently long to focus the attention of donor countries, which were willing to push for environmental reforms. *Safeguard policies*, a type of administrative procedure, were put in place that required the multilateral development banks to prevent environmental damages in their infrastructure, forestry, and hydropower projects. The environmental safeguard policies require that all projects be assigned to an environmental risk category, each with distinct requirements for preparing projects. These safeguard policies were established at the World Bank and Asian Development Bank in the run-up to the Rio meetings, and immediately following the Rio meeting at the Inter-American Development Bank as part of its Eighth General Resource Increase (Large 2005; Board of Governors 1994). The safeguard policies required the multilateral development banks to assess the negative environmental impacts of development projects before approving projects, to prevent environmental damages from occurring during the implementation of projects, and to consult with local people about their environmental concerns.

At the same time, staff at the multilateral development banks developed new types of projects that aimed to address environmental concerns of global proportions, including ozone depletion, biodiversity conservation, and climate change mitigation (Hicks et al. 2008, 189). I call these types of projects *global environment-improving projects*, since their primary purpose is to address transboundary issues of direct concern to donor countries. In the aftermath of the Rio meetings, donor countries looked to the multilateral development banks to coordinate the financing of international environmental efforts, even when civil society groups opposed the involvement of these multilateral organizations (Shabecoff 1990). When rich countries came together to discuss financing assistance for less-developed nations in line with Rio commitments, they decided to channel the initial $2 billion through the Global Environment Facility, the United Nations Environment Program, and the World Bank (Lewis 1994).

The new environmental offices and divisions at the multilateral development banks expanded rapidly to accommodate the influx of resources for global environment-improving programs. Indeed, the management of the multilateral development banks actively sought to attract significant new resources for these types of operations. While these new departments did not change the multilateral development banks into paragons of environmental responsibility (Nielson and Tierney 2003; Gutner 2005), they had a significant influence on MDB assistance strategies. To this day, the organization-wide assistance strategies at all of the multilateral development banks prioritize global environmental issues, at least formally. As a result, the multilateral development banks have become the primary conduits of international environmental assistance (Hicks et al. 2008, 28).

Finally, the environmental mandates of the multilateral development banks recognized that economic development produces environmental damages that are primarily domestic. World Bank staff, for example, emphasized the link between health, poverty, and local environmental conditions in the 1992 World Development Report (World Bank 1992). While both donor and borrower states have been interested in addressing environmental issues such as sanitation and sewerage, abatement of industrial pollution, management of solid waste, and soil conservation, the benefits of doing so primarily accrue to the borrowing country. I call these types of operations *local environment-improving projects*. As I will argue in later chapters, the lending preferences of donor countries are different for global and local environment-improving projects, which influences the ability of the multilateral development banks to practice selectivity.

These three types of projects are different on a number of dimensions that are likely to be important determinates of whether selectivity can be practiced within country portfolios: the interest of donor states; the demand by borrowing countries; the procedures that regulate approval; and the types of information that are routinely gathered about performance. Differences along these dimensions permit testing of specific hypotheses about when the tensions between strategic and development concerns can be overcome in development finance. Before proceeding to these tests, the next chapter presents the core theory of this book about how information can be used to manage discretion at international organizations.

3

Addressing the Problem of Performance

A PRINCIPAL-AGENT FRAMEWORK

While selectivity *within* the portfolios of individual countries might resolve some of the tensions between the strategic and development goals of aid, it is not easy to practice. Selectivity requires good information about what projects succeed and what projects fail in particular countries. It also requires that staff at aid agencies have incentives to update allocation decisions in light of this information. Even when the member states in the multilateral development banks would like to improve development outcomes, which may not always be their strongest incentive, they cannot simply mandate selectivity because it is difficult for them to monitor decisions by the bank staff. Because member states cannot easily monitor decision-making and operations at international organizations, it is difficult to ensure that management and staff respond to mandates and directives.

In this chapter, I present a principal-agent framework that more precisely describes the challenges involved with generating and using information about results to promote selectivity. This framework also helps illustrate the trade-offs involved in granting international organizations discretion. Building on this framework, the core argument of this book is that member states are able to manage discretion and promote selectivity when they (1) generate information about the outcomes of past decisions and (2) use that information to raise the costs of making decisions that have been unsuccessful or encourage decisions that have been successful. While it may seem easy enough to generate and use information about results, both steps can be difficult and costly. In isolation, neither step will maximize the benefits of delegation to international organizations. Information will be disregarded if policies and procedures do not create incentives to use it. Policies and procedures cannot selectively limit decisions that result in bad outcomes and promote the decisions that result in good outcomes unless they are applied based on credible information about performance.

The challenge of promoting selectivity reflects more general concerns about managing international organizations to take advantage of delegation (see Hawkins et al. 2006a). In recent years, international relations scholars have delved more seriously into the politics of performance at international organizations. Despite the recognition that some international organizations are far more effective at carrying out the tasks that have been delegated to them than others, the internal and external factors that contribute to this variation are poorly understood. Possible factors that influence IO performance include bureaucratic culture, organizational resources, competing member state interests, incoherent mandates, management practices, and information problems (Gutner and Thompson 2010).

Less is known about the strategies that states employ to overcome problems that can arise when they rely on international organizations. Gutner and Thompson (2010, 245) outline the need to explain variation in the performance of international organizations, specifically since "there is a pressing need for IOs to better address old problems and to take on a growing list of new ones." They argue that it has been difficult to research variation in the performance of international organizations because of vast differences in outcomes between different international organizations and the difficulty of identifying cause-and-effect relationships in complex governance environments. Because multilateral development banks all allocate projects and collect information about the outcomes of these projects, they offer an excellent domain to understand how management efforts by states contribute to variation in the performance of international organizations.

Drawing from research on the challenges of generating information and using it to change the incentives of staff at other types of large organizations, I derive testable hypotheses about the policies and procedures that are likely to succeed at reaping the benefits of discretion without the risks to performance inherent to discretion. I test these hypotheses in the chapters that follow. The multilateral development banks offer a unique ground for generating and testing theories of performance because they attempt to achieve similar outcomes, those outcomes can be measured systematically, and variations in policies and procedures intended to improve performance exist between organizations, countries, and time periods.

Principal-agent theory offers a useful point of departure for describing the relationships between member states, the management of international organizations, and the frontline staff of international organizations. At each relationship in this chain, resources and authority are granted from the higher level to decision-makers at the lower level, with a mandate to achieve some outcome. The fundamental feature of delegation relationships is "a conditional grant of authority from a *principal* to an *agent* that empowers the latter to act on behalf of the former" (Hawkins et al. 2006b, 7). Examples of this relationship in political contexts include legislative delegation to executive agencies (Weingast and Moran 1983), public delegation of war-making powers to executive branches (Downs and Rocke 1994), the delegation of shared defense functions to military allies (Lake 1996), and the delegation of authority to finance development to the multilateral development banks (Nielson and Tierney 2003). In each relationship, a principal empowers an agent to act on its behalf because doing so allows the principal to better achieve its interests than would acting alone. Principals expect to do better because agents possess some combination of organizational, coordination, information, and technical advantages.

The delegation of authority and resources to the multilateral development banks is a classic example of a principal-agent relationship in international relations (Nielson and Tierney 2003; Milner 2006). The multilateral development banks, like other international organizations, derive the authority and resources to take actions from their member countries. States collectively created the multilateral development banks and delegated substantial authority and resources to the multilateral development banks so that they could design and implement development programs around the world.[1] In return, member states would like the multilateral development banks to achieve development outcomes that are difficult for the member states to achieve themselves.

The delegation relationship does not always lead to the problem of performance described in the first chapter. The problem of performance arises when the preferences of the agent do not align with the preferences of the principal, a condition I call *divergent preferences*. Divergent preferences have too many origins to outline completely in the case of international organizations, but most deal with the incentives of individuals who make up the organizations. These interests include financial gain, lower expenditure of effort, maintaining the status quo, or professional prestige. As Ness and Brechin (1988, 247) write about international organizations, "They are live collectivities interacting with their environments, and they contain members who seek to use the organizations for their own ends." For the particular application considered in this book, several reasons for divergent preferences are worth noting.

The management of international organizations may seek to grow and control resources (Vaubel, Dreher, and Soylu 2007). The professional norms and policy preferences of agents might clash with the policies that are mandated by lawmakers (Meier and O'Toole 2006; Sabatier and Loomis 1995). Agents might like controlling the resources delegated to them, but they might not want to expend effort to carry out the mandates that accompany those resources (Dejong, Forsythe, and Lundholm 1985). This problem is endemic to public service agencies in many poorly governed countries (Keefer and Khemani 2005). Agents might have incentives to act in ways that strengthen their hold on power and policymaking. For example, military leaders have advantages in gaining access to public resources, which often enable them to gain greater control of political institutions over time, rather than acting according to legislative preferences (Mbaku 1991). Finally, agents might simply use delegated public resources for private gain, giving rise to corruption and graft (Bardhan 1997). While divergent preferences may arise for a variety of reasons, they all leave the principal with the problem of controlling their agent.

Divergent preferences lead to problems of performance in a delegation relationship. Most directly, an agent might use the authority and resources delegated to it to pursue its own interests, rather than the interests of the principal. The problem for the principal is that it may be difficult to observe when the agent acts on divergent preferences. In a seminal article, Eisenhardt describes the information problem at the heart of managing divergent preferences: "(a) the desires or goals of the principal and agent conflict and (b) it is difficult or expensive for the principal to verify what the agent is actually doing. The problem here is that the principal cannot verify that the agent has behaved appropriately" (1989, 58). If a principal could observe each and every action taken by their agent without cost and could effectively sanction the agent for acting on divergent preferences, then the problem of control in a delegation relationship would be less of a challenge. Principals, however, have difficulty observing the actions of their agents in many cases. Agents might be mandated to carry out tasks that are not readily observable, since they are implemented repeatedly in dispersed settings. For example, when legislative bodies delegate control over monetary resources to bureaucrats and accounting standards are poor, it can be very difficult to trace when public officials use resources for private gain (Dorotinsky and Floyd 2004). This is an information problem and contributes to endemic corruption in many countries around the world, even when agents have limited discretion about how to achieve the principal's goals.

When agents have discretion about how to carry out their mandate, other types of information problems arise. Principals often delegate resources to agents because they have technical expertise about how to use resources to best achieve the interests of the principal. For example, executive agencies are often given substantial leeway to write specific rules and regulations under the authority of umbrella laws because they have more technical capacity than legislators (Epstein and O'Halloran 1994). International organizations, like the multilateral development banks considered in this book, are given substantial flexibility on how to use the resources for development purposes since they assemble highly trained technical staff. Even if principals can observe the actions of their agents, they may not possess the technical expertise necessary to assess whether their agents are acting with the mandate or their own private interests in mind. Indeed, past research has highlighted how agent expertise poses a significant barrier to effective control by principals in policymaking settings (Barnett and Finnemore 1999). When divergent preferences are present, technical uncertainty raises the possibility that any problems of performance will not be detected until much later, when the outcomes of current choices are realized. Even then, it will not always be clear whether realized problematic outcomes are a product of shirking agents or the inherent uncertainty of decision-making in complex settings.

Indeed, the challenges of information asymmetries motivate much of the research on international organizations. In an important early study, Pollack writes that "monitoring and sanctioning are costly to member state principals," which provides a way for international organizations like the European Commission to act independently of the EU's member governments and influence European integration (1997, 101). Likewise, Barnett and Finnemore argue that "international organizations have become autonomous because of their embodiment of technical rationality and control over information" (1999, 709). State principals may delegate to international organizations precisely because the latter are able to coordinate specialized expertise better, making it even more difficult for donor states to understand what activities best achieve their interests (Hawkins et al. 2006b, 13–15). For example, Lipson (2010) finds that because the relationship between UN peacekeeping activities and outcomes is highly ambiguous, it is almost impossible for member states to assess and respond to performance. Similarly, Vreeland (2006) argues that it has been difficult for states to insist on reforms at the International Monetary Fund because they do not understand the reasons why programs succeed. Under conditions of uncertainty, international organizations have substantial leeway to act counter to the interests of their member states.

Even if monitoring and evaluation provide principals with the information they need to identify when their agents are acting on divergent preferences or are not updating their practices to reflect new information, principals may not have tools to steer their agents to act in the ways they want. States may find it difficult to withdraw from the delegation relationship. At the domestic level, legislatures cannot simply fire executive agencies. In parallel at the international level, member states in international organizations rarely find it advantageous to withdraw membership.

In terms of managing the management, research on the design of international organizations shows that bureaucrats resist state control. For example, Johnson (2013) looks across new international organizations and finds that when bureaucrats are involved in their design, the resulting organizations tend to have fewer features that promote state control, such as veto points in operational or financial decision-making. Parallel research on large, public organizations finds that the incentive for management to maintain autonomy is a strong incentive (Carpenter 2001). The drive for autonomy and resources comes from a number of mechanisms, including the desire for prestige (Teodoro 2011, 65–67), the ease of maintaining the status quo (Villadsen 2012), and the pursuit of professional or social norms unique to the organization (Fortmann 1990; Ringquist 1995; Meier and O'Toole 2006). While my present goal is not to outline and distinguish between the reasons why organizations pursue autonomy, it is important to note that this incentive is prominent at many organizations.

The multilateral development banks are large organizations and are difficult to manage, like all kinds of organizations with complex chains of delegation, internal cultures, and different types of individual staff incentives (Gutner 2005; Vaubel 2006). In practice, member states in the multilateral development banks work with a select few points of management and are not involved in regular interactions with thousands of operational and frontline staff, who are only indirectly controlled. Even if they are able to perfectly manage the management, the challenge of managing the staff remains. As depicted in figure 3.1, states are one step removed from the direct management of the individuals who design and implement programs.

Instead, member states have to rely on the management of the multilateral development banks with whom they have direct contact. In the principal-agent framework, this is often referred to as a "chain of delegation," since there are multiple sequential delegation relationships that have the possibility for agent slack (Vaubel 2006). The challenge of ensuring results across sequential relationships based on

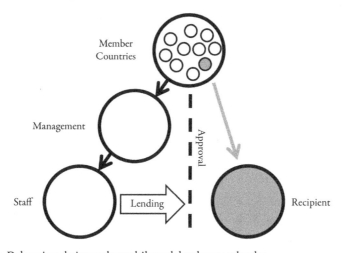

FIGURE 3.1 Delegation chains at the multilateral development banks

delegation, especially when lines of responsibility are complex, networked, and blurred, presents particular problems. Recently, scholars of international organizations have begun exploring this complexity, for example, by defining international organizations as "complex agents" that have various internal actors with different levels of autonomy from member states (Elsig 2014). Indeed, the management structure of the multilateral development banks has moved away from a clear hierarchy (Independent Evaluation Group 2012).

The large research tradition on "street-level bureaucrats" highlights some of the challenges of getting staff to implement mandates, particularly the numerous and oftentimes competing demands placed on frontline staff (Lipsky 2010). A recent review of decentralization to embassies for the operations of Danish aid projects finds that frontline staff are often overburdened with many goals and administrative commitments, which has caused some troubles with maintaining focus on high-level strategic objectives (Engberg-Pedersen 2014). Research on the challenge of simultaneously managing multiple goals at public agencies finds that attention can become scattered. More effective management strategies often focus on a limited set of goals (Resh and Pitts 2013). When frontline staff are tasked with addressing many competing demands, they often prioritize goals that lead to the greatest career benefits (Teodoro 2011).

The challenge of managing the implementation of projects and programs becomes even more difficult as projects move into the implementation stage. The staff at multilateral development banks are formally in charge of supervising implementing partners, which are oftentimes government agencies in the recipient country. These implementing partners are primarily responsible to domestic parties, particularly the government ministries that conclude negotiations with the multilateral development banks. This means that after projects are approved, the contractors in charge of implementation often face greater accountability pressures at the domestic level than they do from the staff at multilateral development banks.

In the worst cases, this leads to corruption. For example, US and European Union officials estimated that at least half of all foreign aid for reconstruction and development that flowed into Afghanistan following the ouster of the Taliban regime was lost to corrupt officials (Chamberlain 2007). In 2012, Ireland, Norway, Sweden, and Denmark suspended aid to Uganda after an auditor found that more than 12 million euros intended to build infrastructure in the north of the country had been diverted to corrupt politicians after being disbursed to government accounts (Lynch 2012). In more benign cases, this can lead to projects moving in directions that were not supported by the full membership of international organizations. For example, Australia has had persistent problems ensuring that its aid to Fiji is not diverted to the military or that aid earmarked for reconstruction is not diverted to the general budget (Keohane 1988; Crawford 1988; *Fiji Times* 2008). Once funds leave the accounts of donor organizations, it becomes very difficult to monitor and control actions taken by counterparts at recipient governments.

An additional challenge of managing these large organizations is that member states do not always agree on what type of control mechanism is needed or how stringently it should be applied. For many types of international organizations, including multinational courts, principals have limited recontracting abilities because it is difficult to create broad agreement to remake international organizations, leaving "exit" as the only strategy in many cases (Alter 2006). Member states in the multilateral development banks do not have uniform interests, which may make it difficult to coordinate competing demands for different types of performance at the board level (Lyne, Nielson, and Tierney 2009; Waterman and Meier 1998). For instance, when the World Bank Inspection Panel was established to provide civil society groups an institutionalized way to submit complaints, there was significant disagreement among member countries about which allegations to investigate (Clark 2003, 11–15). At the African Development Bank and Inter-American Development Bank, donor states hold a minority of shares, which has resulted in their inability to maintain a strong focus on environmental reforms (staff interviews with author).[2] When member states hand down competing goals, multilateral development banks may find it difficult to manage performance across these goals.

Researchers working on other areas of state-IO relations have found that member states sometimes fail to produce sufficient incentives for IO staff to change their practices, despite clear preferences on the part of member states. Pollack and Hafner-Burton (2010) found, for example, that gender mainstreaming policies promoted by member states have had limited effects in the European Commission because they fail to provide "hard incentives" for staff to change their practices. Other studies across a variety of contexts have found that sanctioning is very costly for member states, even when they have information about poor performance (Pollack 1997; Elgie 2002; Wilks 2005). These variations suggest that external accountability relationships influence the development of internal practices, and potentially norms, about performance in meeting member state mandates (Johns 2007; Reinalda and Verbeek 2004; Elsig 2010).

In particular, international organizations may not be achieving all their mandates, but on net still bring benefits to the states that support them. In these cases, member states in international organizations have few credible ways to sanction their agents for failing to carry out their mandates. Because IO activities serve multiple purposes, shutting down programs for poor performance along certain criteria can harm the overall interests of member states. In addition, even if member states in international organizations are able to monitor organization-level performance, it can be difficult to monitor and sanction individual decisions and staff.

A fundamental issue for the multilateral development banks considered in this book is that they exist to transfer development resources to less-developed countries, many of which suffer from significant governance problems. As Easterly argues, "The success of past aid to follow conditions and the failure of past aid to follow conditions are both taken as justification for future aid" (2003, 38). Given that a primary function of the multilateral development banks is to make investments where private sector lending is unavailable, the banks have only been willing to cease all engagement with particular countries in extraordinary circumstances.[3] Donor states and staff at the development banks often view poor outcomes as necessary costs on the path to long-term development in recipient countries. Because donor states are reluctant to withdraw all development support for poor performance, they often lack tools to ensure that the multilateral development banks are responsive to past performance, short of threatening to withhold resources.

The principal-agent model offers a useful point of departure for considering the mechanisms that can be used to control agents that are delegated responsibilities and resources at multiple levels. But it does not offer a complete picture. In developing and explaining when international organizations like the multilateral development banks practice selectivity, particular attention needs to be paid to the sources of divergent preferences. Control mechanisms must offer information about when agents are acting on those preferences and must be sufficiently strong to change behaviors that are driven by strong incentives. The particular configuration of preferences and points of control will be the focus of the next section, where I develop the hypotheses that will drive the empirical chapters that follow.

MANAGING DISCRETION

While the principal-agent framework helps to describe relationships between member states, management, and staff at international organizations, it does not directly speak to the core trade-off of managing a relationship based on delegation. If principals control agents by limiting the choices they can make, then they are also likely to decrease the ability of their agents to use technical expertise. This is one of the core reasons to delegate resources and authority in the first place. Kathleen Bawn, writing about domestic bureaucracies, sums up this trade-off:

> The problem is that administrative procedures designed to prevent bureaucratic drift also limit the agency's ability to research policy consequences or to make decisions that reflect its expertise. . . . The degree of agency independence on any particular policy reflects the legislature's willingness to trade uncertainty about policy consequences for uncertainty about agency behavior. (1995, 63)

The challenge for principals is finding ways to increase control of agent behavior in ways that do not significantly reduce the benefits of delegation and discretion. Since research in the principal-agent tradition in international relations has not focused on the mechanisms available to decrease the size of this trade-off, I build from recent research on bureaucratic control, public administration, and organizational management to generate hypotheses. In doing so, I seek to demonstrate that states do not need to eliminate discretion to exert control. They have ways to manage discretion. Existing research mostly finds that control should be difficult because of the limited ability of states to recontract following delegation and the significant information problems involved with delegation (Alter 2006; Cortell and Peterson 2006; Dahl 1999; Vaubel 2006). I argue that finer tools exist that allow states to manage discretion without forgoing the benefits of discretion. The presence of these tools is likely to increase the performance of international organizations.

In his book *Bureaucratic Ambition* (2011, 53–55), Manuel Teodoro highlights how the relationships between political principals and bureaucratic agents vary widely. One possibility is the standard principal-agent relationship, where principals have well-specified preferences over outcomes and clear expectations about what is required to achieve those outcomes. Alternatively, the expectations about the relationship might be described as a client-professional relationship, where expertise and judgment are precisely the qualities that politicians, or in this case member states, would like to gain. Principals that enter the delegation relationship vary on the degree to which they depend on professional judgment and expertise, and are likely to structure a delegation relationship differently based on their expectations and needs. As Huber and Shipan (2002) argue, principals are often deliberate about the decision to grant discretion to agents, depending on the alignment of interests and the need for technical expertise.

Consider the possible value of decreasing the trade-off between discretion and control in abstract terms. Any decision made by an agent has some uncertainty in the outcome that is likely to result, in this case represented by ranges of probable outcomes A, B, and C (figure 3.2). When a principal grants decision-making authority to an agent, the agent can make choices that lead both to good and to bad outcomes. A principal makes the choice to grant either low or high discretion to an agent, who might have divergent preferences to use resources and authority for private gain.

If principals grant little discretion regarding the use of delegated resources or eliminate discretion altogether, they are likely to lower the probability of both very good and very poor outcomes. In figure 3.2, this is represented by the elimination of choices available to agents that are likely to lead to outcomes in areas A and C. Indeed, the core challenge for principals of all types of organizations is not to put

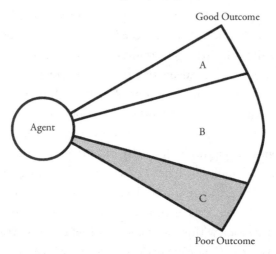

FIGURE 3.2 Managing agent discretion to avoid poor outcomes

Note: The challenge for the principal is to manage discretion in ways that avoid poor outcomes C without also forgoing the opportunity for good outcomes A obtained through the innovation and experimentation permissible with discretion.

in place control mechanisms that eliminate the possibility for the beneficial use of discretion. Landau and Stout (1979, 155) describe the trade-off in particularly lucid terms: "Time and time again, control systems, imposed in the name of error prevention, result only in the elimination of search procedures, the curtailment of freedom to analyze, and a general inability to detect and correct error."

This occurs because the agent cannot use resources for the most egregious types of private gain, but might also be limited in making innovative decisions that take advantage of technical expertise and coordinating capacity for better performance. Control mechanisms put in place to manage discretion seek to decrease the probability that bad outcomes will occur repeatedly in specific domains of decision-making, in this case the range of outcomes represented in C, without decreasing the choice set for domains of decision-making where discretion has not led to bad outcomes. In this way, an effective control mechanism aims to reduce *repeated errors*, rather than well-calculated risks that take advantage of either new opportunities with higher uncertainty or decisions that are known to be lower risk because outcomes have been successfully achieved previously. In the context of development finance, this means that the management of discretion should not stunt innovation and experimentation; it should ensure that future decisions take into account the successes and failures of innovative or experimental decisions.

Indeed, principals have a variety of oversight and control mechanisms for international organizations following delegation, many of which do not require exit from the delegation contract but rather seek to avoid repeated mistakes and bad outcomes. Principals can require that their agents carry out procedures that reveal divergent preferences, without precluding the full range of choices. Principals can enlist the help of specialized monitors or auditors to evaluate whether their agent is shirking and increase audits in areas where outcomes have been poor previously. Principals can use external monitoring, such as that provided by interest groups, to overcome information problems. Public agencies and international organizations now routinely have strong monitoring and evaluation functions built into programs and activities. Principals can change the mandate of their agent in light of information about performance and decreased uncertainty as part of strategic planning.

In sum, principals are not helpless in the face of agency problems. Indeed, a principal's decision to delegate authority and resources is partly based on the options that they have for control and oversight following delegation. If a principal anticipates agency problems, but can oversee its agent at low costs, then it is more likely to delegate. If on the other hand, the principal has no good way to control the agent, then the principal might not delegate at all. Principals in other settings certainly make the decision to delegate with oversight and control mechanisms in mind. For example, legislative bodies give different executive agencies widely varying levels of discretion, in part based on how well agency decisions can be managed (McCubbins 1985). It is necessary to account for oversight and control mechanisms not only to explain the performance of agents, but also to explain the origins of the delegation relationship. A persistent theme in research on bureaucracies and international organizations is a need to identify when different types of control mechanisms will emerge and what their effects will be (Huber and Shipan 2000).

The challenge of managing discretion at public bureaucracies has been discussed for a long time, but the insights generated from this work have not been systematically applied to international organizations, which operate under different political and institutional constraints. Unfortunately, we have little systematic knowledge about the efficacy of different oversight and control mechanisms at international organizations. Instead, existing research has sought to explain why states delegate to international organizations and how the delegation relationship can lead to suboptimal outcomes (Barnett and Finnemore 1999; Hawkins et al. 2006a). This offers the opportunity to build strategies from research in public administration, bureaucratic control, and organizational management that might prove successful in managing international organizations. I consider four strategies in particular: administrative procedures, accountability mechanisms, project evaluation, and strategic planning.

ADMINISTRATIVE PROCEDURES

When a principal delegates authority and resources to an agent, it also has the ability to set rules for how the agent will use the delegated authority and resources. These rules may be very specific, or they may leave the agent with considerable discretion. For instance, military alliances typically have strict rules and procedures that govern the use of military resources, since states are not willing to leave core security functions to the discretion of agents that may not have aligned preferences (Cortell and Peterson 2006). Other times, member states give considerable discretion to international organizations, because they seek to take advantage of technical expertise (Barnett and Finnemore 2005). The multilateral development banks are perhaps the best example of international delegation with significant discretion, since the multilateral development banks have virtually no restrictions on the types of projects that they can pursue with different borrowing countries. However, projects must undergo economic, social, and environmental planning and review procedures before they are approved.

In domestic settings, legislatures often overcome problems of performance that arise from discretion by mandating that executive agencies follow certain types of procedures when carrying out their programs (McCubbins and Page 1987; McCubbins, Noll, and Weingast 1987; Gailmard 2009). For example, legislative bodies can allow executive agencies to write rules and regulations, but require public hearings and economic studies before the rules and regulations are finalized (Steelman 1999). This can make rules that run counter to strong public interests easier to identify. In other cases, procedural controls are substantially tighter. For example, the military might be given very specific directions from civilian commanders and be required to seek explicit approval for any deviations from a mandated plan. Procedures often do not summarily prohibit actions by an agent, but instead make it easier for principals to monitor whether decisions align with mandates. The procedures thus make it more difficult for agents to act on divergent preferences.

Oftentimes, principals seek to achieve better performance by complementing procedures with specialized offices that must approve the results of reviews and plans. For example, audit offices in public bureaucracies ensure that financial resources are used according to rules and procedures that are set out by legislatures. By mandating certain observable procedures that are supposed to be associated with performance of the mandate and then empowering specialized monitors to ensure that those procedures are carried out, the principal can avoid the need for active oversight, assuming auditors are sufficiently empowered to sanction individual staff or departments that run afoul of financial rules. Additionally, principals can require that their agents themselves complete additional reviews in areas where divergent preferences are likely. In the United States, for example, infrastructure projects that involve federal land are required to undergo environmental impact assessments. These assessments do not disqualify projects from being permitted, but they do change costs to government employees for making decisions without due diligence, as they raise the shadow of oversight by increasing detection (Bailey 1997).

Member states in international organizations have often responded to performance problems by altering administrative procedures as well. In 1989, the Office of the United Nations High Commissioner for Refugees faced an unprecedented cut in its budget and staff after it expanded its programs for refugees beyond what member states preferred. It was forced to accept new procedures for the repatriation of refugees, which resulted in more refugees being returned to their home country (Barnett and Finnemore 2004, 95). In 2011, the World Health Organization launched a reform process to improve its performance in meeting public health goals, particularly by adopting new procedures that required program goals to be clearly specified (World Health Organization 2012). At the multilateral development banks, the environmental performance issues brought to light by the Narmada Dam controversy instigated a wave of policy reforms, including the requirement for strong environmental impact assessments before risky projects and the expansion of an environmental office that was tasked with ensuring that these procedures are carried out (Nielson and Tierney 2003). I ask whether these procedures make it easier to monitor the multilateral development banks and whether they constrain the approval imperative that often leads to poor environmental outcomes. Existing research has suggested that procedures help member states measure performance, perhaps supporting a move toward better performance (Gutner 2002, 2005).

Existing research is rarely based on a systematic investigation of the decisions of organizations subject to procedures. I contend that administrative procedures like the safeguard policies should at the very least make the multilateral development banks responsive to past performance, since they raise the cost of approving environmentally risky projects in countries that have not implemented safeguards well in the past. Like Pollack and Hafner-Burton (2010), I argue that when administrative procedures provide sufficient "hard incentives" for staff because they set measurable standards that can be monitored, they should constrain repeated poor decisions. I test the proposition that safeguard policies at the multilateral development banks have decreased the approval of environmentally risky projects in countries that have a record of running afoul of safeguard procedures.

Hypothesis: Member states induce selectivity in decisions about allocation when they create procedures that make it costly for staff to pursue environmentally risky projects in countries with poor records of implementing environmental safeguards (chapter 4).

ACCOUNTABILITY MECHANISMS

While administrative procedures might constrain certain types of decisions that contribute to poor performance, they have not eliminated performance problems related to the management of negative environmental outcomes at the multilateral development banks (Gutner 2002; Independent Evaluation Group 2010b). While donor countries are not in the position to monitor the implementation of environmental management plans in every project, they have been very interested in avoiding "disaster projects" that create an outcry among their own citizens. Although administrative procedures might be able to change staff incentives to approve projects, they might not lead to better implementation after approval. Most safeguard policies revolve around the creation of environmental management plans during project design. Much less effort is spent on actively auditing these plans during project implementation. It may even be difficult for the multilateral development banks to monitor this type of performance, since staff are not digging roads, building power plants, and so on, but rather contracting out many of these services. Thus, even MDB staff are one step removed from implementing activities to achieve environmental goals (Gutner 2005). This means that even if administrative policies can constrain the approval imperative, donor states might benefit by enhancing their ability to monitor the implementation of projects.

In domestic settings, it has long been recognized that legislative bodies can benefit from external monitors like citizen groups, who enhance their oversight capabilities. In particular, when external monitors have interests that align with the principals and the ability to provide monitoring independently, they can facilitate "fire-alarm oversight" (McCubbins and Schwartz 1984). Since monitoring is costly for legislative bodies, especially given the myriad of activities that are carried out by executive agencies every day, it can be a better strategy to allow external groups to bring to attention activities that diverge from legislative preferences. This way, legislative bodies do not have to undertake costly monitoring and can take credit for responding to constituent demands. The key element of this arrangement is that external groups must be able to monitor the types of actions that run afoul of principals' preferences. For example, citizens have been successful at driving responses from municipal governments by submitting complaints about observable environmental violations like uncollected waste, unmanaged lots, and litter (Jones et al. 1977). In other cases, such as ensuring that public resources are not lost to corruption, this kind of monitoring can be very difficult. However, even in this more difficult context, examples exist where citizen groups have gained access to financial information of public agencies, allowing them to independently monitor expenditures and reduce corruption (Goetz and Jenkins 2001).

At the international level, nongovernmental organizations play important roles in monitoring cooperative arrangements between states. Like domestic settings, NGOs can monitor whether states abide by agreements, which can make bargaining easier by facilitating credible commitments (Princen and Finger 1994; Pallas and Urpelainen 2012; Raustiala 1997). However, while the role of NGOs in monitoring arrangements has been investigated, the role that NGOs might play in enhancing performance at international organizations is not well understood. Over the last two decades, civil society groups have become increasingly active in monitoring international organizations, especially those involved in economic development and globalization (Ackerman 2004). Accountability mechanisms, which are formal processes that allow civil society groups to raise performance problems, have grown more common (Grigorescu 2010). These mechanisms provide civil society groups formal ways to seek accountability, avoiding perhaps the costly process of appealing to states for accountability in informal ways (Keck and Sikkink 1998; Grant and Keohane 2005). Thus, I explore the extent to which NGOs are available to provide monitoring of MDB performance in ways that complement oversight by states and constrain the approval of projects that are likely to have performance problems.

Still, NGOs face limitations in monitoring the performance of international organizations in many instances. Just like states, they face problems observing the actions of international organizations (Ascher 1983; Hawkins et al. 2006b; Woods and Narlikar 2001). Thus, I expect NGO oversight through accountability mechanisms to have an effect on lending decisions only when NGOs are available, such as when environmental NGOs are already a prominent part of civil society and do not face political repression in their home country. I explore the extent to which civil society monitoring can help member states control international organizations in light of performance problems raised by delegation and the difficulty of monitoring.

Hypothesis: External monitors can enhance state oversight by providing information about implementation problems through accountability mechanisms, thereby inducing selectivity, but only when states have an existing interest in providing oversight for the actions that are subject to monitoring (chapter 5).

OPERATIONS EVALUATION

While accountability mechanisms can generate information about the types of projects that are likely to face opposition from civil society groups, not all problems in delegation come from monitoring and oversight difficulties. Researchers have also called attention to the importance of *uncertainty* in principal-agent relations. For example, Nilakant and Rao (1994) challenge the idea that divergent preferences are the key source of performance problems by agents in many circumstances. Principals, whether they are corporate boards or member states, rely on agents for technical expertise that allows them to operate effectively under conditions of uncertainty. Business managers must navigate changing market environments, emerging competitive threats, and uncertain business forecasts. Likewise, international organizations must operate in countries with unstable political, economic, and institutional conditions. Under these conditions, Nilakant and Rao argue, performance problems come about more often through "incomplete knowledge about the effort-outcome relationship" than divergent preferences (1994, 649). Many of the performance problems associated with agent shirking can be alternatively explained by uncertainty faced by the agent (Hendry 2002). Solving monitoring and oversight problems may be less applicable than establishing management systems that deal effectively with uncertainty by prompting agents to update their practices based on new information.

This is a two-pronged problem: (1) generating useful information and (2) responding to information. Evaluation is a primary tool to generate useful information that helps decision-makers deal with uncertainty. Indeed, professional evaluators have recognized that one of the most important functions of an evaluation is "uncertainty reduction" (Leviton 2003, 530–31). Many times decision-making in complex environments is based on experience and intuition. While agents are relied on precisely because they have the capacity to derive better assumptions and predictions about their working environment, like all people they take mental shortcuts and have bounded knowledge about what results their actions will cause. Evaluations can expand the availability of relevant information, challenge assumptions about the "effort-outcome" relationship, and analyze whether the actions routinely chosen by decision-makers are appropriate to their environment. Specific to international development organizations, Forss and Samset (1999) argue that evaluations can play a useful role when they cause decision-makers to reflect on uncertainty and send strong signals about what has been learned about past operations.

Many evaluators at the multilateral development banks see their role in this way. For example, a report prepared for discussion by member states of the Asian Development Bank highlighted the important role of evaluation in ensuring scarce resources are used wisely:

> Operations Evaluation Department undertakes evaluation activities to help the ADB management and decision-makers in developing member countries who are responsible for planning, designing, and implementing projects and

programs to understand whether resources are well spent, and whether the planned outcomes are achieved. The principal goals of evaluation are to distill lessons learned for future operations . . . to ensure accountability for the use of resources for improving development effectiveness. (Asian Development Bank 2003, 1)

Just because information is available that helps reduce uncertainty does not mean that agents will automatically respond to new information. The use of evaluation information depends critically on the political preferences not only of the evaluation unit itself, but of the decision-makers and political principals that use evaluation information (Weiss 1973, 1988, 1998). In many cases, political actors have incentives to underinvest in information because new information might challenge their preferred mode of action (Pritchett 2002). In some cases, legislative bodies may even want executive agencies to take the blame for failed policies by attributing failure to incompetence in implementation rather than uncertainty, a process that Kiewiet and McCubbins (1991) call the "abdication hypothesis." Scholars have been skeptical that evaluation alone can improve agency behavior unless it is coupled with pressure from principals that deals with organizational inertia (Torres and Preskill 2001; Cronbach et al. 1980). Staff members at international organizations may have their own preferences that limit updating. Indeed, past research has shown that internal cultures can develop within international organizations based on professional norms and agreed standards of practice (Barnett and Finnemore 1999).

At the multilateral development banks, there is an additional reason to doubt that evaluations of individual projects will influence future lending decisions. Member states have limited capacity to monitor everything that happens at the multilateral development banks. Thus, while evaluations might produce new information that helps decision-makers independently deal with uncertainty, evaluations of individual projects are generally below the level of state attention. At many of the multilateral development banks considered in this book, there is no formal process by which member states assess either the findings of project evaluations or management responses to project evaluations. Because formal mechanisms for updating are not present, I can test whether information, in the absence of state engagement, is sufficient to change allocation decisions.

To isolate the role that evaluation might play in addressing uncertainty and subsequently decisions about allocation, I examine environment-improving lending. Donor states have put significant pressure on the multilateral development banks to scale up lending in this sector. Because donor states have shown little appetite to limit environmental projects, even in countries with poor performance, any changes to allocation are likely driven by information provision and updating. Specifically,

I examine whether the results in project evaluations change decisions about the allocation of projects with primarily global or primarily local benefits. For projects with global benefits, all parties gain by allocating more projects, so information about performance does not reduce uncertainty in a way that affects allocation. For projects with local benefits, borrowing countries offer a control point for allocation, as they are more likely to request projects that have proved to be successful. Thus, I expect that project evaluations will mainly have an effect on allocation decisions about projects with local benefits.

> **Hypothesis:** Evaluation will not induce selectivity when donor states prioritize new lending, but can help borrowing countries identify successful programs that meet local demands by overcoming uncertainty (chapter 6).

STRATEGIC PLANNING

Past research also suggests that evaluation is likely to have the most impact on organizations when it is integrated into relevant decision-making processes (Mathison 1994; Kirkhart 2000; Torres and Preskill 2001). One difficulty of making the multilateral development banks more responsive to performance is that member states have little direct involvement with day-to-day decisions at the multilateral development banks (Weaver 2008). Only the very largest countries have permanent missions to the multilateral development banks, and those missions usually have a very small staff. This makes micromanagement and oversight practically impossible for member states. Instead, member states must rely on organization-wide policy and high-level strategic decisions to wield influence. While it is not automatic that international bureaucrats will perfectly implement high-level strategic decisions, it is the case that member states can impose serious budget and policy changes on international organizations if they stray too far from strategic preferences of powerful member states (Barnett and Finnemore 2004). Thus, evaluations that are integrated into high-level decisions about lending might offer a mechanism that induces selectivity.

Perhaps even more important than having a lever of influence, strategic planning can reduce uncertainty among both member states and operational staff about the types of projects and programs that will effectively achieve the goals of member states. Unlike project evaluations, states can effectively engage. The multilateral development banks, like many large, international organizations, work in complex environments with high levels of uncertainty. Host governments change. Economic shocks emerge. Technical and cost projections must be modified. Indeed, the success of development organizations depends in part on the ability of decision-makers to understand and respond to uncertainty in a proactive way. Many of the project appraisals at the multilateral development banks document "threats to development" and other scenarios that might put operations at risk.

Many times plans to deal with uncertainty are based on expertise and assumption. Indeed, uncertainty is one of the core challenges facing organizations, and strategic planning can offer one of the best ways to deal with that uncertainty (Bryson, Crosby, and Bryson 2009). One of the main benefits of engaging in strategic planning for all types of organizations is the opportunity for decision-makers to challenge their own judgments and assumptions (Barnes 1984). In fact, the relationship between principals and agents need not be adversarial but can be based on discovering sources of effectiveness under conditions of uncertainty. Over time, a systematic approach to uncertainty through strategic planning can create more collaborative relationships between principals and agents around discovering solutions to problems of uncertainty. Berry and Wechsler (1995) found, for example, that US states that engaged in strategic planning developed better systems of accountability and results measurement over time as a side consequence.

Thus, high-level evaluations and strategic planning may be better able to induce responsiveness to past performance because they are explicitly embedded within decision processes that involve member states. This stands in opposition to decisions about the design of projects that are predominately driven by staff at the multilateral development banks. Evaluation has a much greater impact when it meets the needs of decision-makers (Weiss 1988, 1998). Thus, evaluations that assess whether decisions made in consultation with member states are actually meeting member state preferences have the potential to offer performance information in a setting directly linked to future decisions about lending. To the extent that lending programs are not successful at meeting member state preferences, member states have the information necessary to prompt a change in direction. Strategic planning and evaluation offers a chance to synthesize information about performance in complex organizations (Miller and Cardinal 1994). In addition, high-level evaluations might challenge the assumptions of states about the kinds of lending programs that will produce the most desired impact.

At international organizations, existing research supports the notion that evaluations intended to inform *member states* about outcomes are most influential. For example, an assessment of the most influential evaluations at the World Bank shows that strategic planning had the potential to define the meso-level preferences of principals for certain policy and programming choices (Operations Evaluation Department 2004). Likewise, an evaluation of influential evaluations at the Asian Development Bank found that member states are most likely to respond to information about large strategic decisions and directions (Operations Evaluation

Department 2007e). An assessment of the evaluation function at the International Monetary Fund similarly found that broad, high-level evaluations are most suitable for gaining the attention of member states (Lissakers, Husain, and Woods 2006). Evaluations that appeal directly to state principals appear to have the most influence on future decisions.

Thus, I will examine how evaluations of multiyear lending portfolios in individual countries affect future lending decisions. One of the most important operational decisions that involve member states at the multilateral development banks is the establishment of multiyear country assistance strategies. Country evaluations are intended to feed into this strategic planning process, and thus offer information that may be more useful and consequential to lending decisions. By examining how future lending reflects the results of country evaluations, I will be able to test whether evaluation solves information problems for member states that are actually in a position to steer course corrections.

Thus, while donor states have expressed a strong preference for expanded environmental lending, country-level evaluations that provide information about the relative effectiveness of that policy preference might change the preferences of donor states. Specifically, they might cause the members states in international organizations to change the mandates they hand down to operational staff. Ironically, although strategic planners and evaluators emphasize the importance of responding to new data about the effectiveness of decisions, little previous research explicitly evaluates whether strategic planning improves decision-making (Mintzberg 1994). Some research has been pessimistic about the role of strategic planning in improving organizational performance, because it can blind organizations to new and unexpected opportunities by focusing on past performance (Miller and Cardinal 1994). In the context of development lending, this reflects a basic issue with evaluation; because evaluation is backward looking, it might not be relevant to new decisions.

> **Hypothesis:** High-level evaluations that are integrated into strategic planning processes will prompt selectivity in the allocation of projects (chapter 7).

Before I proceed with the further development and testing of these hypotheses, it is important to be clear that managing discretion is not the same as eliminating discretion. One concern about selectivity and the practice of letting past performance dictate the allocation of future projects is that innovation will be stunted or eliminated. Two points are worth emphasizing. First, nothing about the framework that

I propose for aid allocation suggests that well-considered risks that might result in failure should not be pursued. I only argue that the multilateral development banks should incorporate the information from past outcomes into future decisions. The absence of this kind of learning or updating is a key reason for ineffective development finance. Second, I am not arguing that choices be eliminated based on past outcomes. Instead, management mechanisms should make it easier or harder to approve new projects based on past outcomes. This keeps open the possibility that a type of project that has failed in the past can be pursued after careful consideration and improvements. The goal of selectivity is not to eliminate discretion; it is to create incentives that align the use of discretion with mandates from states.

4

Administrative Procedures

AVOIDING DELAYS WITH ENVIRONMENTALLY
RISKY PROJECTS

BY THE 1980S, environmental groups were up in arms about the environmentally damaging projects being designed and implemented by the multilateral development banks (Schwartzman 1985). Bruce Rich (1994), in his book *Mortgaging the Earth*, described several "disaster projects" funded by the World Bank that contributed to the outcry. The Northwest Region Development Program in Brazil, which funded the construction of highways and feeder roads, caused more than half a million settlers to move into forested areas in the Amazon and produced widespread deforestation (Rich 1994, 26–28). In India, a series of four loans totaling $850 million for the construction of the Singrauli Super Thermal Power Plant resulted in severe mercury pollution in heavily populated areas (Rich 1994, 40–42). The Indonesia Transmigration Project, which sought to alleviate population pressures on the inner islands through the resettlement of people to less populated islands, mobilized 2.3 million settlers and caused 40,000 to 50,000 km^2 of deforestation (Rich 1994, 34–38).

These types of projects highlighted the weaknesses of environmental policies and practices at the multilateral development banks. They also put management at odds with the growing preference of donor countries to mitigate the environmental damages caused by development projects. Large infrastructure projects at the multilateral banks did not frequently have plans to address negative environmental risks. For example, the Asian Development Bank approved the Bali Irrigation

Sector Project in 1981 with a goal of increasing the production of rice in the project area. But without safeguard policies that mandated the mitigation of environmental risks, the project overlooked traditional ways that local people managed water that were "reflected in the local culture and institutions for centuries" (Asian Development Bank 1992, 10). A later evaluation of the project found "the near abandonment of the age-old coordinated Balinese fallow period . . . which resulted in a major increase in both pest problems and pesticide use. The result was widespread contamination and buildup of pest resistance that reduced yield increments and sustainability" (Asian Development Bank 1992, 11). Without policies and procedures that dealt with environmental risks, these types of reports became commonplace, and many development gains were undermined. Even when environmental management plans were written, they were not implemented diligently (Rich 1994; Wade 1997; Bowles and Kormos 1999; Gutner 2002).

The move toward standardized procedures for managing environmental risks was gradual at the multilateral development banks. Before standard policies and procedures were put in place in the early 1990s, environmental assessments were often completed when they had little chance to affect decisions about the design or approval of projects. For example, the Bauchi Township Water Supply Project in Nigeria, approved by the African Development Bank in 1989, did not include activities to deal with the wastewater that would be produced by increased water supply. The results were predictable: "Dirty wastewater stagnated in pools and puddles within the colonies and was a fertile breeding ground for mosquitos and the spread of malaria. . . . Seepage contaminated the shallow open wells causing serious health hazard and vulnerability to epidemics" (Operations Evaluation Department 2000, 12). Surprisingly, this project had an associated environmental assessment. The assessment was too late. According to the postproject evaluation, "The Bank had relatively lower input in the technical preparation of the project and very little time to assess the environment under which it was to be implemented" (Operations Evaluation Department 2000, 1). This problem was not uncommon across the multilateral development banks. In many cases, environmental risk assessments were completed as afterthoughts, well after the associated project was designed and disbursed (e.g., Rich 1994, 44). As one multilateral development bank environment staff wrote, "A Bank's entry point into the borrower's project planning process (and particularly if the borrower is from the private sector) tends to be after the borrower's own identification process, at a point when major decisions about types of investments and siting have already been made" (Kennedy 1999, 3).

The mid-1980s and the early 1990s saw a growing flurry of interest on the part of member states, and especially the United States, in strengthening the environmental policies at the multilateral development banks. In 1984, as the seventh replenishment of the International Development Association was being negotiated, the US Congress held lengthy hearings about the environmental performance of the World Bank that included witnesses from prominent US environmental NGOs like the Sierra Club and the Environmental Defense Fund (US House of Representatives 1984). Almost unanimously, these organizations sought to make replenishment of IDA by the US Congress conditional on the adoption of stronger environmental policies and procedures for dealing with environmental risk. These advocates argued that many development gains would be lost or reversed without attention to the management of environmental risks. With growing effort by advocates to better manage environmental risks, the United States began to change its approach to the approval of projects at the multilateral development banks. For instance, in 1986, the US representative to the World Bank voted against a loan for the Brazilian power sector on environmental grounds (Rich 1994, 137).

In 1989, pressures from the United States for reforms to environmental policies reached a breaking point. A group of US senators threatened to withhold funding for replenishment of the World Bank unless policies were adopted that better addressed environmental risks (Nielson and Tierney 2003). That same year, the US Congress passed the International Development and Finance Act, with provisions (i.e., "Pelosi Amendment") that required the US representatives to the boards of multilateral development banks to vote against any environmentally risky project that did not have an environmental impact assessment released for at least 120 days prior to a vote. Facing these threats, the World Bank adopted new policies to safeguard the environment during the design and implementation of projects, including an Operational Directive on Environmental Assessment (OD 4.00, annex A) in October 1989, which required environmental assessments for all projects that were likely to have negative environmental impacts (World Bank 1991, 1993b). Likewise, the Asian Development Bank included a requirement for environmental assessments of all projects with negative impacts beginning in the 1988 operations manual (Asian Development Bank 2002). Threats to withhold replenishments to the World Bank continued for the next several years. As Senator Patrick Leahy stated in a March 22, 1990, hearing of the Senate Foreign Operations Subcommittee:

Environmentally problematic projects continue to come forward for Board consideration at the World Bank. I know that you know that we're serious about the environment here, and that's something that's very much of a bipartisan message here. But I hope the World Bank economists who might be listening or following this hearing get the message. I'm going to be very reluctant to support any contribution to the World Bank next year if their environmental image doesn't improve and if their environmental sensitivity doesn't dramatically improve. (US Senate 1990)

Pressures in the US Congress for better environmental practices at the multilateral development banks, and the World Bank in particular, did not let up. When it came time to vote on another replenishment in 1994, Congress withheld $1 billion from the World Bank and made its contribution contingent on further environmental reforms (Nielson and Tierney 2003).

New environmental policies and procedures clashed with existing incentives. The multilateral development banks and their individual staff had (and still have) strong incentives to meet lending and disbursement targets (Asian Development Bank 1994, v; Operations Evaluation Department 2006; Wapenhans 1992). Environmentally risky projects tended to be large, allowing staff to meet these targets quickly. With the adoption of safeguard policies, development banks faced new risks that the time required to design projects would be lengthened, that rates of disbursement would decrease, and that a higher proportion of scarce organizational resources would have to be devoted to assessing and monitoring environmental impacts during project implementation (World Bank 2001; Operations Evaluation Department 2006). It was and still is often advantageous for staff to avoid these time-consuming requirements. This is a problem for member states with an interest in environmental performance, because they cannot easily monitor the implementation of environmental management plans across hundreds of projects and countries. The relevant question, then, is whether or not the procedures put in place by safeguard policies have overcome this problem and promoted selectivity about risky projects.

The environmental safeguard policies that were adopted by the multilateral development banks in the early 1990s imposed new and costly planning requirements on the large dam, road, and irrigation projects that had traditionally been the core of lending by the multilateral banks. These new policies attempted to prevent environmental problems, by ensuring that projects were designed to meet the environmental preferences of donor countries. They also established a yardstick to measure implementation during the course of projects. After 1989, the multilateral development banks were under clear directives from their member states to draft and implement environmental management plans that would prevent negative environmental outcomes. Since the United States precommitted to voting against any project that did not have an environmental impact assessment and management plan available for public scrutiny for at least 120 days, consideration of environmental risks became a binding directive for staff during the design of new operations.

These efforts might not work, since they clash with directives to approve a certain amount of lending each year. Observers have expressed deep doubts that international organizations can be controlled when different states have different preferences about outcomes, particularly when there are significant trade-offs between multiple desirable outcomes (Gutner 2002; Copelovitch 2010). I have argued that states can steer the discretion they grant to international organizations when they (1) harness information about the outcomes of past decisions and (2) use that information to raise costs of making decisions that have been unsuccessful and decrease the costs of making decisions that have been successful. Safeguard procedures that seek to decrease environmental harms have the potential to meet these conditions, since the cost of passing them is likely to be higher when past performance is poor. Information from evaluations might selectively raise the costs of pursuing projects that have been unsuccessful. These conditions are met for the World Bank and the Asian Development Bank, but not for the African Development Bank or the Inter-American Development Bank.

Member states that are interested in preventing environmental harms face difficulties involved with monitoring the implementation of environmental management plans, regardless of the formal policies put in place. In particular, they cannot visit the thousands of field sites where projects are implemented. They need to empower specialized staff to delay project preparation based on information about performance. In the case of environmental harms, offices of environmental specialists were established to support the implementation of environmental safeguards. While these offices do not have regular access to field sites, they do have the ability to delay projects based on risks that are not addressed in management plans. By empowering environmental staff to manage procedural requirements, member states might make allocation responsive to performance for two reasons. First, the MDB's board simply will not consider a project until an environmental assessment is produced. Second, the specialized environmental offices are not under pressure to meet lending targets. These two changes make it more costly for operational staff to approve and administer environmentally risky projects in general.

However, to induce selectivity, the environmental offices responsible for administering the safeguard policies must not limit discretion of the agent entirely. Instead, they must find ways to selectively steer discretion when previous performance indicates that there are serious risks to achieving the mandates passed down by states. Since the ultimate responsibility for implementing safeguard policies falls to borrowing countries, operational staff cannot meet safeguard requirements without cooperation from borrowing countries. Since staff have strong incentives to approve projects without delay, they are less likely to pursue projects when they anticipate significant delays that are outside their control. Given this possibility, I argue that the staff have strong incentives to use information on past safeguard performance when making decisions about environmentally risky financing.

SAFEGUARD POLICIES AND INCENTIVES TO LEND
A Brief History of Environmental Safeguard Policies

Through the 1970s and 1980s, the portfolios of the multilateral development banks consisted largely of environmentally risky projects: large dams, new roads, large-scale irrigation schemes, energy generation facilities, and projects that extracted natural resources. According to the AidData database (Tierney et al. 2011), the World Bank supported 114 hydropower projects with $11.9 billion in financing between 1980 and 1994.[1] The World Bank's own project database identifies $15.9 billion of environmentally risky financing committed between 1990 and 1994, split between such sectors as roads, hydropower, and irrigation. Between 1980 and 1994, the ADB approved 22 loans for hydropower plants totaling almost $1.5 billion (Asian Development Bank 1999, appendix 1). According to Hicks and colleagues (2008, 198–99), the amount of ADB financing directed to "dirty" projects was 10 times the financing allocated to environmental projects from 1980 to 1991, before safeguard policies were in place.

Staff had clear incentives to prefer these types of projects. Before the safeguard policies, a successful career at the multilateral development banks was built on the approval of new operations, and specifically projects that were large and economized on design and preparation costs. Large infrastructure projects generally fit these criteria. The technology behind these projects was well established, which led to faster preparation times in many instances. Thus, prior to safeguard policies, a large share of the financing provided by the multilateral development banks focused on the large infrastructure projects that are also most risky in terms of environmental and social impacts.

The growing attention to the negative environmental consequences of these projects in the mid-1980s and early 1990s from donor countries, as described in the previous section, created demand for an array of new environmental policies and procedures, which were dubbed "safeguard policies" or simply "safeguards" at the multilateral development banks. All of the multilateral development banks adopted safeguard policies during the late 1980s and early 1990s, in response to pressures from donor countries. Pressures from donor countries and the adoption of safeguard policies corresponded to the increased attention that was paid to the relationship between environment and development around the world leading up to the 1992 Earth Summit in Rio de Janeiro. The declaration, signed by heads of state around the world, contained a number of principles. People should be fully informed and participate in managing environmental risks that impact them. Environmental impact assessments should be routine as part of development. Victims of environmental degradation should be appropriately compensated. While the strength of these global norms grew, the challenge of putting them into practice remained.

Safeguard policies attempted to do this in concrete ways. While the exact language and specific procedural requirements of safeguard policies vary across the multilateral development banks, all safeguard policies include two core elements. First, all safeguard policies require that an environmental risk category be assigned to projects at the early stages of the design process, based on expectations about environmental harms. This category is typically assigned by environmental staff. Second, for the riskiest projects, an environmental impact assessment and appropriate management plan must be completed before a project is eligible for approval. The rollout of these policies followed slightly different timelines at the multilateral banks, but all took place following international pressure to put into practice the emerging global norms about environmental protection.

The World Bank first adopted a policy statement about environmental management in 1984 (Operations Manual Statement 2.36, cited in World Bank 1993b). This policy statement encouraged operational staff to consider the environmental consequences of development projects and incorporate appropriate mitigation measures. To implement these goals, an Environment Department was established in 1987, in addition to Environment Divisions in each of the four regions (World Bank 1993b). This reform laid the groundwork for a formal safeguard policy, the Operational Directive on Environmental Assessment (OD 4.00, annex A), which was established in 1989. In 1991, the *Environmental Assessment Sourcebook* was first released and included detailed procedures for assessing the potential consequences of development projects as required by the 1989 policy. In particular, all projects had to be categorized according to their environmental risk, and environmental assessments were required for the riskiest projects.

The Asian Development Bank adopted environmental safeguard policies on a very similar timeline. Prior to 1987, the ADB did not have policies or guidelines in place to assess and mitigate the negative environmental impacts of its lending portfolio. In 1987, the Environmental Unit was established with responsibility for developing guidelines on managing environmental risks (Turnham 1991). By 1988, the ADB operations manual, which sets guidelines that staff must follow when designing and implementing projects, formally required environmental assessments for environmentally risky projects (as cited in Asian Development Bank 2002). Throughout the early 1990s, the ADB clarified and strengthened its safeguard procedures. Relevant policies and procedures included the 1993

Environmental Assessment Guidelines, the 1995 Bank Policy on Forestry, and the establishment of an Inspection Panel in 1995 to ensure that external grievances, including those related to environmental harm, would be addressed by the ADB.[2] By 2002, the ADB adopted a unified Environment Policy that required environmental planning and management as part of all projects with environmental risks.[3] Taken together, these policies increased the time and resources required to approve and implement environmentally risky lending across the ADB lending portfolio (Operations Evaluation Department 2006).

The African Development Bank first adopted an environmental safeguards policy in 1990 and developed Environmental Assessment Guidelines in 1992 (African Development Bank 2001). These procedures required several actions similar to the other multilateral banks: (1) operational departments assign environmental risk category to projects; (2) borrowing country governments are responsible for developing environmental management plans for projects that have environmental risks; (3) the sustainable development unit must clear the environmental management plans; (4) environmental management plans are included in loan covenants; and (5) borrowing countries are responsible for implementing the environmental management plan. While the African Development Bank environmental safeguard policy was similar on paper, as will be discussed below, its implementation was much weaker than similar policies at the World Bank or Asian Development Bank. From 2000 to 2009, a decade after safeguard policies were adopted, less than half of projects were being assigned environmental risk categories, even though this was required by the environmental safeguard policy.[4]

Like the other multilateral development banks, the Inter-American Development Bank began formally considering the environmental impacts of its operations in the decade prior to the establishment of more formal procedures. Beginning in 1983, an Environment Committee was established at the management level to review the environmental impacts of IADB operations (Inter-American Development Bank 1996). During this time the use of environmental impact assessments became more common, though formal procedures had not yet taken root. The move to formalize environmental safeguard procedures followed the other multilateral development banks during the eighth replenishment of the IADB concessional lending arm in 1994. During this replenishment the IADB committed to "develop and update environment-related guidelines in the context of consultation and dialogue with relevant segments of the public" (Board of Governors 1994). Following this commitment, the Environment Committee was changed to the Committee on Environment and Social Impact (CESI). In addition to clearer environmental guidelines, procedural changes also required that project documents prepared as part of the approval process "contain an environmental chapter and/or annex approved by the CESI"

(Inter-American Development Bank 1996). As with the other banks, these changes established an additional process that could delay the approval of any project.

All of these new procedures aimed to limit the environmental damages caused by development projects. They also created a new type of project—the environmentally risky project that required a full environmental impact assessment and a management plan based on that assessment. These category A or I projects—the riskiest classification—are designated based on whether initial design documents anticipate environmental damages that are significant. This classification made it easier for member states to identify the projects that might require closer oversight. The branches of the development banks that provide lending to the private sector within eligible recipient countries, including the European Bank for Reconstruction and Development, established similar policies that were modified to fit the challenges of regulating the environmental performance when private firms and financial institutions are the direct program leads. Here I consider the policies relevant to multilateral development bank lending to governments.

Controlling Agent Discretion with Administrative Procedures

Political principals often use more stringent procedures and limit discretion when the cost of oversight is high (Bawn 1997) and the potential for conflict with preferences of the agent is large (Huber and Shipan 2000). Member states cannot easily monitor the hundreds of environmentally risky projects that are being planned or implemented, even if they have an interest in limiting environmental harms from these projects. By establishing safeguard policies at the multilateral development banks, donor countries made oversight easier and more automatic. Environmental units have the ability to delay the approval of a project if social and environmental risks were not adequately addressed in the design of a project and in the analysis contained in these assessments. These policies did not fundamentally limit discretion, but they did weigh on decisions about which projects to pursue in particular countries, by improving the conditions for effective oversight by member states and specialized environmental units.

The use of procedures to manage discretion has generated attention in other domains, which provides a useful point of reference for safeguard policies at the multilateral development banks. As highlighted in research on domestic bureaucracies, political principals use procedures to require that agents justify and review their decisions (see McCubbins, Noll, and Weingast 1987). For example, Matthew Potoski finds that US states are more likely to require bureaucratic agencies to complete and report policy analyses when they are tasked with creating policy to deal with more complex problems. He suggests that under conditions of technical uncertainty, procedures that require these analyses are used to "produce information and improve conditions for legislative oversight" (1999, 634). David Spence (1999) found that the 1986 Electric Consumers Protection Act in the United States that required the Federal Energy Regulatory Commission (FERC) to provide documented responses to recommendations made by federal and state natural resource management agencies caused FERC to require more environmentally friendly conditions in hydroelectric licenses even though these conditions were not strictly mandated. Spence concluded that procedures made certain types of decisions that disregarded the advice of natural resource management agencies more costly and visible, which improved legislative control.

Since environmental management plans that are part of the safeguard policies at the multilateral development banks specify clear and observable actions that agents must complete when making certain types of decisions, they decrease uncertainty about what should be monitored and what constitutes acceptable performance. They also raise the cost of making certain decisions, potentially in ways that are related to past performance. These two effects can give rise to selectivity.

Lending Incentives Created by Safeguard Policies

Previous research has highlighted the mixed incentives that donors have to allocate projects based on the past performance of recipients. On the one hand, MDB budgets are partly determined by whether their primary shareholding members perceive programming to be effective and aligned with their interests (Fleck and Kilby 2006). As a consequence, the multilateral development banks have been under pressure to demonstrate performance, including successful mitigation of environmental damages, in order to maintain and increase their lending resources during concessional fund replenishments and general capital increases (Park 2005; Weaver 2007).

On the other hand, some scholars have suggested that development organizations face the "budget pressure" problem, which requires them to fully disburse all funds regardless of performance to maintain or increase future budgets (Svensson 2003). In addition, career progression for staff often depends on steering large projects through the approval pipeline (Weaver 2008). These incentives create a strong internal "loan approval culture" that values the approval and disbursement of loans above most other outcomes (Wapenhans 1992). Operational staff are rewarded in terms of promotion, salary, and internal prestige based on the projects they steer to approval. Because staff rotate between different offices over the course of their careers, the results of the projects they steer to approval infrequently follow them. With incentives based on the approval of projects, staff are discouraged from pursuing any project that might result in delayed approval.

To the extent that administrative procedures interact with these incentives, particularly by causing delays to projects in countries with a history of poor implementation, they might change decisions about the allocation of projects. Given that staff incentives are based on loan approvals and that portfolio outcomes have traditionally been evaluated using economic metrics, absent administrative procedures that make environmental considerations a relevant part of the costs to approving and administering projects, operational staff have incentives to de-emphasize the environmental consequences of projects (Gutner 2005). This is precisely how safeguard policies change allocation practices. During the design phase of the project cycle, environmental policies can significantly delay the preparation and approval of projects. Thus, the adoption of safeguard policies has significantly increased the incentives to respond to past performance, as past performance within a particular borrowing country is likely to be a signal of the delays that will be faced during the preparation of new projects, and potentially with the disbursement of funds. These incentives are laid out very clearly in a recent evaluation of the ADB safeguards policy:

> There is recurring evidence of lending decisions being actively directed to avoid projects that might trigger environmental procedures. . . . The decision to avoid environmentally sensitive projects is a rational response of ADB staff, given the existing incentive structure. Often this approach is preferred by the governments, as it fits their desire to expedite project processing and minimize project delays and the associated payment of interest and commitment charges. ADB staff have incentives to gain recognition for project approval, as this impacts on career progression. Environmental safeguard procedures can frustrate this, especially where there is a clash between ADB and national procedures. From the perspective of individual ADB staff and [executing agencies], it makes good sense to avoid or circumvent the environmental safeguard procedures. (Operations Evaluation Department 2006, 57)

Indeed, the first World Bank review of environmental assessment procedures found that environmental assessments could take up to 30 weeks of the project task leader's time (1993a, vii). Similarly, a 2001 World Bank study found that the implementation of safeguard policies, together with requirements for stronger accounting practices, increased administrative costs an average of 20% for projects (World Bank 2001). An evaluation brief completed by the Operations Evaluation Department found that "there is anecdotal evidence that some managers are discouraging their staff from tackling operations involving safeguard policies" (Operations Evaluation Department 2001d, 1). The same evaluation brief reported that 55% of staff with experience with forestry projects reported that environmental safeguard policies were a key reason for declining investment in the forestry sector. As a 1997 World Bank review of safeguard policies reported, "Components that would have caused significant adverse environmental impacts are often eliminated, or significantly altered in size and scope at the time of project identification and environmental screening" (1997, 50). An Independent Evaluation Group evaluation of safeguard policies at the World Bank reports survey data that reinforce these findings:

> Client feedback about the deterrent effect of safeguards was confirmed by the staff survey. Bank-wide, 38 percent of task team leaders, 72 percent of social specialists, and 55 percent of environmental specialists have encountered clients who wanted to avoid all or part of a project because of safeguard policies. The impact of this chilling effect was reported by a majority of team leaders from Latin America and the Caribbean and over 40 percent from East Asia and Pacific and South Asia, which have the most active safeguard portfolios. Almost a fifth of team leaders had encountered a situation where the team revised the scope or design of a project to avoid being classified as category A because this high-risk category leads to higher levels of scrutiny and higher costs. (Independent Evaluation Group 2010b, 46)

While staff at the multilateral development banks have discretion to choose environmentally risky projects, they rely on implementing agencies in the borrowing country to carry them out later. The only direct role they play in implementation is regular oversight missions. Thus, although the multilateral development banks are responsible for meeting the demands of donor countries to safeguard the environment during the implementation of projects, meeting these goals is not entirely or even mostly in their hands. This challenges the idea that safeguard procedures can eliminate the negative outcomes that they are intended to address. Indeed, a scan of the available data in recent years indicates that problems with implementation have not been eliminated (see figure 4.2). Thus, the reaction of staff at the multilateral banks to safeguard procedures should be based partly on the record of borrowing countries. To the extent that borrowing countries have not implemented safeguard policies well and this information is available, staff should want to avoid risky projects where they know they will face more oversight and delay.

When considering environmentally risky lending in countries with a strong record of implementation, staff at the multilateral development banks can have more confidence that project preparation, including environmental assessments, will be completed in a timely manner. This allows staff to meet lending targets. Since the implementation of environmental assessments is the responsibility of the borrowing country, avoiding poorly performing borrowers is one of the only ways that staff can control preparation costs and delays associated with environmental risks. Indeed, a recent ADB evaluation found that mitigating the negative environmental impacts of development projects depends critically on the capacity and willingness of the borrowing country to follow through with environmental management and mitigation measures (Operations Evaluation Department 2006). In addition, the speed of loan disbursement is likely to be faster in countries that have a history of good environmental performance. The cost of supervision will also be lower. The pursuit of environmentally risky projects in high-performing countries is less likely to cause negative attention from donor countries (Khagram 2004; Rich 1990). Since infrastructure and agriculture loans are typically large and economize on preparation costs (Deininger, Squire, and Basu 1998, 395), it may even be the case that good implementation of safeguard policies will lead to more infrastructure and other risky lending.

In addition to the incentives that safeguard policies create for MDB staff, there is evidence that borrowing countries themselves have sought other sources of financing for development projects when they experience significant approval and disbursement delays due to safeguard policies. This is an additional point of decision-making that might use information about past outcomes to make decisions about similar projects in the future. For example, the 2007 ADB Country Assistance Program evaluation for India reported:

> Concerns of the [Government of India and executing agencies] regarding the scope and detail of safeguard requirements are becoming a factor in their perceptions of ADB assistance. Safeguard-related issues are seen to cause substantial implementation delays, particularly in the transport sector. . . . The transport sector assistance program evaluation observed that [Government of India] and ADB officials try to avoid projects with major environment/resettlement/land issues and focus, for example, on rehabilitation projects, which can be categorized as category "B" [lower-risk] projects, rather than on new roads. (Operations Evaluation Department 2007c, 35)

Given that environmental safeguard policies have created incentives to avoid environmentally risky projects, especially in borrowing countries that have not shown the capacity to properly implement environmental management plans, I test the following hypotheses:

Hypothesis 1: Development banks will approve fewer and smaller environmentally risky projects in borrowing countries that have poor records implementing safeguard procedures, when the donor states most interested in environmental outcomes have a majority on the board.

Implication 1a: An MDB is less likely to approve an environmentally risky project during a given year for an eligible borrower that has a poor record of safeguard implementation, as compared to a borrower that has a good record, when strong safeguard policies are in place.

Implication 1b: Given that an MDB approves an environmentally risky project during a particular year, the approved project value will be lower for a borrower that has a poor record of safeguard implementation, as compared to a borrower that has a good record, when strong safeguard policies are in place.

CASE STUDIES: ADMINISTRATIVE PROCEDURES AND STAFF INCENTIVES

Because the choices about whether or not to pursue potential projects are not documented, it is difficult to directly observe how safeguard policies affect the allocation of projects. Once a project is formally identified and enters the stream of documentation, it is almost always approved. Prior to being identified in a documented way, negotiations between staff at the multilateral development banks and recipient counterparts about what projects to pursue are informal and confidential. Given these constraints, I compile qualitative evidence about the mechanisms that make the multilateral development banks responsive to administrative procedures in two steps. First, I assess whether staff at the development banks report sensitivity to delays and the avoidance of risky projects when interviewed. Second, using a case study of the process of approving a large, environmentally risky dam project, I show that safeguard policies can create very significant delays that are costly for both staff at the multilateral development banks and recipient governments.

In combination, these streams of qualitative evidence illustrate the way in which states can use policies and procedures to ensure that international organizations update their practices with new information about the outcomes of decisions made under uncertainty. Like research on legislative control of federal agencies (e.g., Spence 1999), I find that administrative procedures can induce this response when they raise the costs of specific types of decisions, even though discretion is still available to the agent. Since it is not possible to test whether the logic of administrative control through procedure is systematic across the multilateral development banks with only one case study, I then proceed to test the observable implication that recipient countries with poor records of implementation are less likely to receive environmentally risky projects in the future.

The Costs of Delays: Staff Perspectives at the Multilateral Development Banks

One way to find out whether staff at multilateral development banks and their counterpart ministries are sensitive to delays is to ask them. Accordingly, I spent several weeks conducting interviews at the headquarters of the World Bank, Inter-American Development Bank, Asian Development Bank, and African Development Bank. While visiting these organizations, I sought to conduct interviews with as many types of staff and offices as possible, a technique often referred to as "maximum variation sampling" (Teddlie and Yu 2007). The goal of maximum variation sampling is to uncover the full range of responses to a similar question. When conducting interviews, I met with a wide range of evaluation, policy, and operational staff at each of the multilateral development banks. When different types of interviewees provide similar statements about the incentives at work when deciding on projects, conclusions based on interviews are likely to be robust.

In total, I conducted interviews with 54 individuals across the four multilateral development banks that are considered in this book. Because I could not ensure that any particular individual or unit at the multilateral development banks would be available to speak with me during my visits, an approach to interviews based on the maximum variation in sampling allowed me to probe the consistency of information from different sources and explore any anomalous statements. Each interview was based on a consistent template, to ensure that there was comparability of information across interviewees of different types. This method is often referred to as "semistructured interviews." I asked questions about the ways that staff in different parts of these organizations respond to safeguard policies, how information about safeguard performance is collected and transmitted within the different multilateral development banks, and when and why staff have incentives to respond to information about performance. For a full outline of the semistructured interview template, see appendix 1. While my interviews followed a consistent template, I left time and space to discuss issues that I did not anticipate.

At both the World Bank and the Asian Development Bank, operational staff reported that the "hassle factor" of complying with environmental safeguard policies steered them away from projects with high risks or risky components in countries that had records of poor performance. According to these staff, decisions about high-risk projects are driven by expectations about delays in the approval and implementation of projects. Operational staff have incentives to pursue projects that can be approved quickly, since getting new projects approved is the bedrock of a successful career for staff at the multilateral development banks. One staff member at the Asian Development Bank pinpointed the role of "procedural compliance" in deterring staff from pursuing projects with high environmental risks. At the Asian

Development Bank, the "checklist" of items that must be completed when a project is flagged as risky is perceived as extremely onerous and demands a high amount of staff time. Staff are able to reduce the risk of delay when they work with well-functioning government agencies that have shown an ability to successfully implement projects and complete these steps.

Operational staff at both the World Bank and the Asian Development Bank reported that they often pursue lower-risk projects when they have concerns that safeguard requirements will disrupt or delay the approval of a project. Because career advancement is strongly related to the approval of projects, interviewees at both the World Bank and Asian Development Bank reported that they sometimes avoid the components of projects that are likely to trigger safeguard procedures and cause delays in approval. In both cases, operational staff reported incentives to have infrastructure projects assigned to environmental risk category B, which does not require a full environmental impact assessment and environmental management plan in most cases. For example, one transportation staff member at the Asian Development Bank reported that highway projects are often classified as "rehabilitation" projects on existing right of ways, even if project activities are substantially similar to building a new road (e.g., unimproved road to expressway). In this way, the transportation unit does not have to complete the environmental impact assessment required for risky projects, but rather the less onerous "initial environmental assessment" for the less risky category B projects.

Another way that staff circumvent safeguard policies is to fund only the less risky parts of larger projects. One operational staff member in energy at the World Bank indicated that it has been common practice to finance the transmission lines from power-generating facilities, rather than the facilities themselves. At the Asian Development Bank, transportation staff often seek to finance the less risky portions of larger road projects, such as those that do not pass through sensitive ecological areas or national parks, knowing full well that the borrowing country in question will find other sources of financing to cover these more risky portions of the project.[5] For example, the ADB was considering financing improvement to the Mumbai airport, but because significant safeguard issues were raised with regards to resettlement and environmental management, the ADB instead moved forward with financing for a transportation framework that included roads and rail linking the Mumbai airport to surrounding areas.

A borrowing country's past performance implementing environmental safeguard procedures is a strong signal to staff about the delays that might be faced when seeking the approval of environmentally risky projects. Since the implementation of safeguard policies is still basically the responsibility of the borrowing country (Operations Evaluation Department 2006; Independent Evaluation

Group 2010b), failure by a borrowing country to carry out safeguard requirements in past operations indicates that more time and resources will need to be devoted to designing, implementing, and supervising safeguard issues in future projects. Indeed, operational staff indicated that borrowers who failed to properly implement safeguard policies in past operations required greater implementation support and supervision in future projects. Thus, when safeguard policies are not successfully implemented in past operations, it can create a "chilling" effect among operational staff who are accountable for using scarce administrative resources to approve projects.

For example, operational staff at the Asian Development Bank described the onerous process of obtaining a "safeguard compliance memo" from the Environment and Social Safeguards Division before a project would be considered for approval by the board. Operational staff reported instances where they were sent down to the safeguards division to "camp out" and wait for the approval of the safeguard compliance memo. This process can delay approvals by bumping a project to a new board meeting several weeks or months in the future when the memo is not complete by the internal deadline. Some staff reported that higher-level operational management will sometimes tacitly pressure the safeguards division to release a safeguards compliance memo that does not require significant changes to project design. These statements demonstrate that the process of achieving safeguard clearance while projects are in preparation can take considerable effort.

In addition to having safeguard measures formally approved by safeguard units, other time-consuming operational practices have been put in place to ensure that projects are designed with safeguards in mind. At the Asian Development Bank, operational staff report an onerous "box-checking" exercise that must be completed when designing any project with environmental risks. For example, the mandated procedures for conducting environmental impact assessments at the Asian Development Bank are based on a 13-chapter, 356-page manual that includes a 72-item checklist of the criteria that will be used to review and approve an environmental impact assessment (Lohani et al. 1997). The corresponding manual at the World Bank has 10 chapters and includes a checklist based on 20 separate operational policies (each with its own requirements), all of which must be accounted for when designing an environmental assessment and environmental management plan (World Bank 1999). Given that responsibility for carrying out these procedures largely rests with the borrowing country, past performance is an excellent indication of the speed at which these requirements will be fulfilled.

In terms of learning from the outcomes of past projects through project evaluations and other project completion assessments, one operational manager at the Asian Development Bank believed the most significant "learning" for operational staff was that they should not get involved in projects that will be unnecessarily difficult. Many operational departments have learned that scarce administrative resources are best spent by "avoiding the hassle of category A projects," according to the same operational manager. The learning that takes place within operational units is thus about the types of projects that are likely to face significant delays in the design stage. At both the World Bank and Asian Development Bank, certain types of projects are now seen as universally too risky, such as large hydropower projects and coal-fired power plants. For slightly less risky projects, teams at the development banks learn about the civil society opposition they will face when pursuing different types of projects. Operational staff reported that an active and critical civil society is a key determinant of the delays faced when designing and implementing environmentally risky infrastructure or energy projects. One ADB staff member indicated that this is a primary reason why India has received fewer environmentally risky projects over time than China, given that strong opposition to environmentally risky projects in India is all but guaranteed.

Safeguard Policies Create Delays: The Nam Theun II Dam in Laos

It is not enough that staff are sensitive to delays; the administrative procedures that are established to steer the multilateral development banks away from projects where risks cannot be properly managed must cause delays. And it is not enough that safeguard policies cause delays, they must cause delays on the basis of past performance of the implementing agency in the host country. Since staff have incentives to avoid delays, as outlined above, policies that make delays more likely when performance is expected or revealed to be weak in a particular borrowing country will align the allocation of aid projects with expected results. Since it is not possible to observe the negotiations that lead to the decision to pursue individual projects, I turn to a high-profile case that illustrates how safeguard policies can cause delays on the basis of expected and revealed performance of the recipient government. That case is the Nam Theun II Dam in Laos.

Laos is one of the poorest countries in the world, with per capita income in the 1980s ranging between $200 and $250.[6] The country is landlocked and has few opportunities to engage in the international commerce that has been a boon to Southeast Asia in recent decades. The American-Vietnamese war and prolong bombings by American forces destroyed much of Laos's infrastructure. But Laos has abundant precipitation, steep mountains, and proximity to some of the fastest-growing economies in the world. This combination makes the production and sale of hydropower a significant economic opportunity for Laos, especially for generating foreign exchange. However, with extremely low levels of development, in-country technical capacity, and capital, Laos needed to look abroad to develop its hydropower potential.

This is when the World Bank and the Asian Development Bank, along with a host of other private financial institutions, stepped onto the scene in 1993. The linchpin of hydropower development in Laos was the Nam Theun II hydropower project in the Theun River basin, with a total cost approaching $1.3 billion. The total costs of constructing the dam amounted to approximately one year's worth of GDP for Laos and three years of the government's budget (Sexton 1996a). The project was expected to significantly increase the capacity of Laos to export energy, boosting government revenue and promoting development in the process. As a landlocked country with few other resources, World Bank staff agreed that hydropower was critical to Laos's development.

The timing of Nam Theun II was sensitive for the multilateral development banks, and especially the World Bank. Criticism of the project to build the Narmada Dam in India, which had precipitated an international outcry about the negative social and environmental effects of donor-supported hydropower, had reached fevered pitch. The World Bank was going through a process to create a new accountability mechanism (discussed in the next chapter) to avoid "disaster projects" that had generated so much bad press for the World Bank. This heightened attention to environmental risks generated extra scrutiny for hydropower projects around the world, especially those that were financed with support from donor agencies.

Under this heightened scrutiny, the World Bank approached Nam Theun II more cautiously than might have been expected previously, even though it agreed to formally consider the project for approval beginning in 1993. Financing from the World Bank was critical for guaranteeing the participation of private financial firms, including Barclays, Deutsche Bank, and the French Société Générale. However, in November 1995, the World Bank delayed approval of the projects because it "was not satisfied with existing studies" and requested that additional studies of environmental and social costs be completed that included an analysis of alternatives to the project (Sexton 1996a).

This delay threw the project into disarray. The economic viability of the project was based on an agreement from Thailand to purchase power at a set rate. In 1996, while the World Bank was "going over [the Nam Theun II project] with a fine toothed comb," Thailand was reconsidering its options and threatened to withdraw from the purchase agreement. In October 1996, Thailand withdrew its offer to purchase power from the dam project, "since the project was two years delayed owing to environmental reviews" (Sexton 1996b). With Thailand backing away from the project, looming questions emerged about whether the project would ever be economically and environmentally viable. Although the World Bank indicated that it was still committed to the project under the correct environmental conditions, it also indicated that it would not provide final approval for the project until late 1997, after the completion of further environmental impact assessments (Torode 1996).

With uncertainty about the project looming, it was unclear whether the project would ever be approved. In 1997, the World Dams Forum was held in Geneva to consider dam projects more generally. As reporter Stephanie Flanders (1997) wrote, "Everyone . . . could see the merit of trying to see to it that fewer environmentally costly dams were built and fewer beneficial projects were subject to delays." As 1997 closed, the World Bank had still not made a decision to approve the project despite four years of careful environmental and social studies conducted with the goal of mitigating risks.

As the delays went on, the financial crisis hit Southeast Asia, with Thailand hit especially hard. In 1998, Thailand delayed its commitment to purchase power from Nam Theun II again, even after it had renegotiated a purchase agreement. The Thai economy slowed during the financial crisis, and it was not clear that there was demand for all of the power that it had agreed to purchase. Yet the delays were not done. In 1998, the World Bank appointed an "international advisory group" to consider the environmental consequences of the dam, and by the end of the year still no decision had been made about whether to move forward (*Water Power and Dam Construction* 1998). Delays continued for more years as the president of the World Bank announced a general move away from large dam projects following the release of the World Commission on Dams report in 2000 (Redfern 2000). With support for large hydropower projects waning and the economic climate in the region weak, final approval for the project was delayed until 2005, more than a decade after the Nam Theun II project had entered the World Bank project pipeline. When the project was finally approved, World Bank president James Wolfensohn stated plainly the difficulty and delays involved with financing and implementing such a project:

> We have spent the best part of a decade studying the project and evaluating the risks. In fact, we have been advised by some independent experts that we have studied it for too long, and been too focused on possible risks. But because it involves resettlement of people, because it impacts not one but two rivers, and because it is so vital for the future of the country, we believe these risks need the utmost attention. Our decision, after a lot of deliberation, is that the risks can be managed; in fact, one major reason we are involved is to help manage those risks. (World Bank 2005[7])

In the aftermath of the project, staff at both the World Bank and the Asian Development Bank were clearly deterred from pursuing similar projects, in both their public statements and anonymous data that I collected during interviews. One energy specialist at the Asian Development Bank I interviewed reported that the Nam Theun II project has been an attempt by the ADB to constructively engage in the hydropower sector after the controversies of the 1990s, but that the experience had not left the bank keen to pursue very large projects that would almost certainly face delays. An evaluator at the Asian Development Bank likewise reported that Nam Theun II was an attempt to engage constructively in the hydropower sector after this sector had been largely avoided during the 1990s. Nonetheless, the bank had learned how difficult it was to pursue such projects in light of the controversy they generate and the number of procedures that must be followed before approval.

In an edited volume that reviews the World Bank experiences with the Nam Theun II project, similar concerns are expressed about World Bank involvement in future infrastructure projects of this scale. Serra, Segal, and Chopra (2011, 97), all World Bank alumni with ties to the project, report that private and public sector partners were turned off by the bank's participation in this type of project: "Private and public partners' perceptions of the World Bank are not uniform, but some indicated that they would prefer to fund large infrastructure projects in East Asia without the World Bank." Likewise, a team from the Duke Center for International Development that held a workshop with the project team suggests that the management and oversight costs within the World Bank were too high to be easily replicated in future operations:

> Establishing the project oversight group [of senior management] helped build and manage consensus within the World Bank ... The amount of time and attention to detail that characterized the group's meetings made these meetings very costly, however, suggesting that such groups may be replicable only in very special circumstances in the future. (Duke Center for International Development 2011, 144)

The Nam Theun II Dam project is clearly an extreme case of delays caused by environmental policies, but it illustrates the basic logic of how administrative procedures can control the types of outcomes that member states in international organizations would like to avoid, while maintaining the discretion necessary to take advantage of the technical and coordination capacities of international organizations. Staff have incentives to avoid delays in the approval of projects, which conflict with their mandate to approve and disburse development financing. Environmental safeguard policies have made it selectively more difficult to approve projects in certain countries, particularly where the expectation for implementing safeguard policies is low. Additionally, the safeguard policies empowered a new type of office within the multilateral development banks that has the capacity to ensure that trade-offs between environmental protection and project approval are managed according to the preferences of member states. Next, I turn to whether this kind of effect is systematic across the multilateral development banks.

DATA AND MODEL SPECIFICATION

While a case study can provide evidence about *how* administrative procedures can constrain risky decisions by multilateral development banks, a single case might not be representative of the lending process more generally. Having explored the mechanism by which safeguard policies might change multilateral bank staff and recipient country preferences, I test whether past performance in implementing environmentally risky operations is related to the approval of future environmentally risky projects systematically. Since the relative share of environmentally risky projects has not significantly decreased during the time period considered (Independent Evaluation Group 2010b), any effect that safeguard policies have had on allocation will be found in the mix of projects approved for specific countries.

Outcome Variable: Approval and Allocation of Environmentally Risky Projects

Two features of the approval process are potentially important. First, the decision to approve an environmentally risky project during a given year provides information about how the multilateral development banks screen projects in different borrowing countries. Second, the size of approved projects indicates the relative priorities of the multilateral development banks when compared to their total budget constraints. Larger projects are likely to be more valuable to borrowing countries.

To examine the types of projects that are relevant to environmental safeguard policies, I compiled the environmental risk rating that was assigned to every project approved by the World Bank from 1990 to 2009 and the Asian Development Bank from 1990 to 2007 using project approval documents and available project databases. I obtained risk categorization data directly from the African Development Bank for the period 2000–2009. Across all of the multilateral banks, environmentally risky financing comprises between 10% and 20% of total portfolios over time (figure 4.1). Generally, the multilateral development banks categorize projects according to whether they are expected to have a high, a moderate, or no negative impact on the environment. For the analysis presented below, I consider environmentally risky projects to be all projects that have been flagged for high impacts and that are not primarily intended to improve environmental management according to the project description (World Bank and ADB category A, African Development

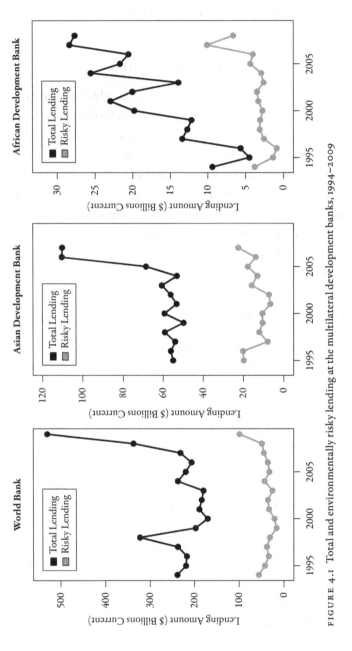

FIGURE 4.1 Total and environmentally risky lending at the multilateral development banks, 1994–2009

Bank category I).[8] As I review in chapter 6, the multilateral development banks face little pressure to be selective about their environment-improving operations, so these projects are not considered in this analysis because they trigger environmental studies for a different reason. Although "green" risky projects face the same environmental procedures, they are unlikely to face the same level of scrutiny and pressure from donor countries and the units tasked with preventing environmental harms within the multilateral development banks.

Measuring Past Safeguard Performance

Reflecting the importance donor countries have placed on mitigating negative environmental impacts, evaluation departments at the multilateral development banks have routinely evaluated the implementation of environmental safeguard procedures in both project and thematic evaluations.[9] For this chapter, I focus on how the World Bank, Asian Development Bank, and African Development Bank have responded to performance in implementing environmental safeguards as reported in project evaluations since 1990.[10] Project evaluations are written for approximately 25% of completed projects and are the most basic building block for higher-level evaluations at all of the multilateral development banks considered in this chapter. In many project evaluations, a dedicated section evaluates whether environmental safeguards were properly implemented.

To compile information about safeguard performance in a systematic way, I assembled a team of research assistants to code textual statements in evaluation documents using a four-point scale (table 4.1). The four-point scale is based on any available evaluation that documented how closely the implementing agencies adhered to environmental safeguard policies. Two coders independently coded every project evaluation, and I determined the final coding when there were discrepancies between the coders.[11] By coding safeguard implementation performance in terms of the adherence to well-defined standards, I produce a comparable measure of performance across a large number of projects. All of the multilateral development banks considered in this book adopted similar standards that seek to limit unmanaged environmental harms. As a result, the presence of unmanaged environmental harms in postproject evaluations offers an easily recognized and consistent measure of adherence to procedures. Donor countries also have difficulty collecting this type of information in the absence of an evaluation process that visits the field. While scholars studying international environmental politics have long discussed the difficulty of defining effectiveness in empirical research (Keohane, Haas, and Levy 1993; Young and Levy 1999; Gerlak 2004), in this case, creating a comparable measure of performance is aided by the relatively uniform policies and procedures.

TABLE 4.1
CODING CRITERIA FOR PERFORMANCE IMPLEMENTING SAFEGUARD PROCEDURES

Coding	Meaning	Criteria	Example text
4	Highly satisfactory	Exceeds safeguard requirements or conditions; specifically mentioned for outstanding safeguard performance; efforts significantly improve environmental outcomes as compared to preapproval expectations.	"The government has renewed its commitment to tackling environmental problems . . . the policy of providing continuous training to staff has guaranteed the smooth implementation and operation of the project. Risk factors have been minimal particularly from environmental point of view. In fact, the supply of natural gas has enhanced the environmental benefits of the project" (African Development Bank, Egypt, El Arish Power Project).
3	Satisfactory	Meets all safeguard requirements or conditions with only minor exceptions observed; summary statement of performance is positive.	"Neither project had any obvious negative impacts on the environment. . . . Water schemes visited appeared to have no major environmental problems. Drainage work appeared to have had a positive impact in the few sites visited" (World Bank, Indonesia, PPAR No. 35585).

2	Partly satisfactory	Meets some safeguard requirements or conditions with significant deficiencies observed; does not meet monitoring or evaluation standards in projects with no discernible environmental impacts; summary statement of performance is negative.	"The [evaluation mission] did not discern any environmental impact of subprojects . . . the [evaluation mission] was informed by some subborrowers that they were not required to assess the environmental impacts . . . the [participating financial institutions] generally submitted inadequate environment-related information. ADB should have more diligently reviewed the environmental aspects of subprojects" (Asian Development Bank, Pakistan, PPAR No. 23341).
1	Unsatisfactory	Does not meet most environmental goals or conditions with major deficiencies observed in most areas; outright noncompliance with environmental loan conditions and/or non-achievement of safeguard requirements.	". . . failure to protect biodiversity. . . . The final version of the environmental impact report made no references to a possible dropping of [critical habitat for endangered fauna from the project area]. Despite concerns expressed by the Bank's Environmental Advisor, Operations went ahead . . . ignoring the concerns about the loss of wildlife habitat" (World Bank, Sri Lanka, PPAR No. 29489).
NA	Not available	Project has no safeguard requirements, or insufficient information is available in evaluation report to assess recipient performance.	

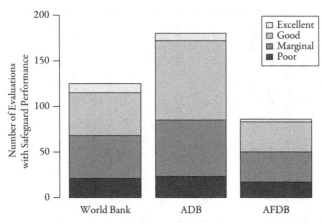

FIGURE 4.2 Evaluations with information about performance implementing environmental safeguards

As might be expected, the data reveal mixed performance in implementing environmental safeguard policies, with approximately half of relevant project evaluations finding major implementation problems with safeguards or outright noncompliance (figure 4.2). This opens the opportunity for all of the multilateral development banks to respond to performance information related to environmental risks in their future decisions. In addition to collecting the outcome data displayed in figure 4.2, our team also collected data on whether problems in project design led to performance problems later, thereby relieving the borrower of some responsibility.

For modeling purposes, I create three predictor variables from the data displayed in figure 4.2. All project evaluations that have satisfactory or highly satisfactory safeguard outcomes are included in the variable *NO. EVALS W/SAFEGUARD SUCCESS*, which is the count of good outcomes in a particular country during the previous five years. Similarly, the variable *NO. EVALS W/SAFEGUARD FAILURE* refers to the number of evaluations that report poor safeguard outcomes during the previous five years. For the Asian Development Bank, which has many older project evaluations that evaluate environmental performance for projects approved prior to the adoption of environmental safeguard policies, I exclude instances of safeguard failures that are attributed primarily to design decisions at the time, since these failures could be more easily corrected when pursuing future projects.

Control Variables

I use several control variables to account for other factors that drive lending decisions (as reviewed in chapter 2). During interviews at the multilateral development banks, staff suggested that opposition from civil society to environmentally risky projects was a key determinant of whether such projects would be pursued. Indeed, civil society opposition has been a primary reason why environmentally risky projects are either delayed or canceled (Khagram 2004; Fox and Brown 1998). Thus, I include the Freedom House index of political liberties (*FEWER POLITICAL LIBERTIES*) to control for the ability and potential for civil society to mobilize against risky projects.[12]

I also expect the multilateral development banks to allocate projects based on the development status of particular borrowers. Thus, I control for characteristics of each borrowing country's lending portfolio. First, I use the percentage of total lending that is concessional in each country-year (*CONCESSIONAL*) as a control variable, because risky projects tend to be large infrastructure projects that are funded through market-rate lending for middle-income countries with low external debt. Second, borrowing countries that receive more projects are also more likely to receive at least one project that is flagged as environmentally risky, thus the variable *NO. PROJECTS PREV 5 YRS* controls for the overall size of the country portfolio in the approval models. In the allocation stage models, *PORTFOLIO SIZE* controls for the overall lending amount allocated to a country that same year, again to account for the association between portfolio size and project size in recipient countries. This variable also controls for potential fluctuations in total MDB lending amounts and currency inflation.[13]

Modeling Approach

Many empirical studies of aid allocation consider separately the decision to approve projects and the decision about the size of projects once they are approved (Cingranelli and Pasquarello 1985; Neumayer 2003; Hicks et al. 2008). I follow a similar approach. All environmentally risky projects regardless of size must go through the same set of environmental safeguard procedures. Thus, staff might make decisions about pursuing risky projects without consideration of their size, given uniform preparation requirements across projects. I refer to this as the "approval" stage and model whether donors screen projects based on variables of theoretical interest. The outcome is a binary variable that indicates whether or not an environmentally risky project is approved in a particular country and year. After the approval stage, decision-makers may adjust the size of the project in light of environmental risks, since larger projects may have higher risks. In this "allocation" stage, I model whether the size of environmentally risky projects increases or decreases based on past environmental performance.

Approval Model. For the "approval" model, I code each country-year as a binary variable to indicate whether each MDB approved at least one environmentally risky project during that year. Only years when a borrowing country receives at least one project of any type are included in the panel. I adopt a more conservative modeling approach than many researchers by accounting for temporal dependence among observations and country-effects within the logistic model. Since MDB operational departments are often organized by country, it may be the case that there are regular spacing intervals between projects or that the country program loses the staff expertise to approve and manage certain types of projects over time. Thus, I follow Beck, Katz, and Tucker (1998) and include dummy variables (*TIME DUMMIES*) for each time interval since the last approval of an environmentally risky project.[14] It is also possible that there are consistent country-effects that are not modeled with the control variables. Since a fixed-effects model is not identified because some of the countries do not have variation in the dependent variable (no risky projects are approved during the sample period), I employ a random-intercept model estimated by Laplace approximation to account for unobserved differences between countries (Gelman and Hill 2007, ch. 14).

Allocation Model. For the allocation stage of the model, the dependent variable is the amount of financing that was flagged as environmentally risky, given that at least one such project was received during the country-year. Following a modeling strategy similar to that above, I employ a random-intercept linear model to account for unobserved differences between countries (Gelman and Hill 2007, ch. 13).

MODEL RESULTS
Approval Decisions

The results of the approval stage model provide support for the hypothesis that the World Bank and Asian Development Bank respond to a borrowing country's performance in implementing environmental safeguards, controlling for other variables that also influence the allocation of environmentally risky projects. In all models, both the World Bank and Asian Development Bank are less likely to approve at least one environmentally risky project for countries with a poor record of implementing environmental safeguards (table 4.2, Models 1a–2b).[15] It might be the case that countries chosen for project evaluations are unlike countries that do not have project evaluations. For example, countries with evaluations typically have larger portfolios and might expect to face greater scrutiny from major donor countries as a result. This might cause them to choose certain types of projects where success is more likely or to put additional effort into implementation. To guard against the possibility that the results are driven by selection into evaluation, I additionally examine how the approval of environmentally risky projects changes only for those countries covered by a project evaluation in the last five years. Since these effects are

TABLE 4.2
APPROVAL DECISIONS ABOUT ENVIRONMENTALLY RISKY PROJECTS

Model	1a	1b	2a	2b	3a	3b
MDB	World	World	Asian	Asian	African	African
Outcome variable	Dirty "A"	Dirty "A"	Dirty "A"	Dirty "A"	Risky sector	Risky sector
NO. EVALS W/ SAFEGUARD FAILURE	−0.62* (0.41)	−1.16** (0.43)	−1.04** (0.52)	−1.01** (0.51)	0.29 (0.33)	−0.04 (0.34)
NO. EVALS W/ SAFEGUARD SUCCESS	0.36** (0.16)	0.18 (0.16)	0.10 (0.15)	0.07 (0.15)	0.23* (0.17)	0.15 (0.18)
FEWER POLITICAL LIBERTIES	0.21** (0.06)	0.29** (0.09)	0.16 (0.11)	0.12 (0.13)	−0.01 (0.06)	−0.03 (0.08)
CONCESSIONAL	−0.81** (0.25)	−1.20** (0.34)	−0.19 (0.53)	0.34 (0.66)	−0.21 (0.23)	−0.15 (0.33)
NO. PROJECTS PREV 5 YRS	0.06** (0.01)	0.08** (0.02)	0.03** (0.01)	0.03** (0.01)		
TIME DUMMIES	all neg., 3+**	4+**	4+**	2–4+ neg.		
NO. RISKY TYPE 5 YRS					0.17** (0.06)	0.07 (0.07)
Random intercept variance	0.63	0.00	0.00	0.00	0.00	0.00
Data subset	Full panel	With evaluation	Full panel	With evaluation	Full panel	With evaluation
Observations (countries)	1,450 (136)	347 (74)	281 (37)	190 (26)	457 (52)	257 (38)
Residual deviance	1,081	299.4	167.2	131.8	592.4	352.5
Null Deviance	1,141	348.0	198.8	159.3	602.5	355.5

Note: All models are random-intercept logistic regression estimated by Laplace approximation. Null deviance is calculated using random intercept and time dummies.

Statistical significance of one-tailed hypothesis test: $^{*}p < .1$, $^{**}p < .05$.

consistent across both the full panel and a restricted subset of country-years covered by at least one evaluation, selection into evaluation does not account for the results.

In contrast, the satisfactory implementation of safeguard policies does not produce consistent evidence increased approval of environmentally risky projects, an effect that appears only in the full World Bank panel (table 4.2, Model 1a). Collinearity between evaluation variables is not driving the main result about negative information, which is robust to dropping the number of evaluations with positive information, but not vice versa. These results support Implication 1a, which states that multilateral development banks approve environmentally risky projects according to the previous safeguard performance of borrowing countries.[16]

Several other factors are associated with approval decisions about environmentally risky projects. Borrowing countries that have low levels of political rights are more likely to receive environmentally risky projects at the World Bank, indicating that opposition from civil society either decreases borrowing country demand for risky projects or bank staff incentives to pursue risky projects. These possibilities will be the subject of the next chapter. Also as expected, the number of projects in each borrower's portfolio has a large and significant impact on the probability of receiving environmentally risky lending during any given year. There is also a very clear temporal dependence in the data. Once environmentally risky projects are not financed for a long time, they are less likely to be financed in the period under consideration. In addition, time dummies control for countries that never or only infrequently receive environmentally risky projects because of unobservable country characteristics.

To aid substantive interpretation of these model results, figure 4.3 displays the model fit and the 90% confidence interval for the substantive effect of a negative evaluation, based on Model 2a for the Asian Development Bank. To produce the effect, I draw randomly from the estimated distribution of every model coefficient, set each model variable to the mean of the sample for continuous variables or the median of the sample for discrete variables, vary the levels of *NO. EVALS W/SAFEGUARD FAILURE* and *NO. PROJECTS PREV 5 YRS*, and predict the outcome based on the estimated model.[17] In this way, the effect interval shows how poor safeguard implementation influences the predicted probability of receiving an environmentally risky project during a given year, accounting for total model uncertainty. As can be seen in figure 4.3, failing to implement safeguard measures when no design problems are noted decreases the probability of receiving an environmentally risky project between 20% and 60%.

It appears that both the World Bank and Asian Development Bank respond to the records of borrowing countries of implementing safeguards. This result is likely driven by the cost to approve environmentally risky projects in countries with poor

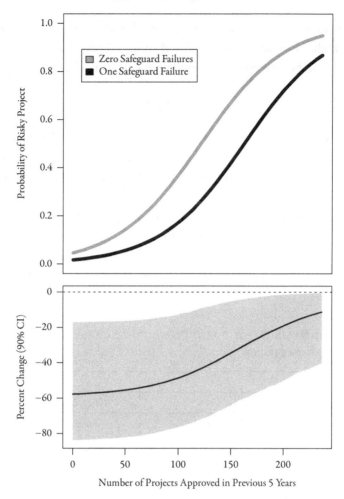

FIGURE 4.3 The effects of failures to implement environmental safeguards and portfolio size on the approval of environmentally risky projects at the Asian Development Bank

Note: This plot shows predictions from Model 2a. The top panel displays the probability of receiving at least one environmentally risky project. The bottom panel shows the effect size of failed implementation as a percentage with a 90% confidence interval.

performance, given how oversight procedures are applied. In contrast, the African Development Bank exhibits very different behavior. As can be seen in Model 3a, I do not find evidence that approval decisions at the African Development Bank respond to a country's record of implementing environmental safeguard procedures. In this case, the dependent variable is not category A projects, but sectors that are defined as "strictly dirty" by Hicks et al. (2008, 271).[18] Borrowing countries that are evaluated as having poor safeguard performance do not receive fewer projects in the future. This result indicates weaker safeguard practices at the African Development Bank, likely resulting from less oversight and control by donor countries. As more stringent environmental policies have recently become a regular part of AFDB operations, with the associated approval and administration costs applied more systematically, it will be interesting to see whether this result changes.

Allocation Decisions

Thus far, I have only examined how past performance in implementing environmental safeguards influences the probability of receiving at least one environmentally risky project in a particular year, regardless of the actual project value. It may be the case that the multilateral development banks not only screen their projects based on past performance at implementing safeguards, but also approve larger and thus more complex projects for borrowers that have a good record. In table 4.3, Models 4–5, I do not find support for Implication 1b, which states that borrowing countries with good safeguard implementation should receive greater amounts of

TABLE 4.3

ALLOCATION AMOUNTS FOR ENVIRONMENTALLY RISKY PROJECTS
IN YEARS WITH PROJECTS

Model	4	5
MDB	World	Asian
NO. EVALS W/SAFEGUARD FAILURE	−13.7	−28.6
	(66.5)	(121.5)
NO. EVALS W/SAFEGUARD SUCCESS	1.7	14.7
	(14.2)	(17.5)
FEWER POLITICAL LIBERTIES	**21.7****	22.6
	(10.1)	(28.5)
CONCESSIONAL	−45.8	−76.9
	(40.6)	(121.5)
PORTFOLIO SIZE	**0.33****	**0.30****
	(0.02)	(0.11)
TIME DUMMIES	n.s.	n.s.
Random intercept SD	113.6	141.1
Observations	245	45
(countries)	(78)	(15)
Residual deviance	3,300	602.7
Null deviance	3,478	621.6

Note: Both models are random-intercept linear regression of risky project amounts.

Statistical significance of two-tailed hypothesis test: $^{*}p < .1,$ $^{**}p < .05.$

environmentally risky financing, controlling for screening decisions at the previous stage. In no case is either good or poor safeguard implementation performance predicted the amount of risky financing that will be received, given that at least one environmentally risky project is approved during a given year.

This result indicates that safeguard policies primarily affect decisions about what types of projects to pursue, rather than the size of projects that are pursued. This might be expected, given that most projects come into the approval pipeline with a predetermined level of financing, and all projects that trigger safeguards must have impact assessments and management plans regardless of project size. As discussed below, I find no evidence in interviews that project sizes are altered because of past safeguard performance. Instead, MDB staff choose different types of projects if environmental risks are too costly owing to safeguard procedures and the expected performance of borrowers.

DISCUSSION
Safeguard Policies and Information

A point of consensus between interviewees across the multilateral developments banks is that there are no formal, institutionalized procedures that require direct responses to information about performance in project evaluations. For example, a World Bank evaluator indicated that very few project evaluations are formally considered at the sub-board Committee on Development Effectiveness and that there is no process to track how the findings of previous project evaluations influence future lending decisions. A former manager at the Asian Development Bank Operations Evaluation Department indicated the usefulness of project evaluations has long been considered problematic within the ADB, given that there is no direct "learning mechanism" in place to transfer findings into allocation decisions or operational practices. As one ADB evaluator commented, any risk aversion to environmentally risky projects is likely to be "much more systematic than any specific project evaluation." When operational staff are considering new operations, they take into account all information about the risks the project will raise and the delays that are likely. The interview data that I collected thus point to an indirect and decentralized response to information about performance, if any.

Despite these doubts about a direct learning effect, some staff members, especially those at the Asian Development Bank, believed that I would find "constructive engagement" based on the records of borrowers. Instead of leaving sectors because of poor safeguard performance, staff members might seek additional technical assistance for safeguard implementation or seek the approval of "easier" projects that are intended to improve capacity to implement risky projects. While this type of engagement is consistent with the model findings presented above, in the future it is important to address whether the multilateral development banks respond to safeguard performance in other observable ways, like allocating greater amounts of technical assistance to deal with capacity problems that previous operations reveal.

Safeguard Policies and Borrowing Country Demand

It is not only staff at multilateral development banks that have responded to environmental safeguard policies. During my interviews, I repeatedly heard that borrowing countries have also been deterred from pursuing environmentally risky projects with the multilateral development banks in recent years because of delays in the approval and implementation of projects. When borrowing countries have access to other sources of financing, whether through commercial lending markets, self-financing infrastructure projects with tax revenue, or other sources of development assistance that do not have onerous safeguard procedures (e.g., Chinese development cooperation), borrowing countries can more quickly and smoothly move projects toward implementation. In several interviews, staff at the multilateral banks reported that borrowing countries frequently question the requirement that environmental impact assessments be posted for 120 days before a project is eligible for board approval.[19] Even more significantly, staff surveys reveal that borrowing countries often drop projects because of safeguards. For example, two-thirds of managers from the Latin America region of the World Bank reported that "some clients had avoided or were dropping a Bank project because of safeguard policies" (Independent Evaluation Group 2010b, 73).

Asian Development Bank operational staff and evaluators cited specific countries that have become less interested in financing environmentally risky projects through the ADB because of delays caused by safeguard policies. For example, one staff member described how the Philippines has moved toward more flexible program lending that provides general support to government ministries, as opposed to project lending that often entails significant delays in implementing safeguard policies. Staff reported a similar trend in borrowing requests from Indonesia. In Southeast Asia, the multilateral development banks used to be the primary financers of large hydropower projects. Because of the significant delays caused by environmental and social safeguard policies, the ADB and World Bank have funded very few large hydropower projects in the region in recent years, despite a growing number of such projects being financed by other sources. Senior operational management at the ADB reported that India has taken the position that it does not want ADB financing for category A projects. A recent $600 million railroad project in India did not move forward because India wanted the project rated as a category

B but the ADB safeguards unit required the full safeguard procedure for a category A project. Eventually in 2011, only a portion of the Railway Sector Investment Program was approved as a category B project.[20]

On the other hand, China continues to receive a large number of category A projects primarily because it has a system in place to handle the safeguard policies of the multilateral development banks. It was reported that China often approaches the multilateral development banks with complete proposals for projects, including the relevant environmental impact assessments. By taking on much of the burden for environmental assessments, China has ensured that significant delays will not be encountered, leaving staff at the multilateral banks to prepare only a desk review. Thus, because China is a high performer and has developed a domestic system to handle safeguard procedures, it is unlikely to face the delays that are frequent with low-performing countries. Staff working at the multilateral development banks are likely to see risky projects in China as having low risks for delay. In addition, China has shown the propensity to self-finance projects that are especially risky.

Contrast with the African Development Bank

I do not find any evidence that the African Development Bank responds to safeguard performance as do the World Bank and Asian Development Bank. This contrast presents an opportunity to examine the role of policy choices and administrative procedures in driving selectivity. Whereas the World Bank and Asian Development Bank both have formalized safeguard policies that cause observable delays in project approval and implementation, the African Development Bank had much weaker safeguard procedures during the time period considered here. When the African Development Bank went through a restructuring in 2007–2008, a Safeguard Unit was created to ensure diligent implementation of safeguard procedures. When I met with this unit, staff indicated that prior to 2008, there was very little institutional ability within the African Development Bank to ensure the proper implementation of safeguard policies. This problem was systematic both for preparation and for implementation of projects. Prior to 2008, completion reports were written for only 8% of projects, and more than 40% of the AFDB portfolio was considered to be at risk of failure. Given the state of the portfolio, the Safeguards Unit was skeptical that the safeguard procedures were a serious priority during the time period considered in this research.

When I spoke with operational staff at the African Development Bank, I was met with significant skepticism that safeguard procedures cause delays in project approval and implementation, or that safeguard policies had significantly shaped approval and allocation decisions. Most operational staff report that addressing the development needs on the African continent was the paramount priority and would be pursued regardless of whether a project was likely to have negative environmental impacts. Operational staff generally regard environmental risks as only a small part of the overall costs of project approval and implementation. One AFDB operational manager stated that "safeguards" was very much a Western, World Bank–inspired term that had little relevance to decisions made in the context of African development finance. Instead, safeguards are viewed as just another procedure followed during project preparation, with little possibility for significant delay.

Many operational staff at the African Development Bank were unable to recall specific instances of satisfactory or poor implementation of safeguards. Instead, most staff indicated that the majority of administrative effort required by safeguard policies occurred during project preparation. For example, one staff member who had been a task leader for transportation projects indicated that he was not able to comment about the track record of safeguard implementation during projects, since there had been no systematic review of safeguard performance. In many cases, project teams use consultants to both write and supervise the implementation of environmental management plans. Because of the difficulty of implementing projects in many countries, one staff member commented that management is less concerned with projects that are out of compliance with safeguard procedures than they are about having a plan to deal with noncompliance. Accordingly, there were few reports of disbursement delays owing to problems with safeguard procedures.

In addition, AFDB staff reported that they do not feel significant pressure from civil society groups to minimize projects' environmental impact. One operational staff member stated that the World Bank is always afraid of civil society groups, particularly international environmental NGOs, whereas staff at the AFDB are "not afraid." For example, there was a large hydropower project called Gibe III in Ethiopia to be jointly financed by the World Bank and African Development Bank. The International Rivers Network, an international NGO based in the United States, demanded that additional environmental studies be carried out prior to the project being approved. Whereas the African Development Bank was ready to go forward with the project after carrying out its own internal safeguard procedures, the World Bank insisted on more studies in line with the International Rivers Network request. In the end, the project was "lost" because Ethiopia and the World Bank considered the safeguard issues to be too much of a constraint on the project. There are indications that China will finance the project instead, with very few safeguards in place (Rice 2010).

As the implementation of safeguard procedures becomes more stringent, it will be interesting to test whether the African Development Bank also responds to information about performance. Slowly, environmental risks are becoming more prominent in high-level discussions at the AFDB. During recent replenishment meetings, safeguard issues figured prominently into donor country demands for continued support of the AFDB.[21] In addition, the Independent Review Mechanism that received complaints from civil society groups about performance has reviewed environmentally risky projects, such as the project to build the Bujagali Dam in Uganda. Some operational staff have reported the need to spend more time studying and implementing environmental procedures as a result.

CONCLUSIONS AND IMPLICATIONS

There is a deep skepticism that donor agencies and multilateral development banks can be made responsive to their past performance. This skepticism lies at the heart of concerns that aid is not up to the task of successfully addressing development issues (Gibson et al. 2005). At the multilateral development banks, the skepticism finds its root in a system of incentives that favors the rapid approval of projects over the careful selection of projects in light of their past performance. Responding to performance information has been repeatedly highlighted as key to achieving favorable outcomes in development assistance. If financing decisions are not adjusted to reflect performance, borrowers do not have incentives to comply with costly procedures and policies, such as strict financial accounting or proactive environmental management (Collier et al. 1997; Guillaumont and Chauvet 2001). Environmental performance is among the most classic examples of this delegation problem.

In this chapter, I asked whether safeguard procedures have been able to steer the multilateral development banks away from environmentally risky projects in countries where past performance has been poor. By requiring the multilateral development banks to produce environmental assessments and management plans prior to considering new environmentally risky projects, the member states at the multilateral development banks accomplished two things. First, they made it easy to monitor that the banks had plans to achieve their preferences. Second, and more importantly, they made it costly for operational staff to approve environmentally risky projects because specialized environmental units have the ability to stall the approval of projects if environmental assessments and management plans are weak. The potential for delays is pronounced in countries with poor records. Thus, administrative procedures may help to overcome the difficult problem that donor states face in monitoring environmental performance of hundreds of environmentally risky projects around the world. This possibility offers a response to general skepticism that international development organizations are able to practice selectivity.

The kind of selectivity where the multilateral development banks avoid projects with significant risks when staff cannot show a clear plan to manage risk is precisely the kind of control that member states would like to exert. Nothing about the safeguard policies seeks to make projects with environmental risks impossible or even less likely. Rather, making staff generate a credible plan to manage risk has two functions. For risky projects with manageable risks, such as when the borrowing country is high-performing, procedural requirements reduce the probability that agents will be able to shirk during implementation, while not eliminating discretion about choosing projects that are likely to have the greatest development impact. For operations without manageable risks, such as when the borrowing government does not have demonstrated capacity or willingness to manage environmental risks, the requirement to generate a credible plan serves as a barrier to approval. The safeguard policies manage discretion, rather than eliminate it.

To this point, most empirical studies that examine when and why donors are selective have examined only macroindicators of recipient governance and aggregate flows of development assistance. I have taken a different approach by systematically examining how multilateral development banks respond to project-level performance information about the past implementation of environmental safeguards when approving and allocating environmentally risky lending. I find evidence that both the World Bank and Asian Development Bank screen projects based on the past performance of borrowing countries. This finding demonstrates that state principals can use administrative procedures to incentivize certain types of actions and raise the shadow of oversight, in this case by making it costly to disregard past performance. To do so does not require active project-by-project oversight. The environmental safeguard policies that have been put in place at the multilateral development banks increase the costs to design, approve, and administer environmentally risky projects. Operational staff can take cues from past performance about the magnitude of these costs for specific borrowing countries. For staff and management at the multilateral development banks, the costs of administering and supervising safeguard policies are higher for borrowing countries that have a history of poor performance than they are for countries that have a history of satisfactory performance. In this way, procedures change the costs of approving projects in line with past performance.

Given the difficulty that development organizations have had in practicing conditionality at the project level and performance-based allocation at the aggregate level, this finding speaks to the importance of having administrative policies in place that systematically make it more costly for donor organizations to approve projects that have not been successful in the past. This lesson need not be limited to environmental performance. Policies that attempt to support selectivity are likely to have the greatest influence when they are linked to core operational incentives, which are often to meet lending or grant-making targets (Operations Evaluation Department 2006). Development organizations might establish policies requiring more intensive (and expensive) preparatory analytical work and supervision of projects in countries with a history of poor performance in particular areas. This might not only increase the quality of projects, but also induce development organizations to select the projects that have succeeded in the past in order to avoid projects with high administrative costs.

Another important implication of the findings presented here is that selectivity may be more easily implemented by development organizations that have flexible portfolios consisting of different project types. Discretion is a condition for more focused types of selectivity. Since it is difficult to implement conditionality through disbursements within a single project (Svensson 2003), and organization-wide allocation practices are often slow to change (Nielson and Tierney 2003; Gutner 2005), development organizations are likely to be most effective when they adjust portfolio composition at the country level. Future work on performance-based and selective allocation practices should explore the possibility of practicing selectivity within country portfolios. To support selectivity at this level, project evaluations should routinely include detailed information about the performance of goals identified in country-level assistance strategies. In terms of the environment, this means that more detailed performance information is needed at the project level for recipients with identified needs for environmentally risky projects. Just as it is standard procedure to conduct environmental impact assessments for high-risk projects before approval, it should be standard to conduct environmental reviews following the completion of high-impact projects. This would ensure that the information necessary to mitigate risks is available, given that policies are in place to incentivize the use of information.

Within the international relations literature on institutional design, scholars have inquired about the types of design features of international organizations that can improve performance. In particular, scholars have been interested in understanding how the rules for controlling the behavior of international organizations operate (Koremenos, Lipson, and Snidal 2001). In terms of environmental policies, project-by-project oversight is not possible for the donor countries of the multilateral development banks (Weaver 2008). The results here show that by designing organizations with internal units that check divergent preferences (maximize lending versus mitigate environmental damages) can be a key way to relieve state principals from the burden of providing oversight. In the case of safeguard policies, donor countries have created a system of passive checks and balances within the multilateral development banks that incentivize responses to performance. Both practitioners and scholars have become interested in the performance of international organizations, and more attention can be paid to how internal procedures can enhance oversight and improve performance.

However, owing to the delays caused by safeguard policies during the design and approval of projects, there has been a large push, especially from borrowing countries, to streamline planning and safeguard requirements. For example, the Asian Development Bank is currently undergoing reforms that would decrease project preparation time by half, which some staff believed would come at the expense of environmental risk mitigation (Asian Development Bank 2009). This may decrease the incentives that staff have to actively take cues from the records of borrowing countries. In addition, more borrowing countries are exercising their "exit options" by choosing to look elsewhere for environmentally risky financing because of safeguard policies. Many operational staff I spoke with at both the World Bank and the Asian Development Bank highlighted the risks of driving borrowing countries to financing sources that require no environmental safeguards. As more commercial financing is available to middle-income countries, this becomes a distinct possibility.[22]

One trend that might preserve the incentives created by safeguard policies is the piloting of "country systems" for the implementation of environmental safeguards. The multilateral development banks have recognized that for certain high-performing countries, the safeguard policies add substantial administrative burdens without adding much value in terms of outcomes (Independent Evaluation Department 2009; Independent Evaluation Group 2010b). For these countries, both the World Bank and the Asian Development Bank are allowing the country to certify and implement safeguard mitigation measures according to their own procedures. In many cases, high-performing countries have complained that they must duplicate efforts under blanket safeguard procedures because projects must pass through both their own safeguard procedures and a separate set of procedures mandated by the multilateral development banks. Ending the later requirements based on performance has the potential to incentivize countries to adopt strong policies of their own and implement them well in order to qualify for participation in country safeguard systems. This would also incentivize staff to pursue environmentally risky projects in countries with high safeguard performance. However, care needs to be taken to ensure continuous high performance once countries transition to country systems in order for these incentives to be preserved.

More broadly, the results of this chapter speak to the importance of administrative procedures as a method that political principals can use to control bureaucratic agencies. Administrative procedures have two particularly important functions.

Principals can mandate actions to steer agent decisions by making certain decisions more or less costly. In addition, they decrease the cost of monitoring to political principals and make it possible to delegate the responsibility for the monitoring and enforcement components of oversight. As is the case in domestic settings (Baber 1983; Barzelay 1997; Kelly 2003), this means that there are clear advantages to creating departments within international organizations with specialized monitoring and enforcement authority when divergent preferences are a problem. Administrative procedures support the work of such departments. At international organizations, for example, it may be the case that problems in mainstreaming gender analysis into development programs could be facilitated by specific administrative processes that require plans to be drawn up and evaluated by specialized monitoring bodies (Pollack and Hafner-Burton 2010). Monitoring departments, such as financial control offices, are already common in international organizations and other bureaucracies.

When speaking to staff at the multilateral development banks about environmental safeguard policies, it was clear that, in addition to the incentives brought about by differences in compliance costs at the country level, the threat of being subjected to high-profile citizen complaints might drive allocation and approval decisions. Recognizing the environmental failures of the 1980s, three development banks established inspection mechanisms that allowed civil society groups to formally petition for redress when safeguard procedures are not properly implemented. Thus, in addition to the incentives created by organization-wide administrative procedures, the availability of oversight from nonstate actors and the cost of sanctioning might have an additional effect on the allocation of environmentally risky projects. The next chapter explores these possibilities.

It was hoped that this citizen driven process would provide some means of holding the bank accountable to the people affected by its lending decisions, and that having such a mechanism in place would lead to the avoidance of further disastrous projects.

CLARK 2003, 2

5

Accountability Mechanisms

CIVIL SOCIETY CLAIMS FOR ENVIRONMENTAL

PERFORMANCE

INFORMATION ABOUT THE performance of the multilateral development banks that comes directly from local people might fill gaps left by project evaluations. Project evaluations are only available for a minority of projects. Therefore, project evaluations might not fully capture the experiences of local people, especially since they often focus on inputs and procedures that can be assessed by desk review, rather than direct observations of outcomes on the ground (Uphoff 1992). Sourcing local information about the outcomes of projects and the implementation of safeguard procedures might provide an alternative pathway to better performance and more selective decisions about the allocation of development assistance. This chapter assesses whether the establishment of citizen complaint mechanisms has provided a different pathway to selectivity.

It is often challenging for local people and civil society groups to have their voices heard at international organizations, which are accountable to states. To have a voice at international organizations, civil society groups have to find the support of powerful states, which can be difficult in many circumstances. At the domestic level, governments face accountability through the ballot box or even revolution. For international organizations, no direct pathway of accountability is similarly available. One of the clearest manifestations of this problem occurs at aid agencies. Scholars, practitioners, and NGOs have all lamented the broken "feedback loop" between the supposed beneficiaries of aid projects and the organizations tasked with managing projects (Jacobs 2010).

These concerns have not escaped the attention of donor states to the multilateral development banks. Recognizing the limitations of safeguard procedures without monitoring, the multilateral development banks all adopted accountability mechanisms that accept feedback and monitoring from civil society groups. Since local people are often directly able to monitor the implementation of environmentally risky projects, they may provide crucial information about performance. As McCubbins and Schwartz (1984) have proposed for domestic bureaucracies, civil society groups might provide "fire alarm" monitoring of projects that go awry during implementation. Not only do civil society groups have the most at stake in the environmental performance of development projects, but they are also best positioned to monitor whether projects actually live up to the environmental requirements set by safeguard procedures. The multilateral development banks offer an excellent test of this possibility, since they have all established mechanisms that encourage "fire alarm" monitoring of safeguard policies. Accountability mechanisms might promote selectivity by driving environmentally risky projects away from countries that implement them poorly, as revealed by local people.

Accountability mechanisms grew out of widespread opposition by civil society groups to environmentally risky projects in the late 1980s. A large dam project in India was the spark. The Narmada Dam project, which was approved for financing by the World Bank in 1985, mobilized civil society groups around the world. Civil society groups highlighted that thousands of people would lose their homes as a result of the project and that vast areas of natural and agricultural land would be inundated by construction of the dam. Indian and international civil society groups joined together to advocate for cancelation of the project. In India, this mobilization led to marches of hundreds of thousands of people and civil disobedience throughout areas that were scheduled for inundation (Clark 2003). These protests were supported by civil society organizations around the world, leading to legislative hearings in donor countries about the environmental and social practices of the World Bank. Among the most important issues raised by this attention was the lack of recourse for private citizens and civil society groups that were negatively impacted by lending decisions at the World Bank and the other multilateral development banks.

In response to protests and pressure from donor countries, the World Bank agreed to form an independent commission to review the Narmada project. The commission found systematic flaws in planning, design, and implementation, reinforcing the claims of civil society groups (Morse and Berger 1992). In 1993, facing growing criticism from both major donor countries and civil society groups, the World Bank canceled its support for the Narmada project at the request of India.

In the following year, NGOs and some donor countries pushed the World Bank to establish a permanent commission that would be available to review complaints from civil society about poor implementation of environmental and social policies. In 1994, as part of the 10th International Development Association (IDA) replenishment, the United States insisted that the World Bank adopt an accountability mechanism. Following a series of oversight hearings in the US Congress about World Bank environmental and social policies, a permanent Inspection Panel was established at the World Bank.[1] The Inter-American Development Bank and the Asian Development Bank adopted similar reforms in a matter of months (McGill 2001; Miller 2001; Nelson 2001).

Scholars of international relations have long been interested in the mechanisms available to hold international organizations accountable for performance. Given the long chains of delegation between states and international organizations and the inability of states to monitor performance in many instances, accountability at international organizations is generally weak (Lyne, Nielson, and Tierney 2006; Nye 2001; Gutner and Thompson 2010). As Grant and Keohane write, one of the major questions about the governance of international organizations is "What kinds of accountability mechanisms are likely to be effective in constraining international organizations such as the World Bank and International Monetary Fund?" (2005, 30). Establishment of accountability mechanisms at the World Bank and the other multilateral development banks is remarkable because states have typically reserved sole authority to hold international organizations accountable for performance (Clark 2003, 9). Civil society groups that wish to challenge the actions of international organizations face the difficult task of appealing to member states of international organizations, which are not always receptive to their claims (Woods 2001; Keck and Sikkink 1998). This means that civil society groups must often resort to challenging the reputation of international organizations to induce sympathetic states to press for reforms or better performance (Grant and Keohane 2005). Inspection Panels open the possibility for a more direct form of accountability and decrease the costs to civil society groups that would like to change the actions of the multilateral development banks.

To this day, the establishment of accountability mechanisms at the multilateral development banks is one of the most important attempts to overcome monitoring problems at international organizations. In essence, the inspection process provides civil society groups with a high-level, visible forum to reveal instances of poor environmental and social performance by the multilateral development banks. When an inspection claim is received from a civil society group, the claim is made public and the panel determines whether the claim is eligible for investigation.[2] If the claimant is found to be eligible, initial reports about the case are send to the board, which consists of representatives of member states, for approval of a formal investigation. Owing to this high-level attention, management and staff at development banks generally spend large amounts of time and resources defending bank actions when an investigation is approved. If the Inspection Panel finds evidence that environmental or social policies were not properly implemented, it will make recommendations for remedial actions, which can impose further costs on management. In addition, because of significant board involvement throughout the inspection process, claims can seriously damage the international reputation of multilateral development banks, making it difficult to secure resources from donor countries in ongoing replenishment and capital increase negotiations.[3]

A critically important feature of the MDB accountability mechanisms is that the consent of any member country or the borrowing country is not required for a request to be filed. Because inspection requests automatically set in motion a number of costly steps for the multilateral development banks, the inspection process allows civil society groups to impose substantial costs on the multilateral development banks for poor implementation of environmental safeguards without needing to first find sympathetic states. It remains an open question whether this type of monitoring and accountability mechanism can induce the multilateral development banks to become more selective about the countries where they will pursue environmentally risky projects.

The primary type of claim from civil society groups at these Inspection Panels concerns the poor implementation of environmental and social safeguards (Treakle, Fox, and Clark 2003, 251). While it has been recognized that civil society groups can provide important monitoring functions to states (Dai 2007; Steffek and Ferretti 2009), rarely do civil society groups from less-developed countries have the ability to publicize their grievances about IO performance in ways that attract significant attention from member states and cause offending international organizations to incur large financial and operational costs. From the perspective of civil society groups, two types of successful outcomes might come about because of inspection claims. First, the board might require projects to be implemented differently or corrected when civil society grievances are found to be legitimate. Second, the multilateral development banks might be more selective about similar types of projects in future periods. The first outcome is a given; the second outcome is the primary question considered in this chapter: *can civil society claims for environmental performance make the multilateral development banks more selective about the allocation of environmentally risky projects?* I show that accountability mechanisms change the allocation practices of the World Bank when monitors are available and when information from monitors creates problems and delays for staff.

CIVIL SOCIETY AND ACCOUNTABILITY OF INTERNATIONAL
ORGANIZATIONS FOR PERFORMANCE

States make international organizations accountable and responsive to results by imposing costs and rewards that are aligned with performance. For example, states can decrease resources to international organizations that fail to meet certain performance standards (Crane and Dusenberry 2004). In 1998, member states of the United Nations drastically and surprisingly cut the budget for the United Nations High Commissioner on Refugees, owing to perceptions about inefficiency and impacts of costly resettlement programs being planned by the commission (Barnett and Finnemore 2004, 95). In the late 1980s, the United States cut the budgets of several international organizations that it deemed not to be acting in accordance with American interests (Adams 1988). Most prominently, the United States withdrew most of its budget support to the United Nations Food and Agriculture Organization (FAO) over a clash with the organization's leadership about the direction of its agriculture programs and the efficiency of its operations. The loss of resources drastically scaled back FAO operations (Lewis 1988; Lanig 1995). States are also able to change the mandates of international organizations and restrict their activities in response to poor performance or grant international organizations greater authority and resources in response to satisfactory performance (Jupille and Snidal 2006). A prominent example of this form of accountability is the periodic replenishments and capital increases that are negotiated between states and multilateral development banks. The concessional financing windows of the multilateral development banks that lend to poor countries require new infusions of resources on a frequent basis. This gives donor states significant leverage to push for policy changes (see Andersen, Hansen, and Markussen 2006). Even the financing windows that lend at market rates to middle-income countries must receive capital increases to increase their lending.

Despite these possibilities, overt accountability where states sanction international organizations on the basis of performance is less frequent than might be expected (Reinisch 2001; Grant and Keohane 2005). For international organizations involved with development assistance, this lack of accountability has been cited as a key reason for poor performance (Wenar 2006). A main reason for the lack of accountability at multilateral development organizations is that states cannot monitor the many activities being implemented around the world (Weaver 2008). As a consequence, states do not always have good information on which to base sanctions. For development projects, private citizens and domestic civil society groups are often best positioned to monitor performance and outcomes. Indeed, an executive director from a donor country to the Asian Development Bank that I interviewed for this project emphasized that civil society groups serve as "watchdogs," since a member country has limited capacity to monitor hundreds of active projects.

Indeed, civil society groups might fill a more general void in the monitoring of international organizations. With the expansion of information technologies, civil society groups have dramatically expanded their reach into the international sphere (Keck and Sikkink 1998). Civil society groups now organize and gather in protest at many international meetings of state delegates (Clark, Friedman, and Hochstetler 1998). Because of their outspoken advocacy, civil society groups have been successful at gaining access to international meetings of state delegates, both as observers and as participants (Bernauer and Betzold 2012; Böhmelt 2012). In some cases, like the United Nations Framework Convention on Climate Change, civil society groups are even being included in state delegations (Mathews 1997). Civil society groups can provide states with low-cost monitoring of international organizations, thereby enabling more vigorous state responses to lapses in performance (Dai 2007; Steffek and Ferretti 2009). Civil society groups can even impose major reputational and operational costs on international organizations when they are able to capture state attention (Simmons 1998; Khagram 2004).

The multilateral development banks and other international financial institutions have a particularly vibrant constellation of civil society groups that monitor their activities and seek accountability for poor performance. The World Bank has been the focus of much civil society attention, given its prominent development programs around the world and its central role in the neoliberal policy agenda of Western countries in the 1970s and 1980s. Civil society groups have sought substantial policy reforms over time at the World Bank, especially for environmental management (Rich 1990; Nelson 1996; Wade 1997). Not only have Western civil society groups gained prominent roles as advocates for World Bank reforms, but they have also supported grassroots monitoring by local civil society groups. Some observers credit these efforts for bringing about environmental reforms at the World Bank (Wade 1997; Fox and Brown 1998). Civil society organizations gave states both information and the political pressure needed to pursue broader reforms.

Still, recent research has been skeptical of the role that civil society groups play in providing actionable information to states, at least as part of official delegations to international meetings. As an alternative explanation, Böhmelt (2012) suggests that states include civil society groups in climate negotiations to head off criticism at the domestic level and make agreements easier to sell to domestic interest groups. In relation to international organizations, Grigorescu (2007) finds that organizations with more democratic states are more likely to adopt access to information policies that benefit the public and NGOs, likely because of the need to increase the legitimacy of international organizations to domestic audiences. Likewise, Raustalia (1997) argues that states include NGOs in global environmental negotiations in part to signal to domestic audiences and reduce the chance that opposition to the ratification of agreements will arise later. Almost all existing research has examined how states include NGOs in international negotiations as a signaling device. How states interact with civil society groups in foreign countries that do not have any direct political leverage in their home country is not clear.

Long chains of delegation and the challenges of international advocacy make it difficult for civil society groups to seek recourse for actions by international organizations that harm them, despite their willingness to seek accountability. Many times, groups without significant communication and travel resources lack the ability to participate in the decision-making of international organizations (Keck and Sikkink 1998; Acuña and Tuozzo 2000). Their home states can be unreceptive to their concerns because elite preferences are different from local preferences, especially when it comes to national-scale development planning (Boone 1996; Feyzioglu, Swaroop, and Zhu 1998). Because civil society groups from less-developed countries have not traditionally been able to participate effectively in decision-making of international organizations, various scholars have been concerned that international organizations have a "democratic deficit" (Nye 2001; Stutzer and Frey 2005). It is possible that accountability mechanisms might make the multilateral development banks more responsive to their past performance by solving information problems for states that have a real interest and ability to allocate risky projects selectively.

Introduction to the Inspection Panels at the Multilateral Development Banks

The establishment of the Inspection Panels at the multilateral development banks is one of the most significant and direct attempts to promote accountability at international organizations.[4] The inspection process provides states with "fire alarm" oversight of performance related to implementation of safeguard policies (McCubbins and Schwartz 1984). While there are certainly systematic barriers to participation in the inspection process (e.g., transaction cost of formulating a claim or a previous attempt to address the issue with MDB management), a group of any size can submit a claim, and if the group is determined to be eligible, that claim will receive the attention of member states through the board. At their core, the inspection processes have created an avenue for civil society claims to be amplified and formalized at the international level, which may solve information problems of donors states. In turn, member states can use this information in their negotiations with the multilateral development banks for resources and to enhance their oversight of activities.

While the formal rules governing Inspection Panel claims at the various multilateral development banks are documented extensively elsewhere, it is worth noting the main elements of the claims process that can be generalized across the multilateral development banks.[5] All of the multilateral development banks have established policies about the environmental and social safeguards that must be carried out during the design and implementation of every project, for example, the completion of an environmental impact assessment when a project is likely to cause negative environmental damages. If a group of people is negatively affected by an MDB project because these policies are not carried out with due diligence, they can file a claim to the Inspection Panel, which will investigate whether policies have been violated. The Inspection Panels are structured in a variety of ways, but generally consist of external experts with a mix of nationalities.

Owing to the negative attention from donor states and the significant resources that are required to respond to inspection requests, both the management of the multilateral banks and the borrowing country have routinely sought to have inspection requests declared ineligible (Clark 2003, 12–13). They rarely succeed in doing so when grievances pass minimum eligibility rules. The most important of these rules is a claim of direct and material harm, as well as a documented attempt by the claimants to resolve the matter with relevant operational staff. If the Inspection Panel determines that the claimants are eligible and the board approves a recommendation for an inspection investigation, then the panel conducts a formal investigation, which includes field visits, interviews with the claimants and bank staff, and a review of project documents. Based on the investigation, the panel produces a public report that documents any policy violations and makes recommendations for remedial activities. Civil society groups are not able to demand specific compensatory actions from the multilateral development banks as part of this process (Fox and Treakle 2003, 282–83; Steffek and Ferretti 2009, 41). Thus, the inspection process alerts member states and other interest groups to instances of poor performance, but ultimately depends on member states ("the board") to approve remedial actions for any specific project or any broader changes to policy and practice that might affect future decisions about allocation. The board chooses whether or not to adopt recommendations made by the Inspection Panels, and if they are adopted, they become a binding directive for management. While authors have noted that this long chain of events may decrease the effectiveness of panels in providing accountability (Fox 2000; Fox and Treakle 2003), the systematic impact of this accountability mechanism on allocation decisions about projects has not been examined. Most existing studies of the inspection process rely on single cases examined at great depth (Clark, Fox, and Treakle 2003).

The Inspection Panel might change the incentives surrounding project allocation for several reasons. The multilateral development banks have run into problems with replenishment and capital increases because of negative attention raised by inspection cases. During replenishment meetings, inspection cases frequently prompt donors to pursue policy changes that involve stronger environmental and social protections for local people.[6] A staff member involved with coordinating management responses to inspection cases reported that preparation of a response takes a great deal of time and care in order to avoid upsetting donor relations. According to another operational staff member, departments try to avoid projects that can trigger inspection cases because they take up management and staff time for months, which detracts from the ability of higher-level management to "push the pipeline" and reach lending goals.

At the individual level, inspection cases can create important career barriers for operational staff. As one operational staff member at the World Bank reported, there is a high level of "neck protection" among staff at the World Bank. Individuals who design projects that enter the inspection process carry an informal stigma for the rest of their career. While staff cannot avoid the risks associated with inspection investigations entirely, teams that design projects often avoid components of projects that might lead to significant risks when history indicates that requests are likely. Because individual incentives are closely linked to the approval of new projects, staff at the Asian Development Bank reported that they avoid certain types of projects in the transportation sector when civil society opposition is likely, as this can lead to significant delays in the approval of new operations. When the inspection function was first considered at the World Bank, misgivings about the avoidance of projects were a central part of opposition to this new accountability mechanism (World Bank 2001).

To understand when and why accountability mechanisms constrain international organizations, we must know two things. First, when will external groups provide monitoring and submit complaints through an accountability mechanism? Second, under what conditions do complaints submitted through accountability mechanisms impose costs sufficient to make international organizations less likely to pursue offending actions in the future? On the first question, I argue that the provision of fire-alarm monitoring through accountability mechanisms is most likely when civil society groups face low monitoring costs and are able to reveal monitoring information without threat of repression in their home country. On the second question, I argue that accountability mechanisms are most likely to constrain the actions of international organizations when they enhance the oversight capabilities of states that have an interest in the same type of performance as the claimants.

Provision of Inspection Panel Requests

To understand whether civil society monitoring can drive selectivity related to environmentally risky projects and thus improve the way that discretion is utilized by the development banks, it is first necessary to explain when and why civil society groups will provide monitoring. One factor that may account for inspection requests is the availability of a strong civil society. When civil society is already organized or has the ability to organize quickly around the relevant issue, civil society groups are more likely to serve as monitors. To the extent that local advocacy groups already monitor the relevant issue, monitoring is more likely to be provided. Since violations of environmental policies are the most common element of inspection requests, I hypothesize that countries with more environmental NGOs should produce more inspection requests:

Hypothesis 1a: Borrowing countries will more likely be subject to an inspection request in any given year as the number of environmental NGOs increases.

Civil society groups are not available to provide monitoring in many authoritarian or semiauthoritarian countries, and therefore may not be able to use accountability mechanisms. Civil society groups may lack the ability or legal right to organize in ways necessary to produce an inspection claim, which must include multiple households. Citizens in places with fewer political freedoms may lack information about their options, since they have fewer links with international civil society organizations (Linaweaver 2003). In addition, Inspection Panel investigations often delay the disbursement of lending projects, which may harm the borrowing country. Under these conditions, authoritarian borrowing countries may repress claims for inspection (Ho 2001). If civil society groups are not available to seek recourse in many places where the multilateral development banks operate, the promise of the Inspection Panel to promote better environmental performance would be circumscribed. This logic of availability leads to the following hypothesis:

Hypothesis 1b: Borrowing countries that protect political rights will more likely be subject to an inspection request in any given year.

Both the multilateral development banks and civil society groups might learn from past inspection investigations. The multilateral development banks might respond to previous requests by ensuring better safeguard policy implementation in future periods, rather than avoiding projects with environmental risks. Indeed, none of the Inspection Panel charter documents envision a situation where the establishment of the inspection process would change allocation practices, but rather that management would be accountable for diligently implementing operational policies.[7] One of the reasons why international development organizations have not been responsive to their mistakes is that internal incentives reward continued project approvals, rather than responses to lessons of past operations (Biggs and Smith 2003). The Inspection Panels made the costs of noncompliance with environmental safeguard policies high for staff and management, both for the implementation of the project in question and in terms of scrutiny of future projects. These costs create incentives to choose projects where safeguard policies can be carried out with due diligence.

All of the multilateral development banks have placed a great deal of emphasis on becoming "learning organizations," mainly through increased transparency about their successes and failures (Ellerman 1999; Asian Development Bank 2009). One of the most difficult parts of creating a "learning culture" within complex organizations is the lack of incentives to share and learn from failed operations (Storey and Barnett 2000). In a way, establishment of the inspection process has forced the multilateral development banks to deal directly with instances where they failed to ensure that environmental and social safeguard policies are implemented well. Thus, the inspection processes may have promoted "learning by doing," whereby the multilateral development banks become more acutely aware of the risks associated with their programs in particular countries and adjust to these risks.

On the other hand, civil society groups might learn about the political efficacy of filing requests based on past cases. Since inspection requests are often followed by concessions from the MDB management, either to head off full inspections or as required by recommendations from the Inspection Panel, civil society groups in particular countries might be successful at spreading knowledge of this mechanism. A similar phenomenon of learning about successful advocacy strategies through formal institutions has been found for World Trade Organization dispute filings (Bermeo 2010). In addition, the multilateral development banks might find it difficult to be selective about environmentally risky projects in some countries despite previous inspections, owing to borrowing country priorities. In these countries, the risks of inspection requests do not overwhelm the expected benefits of pursuing risky projects, leading to repeated inspection requests over time. These competing propositions lead to the following testable hypothesis:

Hypothesis 2: Borrowing countries that have experienced previous inspection requests or investigations will be more/less likely to have their projects subjected to additional inspection requests and investigations in future periods.

Inspection Panel and Selectivity

After testing hypotheses about the provision of monitoring through the Inspection Panel, it is necessary to understand the effect of this monitoring on decisions about allocation. Given that inspection documents are made publicly available and receive immediate, high-level attention from member states, management at the multilateral banks and representatives from many borrowing countries have feared that establishment of the Inspection Panels would make the multilateral development banks systematically *risk-averse* about infrastructure projects that are important for economic development (World Bank 2001).[8] I explore whether the inspection process creates selectivity within country portfolios, rather than a systematic decrease in environmentally risky lending.

Environmentally risky projects are beneficial to the multilateral development banks for two reasons. First, environmentally risky projects tend to be large infrastructure projects that are an efficient use of scarce administrative resources, because they quickly meet lending targets and potentially avoid the need to steer multiple smaller projects through the approval process. Second, infrastructure projects have generally achieved output targets more successfully because implementation involves physical outputs that can often be sourced from contractors, rather than more difficult institutional goals of reform programs that require a great deal of borrowing country commitment (Freeman 2009).

Concerns about the inspection process causing systematic risk aversion have been voiced both inside and outside the multilateral development banks, and especially for the World Bank. Shihata (2000, 230), a World Bank insider, writes that there are two primary risks involved with establishing the Inspection Panel. First, there was a perceived risk that "the establishment of the Panel might have a deterrent effect on Bank's staff, causing them to be over-concerned with following the rules and procedures and less innovative in their work." In other words, discretion to pursue environmentally risky projects would not be managed, it would be eliminated. Second, borrowing countries have resisted the establishment of Inspection Panels because of fears that they "internationalize" disputes with private citizens that should be handled domestically, making borrowers less likely to pursue projects with environmental risks through the multilateral development banks. This might result in borrowing countries seeking financing for risky projects from sources that do not require any safeguards.[9]

While years of data show that the multilateral development banks have not systematically decreased lending for environmentally risky projects (see figure 4.1), donor states have shown a willingness to authorize inspections and sanction multilateral development banks for poor environmental performance revealed through accountability mechanisms. For example, the United States and some European countries have consistently voted to authorize inspections despite opposition from borrowing countries (Fox 2000, 303–5). In some instances, inspection cases have resulted in hearings from the US Congress and other legislative bodies.[10] Discussions of inspection cases and other "disaster projects" frequently arise as part of replenishment negotiations for the concessional lending windows of the development banks and often lead to calls for reforms at the development banks (Nielson and Tierney 2003). Thus, establishment of the Inspection Panels might have created a strong reluctance to pursue environmentally risky projects in countries that have been subject to complaints by civil society groups.

I test whether inspection cases make the allocation of environmentally risky projects less likely for recipient countries that receive lending with different levels of oversight from donor countries. The International Development Association (IDA) at the World Bank makes loans below market rates and thus requires regular replenishment of funds from donor states to continue its lending operations. During replenishment meetings, inspection cases are frequently used by member states to pursue policy changes that involve stronger environmental and social protections for local people. Given that the IDA depends critically on replenishments from donor states, the World Bank should be much less likely to pursue environmentally risky projects with countries that borrow from the IDA following an inspection case.

In contrast, the International Bank for Reconstruction and Development (IBRD) makes loans at market rates and covers the costs of its operations without periodic replenishments from donor states. The IBRD did not go through a single capital increase supported by donor states during 1994–2009, the time period considered in the analysis below.[11] Recipient countries that borrow from IBRD tend to be middle-income countries with good credit and access to commercial bond markets. This means that borrowing countries are much more active at setting their IBRD lending priorities and less likely to be pressured by the World Bank to accept investments preferred by donor states. While the inspection process may have a similar effect on lending to these countries, it may also be the case that donor states exercise less leverage over lending at the IBRD following inspection cases.

Hypothesis 3a: Multilateral development banks will be less likely to approve an environmentally risky project for a country that receives concessional lending, where a previous project has been subjected to an Inspection Panel case.

Hypothesis 3b: Multilateral development banks will not be less likely to approve an environmentally risky project for a country that receives nonconcessional lending, where a previous project has been subjected to an Inspection Panel case.

Hypothesis 4: Given that a multilateral development bank approves an environmentally risky project in a given year, the amount of environmentally risky financing will be lower for a country where a previous project has been subjected to an Inspection Panel investigation.

CASE STUDY: THE INSPECTION PANEL

AND HYDROPOWER IN NEPAL

The 402 MW hydropower project in the Arun Valley of Nepal, known as Arun III, was the first World Bank project to be subjected to an Inspection Panel investigation. As the first Inspection Panel case, Arun III offers a chance to see how the World Bank management and staff, accustomed to an operational environment without a citizen accountability mechanism, reacted to an institutional shock. Since the project was planned before the Inspection Panel was created, there are particular gains to be made in assessing how the World Bank changed its operational focus and its lending behavior by comparing lending before and after this new type of monitoring.

Nepal is a poor, mountainous country with incredible potential for hydropower. In the early 1990s, when Arun III was being planned, Nepal's domestic energy demand was growing. Nepal was also seeking opportunities to generate foreign reserves by selling energy to neighboring countries like India. Little of the countryside was electrified, and social services were limited or nonexistent. In this context, the Nepal government, supported by private contractors, began planning for a new wave of hydropower projects across the country to support economic growth, improve access to electricity, and generate foreign reserves. Arun III was a primary component of a medium-term plan to achieve these goals and was identified as a least-cost project to expand energy production both for domestic use and for foreign sale (World Bank 1989; SARI/Energy 2002).

As was the case for many other poor countries, international donor organizations played a primary role in financing large-scale infrastructure. For Arun III, the World Bank's International Development Association began negotiations with Nepal in the late 1980s to support the broader push to increase energy generation. The Arun III project was the center of these negotiations. In particular, the World Bank appraised a $32 million concessional credit to the government of Nepal to fund an access road to the Arun III construction site in 1989 (World Bank 1989). Because the dam site was relatively remote and logistically difficult to reach, improving access was a precondition to constructing a dam. The World Bank credit was the first in a series of commitments to support hydropower in Nepal.

In 1994, several years after the Arun III access road was approved for financing and a consortium of organizations was moving toward the approval of financing for the hydroelectric dam itself, a group of Nepali NGOs calling themselves the Arun Concerned Group, supported by a coalition of international NGOs, filed a request for inspection. The request alleged that environmental and social policies of the World Bank had been disregarded, to the determent of local people. The request claimed that compensation had not been paid to households affected by the project and that the construction of the access road and subsequent dam was likely to have impacts on forests and ecosystems that had not been addressed in the planning documents. Regarding the environmental impacts, the request for inspection noted a particularly troubling section of the environmental assessment conducted before the access road was built, which stated that "serving the needs of the population in the general area through which the road will pass is a secondary consideration." The request goes on to note that "the cumulative impacts in the Arun valley of Arun III . . . have not been evaluated" (Arun Concerned Group 1994).

The World Bank management and Nepali government at first defended the project. However, it quickly became clear that this defense was not uniform inside the bank. In September 1994, the division chief of the South Asia Region at the World Bank, Martin Karcher, resigned from the World Bank in protest of this project, which he claimed would require too much investment by the Nepali government, significantly detracting from other economic and social goals (Udall 1995). With attention being paid to the claims at high levels of the World Bank, it quickly became clear that concerns were not simply being shrugged off, as many activists had claimed the World Bank would do in earlier years.

The board of directors of the World Bank, the body made up of representatives from the shareholder countries and that is often considered to be controlled by donor countries, agreed in 1995 that a full investigation of the project should occur before the project would move forward. The June 1995 inspection investigation found that the Arun III access road project failed to meet World Bank policy in multiple ways. In particular, the project was approved for construction before the environmental impact assessment had been completed, which would prevent a more proactive approach to environmental management. The investigation also found issues with resettlement for the local people who were displaced by the access road that was being built under the IDA credit.

While the inspection investigation did not mandate the project be stopped, it did bring a pause to implementation. Following the Inspection Panel report, a second analysis of the project was commissioned by the World Bank to explore how the project fit within Nepal's broader development plans. It was run by Maurice Strong, former secretary general of the United Nations Conference on Environment and Development. This report concluded that Nepal would not likely be able to absorb a project of such great size and that the project was likely to divert public resources away from more pressing development needs. In light of both the Inspection Panel report and the Strong report, World Bank president James Wolfensohn cancelled the project "in agreement with the Government of Nepal." A project that had been through many years of the planning process was now dead in the water because of concerns raised by local civil society organizations, with major support from international civil society organizations. Importantly, similar projects not subject to the Inspection Panel were moving forward in other countries. For example, the World Bank helped finance the large Ghazi-Barotha Dam in Pakistan at about the same time, with few delays (Khawaja 2001).

After the Arun III Hydropower Project in Nepal went through the inspection process, the World Bank not only withdrew from the project, but also did not approve direct lending in the hydropower sector in Nepal for the next decade. Instead, it shifted focus to supporting and facilitating private sector investment in hydropower, which did not raise the same challenges. The World Bank moved to support hydropower in Nepal through the International Financial Corporation (IFC), the branch of the World Bank that makes loans to the private sector to support investment in developing countries. In January 1996, for example, the IFC and the Asian Development Bank signed an agreement to support the Khimiti I Hydropower Project in Nepal, to be built and operated by a Norwegian utility company. Similar support was made available through the IFC for the Bhote Koshi power plant. But the emphasis of this support shifted markedly toward facilitating private sector involvement, in line with energy sector plans drawn up by the government of Nepal.

The 1996 country assistance strategy for Nepal, which outlined World Bank lending priorities following the Arun III inspection case, focused on policy consultations and investment facilitation "to promote and catalyze private investment in technically, economically, environmentally, and socially sound [hydropower] projects" (World Bank 1996, 16). At the same time, the World Bank was considering a new Nepal Power Development Project, which would invest in grid transmission and distribution infrastructure. Unlike the Arun III project, extensive environmental assessments were conducted throughout the late 1990s in connection with this project, totaling seven volumes examining different environmental implications of the project. The team tasked with preparing the project worked with local people, and it was clear from the 2003 project appraisal report that lessons had been learned. That report gave the following statement in the "lessons learned" section:

> Past experience of hydro development has led to the design and implementation of a transparent and participatory process for the selection of hydro projects as an integral part of project preparation. Consultation with the stakeholders in

Nepal in general, and the project affected people in particular, has been made an integral part of the preparatory process. (World Bank 2003a, 16)

Even with this assessment in place, approval of the Nepal Power Development Project was delayed until 2003, and the scope of World Bank support was further reduced "from investment support for hydropower development to technical assistance."[12] All the while, the government of Nepal shifted its focus toward attracting private investment for the Arun project that was not successfully funded by the World Bank after the inspection case. For example, as early as 1996 Nepal began inviting bids from the private sector to build and operate the Arun project (*Financial Times* 1996). In 2000, the EurOrient Investment Banking Group entered an agreement to build the Arun III project, but this later failed because EurOrient was unable to complete a power purchase agreement with India, providing further evidence that the World Bank had rushed into a project that was not viable (*International Water Power and Dam Construction* 2002). The Arun III dam has yet to be built, though plans are in place to move forward with Indian financing, almost 30 years after the project was first considered. The Inspection Panel process instigated this long delay and reconsideration.

As this example shows, the Inspection Panel serves the dual purpose of correcting implementation problems for active projects and alerting member states to risks in future operations. Whereas these same groups had been active in protesting the Arun III project for years (Bhattarai 1994), the Inspection Panel gave them the ability to halt a large and politically important project that was under consideration at the World Bank. The World Bank moved away from funding these large, controversial projects. Instead, it looked to support the government of Nepal in attracting private financing. The inspection case also resulted in projects that took environmental impacts much more seriously over a number of years before approval. Thus, by alerting the World Bank to issues particular to the place, the Inspection Panel contributed to changes both within the individual project and outside the project.

MODELING ENVIRONMENTAL PERFORMANCE AND REQUESTS
FOR INSPECTION INVESTIGATIONS
Description of Inspection Requests and Findings, 1994–2008

Previous studies have documented individual inspection cases in great detail (e.g., Clark, Fox, and Treakle 2003). The vast majority of inspection cases have been requested for World Bank projects, likely owing to its large portfolio and propensity to attract international attention (figure 5.1). For the purposes of this analysis, the

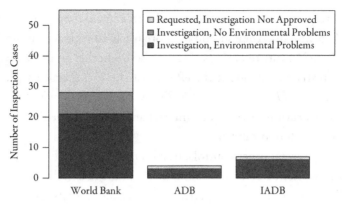

FIGURE 5.1 Inspection cases involving environmental claims at the multilateral development banks, 1994–2008

African Development Bank is excluded because approval for an inspection function was only finalized in 2004, and it took until 2007 for the first claim to be filed. The inspection cases displayed in figure 5.1 are spread across many countries, with 30 borrowing countries experiencing requests at the World Bank, four borrowing countries experiencing requests at the Asian Development Bank, and four borrowing countries experiencing requests at the Inter-American Development Bank. Thus, there are not sufficient cases at either the Asian Development Bank or Inter-American Development Bank for modeling purposes, but I do consider evidence from staff interviews in the final part of this chapter.

Predictor Variables and Specification

The purpose of the first set of models is to test hypotheses about the supply of inspection requests. I use the number of environmental NGOs (*NO. ENGOs*) as documented in various editions of the *Environment Encyclopedia and Directory* as a measure of the civil society activity pertaining to environmental issues in different countries (H1a). To measure when civil society groups are likely to face political repression in their home country for advocacy (H1b), I create a binary variable *POLITICAL REPRESSION* that is positive whenever the Freedom House index of political rights indicates that political rights such as representation, toleration of political discussion, and the ability of the public to lodge complaints with government are highly circumscribed (index value ≥ 5).

Civil society groups might learn about the efficacy and costs of filing requests based on past cases. Since inspection requests are often followed by concessions from the MDB management, either to head off full inspections or as required by remedial directives, civil society groups in particular countries might learn about the opportunities afforded by the Inspection Panel. Once civil society groups have filed a request that successfully results in remedial environmental activities by the World Bank, they should be more likely to seek accountability at the Inspection Panel in future periods (H2). To test whether civil society groups in particular countries learn about the efficacy of the Inspection Panel, I generate the variable *NO. PREVIOUS INSPECTION FINDINGS*, which is a count of the previous inspection cases in a country that required remedial actions by the World Bank at each point in time.

I also include several other control variables that might influence the provision of inspection requests. Borrowing countries that pursue a higher number of risky projects will be more likely to experience inspection requests, given that a risky portfolio provides more opportunities for poor performance. Thus, I control for the number of projects flagged as requiring environmental impact assessments during the five previous years (*NO. RISKY IN PAST 5 YRS*). It may be the case that civil society groups learn from and react to internal evaluations of environmental performance before filing requests. Thus, I include the variable *EVAL W/ SAFEGUARD FAILURE IN PAST 5 YRS*, which is positive whenever a project evaluation completed by the evaluation department found failure to implement environmental safeguard policies during the previous five years (see chapter 4). Finally, it is possible that governments that are effective at implementing policies are more likely to avoid inspection requests, given better policy implementation in general. I use the Worldwide Governance Indicator index of *GOVERNMENT EFFECTIVENESS* to control for this possibility.[13] Since the outcome of interest is a binary variable, I estimate the effect of the predictor and control variables using a standard generalized linear model with a logistic link function.

Model Results

The model results reported in table 5.1 show that the provision of inspection requests has as much to do with the availability of civil society groups as it does with the underlying performance of World Bank projects. Having more environmental civil society groups is a strong predictor that inspection requests will be filed. In addition, it also appears that borrowing countries with fewer political liberties are less likely to face inspection requests, indicating that the ability of civil society groups to organize opposition to policies and projects is important for their ability to provide monitoring. It also seems that civil society groups, rather than the World Bank itself, learn about the efficacy of filing civil society requests. In both models, borrowing countries that experienced previous inspection requests in the past are more likely to experience additional requests in the future. It is also the case that borrowing countries that receive a higher number of environmentally risky projects

TABLE 5.1

REQUESTS FOR INSPECTION INVOLVING ENVIRONMENTAL PERFORMANCE
AT THE WORLD BANK

Model	1a	1b
H1: *NO. ENGOs*	0.04** (0.01)	
H2: *POLITICAL REPRESSION*	−0.76* (0.46)	−0.93** (0.43)
NO. PREVIOUS INSPECTION FINDINGS	0.69* (0.38)	0.86** (0.39)
NO. RISKY IN PAST 5 YRS	0.08** (0.03)	0.09** (0.03)
EVAL W/ SAFEGUARD FAILURE IN PAST 5 YRS	−0.33 (0.95)	−0.52 (1.00)
GOVERNMENT EFFECTIVENESS	−0.65** (0.33)	−0.31 (0.28)
Data subset	Full panel	Full panel
Observations (countries)	1,611 (138)	2,101 (138)
Residual deviance	315.2	367.1
Null deviance	344.9	388.2

Note: All models are generalized linear models with logit link function. Null deviance is calculated using intercept as only predictor

Standard errors in parentheses with statistical significant indicators: * $p < .10$; ** $p < 0.05$ using one-tailed tests for stated, directional hypotheses and two-tailed tests for control variables.

over the previous five years are much more likely to experience inspection requests. Taken together, these results indicate that several baseline conditions make it likely that monitoring is provided to the Inspection Panel—an active civil society engaged in environmental issues, past experiences with inspection requests, and a lending portfolio with numerous environmentally risky projects.

To show the substantive effect of the number of environmental NGOs and the level of political repression on the probability that a borrowing country will face an inspection request during a particular year, I show the model fit and the 90% confidence interval for the effect size, accounting for uncertainty across all of the estimated model coefficients of Model 1a. As shown in figure 5.2, projects in borrowing countries with more environmental NGOs were subject to more inspection requests, regardless of the level of political repression. However, political repression

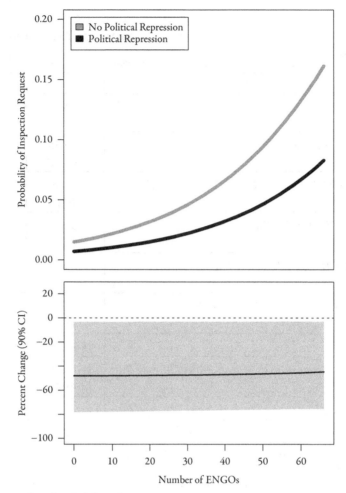

FIGURE 5.2 Predicted probability of an inspection request in a given year accounting for political repression

Note: This plot shows predictions from Model 1a. The top panel displays the probability of an inspection request. The bottom panel shows the effect size of the political repression indicator as a percentage with a 90% confidence interval.

dampened the provision of inspection requests, indicating that not all civil society groups are equally able to take advantage of this mechanism.

Now that it is clear that the provision of monitoring through the Inspection Panel is a function of both the availability of monitors and their ability to stake out political positions, it is important to understand whether this type of monitoring can influence lending decisions. While the results above provide some of the only available systematic evidence about the ability of civil society groups to provide independent monitoring, this type of monitoring may or may not be effective at changing MDB practices, a key consideration in understanding how nonstate actors can promote accountability at the international level and assist with managing the discretion of international organizations.

INSPECTION PANEL CASES AND AVERSION TO ENVIRONMENTALLY RISK LENDING

To model the effect of inspection cases on subsequent lending, I focus on the World Bank. While both the ADB and IADB approve a lot of environmentally risky projects, they have very few accountability cases. This makes analysis using methods that account for the nonrandom provision of inspection requests impossible. For example, the matching method I describe for the World Bank below yields only 30 observations of country-years for the Asian Development Bank, which leads to indeterminate results. For the Inter-American Development Bank, only four countries have experienced inspection cases, and of the seven requests between 1994 and 2008, four requests deal with the same Yacyreta Hydropower Project. Again, analysis of this very limited data set yields indeterminate results. Because the World Bank has a more extensive history of lending in environmentally risky sectors, and because its Inspection Panel has been more active than all the panels at the other multilateral development banks combined, I focus on the World Bank for modeling purposes. I revisit the Asian Development Bank and Inter-American Development Bank using interview data in the last section of this chapter.

The models in this section test whether borrowing countries that have been subjected to previous inspection requests and investigations have a lower probability of receiving an environmentally risky project in subsequent years, and when they do receive a risky project, whether its value is lower (see Hypotheses 3–4). For the approval model, each country-year is coded as a binary variable to indicate whether the World Bank approved an environmentally risky project during that year. The main variables used to test these hypotheses are whether the borrowing country had experienced at least one full investigation related to environmental concerns in the past five years (*INVESTIGATION PREVIOUS 5 YRS*) or whether a request for such an investigation was made (*REQUEST PREVIOUS 5 YRS*).

Since inspection requests are not assigned randomly and covary systematically with the availability of civil society groups and the riskiness of the portfolio for each borrowing country, it is necessary to more explicitly tackle possible selection effects.[14] Control variables in a regression reduce bias in the estimate of a treatment effect only when the controls are weakly related to the treatment variable (Rubin and Thomas 1996). To control for possible selection effects, I adopt a prematching process proposed by Ho and colleagues (2007). The basic goal of this approach is to prune and reweight the data set so that treated observations (i.e., country-years with inspection requests in the past five years) are not observationally different from control observations on average, or more formally:

$$p(X \mid T = 0) = p(X \mid T = 1),$$

where p is the observed probability, X is a matrix of control variables, and T is the treatment state.

There are a variety of matching techniques that can be used to accomplish this goal (Rubin 1973, 1973, 1979; Rubin and Thomas 1996). For this research, I first pre-prune the data set so that the treatment and control observations have common support based on a convex hull test (King and Zeng 2007). In essence, the convex hull test discards treatment or control observations that would require extrapolation to match with the other group.[15] Based on this pruned data set, I use a genetic algorithm to search across different data sets where each treatment observation is matched to one or more control observations so that treatment and control groups are observationally balanced on other potentially confounding variables (for an overview and technical aspects, see Mebane and Sekhon 1998; Sekhon and Grieve 2008; Diamond and Sekhon 2008). This approach does not require any distributional assumptions about the way the treatment and control groups are constructed or which observations are discarded, since it is based entirely on evaluating the balance between treatment and control groups.[16]

To carry out this prematching process, I use the variables that predict the provision of inspection requests presented in table 5.1. Many of these factors might affect both the provision of inspection requests and lending decisions directly, which could confound estimates about the treatment effect of inspection cases. Since I found that both the World Bank and the Asian Development Bank responded strongly to information contained in evaluations in the previous chapter, I include a count of the evaluations completed during the previous five years that indicate failure to implement environmental safeguards (*NO. EVALS W/ SAFEGUARD FAILURE*). Given that opposition to environmentally risky projects originates with civil society groups, it is also possible that the multilateral development banks avoid risky projects in borrowing countries where opposition is likely. Thus, I include a binary variable *POLITICAL REPRESSION* that is positive whenever the Freedom House index of political rights indicates that political rights such as representation, toleration of political discussion, and the ability of the public to lodge complaints with government are highly circumscribed (index value ≥ 5).

Approval and allocation decisions are also likely to be influenced by the demand of the borrowing country for environmentally risky projects. Borrowing countries that receive more risky projects in the previous five years (*NO. RISKY PREVIOUS 5 YRS*) might be more likely to both experience inspection cases and seek more risky projects in the future. Likewise in the allocation model, countries that receive more lending for environmentally risky projects (*AMOUNT RISKY PREVIOUS 5 YRS*) are likely to continue to receive more risky lending. As hypothesized above, countries that primarily receive concessional lending may be more likely to experience changes to lending based on inspection cases than countries that receive nonconcessional lending. Thus, I prematch and model the effect of the variable (*NONCONCESSIONAL*), which is the proportion of total lending during the year under consideration from the IBRD. With this specification, the baseline category in the model is countries that receive entirely concessional IDA lending during the year under consideration.

Inspection Cases and Decisions about Project Approval

As can be seen in table 5.2, country-years in the panel that are covered by inspection requests and investigations are systematically different from country-years that do not receive requests. For example, countries affected by inspection requests and investigations tend to have much more risky portfolios. The standardized mean difference, which measures this discrepancy, is the amount the treatment group is different from the control group measured in standard deviations of the control group. For example, in Model 5a, at the prematching state the treatment group is 0.42 control standard deviations above the control group, but only 0.02 standard deviations different after matching. To arrive at this prematched data set, approximately 90% of control observations with no common support or that do not match well are discarded by the genetic algorithm and are not used for the postmatching analysis that estimates the treatment effect on the treated.

After pruning the data set to obtain control observations that are observationally equivalent to the country-years with inspection requests and investigations, I find significant support for the hypothesis that the inspection process at the World Bank has caused it to be more selective about environmentally risky projects for countries that receive entirely concessional lending (H3a). This result is the baseline coefficient value in table 5.2 on both the *REQUEST* and *INVESTIGATION* variables, which can be interpreted directly when the proportion of nonconcessional borrowing is equal to zero. The interaction term between these treatment variables and the proportion of nonconcessional borrowing is positive and significant, indicating that inspection cases are less likely to decrease environmentally risky lending to countries that borrow mainly from the nonconcessional IBRD window (H3b). More directly, inspection requests no longer have a statistically significant effect (where $p = .10$) on environmentally risk lending when nonconcessional lending is 13% of

TABLE 5.2

POST-MATCHING ESTIMATES OF INSPECTION PANEL REQUESTS
AND INVESTIGATIONS ON THE APPROVAL OF ENVIRONMENTALLY
RISKY PROJECTS AT THE WORLD BANK

Model	2a	2b
MDB	World	World
REQUEST PREVIOUS 5 YRS	−0.88** (0.50)	
INVESTIGATION PREVIOUS 5 YRS		−1.33** (0.57)
NONCONCESSIONAL	−0.53 (0.67) pre: 0.21 post: −0.01	−0.57 (0.89) pre: 0.01 post: −0.03
REQUEST / INVESTIGATION × *NONCONCESSIONAL*	1.86** (0.78)	2.27** (1.02)
POLITICAL REPRESSION	0.67 (0.54) pre: −0.19 post: −0.04	0.74 (0.67) pre: 0.08 post: 0.00
GOVERNMENT EFFECTIVENESS	−0.44 (0.50) pre: 0.12 post: −0.00	−0.17 (0.65) pre: −0.21 post: −0.00
NO. SAFEGUARD FAILURES 5 YRS	−2.42 (2.22) pre: −0.06 post: 0.04	−1.55 (1.90) pre: 0.04 post: 0.15
NO. RISKY PREVIOUS 5 YRS	0.60** (0.10) pre: 0.42 post: 0.02	0.47** (0.11) pre: 0.42 post: 0.01
Postmatching observations (countries)	228 (62)	149 (48)
Residual deviance	190.7	129.8
Null deviance	290.5	197.8

Note: Postmatching models are generalized linear models with logistic link function of the presence of an A project. Statistical significant indicators are for one-tailed hypothesis tests: $^*p < .10$; $^{**}p < .05$.

the country's borrowing portfolio, and investigations no longer have a statistically significant effect when nonconcessional lending is 24% of the country's borrowing portfolio.

For countries that receive entirely concessional lending subject to greater oversight by donor countries (38% of all observations in the panel), the effect of experiencing a full inspection investigation is both substantively and statistically stronger than receiving only a request. To aid substantive interpretation of the treatment effect assuming that a country is receiving entirely concessional lending, figure 5.3 shows the predicted probabilities of countries that are and are not subjected to inspection

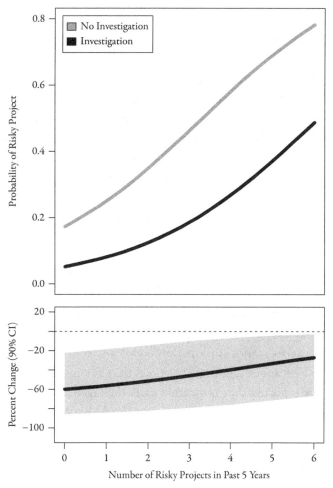

FIGURE 5.3 Effect of inspection investigations on the approval of environmentally risky projects at the World Bank

Note: This plot shows predictions from Model 2b. The top panel displays the probability of receiving at least one environmentally-risky project. The bottom panel shows the effect size of an Inspection Panel investigation as a percentage with a 90% confidence interval.

investigations, along with a measure about the previous environmental riskiness of the portfolio.[17]

It is also possible that inspection investigations would decrease the amount of financing allocated to environmentally risky purposes (H4). I do not find support for this hypothesis. Neither being subjected to an inspection investigation nor having the Inspection Panel confirm poor safeguard implementation decreases the total amount approved for activities that were found to be risky. This finding lends further support to the argument that risk aversion and selectivity primarily operate through project selection, rather than adjustments to the sizes of projects. Instead, the two significant predictors of the size of environmentally risky projects given their approval are fewer political rights and a borrowing country that has a larger lending portfolio overall.

To sum up, the models presented in this section have revealed a number of important findings: (1) Being subjected to inspection investigations *decreases* a country's probability of receiving environmentally risky projects in a future period, given that they receive primarily concessional lending; and (2) being subjected to inspection investigations *does not* decrease the amount of risky financing that a country receives, conditional on it receiving at least one risky project. Considering these results together with the results of the previous section, we can conclude that the inspection process can increase accountability and change allocation decisions when civil society groups are able to avail themselves of the process in countries that face higher levels of oversight from donor states about development lending.

STAFF EXPERIENCES WITH INSPECTION CASES

Staff across the World Bank, Asian Development Bank, and Inter-American Development Bank reported that the inspection processes were likely to be a primary way that performance information about environmentally risky projects impacted decisions about lending (see appendix 1 for interview methodology). Staff commonly reported that inspection cases damaged career prospects. These costs were most frequently emphasized among World Bank evaluators and operational staff. In particular, evaluation staff believed that inspection cases would have more of an impact on lending decisions than evaluation findings. Inspection Panel cases lead to actual costs for operational staff. Inspection requests are unpredictable since they originate from outside of the bank, leading to a much higher degree of caution in implementing environmental safeguard policies than might result from recommendations that come from project evaluations. A recent Inspection Panel case in Albania resulted in the firing of a World Bank staff member, which is almost unheard, and a result that never comes about through evaluation findings.[18]

While staff cannot avoid the risks associated with inspection investigations entirely, design teams often avoid project components that might lead to significant risks of cases. In addition, the World Bank might fund only the lower-impact components of much larger, riskier infrastructure projects.[19] According to another operational staff member, this behavior is elicited because inspection cases take up management and staff time for months, which detracts from the ability of higher-level management to "push the pipeline" and reach lending goals.

Despite the reported behavior of avoiding the most risky components of projects, one of the clearest results of the Inspection Panels has been the establishment of project management systems to avoid inspection cases. For example, according to one staff member, the World Bank Operations Policy and Country Services office has among its primary goals to "keep projects out of the Inspection Panel" by making sure that the board is properly apprised of the risks involved with different policies and that safeguard procedures are implemented with due diligence. One staff member reported that the shareholder states primarily sanction the management of the World Bank through approval and disbursement delays when they are "surprised" by allegations of poor implementation. When this happens, inspection cases tend to become "high profile" and attract significant attention from both donor states and civil society groups. Thus, the World Bank put systems in place to ensure safeguard policies are carried out with due diligence and that environmental risks are transparent to donor countries.[20] These procedures increase the costs of approving and implementing environmentally risky projects.

Among the Asian Development Bank staff that I interviewed, there were a variety of opinions about whether the inspection process has caused "risk aversion," but near universal agreement that specific safeguard procedures had been put in place to avoid the external risks associated with inspection requests. In particular, the Asian Development Bank has created a very detailed "checklist" about the design of projects that is intended to shield staff members from inspection investigations.[21] Many operational staff members reported that the Asian Development Bank follows a Japanese style of management that seeks to address risk through procedure. One staff member stated that 90% of the effort in implementing safeguard procedures occurs during project design. Indeed, this process can be seen as mostly successful, given that there have been very few high-profile inspection cases. One operational staff member reported that the Chashma Right Bank Project, which was designed and approved during 1991–1992, has received the most attention within the ADB over its inspection investigation. However, by the time investigation requests pertaining to this project were received in 2002 and the investigation was completed in 2004, the ADB had already moved away from large-scale irrigation projects. This left little room for the ADB to respond to the inspection investigation in its decisions about lending.

Like staff at the World Bank, Asian Development Bank operational staff reported that they are shying away from project components that might trigger inspection requests. For example, the Asian Development Bank has been involved in the Nam Theun II Dam project for many years now and has devoted an extraordinary amount of resources to ensure that best-practice safeguards are diligently implemented. However, given continued delays and requests by local people for more studies, additional compensation to be paid, and so on, several staff members believed that the ADB would not pursue similar projects in the future. The project to build the Jumana Bridge in Bangladesh has met with significant delays owing to the difficulty of fully implementing safeguard policies. Thus, given the possibility of "losing face" at both the individual and organizational level if an inspection case is triggered, the ADB is forced to undertake costly actions that may be affecting the cost-benefit calculations for large, risky infrastructure projects.[22]

One ADB operational staff member stated that the main impact of the Inspection Panel has been the realization that staff should not pursue projects that are "unnecessarily difficult" in terms of implementing safeguard procedures. I was able to find instances where the Asian Development Bank funded less-risky components of larger projects. For example, one staff member reported that the Asian Development Bank financed a portion of the Laos Northern Economic Corridor Project, but the more risky portion was financed by the Chinese government, which has caused difficulty and calls to coordinate safeguard policies. In addition, the level of civil society engagement on safeguard policies in particular borrowing countries has a large effect on what staff consider to be "unnecessarily difficult," which was reported to be a reason why China has received many more risky projects than India over the past decade.

Several ADB staff reported that Inspection Panel investigations had a "chilling" effect within specific country-sectors. For example, after the Sri Lanka Southern Transport Development case, transportation became a "no touch" sector for staff in Sri Lanka. This inspection investigation may also have slowed lending for transportation across the ADB portfolio. In the future, it will be important to examine the sector effects of inspection cases, as lending decisions may be influenced at this level.

Inter-American Development Bank staff reported less of a reaction to the establishment of an Inspection Panel. One division manager reported that the IADB does not face the same level of NGO or US congressional scrutiny as the World Bank, which is ironically located right down the street. This has resulted in a weaker Environment and Safeguards Unit, because there has been less of a need to put up a robust defense against civil society claims of poor implementation. In addition, unlike the World Bank and Asian Development Bank, less-developed borrowing countries have a majority on the board, which has resulted in less focus on environmental safeguard procedures. However, some operational staff did explain that the Inspection Panel had caused a "chilling" effect at the sector level, specifically as related to hydropower projects, which have been the subject of more than half of requests.

The African Development Bank, which established an Inspection Panel in 2004 and did not process an inspection request until 2007, provides a point of contrast. Operational staff reported a growing recognition that failure to implement safeguard policies would entail financial risks. Still, this recognition is nascent. One director who oversaw an infrastructure group reported that he was "not afraid" of civil society groups like the World Bank. He pointed to the differences in organizational responses to the Gebay III Hydropower Project being cofinanced by the World Bank and the AFDB. The World Bank is still mired in studies about the project because of concerns raised by civil society groups like the International Rivers Network, while the AFDB has been prepared to move forward. This example illustrates that the inspection process is associated with greater attention to safeguard procedures at the World Bank. As the US and Nordic executive directors at the AFDB push the organization to improve safeguard performance and strengthen the inspection process, this kind of attention might also reach the African Development Bank. For example, the Bujagali Hydropower Project recently came up for inspection. The response was to conduct further studies, rather than to abandon the project.

While interviews with staff at the multilateral development banks were generally supportive of the hypothesis that inspection cases affect decisions about environmentally risky lending, several staff were supportive of the conditional effect of inspection cases based on the lending window used by the borrowing country. Middle-income countries that borrow from the IBRD often approach the World Bank with fully developed project proposals, leaving less space for staff and donor representatives to shape lending priorities (author interview at World Bank, 2010). Unlike the IDA, there are no set formulas that determine how much IBRD countries can borrow.[23] These results indicate that in addition to the availability of civil society monitors, closer oversight by countries that are donors to the multilateral banks supports selectivity in the allocation of lending.

CONCLUSIONS

The cross-national and interview data presented in this chapter indicate that civil society monitoring, institutionalized through establishment of Inspection Panels, can play an important role in promoting accountability for performance at the multilateral development banks and drive selectivity. After explicitly addressing factors that might confound the influence of inspection cases on allocation decisions, I find that borrowing countries that experienced inspection requests and investigation and that receive concessional lending are less likely to receive environmentally risky projects in the following five years. This result suggests that environmental civil society groups can induce selectivity for environmentally risky projects at the multilateral development banks when monitoring is combined with oversight.

Selectivity is one indication that environmental performance is taken seriously by decision-makers at the multilateral development banks. Given that the inspection process decreases the number of environmentally risky projects in certain types of countries where monitors are available, these types of accountability mechanisms represent one way that environmental performance can be improved more broadly. By eliminating from the lending portfolio the types of projects that are likely to perform poorly, this mechanism likely raises the overall performance level of the multilateral development banks. Perhaps even more importantly, however, the inspection process creates incentives for selectivity. Just as we should expect staff to avoid projects that are likely to generate requests, we should expect them to implement passable risky projects more diligently to avoid inspection requests. While the data here cannot speak definitely to environmental performance at the project level, they point in the right direction.

More broadly, this finding shows that the threat of sanctioning together with information about performance can induce selectivity at the development banks. Previous research has shown that high-level threats by donor countries to withhold financing have produced environmental policy reforms, but not necessarily the due diligence implementation of these new policies (Nielson and Tierney 2003; Gutner 2005). Because member states of multilateral development banks are not often in a position to gather the type of information necessary for effective oversight of environmental policies, taking advantage of civil society monitoring appears to have been important for enhancing oversight. The results of this chapter indicate that if states wish to more effectively manage discretion at international organizations, enhanced oversight through civil society monitoring is one way forward. As Dai (2007) argues, civil society groups may be particularly adept at providing this type of oversight.

The primary limitation of civil society monitoring is that it is not provided uniformly across all countries. This means that citizens in borrowing countries that repress political rights are not as likely to avail themselves of the inspection process when their interests are harmed. Likewise, in countries that do not have a strong civil society mobilized around environmental issues, inspection requests are less frequent. Under these conditions, civil society monitoring does not provide a substitute for systematic monitoring and evaluation as a way to manage discretion at the multilateral development banks.

Recent reforms at the multilateral development banks will be interesting to watch in light of these results. Both the Asian Development Bank and the African Development Bank have recently updated their inspection processes to include a "consultation phase" between civil society claimants and bank management. This has prevented many projects from automatically going to inspection and may serve to move forward useful, problem-solving consultations or oppositely remove pressures on staff to ensure performance and select projects carefully. Overall, however, it appears that civil society groups can play an important role in providing monitoring and in enhancing oversight at international organizations. This type of activity fills a void in the accountability of international organizations that has long been a source of concern.

6

Project Evaluations

LEARNING WHAT WORKS

EVALUATION IS PERHAPS the most direct tool that principals at all types of organizations use to manage the discretion that they grant to their agents. Evaluations produce information about the outcomes of decisions and reduce uncertainty about cause-and-effect relationships. The technical nature of decision-making by agents makes it difficult for principals to know whether agents are acting in their best interests. When principals are unsure about what kinds of decisions will best achieve their goals and they are likely to discover which decisions are best long after they are made, agents are able to pursue their own interests more easily. For example, despite the wide recognition that programs to improve management of the public sector are unsuccessful unless tailored to specific countries, staff at development organizations continue to pursue "best practice" or "blueprint" reform plans (Andrews 2013; World Bank 2012). Project staff involved with these programs tend to downplay the uncertainty and risks involved in public sector management programs in order to gain quick approval for projects. A recent World Bank evaluation describes an urgent need "to reduce [staff] bias towards best practice priors" that have a limited record of effectiveness and only serve to meet the interests of staff for the quick approval of projects (World Bank 2012, 6).

At the multilateral development banks, evaluations might also allow member countries to detect other instances when decisions by staff are made for reasons of expediency rather than effectiveness. For example, the Asian Development Bank postproject evaluation for the unsuccessful Khulna-Jessore Drainage Rehabilitation Project in Bangladesh, which aimed to improve rural livelihoods through better water management, concluded that poor planning on the part of project staff caused failure: "Project design tends to be rushed and in the process several critical issues are overlooked or undermined. A project that involves the livelihood of a large number of people . . . requires much time for robust consultation and full consideration of local indigenous knowledge systems" (Operations Evaluation Department 2007b, 24). In this case, the evaluation produced information about whether decision-making aligned with the preferences of member countries for effective projects. Facing the possibility of an evaluation like this and the subsequent prospect of punishment, agents might be more likely to act according to the preferences of member states. Evaluations can facilitate oversight.

Even if principals and agents are interested in the same outcomes, it may be unclear how to achieve those outcomes. When both agents and principals are uncertain about cause and effect, shirking on the part of the agent is not necessary for decisions to be made in suboptimal ways. As a recent African Development Bank report on project supervision argues, development financing "is inherently a risky business. High risk environments cannot be avoided by a public sector institution such as the African Development Bank" (2010, 8). One way risks can be managed, however, is to generate and use information about results to design less-risky projects. Evaluation has the benefit of hindsight and can often reveal information about the relationship between decisions and desired outcomes. Responses to this information need not be punitive; when agents have shared interests, evaluations might help decrease uncertainty about future decisions to the extent that the same cause-and-effect relationships are relevant for future decisions. Thus, evaluations can also be used to improve decision-making by overcoming uncertainty, which might promote more careful selection of projects.

For these reasons, international organizations have embraced evaluation as a way to improve decision-making. Almost all international organizations, and especially those with a development mandate, have dedicated offices that conduct evaluations. But evaluations will not automatically improve decision-making. Evaluation might fail as a tool to improve decision-making because member states do not have the incentives or collective tools necessary to engage in oversight after an evaluation. Many times the people or divisions responsible for poor decisions have moved on. Indeed, to the extent that agents do not expect to be present to face accountability based on later evaluations, they are more likely to shirk.

Evaluation might fail as a tool of learning because the uncertainty about cause and effect in the past is no longer relevant. In addition, it is possible that evaluations do not add any new information or might even come to the wrong conclusions about cause-and-effect relationships. Professional evaluators may have less information and data than do decision-makers themselves. This can result in recommendations with little practical value. Even if useful, the information contained in evaluations might not reach decision-makers at the point when information is needed. Even more important, an evaluation might be biased to meet the political needs of the principal that orders the evaluation. As Michaelowa and Borrmann (2006, 315) argue, "If [the evaluator] assumes that the principal has a strong preference for a positive image, he will be inclined to avoid a realistic evaluation in order to please the principal." Given these limitations, evaluation might not facilitate learning by reducing uncertainty.

Finally, evaluations may contain useful information that could be used to improve decision-making, but principals do not have good ways to prompt agents to update their practices and decisions on the basis of this new information. Even when principals would like changes to practices, agents often prefer to maintain the status quo, especially when it comes with autonomy. Management of organizations to maintain the status quo is common across many types of organizations and a key contributor to poor performance, since reforms are often resisted if they do not meet the goals of organizational managers (Hambrick, Geletkanycz, and Fredrickson 1993; Bauer 2012). At international organizations, reform and change are even more difficult because member states must often collectively agree to new practices and policies, which is difficult to achieve.

In this chapter, I examine project evaluation as a means of managing discretion at the multilateral development banks by reducing uncertainty and improving decision-making. Shifting focus from the previous two chapters, I examine the allocation of projects that aim to improve environmental conditions, a type of project that has advantages for testing whether selectivity can be promoted by reducing uncertainty. Recall that I argue discretion can be successfully managed when member states (1) harness information about the outcomes of past decisions; and (2) use that information to raise costs of making decisions that have been unsuccessful or lower the costs of making decisions that have been successful. At the multilateral development banks, donor countries have not wanted to limit environment-improving activities; in fact they have pushed for the opposite. As a consequence, evaluations are likely to have an effect on allocation practices only by reducing uncertainty that limits demand for environment-improving operations from borrowing countries. Because donor countries have not sought to promote selectivity in environment-improving operations, they are not a limiting control point.

Like the previous chapters, I investigate the sequence of lending in relation to information in evaluations. I show that, under pressure to approve environment-improving activities, multilateral development banks can use information about success to convince recipient countries to take on environment-improving activities with clear local benefits. In a placebo test related to this argument, I show that the same type of information is systematically disregarded for projects that primarily have global benefits and fewer local benefits. These results suggest that much of the effort around project evaluation should be directed to meet the information needs of borrowing countries.

ENVIRONMENT-IMPROVING OPERATIONS: A BRIEF HISTORY

An environment-improving project is one that has a primary purpose of maintaining or improving the status of a natural resource or environmental asset. These projects deal with everything from sewers to biodiversity protection. Donor countries have instructed the multilateral development banks to rapidly scale up lending for these types of projects, most notably projects that deal with global concerns like climate change and biodiversity loss. Even the NGOs that have typically been critical of the multilateral development banks have pushed the multilateral development banks to "green" their lending portfolios. For example, the Bank Information Center released an open letter to the incoming World Bank president in 2012 that called for the World Bank to "take the lead in providing affordable energy access to the rural poor by scaling up truly low-carbon, low-impact clean energy markets, and prioritize improvements in end use efficiency over expanding supply."[1] For the most part, the multilateral development banks have responded to these pressures enthusiastically, seeing an opportunity to move into new project areas and gain control of new resources, often without generating significant opposition from civil society groups. Because outside observers and major member states are generally positive about these types of projects, staff face little pressure to be selective or limit allocation.

Indeed, since the early-1990s, the multilateral development banks have become focal points for intergovernmental environmental finance (Findley et al. 2009; Hicks et al. 2008). Since the creation of the Multilateral Fund for the Implementation of the Montreal Protocol in 1991, intergovernmental responses to environmental issues have fallen into a predictable pattern. Developed countries provide concessional grants and loans in exchange for pledges from less-developed countries to improve environmental practices. This basic negotiation outcome has been repeated with the Convention for Biological Diversity, the United Nations Framework Convention on Climate Change, the Stockholm Convention on Persistent Organic Pollutants, and the United Nations Convention to Combat Desertification. The multilateral development banks have been at the heart of many of these agreements, either as formal or as informal channels of financing.

The multilateral development banks have embraced this role for decades. At the 1992 Earth Summit in Rio de Janeiro, developed countries proposed that the World

Bank administer a new window of environmental financing for less-developed countries. President Lewis Preston additionally offered to redirect "not a token amount" of World Bank profits made from the lending to middle-income countries to new environmental programs (Abramson 1992). Since that time, the focus among multilateral development banks on environment-improving projects and operations has increased. All of the multilateral development banks have adopted organizational strategies that prioritize the environment in lending.[2] All have developed specialized environment departments that seek to integrate and prioritize environmental goals in projects. Collectively, the multilateral development banks manage more than half of all environmentally focused official development assistance, and they are the implementing agencies for more than half of the resources controlled by the Global Environment Facility, the main financing mechanism for the largest and most important international environmental agreements.[3]

Donor countries have enthusiastically supported this shift throughout the 1990s and 2000s. By getting the multilateral development banks to finance environmental projects, donor countries not only assuage the demands of activists at home (Lewis 2000, 2003; Rothman and Oliver 1999), but they also have a relatively low-cost way to demonstrate commitment to international environmental issues that have generated widespread attention. For example, in its 2010 *Climate Action Report*, the United States highlighted its contribution "in organizing and supporting the world's response to climate change" through its numerous climate mitigation and adaptation financing programs, many of which are multilateral in nature (US Department of State 2010).

In recent years, a preponderance of new funds for climate change and biodiversity have been established internationally. Donor countries have not pushed the multilateral development banks to be selective about their allocation of environment-improving projects. In fact, the donor states have almost universally pushed the multilateral development banks to rapidly scale up their financing of environmental projects. As the US Treasury Secretary stated in his address to the 2011 World Bank Annual Meeting, "The World Bank and the regional development banks are on the front lines of the globe's most pressing . . . challenges," including actions for "climate change adaptation and prevention."[4] Focus continues to be on the types of projects that generate global environmental goods.

Since the early 1990s, environment-improving programming has increased in two ways. First, the multilateral development banks have undergone a process of "mainstreaming" the environment into their development operations, which is the practice of including environment-improving activities in traditional development projects (Environment Division 1995; Findley et al. 2009; Barrett and Arcese 1995). Second, the multilateral development banks increased their support for stand-alone environment-improving projects, oftentimes cofinancing projects with intergovernmental organizations like the Global Environment Facility (Hicks et al. 2008).

If the multilateral development banks were to be cautious and only finance environment-improving projects or activities in countries with a proven record, then it might be difficult to meet the goals of donor countries to expand into these areas. Many of the worst environmental problems and the lowest levels of capacity to solve them occur in poor countries, which the multilateral development banks are mandated to support. Furthermore, environmental projects are one of the hardest types of aid projects to implement well, many times because of limited recipient country capacity or interest (Operations Evaluation Department 2005b; Buntaine and Parks 2013). It is not clear that pressures to meet lending targets leave room for selectivity, at least in terms of moving away from financing environment-improving projects in countries with poor records.

The shift toward a development portfolio that actively seeks to improve natural resource and environmental conditions raises very serious questions about the ability of the multilateral development banks to practice selectivity in their allocation decisions. As I argued at the outset of the book, the root of many performance problems at the multilateral development banks is the *approval imperative*—the overwhelming incentive that staff at the multilateral development banks have to overlook past performance when it stands in the way of meeting lending goals. One of the great dangers associated with donor pressures for more environmental lending is that the incentives associated with the approval imperative are strengthened.

RESPONDING TO EVALUATIONS OF ENVIRONMENTAL PERFORMANCE

The approval imperative is problematic for environmental lending, since there is ample room for responsiveness to the past results. Environment-improving projects and activities have a mixed implementation record. Borrowing countries have demonstrated everything from negligence to highly satisfactory performance when implementing environment-improving projects and activities. On the negative side, an evaluation completed by the World Bank Operations Evaluation Department in 2005 found that environment-improving projects had one of the lowest success rates across sectors of the lending portfolio (Operations Evaluation Department 2005b). Several World Bank environment-improving projects have become high-profile Inspection Panel cases and were canceled for failing to protect local people from pollution during project implementation.[5] An Asian Development Bank evaluation of joint ADB-GEF projects found examples of unsuccessful environment-improving projects that lacked "adequate owner-ship and clear implementation arrangements, and ... implementation capac-ity of the executing agencies" (Operations Evaluation Department 2007a, vi). These issues were especially pronounced in projects like the Sundarbans Biodiversity Conservation Project, which was evaluated to be ineffective and was canceled because of implementation arrangements that were "inadequate given the weaknesses in governance capacity and practices in Bangladesh" (Operations Evaluation Department 2008, 6).

In contrast, a more recent evaluation of the World Bank portfolio found that more than 80% of pollution management and ozone-related projects successfully achieved their objectives (Independent Evaluation Group 2008). A recent World Bank report showcased projects that led to successful soil and conservation works across more than 200,000 hectares in India, solid waste projects in Bosnia and Herzegovina that improved drinking water quality for more than half of the popu-lation, and renewable energy, zero-emissions projects that electrified communities throughout rural Nepal (World Bank 2010). The Asian Development Bank has also funded several "highly successful" environment-improving projects, including the Shanxi Environmental Improvement Project, which is "seen as [a] nationally impor-tant pilot project which can be replicated at local and national levels and [has] con-tributed to national and provincial environmental policies" (Operations Evaluation Department 2007g, 24). Indeed, reflecting on such stories of success, some scholars have argued that the multilateral development banks are uniquely positioned to finance global public goods like climate change mitigation (Gilbert, Powell, and Vines 1999; World Bank 2007b).

The multilateral development banks have highly mixed records at implementing environment-improving projects and activities, as revealed in independent proj-ect evaluations. Given this mixed performance record, there has been ample room to scale up environment-improving financing in high-performing countries and vice versa. This type of selectivity would ensure that scare financing resources are used efficiently. Of the project evaluations with performance information about environment-improving operations, only 52% of World Bank evaluations, 44% of Asian Development Bank evaluations, and 32% of African Development Bank evaluations find satisfactory or highly satisfactory performance in meeting envi-ronmental goals (figure 6.1). These data corroborate several thematic evaluations completed by MDB evaluation offices that highlight the mixed or "partially satisfac-tory" performance of bank-wide environmental programs (Operations Evaluation Department 2005b; Independent Evaluation Group 2008; Asian Development Bank 2009). Given the mixed nature of environmental performance at the multilat-eral development banks, there are significant opportunities to practice selectivity in

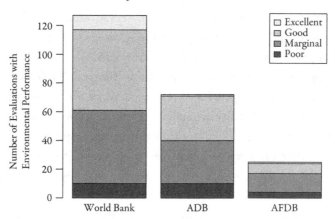

FIGURE 6.1 Evaluations with information about performance implementing environmental goals
Note: Environmental goals attempt to improve the quality of a natural resource or environmental condition.

allocation decisions to improve performance, perhaps by demonstrating to skeptical borrowers that projects can be successful.

While research has explored when environment-improving programs are effective (Haas, Keohane, and Levy 1993; Buntaine and Parks 2013; Connolly 1996; Independent Evaluation Group 2008, ch. 7; Operations Evaluation Department 2007a), donor agencies and organizations have increasingly recognized that projects need to be "demand driven" and designed to align with the unique priorities and capacities of particular borrowing countries (Independent Evaluation Group 2008, xxxv). If this is the case, then identifying the types of projects that can be successful for individual borrowing countries is necessary to make good use of scarce lending resources. Evaluation might overcome uncertainty in identifying the types of operations that can be pursued to meet local needs, even in the absence of a push for selectivity by donor countries.

At all of the multilateral development banks, *independent evaluation* departments have been established to pursue these goals. Independent evaluation is not accountable to the people or programs being evaluated (General Accounting Office 1996; Picciotto 2002). Recognizing that operational staff have few incentives to candidly evaluate the performance of their own projects, member states of the multilateral development banks supported the creation of independent evaluation departments that report directly to shareholder states through the board of directors, rather than to the bank management.[6] Prior to this time, evaluation was usually the work of operational staff themselves, which posed serious problems for generating information that could be used to evaluate the merits of technical decisions made under uncertainty (Wapenhans 1992; Inter-American Development Bank 1993; Asian Development Bank 1994; Knox 1994). Within each of the evaluation departments at the multilateral development banks, greater emphasis has been placed on assessing the environmental results of programming, corresponding to the adoption of strategies that prioritize environmental considerations.

Overcoming uncertainty is not unique to multilateral development banks, or even to international aid agencies. The principals of all kinds of bureaucratic agencies deal with the difficulty of generating information to overcome oversight problems and uncertainty. When multiple parties are responsible for overseeing bureaucracies, there can even be incentives to "freeride" on the monitoring and oversight efforts of others, which can increase the challenge of generating information about performance (Gailmard 2009). In other cases, it has proven difficult to create mechanisms that provide information. For example, the Project on Government Oversight, a nonpartisan think tank and advocacy group in the United States, found that despite the proliferation of inspector general offices in US bureaucracies, they remain understaffed and often are mandated to focus on procedural tasks, rather than pursuing investigations that will promote accountability and information that can be used to overcome uncertainty about policy choices (Project on Government Oversight 2009). In less-developed countries, the lack of information about the performance of public entities relevant to oversight is a primary impediment to economic development. For example, in Nigeria, the lack of information and oversight about the spending of oil revenues is seen by many independent observers as a key impediment to development (*Africa News* 2011).

To demonstrate the dual roles evaluations might play in prompting oversight versus overcoming uncertainty, I distinguish between environmental projects and activities that primarily produce global goods versus those that primarily produce local goods. For clean-energy projects that address global climate change, donor countries have pushed for increased supply of climate investment, often without corresponding demand from borrowing countries. Donor countries do so because the benefits of projects that mitigate global climate change are diffuse and because support for clean-energy financing through the multilateral development banks is a relatively low-cost way to demonstrate international action on climate change. Because of the approval imperative at the multilateral development banks, pressures from donor shareholders to rapidly increase the supply of climate change lending does not create incentives for the MDB staff to be selective about clean-energy projects. In contrast, for urban environment projects that address problems confined within a borrowing country, lending pressure from donor states are lower, since benefits are localized. Under these circumstances, evaluations might help borrowing countries and the operational staff at the multilateral banks identify and decrease uncertainty about the types of projects that can be successfully implemented to achieve local goals.

HYPOTHESES: EVALUATION AND UNCERTAINTY

The core role of staff at the multilateral development banks is to solve the coordination problem between donor countries and recipient countries and approve new projects. Any tool used to manage discretion operates by making it easier or more difficult for staff to find and approve projects that meet the overlapping interests of member states and the specific borrowing country. Because multilateral development banks seek projects that most easily solve the donor-borrower coordination problem, decisions about environment-improving projects must be understood in terms of these external interests.

Donor Countries

Ultimately, the authority of the multilateral development banks to design and disburse development financing is derived from the countries that fund the multilateral development banks. Institutionally this takes place through the board of directors, which comprises country representatives. Voting shares on the board of directors are proportional to the amount that different countries contribute to the multilateral development banks. Because nonborrowing countries contribute more resources to the multilateral development banks than borrowing countries, they have a disproportionate influence on the high-level policy directions and lending strategies of the multilateral development banks. At both the World Bank and Asian Development Bank, nonborrowing countries hold a majority of votes on the board, and can thus largely direct policy. In addition, the United States has the customary role of appointing the president of the World Bank, while Japan has the customary role of appointing the president of the Asian Development Bank (Fleck and Kilby 2006; Harrigan, Wang, and El-Said 2006; Schraeder, Hook, and Taylor 1998). In practice, this gives these two countries a powerful avenue of informal influence and contact with the person responsible for setting and managing the broad lending priorities (see also Stone 2011). Indeed, one operational staff member at the World Bank commented that the United States exerts special influence because the president typically shares a social circle with members of Congress and political appointees.

There are other ways that nonborrowing countries exert strong influence on the assistance strategies of the multilateral development banks. Only the largest shareholder countries at each of the multilateral development banks have their own executive director, which makes it easier for them to exert influence than for smaller countries that must elect directors as groups, thereby facing collective action problems (Lyne, Nielson, and Tierney 2009). As the US Executive Director for the Asian Development Bank told me during a 2009 interview, without the challenge of coordinating the positions of multiple countries for a single board seat, the American executive director can spend more time monitoring and advocating for certain types of lending. In addition, the largest nonborrowing countries contribute a large enough share of the concessional resources that they can seriously disrupt the operations of the multilateral development banks by threatening to withhold funds (Bowles and Kormos 1999). This is a common tactic employed by countries such as the United States. While some borrowing countries also contribute to the multilateral development banks, they typically do not contribute a large enough share to wield this type of influence.

These pressures have influenced the rise of environment-improving lending at the multilateral development banks. Broad increases in environment-improving lending at the multilateral development banks can be traced back to the early 1990s, when there was a proliferation of interest among donor countries, and especially the United States, in reducing the environmental damages of MDB development projects and increasing lending for environment-improving activities (Bowles and Kormos 1999). At the 1992 Rio Earth Summit, an agreement was struck that required donor countries to provide environmental assistance in exchange for the participation of less-developed countries in several international environmental treaties. Donor countries delegated much of the responsibility for implementing and managing environmental assistance to the multilateral development banks. Indeed, the formation of the Environment Department at the World Bank resulted from the United States threatening to withdraw support for the 10th replenishment of the World Bank Group's International Development Association (Nielson and Tierney 2003; Brummer 1992). These pressures from donor countries continue to this day. In 2009, for example, the United States required the ADB to strengthen its environmental safeguards policy and redouble its commitment to environmental lending as preconditions of support for a capital increase, with the US Executive Director on record stating that "a commitment to strengthened safeguards must be clear before any final consideration of an increase in the ADB's capital base" (Gopalakrishnan 2009).

For environment-improving projects, donor countries prefer projects that generate global environmental goods that they cannot generate on their own. Thus, the preferences for lending by donor countries are strongest for environmental problems with transboundary dimensions, such as tropical forest conservation and emissions that contribute to climate change. By supporting lending for global environmental problems, developed donor countries directly accrue some of the benefits. By contrast, investment projects that focus on local environmental issues, such as sewerage or soil erosion, do not directly benefit donor countries. Thus, while these types of local environmental projects have received attention in international forums like the Millennium Development Goals process, they are not as likely to be pushed by donors without corresponding demand from borrowing countries. For these reasons, developed shareholders have the greatest demand for projects that address global issues. When large borrowing countries determine the provision of global public goods, developed shareholder countries must engage them in order to maintain the benefits of global environmental goods, since there are no other available suppliers. The literature on global environmental politics highlights that "the power to destroy" is an important form of leverage within international environmental negotiations (Miller 1995; Sell 1996; Darst 2001). For these reasons, biodiversity conservation and climate change projects remain two lending areas that are substantially "donor driven," as reported by MDB staff in interviews.

This preference for lending is reflected in the statements the multilateral development banks make about their project portfolios related to global environmental goods. For example, the IEG notes "the growing focus on climate change that responds in part to a 2005 request by G8 countries for greater Bank Group international leadership" (Independent Evaluation Group 2008, 77). In a statement to the Asian Development Bank's 40th Annual Meeting in 2007, the Japanese Minister of Finance highlighted climate change as one of the three major challenges in the Asian Pacific and argued that the ADB "should play a vital role in supporting efforts of the member countries to achieve energy efficiency."[7] Indeed, donor countries have been much more interested in the multilateral development banks expanding their environment-improving operations than they are in having the multilateral development banks be selective based on past performance. Although the multilateral development banks are under considerable pressure to demonstrate success to external audiences (Fox and Brown 1998; Ebrahim 2003; Bemelmans-Videc, Lonsdale, and Perrin 2007; Marra 2007), I find no evidence that donor countries are pressuring the multilateral development banks to be selective about environment-improving projects.

Given donor preferences for environment-improving projects, the multilateral development banks must demonstrate that they are "doing something" about the environment. This means persuading borrowing countries to accept projects that might not always be domestic priorities, a noted impediment to achieving environmental goals (Connolly 1996). Because donor countries have not been as critical of failures to achieve environment-improving goals as they have been of failures to mitigate damages associated with development projects, the management of the multilateral development banks are mostly under pressure to demonstrate action rather than results. Indeed, the vast majority of program reports coming out of MDB environment departments focus on inputs and actions (i.e., amount of environment-improving financing; number of operations), as opposed to outcomes and impacts of environment-improving operations (e.g., World Bank 2007a; Asian Development Bank 2009).

Borrowing Countries

Borrowing countries are likely to prioritize environmental activities that have local benefits. Activities with more global benefits must be carefully weighed against relevant opportunity costs of development financing, such as building hospitals, establishing transport networks, and strengthening financial systems. When poverty is widespread, the benefits of additional economic output often exceed the costs of environmental degradation. As development levels rise in countries, so does the willingness to pay for environmental management activities as a matter of public policy, especially in countries with civil liberties and political rights (Torras and Boyce 1998; Selden and Song 1994). In general, environmental activities that do not have strong local benefits are less desirable to countries that borrow from the multilateral development banks. Projects and activities with fewer local benefits include biodiversity protection and the reduction of greenhouse gas emissions. For both of these goals, donor countries reap significant benefits from existence values (Balmford and Whitten 2003) and approval from constituents (Corson 2010). Borrowing countries, on the other hand, must often work against the interests of local people to implement biodiversity protection projects. For example, Gadd (2005) uses interview data in the Laikipia District of Kenya to show that local people often have negative opinions of wildlife conservation programs when direct benefits are low.

Because of these incentives, the demand for environment-improving projects from borrowing countries is often lower than the amount of environmental assistance donor countries would like for multilateral development banks to supply. This is a source of bargaining conflict between donor countries and recipient countries: "Many 'green aid' programs face common predicaments. They are often characterized by conflicts between funders who want to ameliorate regional or global environmental problems and recipients who are more concerned with local issues" (Fairman and Ross 1996, 29). Indeed, a World Bank Environment Department report emphasizes that the "lack of political will" on the part of borrowing countries is one of the most important reasons why environment-improving projects tend to be less successful than other areas of their portfolio (Environment Sector Board 1998, 43; Independent Evaluation Group 2008, 73). Evaluations have highlighted the delicate role that the multilateral development banks must play in order to encourage environment-improving projects:

What the Bank Group can do is ultimately limited by what governments want to borrow or seek policy advice for, even in countries facing serious environmental problems. [Country management units] are nonetheless encouraged to identify strategic entry points in their programs (perhaps in critical sectors such as energy) to help advance the Bank Group's corporate environmental sustainability objectives. (Independent Evaluation Group 2008, 77)

Given the generally lower demand for environment-improving projects, there are three primary reasons why less-developed countries borrow in this area. First, large countries that determine global environmental outcomes, like Brazil and Indonesia with tropical forest conservation, or China and India with greenhouse gas emissions, are under substantial pressure to protect global environmental goods. Oftentimes these large countries have agreed to take action in exchange for low-cost financing from donor organizations (Miller 1995). Thus, globally important countries are likely to borrow for environment-improving projects that address global concerns as a low-cost method for demonstrating action at the international level.

Second, borrowing countries often have specific development projects in mind for financing, but do not have the credit rating or revenue stream that is necessary to borrow for them on international commercial markets. Oftentimes, these projects are brought to the multilateral development banks for consideration, but may not align directly with corporate priorities at the multilateral banks. Thus, there is bargaining to link the development priorities of borrowing countries with complementary environmental projects favored by donor countries. For example, the Asian Development Bank's Greater Mekong Subregion Biodiversity Conservation Corridors Project, which is the ADB's flagship biodiversity program in Southeast Asia, was linked to the approval of the Economic Corridors program that supported regional transportation development (interview, March 2010).

Finally, there are differences in demand for environment-improving projects among borrowing countries. As countries achieve higher per capita income levels, the demand for proactive environmental management as a matter of public policy generally increases. In addition, the management of environmental resources has become a means for political and social stability in some countries facing high levels of degradation (Economy 2004). Thus, in some cases less-developed countries aggressively pursue environmental management. For example, Costa Rica is widely recognized as "a pioneer in incorporating sustainable development into decision making at the national level" (International Institute for Sustainable Development 2004). In addition, as borrowing countries face increasingly severe environmental problems, the benefit of environmental projects increases.

Despite generally lower demand for environment-improving projects, especially those projects that appeal to international constituencies, developing countries often face severe environmental problems that are mostly confined within their own borders. In many countries, domestic constituencies push governments of poor countries to improve sanitation, limit exposure to toxic wastes, and prevent harms to natural resources that are important for their livelihoods. These pressures may be why projects from international donors that mostly have domestic benefits are implemented more successfully on average (Buntaine and Parks 2013). Despite the potential value of these kinds of projects for meeting local needs, the results both politically and environmentally are often uncertain. Implementations problems related to environmental management are rampant in many developing countries (e.g., Birol and Das 2012). The uncertainty that borrowing governments face about what they can accomplish locally with environment-improving projects is likely to be significant.

Approval Decisions for Global Environment-Improving Projects

Less-developed countries have frequently demanded financial and technical support as a condition for protecting global environmental assets such as ozone, biodiversity, and climate (Miller 1995; Williams 2005). Borrowing countries that can substantially impact important global environmental outcomes, like Brazil with tropical forests or China with climate change, usually receive more financing from donors (Hicks et al. 2008, 194; Lewis 2003). This outcome is likely due to the intersection of the lending supply preferences of donor countries and the impetus for large borrowing countries to demonstrate action, even if they deliver poor outcomes.

Given that the primary pressures for global environment-improving projects is driven by a push to demonstrate action quickly, with little selective pressure from either donor or borrower countries, I hypothesize that the allocation of global environment-improving projects and activities will be based on the importance of the borrowing country for achieving global outcomes, rather than the record delivering global outcomes as reported in project evaluations. Because clean-energy projects intended to address global climate change are easily identifiable (as described below), I test the following observable implications about approval decisions:

Hypothesis 1: Allocation decisions about projects and activities that aim to secure global environmental goods will reflect the importance of the borrowing country, rather than information in evaluations about past performance implementing similar projects and activities.

Implication 1a: Multilateral development banks will approve a greater number of clean-energy projects and activities for borrowing countries with high greenhouse gas emissions.

Implication 1b: Multilateral development banks will not change the approval of clean-energy projects and activities based on information in evaluations about the previous implementation of clean-energy projects and activities.

Approval Decisions for Domestic Environment-Improving Projects

Development bank decisions about environment-improving projects that involve local outcomes (e.g., sanitation, solid waste, water pollution) are not as likely to be driven by the lending preferences of donor countries, since these donors have a lower stake in projects that do not generate global goods. Instead, the primary constraint on lending for environment-improving projects with primarily domestic benefits is the demand of the borrowing country. Indeed, a great deal of evidence suggests that projects that do not address the unique needs of borrowing countries are not likely to be favored. A 1998 World Bank report from the Environmentally and Socially Sustainable Development Network states that many environment-improving programs fail because they are "blueprint solutions, which are inappropriate . . . because of the individuality of countries and institutions" (Environment Sector Board 1998, 43).

Fortunately, when projects are "demand driven," they tend to be more successful because the borrowing country is invested in their success (Connolly 1996). Borrowers that achieve success in past operations gain information about the relative benefits of environment-improving operations and face decreased uncertainty about implementation challenges and the potential benefits of certain outcomes. Evaluations that analyze the sources of success may help overcome uncertainty problems that previously prevent a more active lending program for local environmental goods. Because urban environmental projects, which are intended to address localized environmental problems, are easily identifiable (as described below) and represent a large portion of domestically focused environment-improving projects, I test the following hypothesis using approval decisions about urban environment projects:

Hypothesis 2: Development banks will approve environment-improving projects and activities that primarily involve local outcomes (e.g., sanitation, solid waste, pollution abatement) for borrowing countries that have successful evaluations of similar projects and activities.

Implication 2a: Development banks will approve a greater number of urban environmental projects and activities for borrowing countries that have successful evaluations about similar projects and activities.

CASE STUDIES ON EVALUATION, UNCERTAINTY, AND ALLOCATION DECISIONS

To explore these hypotheses, I first examine two case studies and trace whether the flow of information from project evaluations to decisions is consistent with the expectation that operational staff will overlook information when under pressure to allocate projects and that borrowing countries will use information about the performance of projects to overcome uncertainty about whether to pursue additional projects. The distinguishing feature that differentiates the two cases is the source of demand for the project—donor countries or borrowing countries. To trace the flow of information in ways that shed light on causal mechanisms, I first identify cases of both donor-driven and borrower-driven projects that fit the predicted sequence of projects and evaluations outlined in the hypotheses.

For the hypothesis that information about performance in evaluations will be ignored when donors push for projects (H1), I identified an example of two sequential projects that had natural resource conservation goals, with the first project failing to reach goals. The causal logic behind this hypothesis is that project teams are likely to disregard negative information about the performance of natural resource conservation activities when they are under pressure from donor countries to pursue operations related to natural resource conservation. For staff, there is no benefit to being more selective about projects.

For the hypothesis that borrowing countries will use information about performance to overcome uncertainty (H2), I located an example of a water sanitation project with clear local benefits that was repeated after being successful on a first round. Here, I look for evidence that information about the results of the first project decreased uncertainty about the potential benefits of a new approach to programming in the sector, thereby increasing demand for additional projects. For both cases, I chose an example that fit the predicted sequential pattern; the case studies evaluate evidence about mechanisms.

The goal of this approach to selecting case studies is not to generalize about the causal impact of evaluations on allocation decisions. The goal is to assess whether the mechanisms behind the hypotheses are plausible. In the statistical analysis that follows, I turn to the question about whether allocation patterns are consistent with the hypotheses across time and multilateral development banks. This is an example of what Seawright and Gerring (2008, 299) call a *typical case*, "in which the evidence at hand (in the case) is judged according to whether it validates the stipulated causal mechanisms or not." The goal of this approach is to add within-case evidence that is not possible to collect across cases, but can be used to probe causal mechanisms, possibly against alternative mechanisms.

Controlling Bush Fires to Protect Natural Resources in Senegal

With more than half of the population living in rural areas and depending on animal husbandry and agriculture for their livelihoods, rural development has long been a priority for Senegal. Both the World Bank and the African Development Bank supported projects that aimed to increase agriculture and animal husbandry yields starting in the late 1970s.[8] Likewise, various government agencies in Senegal have highlighted rural development as a central component of planning. In the 1970s, a series of decentralization reforms took place to make the rural development plans and policies more responsive to local needs and skills (Vengroff and Johnston 1989). The African Development Bank began funding projects that aimed to conserve natural resources in the 1980s. In particular, the African Development Bank approved the Bushfire Control and Reafforestation project in 1984, which aimed to limit desertification that occurred after vegetation was damaged by bush fires.

The Bushfire Control and Reafforestation project was implemented in 1986, with goals "to limit and control bush fires through fire breaks and control desert encroachment through development of gum Arabic plantations" (1998, ii). To accomplish these goals, the project aimed to create many village-level fire control committees in rural areas, each of which would take responsibility for managing fire breaks that would prevent further desertification. These goals were connected with an emerging policy at the African Development Bank to take natural resource management and conservation into account when planning rural development projects. For example, the 1990 Environmental Policy for the African Development Bank specified not only that mitigation measures should be considered as part of development projects, but also set the AFDB on a course to begin funding "stand-alone environmental projects/programs" in agro-forestry and forestry, water management, and soil conservation (Knox 1994).

These goals failed in the Senegal Bushfire Control and Reafforestation project. The postproject evaluation found that more than 90% of the fire breaks that had been installed during the project had not been maintained only two to three years following the completion of the project (Operations Evaluation Department 1998b). The reason for the failure was clear: local people had not bought into the idea of preventing bush fires. The postproject evaluation reported that "committees took no initiatives to take charge of the project activities, and this calls to question the motivation of the populations" (Operations Evaluation Department 1998b, 1). In addition to the problem that "the populations are not motivated," the Senegalese government did not follow through on its funding commitments to decentralized fire management and did not provide resources for implementation from the Forestry Fund as committed. Poor commitment both from the national government and local populations resulted in a project that was rated "unsuccessful" and the performance of the borrower and the African Development Bank rated as "inadequate."

The most important lesson revealed in the 1998 postproject evaluation completed by the Operations Evaluation Department was that more attention needed to be paid to the institutional aspects of decentralized natural resource management and conservation activities. The 600 fire control committees that were established during the course of the project took no action to maintain fire breaks, which was the key assumption behind project activities. By involving local communities in planning and implementation, the project team sought to find a sustainable and lasting model of natural resource conservation. When this did not happen, the postproject evaluation suggested that any future projects related to fire management should "require the conduct of in-depth socio-economic studies on projects for protection and management of natural resources involving the local populations" (Operations Evaluation Department 1998b, 3). Decentralized natural resource management activities could not assume involvement of poor, rural people in operating and maintaining new types of infrastructure.

Under pressure from donor countries to continue investing in natural resource management and conservation activities, the theoretical prediction about what should happen in the next project is that these lessons should be ignored and similar activities should proceed on the basis of an organization-wide policy to include resource conservation components in projects. This is exactly what happened and in a quite astonishing way. In 2002, the African Development Bank published the appraisal report for the Livestock Support Project II. This project was an explicit follow-up of an earlier livestock husbandry project and aimed to improve the productivity of livestock operations through improved range management, feeding operations, and rural water infrastructure. In addition, the project aimed to retry the same approaches to natural resource management and fire conservation as the Bushfire Control and Reafforestation project that had just been evaluated. In fact, approximately one-third of the project financing aimed to create 1,500 km of fire breaks and vegetation restoration programs by village committees, according to the project appraisal report (African Development Fund 2000).

In the section of the project appraisal that dealt with results and evaluations of previous projects, no mention at all was made of the previously unsuccessful Bushfire Control and Reafforestation project, despite the fact that the evaluation for that project was freshly completed. Perhaps even more strikingly, the project proceeded on the basis of the same decentralized implementation plans that the evaluation had found to be so unsuccessful, with village-level committees being assembled to implement and maintain fire breaks (2000, 20–21). The project appraisal document seems to willfully neglect risks in this approach, stating:

> Perpetuation of the actions undertaken is guaranteed by the project design which is based on participatory approach. The latter will give a more significant responsibility to the people and arouse their participation. The development of organisational and institutional capacity embarked upon through a steady transfer of technical skills and strengthening of potentials to be negotiated and worked out together in order to defend the shared interests, thus, in line with day to day practices where players endeavour to resolve the problems themselves. (African Development Fund 2000, 31)

In the push to incorporate natural resource conservation and vegetation regeneration components into the project, past lessons coming out of a directly relevant evaluation were either ignored or overlooked. If the evaluation in this case had an impact, we would at least observe a different approach to the same goals or a more in-depth response to implementation risks, perhaps through a study of socioeconomic conditions described in the previous evaluation. Instead, this particular sequence of projects shows the potential for new information in evaluation to be ignored under conditions where there are pressures to pursue certain types of activities from donor countries. As I test below, the next step is to understand whether this pattern plays out more generally across the lending portfolios of the multilateral development banks.

Improving Water Supply and Sanitation Services in Indonesia

For environment-improving projects and project components with significant local benefits and less pressure from donor countries, I expect a different response to information about performance that is made available through project evaluations. Many development policies are pursued under conditions of significant uncertainty, with donor support allowing for experimentation and new approaches to be pursued. The expansion of water supply, sanitation, and waste services to villages outside of major population centers in Indonesia was no exception to these challenges. In the 1980s, the development community realized that one of the primary challenges in securing safe water for communities was the provision of operations and maintenance costs following the installation of publically funded infrastructure

(Cotton and Franceys 1988). Many facilities supported by donors fell into disrepair because local governments could not raise sufficient revenue for longer-term operation and maintenance.

The Water Supply and Sanitation in Low-Income Communities Project, supported by the World Bank in Indonesia, aimed to overcome these difficulties by requiring some level of matching contribution from recipient villages in order to be eligible to receive water supply and sanitation infrastructure investments. In a highly experimental plan, the 1993 appraisal report for the project outlined eligibility criteria that included a 20% contribution of the village for operation and maintenance costs (16% in-kind contribution and 4% cash contribution). In addition, to be eligible to receive water supply and sanitation infrastructure investment through the project, a village needed to create a "village action plan." This approach contrasted with previous planning, implementation, and maintenance approaches in Indonesia that favored the completion of physical facilities over planning for long-term maintenance. The appraisal report for the World Bank project characterized previous approaches as

> rigidly tied to uniform, standard designs. The choice of service level and design was dictated by government bureaucrats and their technical experts; and community preferences were not adequately taken into account . . . the selection process for villages did not ensure that they would have the commitment to bear the burden of maintaining and operating the facilities constructed for them by the government. (World Bank 1993c, 5–6)

The new approach was explicitly exploratory in nature, with aims for the "formulation of innovative and replicable approaches (applicable on a large scale) to sustainable rural water supply and sanitation development. The expectation is that the project's initiatives would eventually be incorporated into Indonesia's national policies and programs" (World Bank 1993c, ii). The approach was risky, both for the World Bank and for the relevant government agencies in Indonesia. The Implementation Completion Report (World Bank 2000) for the project recounted that the project was "highly innovative in the way it combined water supply and sanitation" (4) but that "there were obvious risks related to lack of institutional capacity and coordination, especially given its multi-faceted approach" (2). Despite these risks, the Implementation Completion Report found the project to be largely successful, with significant support from relevant government agencies and the communities that opted into the program: "The project received adequate political support at the highest level, and the means for uninterrupted implementation. All necessary institutional and managerial arrangements were put in place and contractual requirements were met, but more importantly perhaps there was strong buy-in by all stakeholders, especially communities which may explain higher than intended coverage in water supply" (World Bank 2000, 13).

The independent evaluation completed by the Operations Evaluation Department in 2001 echoed these same conclusions about the project's results, finding the approach of the project to have led to greater success than the team that designed the project had originally planned, improving water quality in all project areas considered by the evaluation team (2001, 7). The reason ascribed to the success was clear, since the project had "increasingly enlisted the opinions, preferences, and cooperation of consumers in the planning and implementation of its projects. This has been tried only on an exceptional basis under urban projects" (21). The impacts of the project were substantial and unexpectedly positive. While representatives of the Ministry of Health and Ministry of Settlements and Regional Infrastructure both recognized the project as successful and worthy of replication, both identified the complexity of implementation as a major issue affecting long-term plans.

Based on the successful results of this innovative project, the Ministry of Health decided to pursue a second project with the same name, but with slightly simplified implementation procedures. The 2000 appraisal report directly responded to information generated by past projects and draft versions of the postproject evaluations. The same participatory approach was continued, with village action plans required for eligibility to receive water supply and sanitation infrastructure, and 20% matching contributions required for operations and maintenance (16% in-kind and 4% cash contributions). As justification for this approach, the project appraisal document directly noted that the previous project had overcome uncertainty about this type of approach: "Building on the successful aspects of the preceding WSSLIC 1 project as well as those of the related projects . . . the project will adopt a decentralized, community demand-responsive model that channels financial resources and technical assistance directly to village management structures and incorporates contracts for independent monitoring" (Operations Evaluation Department 2001, 5).

At the same time, the project was designed to take into account lessons about complexity and the difficulty of implementing a project with a wide geographic footprint: "The funds channeling was too complicated, involved too many levels of budget, budget administrators and distribution channels. Project administration was also too complicated, involving an excessive number of contracts, agencies and bureaucratic levels of approval, which led to long annual delays in the release of contracts for civil works and technical assistance, and a lack of transparency" (11). As a consequence of these lessons, the project was designed to have clearer lines of accountability and implementation responsibilities within the Ministry of Health, including the creation of a single project management unit.

The project team that designed the project did exactly as predicted for projects that were pursued under considerable uncertainty, but generated substantial learning based on new information. The monitoring and evaluation of the project helped to decrease uncertainty and thus raise demand for an additional project to build on successful outcomes. As the representative for the Ministry of Health said in response to the implementation completion report, "We knew from the evaluation that the project had achieved substantial progress specifically the involvement of communities in planning [and] implementation" (World Bank 2000, 33). Furthermore, the design team for the second stage of the project specifically consulted a number of documents that contributed information and lessons, including a midterm review, draft completion report, and draft evaluation report, independent academic impact studies, and case studies that included information from the first Water Supply and Sanitation in Low-Income Communities Project. This is the causal mechanism expected for projects with local environmental benefits. In the statistical analysis presented below, I ask whether a pattern consistent with this mechanism is observed across the multilateral development banks.

PROJECT EVALUATIONS AND ENVIRONMENTAL PERFORMANCE

To collect the data for a more general analysis of these trends, I assembled a research team that coded implementation performance related to environment-improving targets from every publicly released project evaluation completed between 1990 and 2008. Appendix 1 describes the coding procedures used to collect performance information from project evaluations in greater detail. A combined total of 943 project evaluations have been published, 472 by the World Bank, 283 by the Asian Development Bank, and 188 by the African Development Bank. The Inter-American Development Bank did not produce independent project evaluations during the period under consideration. Of the evaluations, 27% of World Bank, 25% of Asian Development Bank, and 13% of African Development Bank project evaluations contained information about the implementation of environmental goals.

The evaluations are all readily available on the websites of the multilateral development banks. The projects are chosen for evaluation by the development banks based on "purposeful sampling," meaning that priority project areas will have more evaluations. This is appropriate for my research design, since I will assess how information that is available to decision-makers influences approval and allocation decisions. To ensure that the results of the statistical models are not driven by selection into evaluation, robustness is assessed by examining only countries and years that have been subjected to a project evaluation in the relevant time period.

For this chapter, I use two pieces of information from project evaluations: (1) the overall project rating given by evaluators; and (2) the borrower performance at achieving environmental targets, as double-blind coded by our team from independent evaluations. The overall performance rating is already assigned to each project by evaluators based on whether the project reached overall targets (e.g., unsatisfactory, partly satisfactory, satisfactory, highly satisfactory). Our team used the same ordinal scale to code for borrower environmental target implementation performance based on the narrative description of environmental outcomes in project evaluations, if available (see table 6.1).

TABLE 6.1

ENVIRONMENTAL PERFORMANCE CODING CRITERIA

Coding	Meaning	Criteria
4	Highly satisfactory	Exceeds environmental goals or conditions; specifically mentioned for outstanding environmental performance; efforts significantly improve environmental outcomes as compared to preapproval expectations.
3	Satisfactory	Meets all environmental goals or conditions with only minor exceptions observed; summary statement of performance is positive.
2	Partly satisfactory	Meets some environmental goals or conditions with significant deficiencies observed; does not meet monitoring or evaluation standards in projects with no discernible environmental impacts; summary statement of performance is negative.
1	Unsatisfactory	Does not meet most environmental goals or conditions with major deficiencies observed in most areas; outright noncompliance with environmental loan conditions and/or nonachievement of targets.
NA	Not available	Project has no environmental aspects, or insufficient information is available in evaluation to assess recipient performance.

MODELING THE RESPONSE TO ENVIRONMENTAL PERFORMANCE

There are two primary decisions made about the allocation of environment-improving projects. First, a screening decision is made about *whether* to approve an environment-improving project. Second, a decision is made about *how much* financing to approve for an environment-improving project. As with previous chapters, I use a two-stage model to examine these approval and allocation decisions (see e.g., Cingranelli and Pasquarello 1985; Neumayer 2003; Hicks et al. 2008; Buntaine 2011). In the first stage, the decision to approve a clean-energy or urban environment project during a given year is taken to be a binary variable. In the second stage, I model the amount of financing approved for a particular project type *given* that at least one project is approved during a particular time period. See chapter 4 for a more complete specification of this modeling strategy.

Identifying Clean-Energy and Urban Environment Projects

I choose to examine clean-energy and urban environment projects, because they fit my theory about local versus global goods and they are relatively easy to identify. They also represent a large portion of environment-improving financing at the multilateral banks and thus avoid the difficulty associated with modeling rare events (King and Zeng 2001). In both cases, I identified projects and activities using AidData purpose and activity codes and then cross-checked projects against thematic codes assigned by the development banks themselves (Tierney et al. 2011). Each project is assigned one purpose code in the AidData database, which represents "the dominant, immediate sector or subsector each project was designed to target" (AidData 2010, 20). Each project can be assigned multiple activity codes, which include all activities that were undertaken as part of a project. The specific procedures I used to identify projects and activities are as follows.

I classified *clean-energy projects* as those with the renewable energy purpose code in the AidData database, together with at least one activity code that indicates a type of renewable energy besides hydropower. In addition, I included projects with energy efficiency activities and a renewable energy purpose code. Projects that did not have a renewable energy purpose but had either renewable energy activities besides hydropower or energy efficiency activities were coded as projects with clean-energy activities.

I classified *urban environment projects* using a similar procedure. Any approved project that had an AidData purpose code of waste management or disposal,

AidData activity codes for the prevention of air pollution, prevention of water contamination, sewerage, domestic and industrial waste water treatment, or small-system sewerage, or was self-identified by the relevant Environment Department as an urban environment or pollution control project was considered a candidate urban environment project. For each candidate project, I located project appraisal documents and assigned a final urban environment project coding if the primary purpose of the project was to improve environmental conditions in urban areas. I excluded any project that addressed environmental problems in rural areas, multisector water projects that did not have at least 40% of financing directed to environmental purposes, and road projects with stated air pollution management goals.[9] I classified each project as having an urban environmental activity when it had AidData activity codes for the prevention of air pollution, prevention of water contamination, sewerage, domestic and industrial waste water treatment, or small-system sewerage.

Operationalizing Environmental Performance

The main predictor variable of interest in all of the models presented here is the past environmental performance of the particular borrower as measured in project evaluations for the relevant type of project or activity. The coding scheme is described in table 6.1. For the models that predict the approval of clean-energy projects, I create the variables *NO. CLEAN ENERGY SUCCESSFUL* and *NO. CLEAN ENERGY UNSUCCESSFUL*, which are the number of project evaluations during the previous five years that provide the respective information about the performance of clean-energy activities. For the models that predict the approval of urban environment projects, I create the variables *NO. UEI SUCCESSFUL* and *NO. UEI UNSUCCESSFUL*, which are the number of project evaluations during the previous five years that provide the respective information about the performance of urban environment activities.

Controlling for Other Factors

Drawing from the literature on aid allocation, I control for several other factors that might influence approval and allocation decisions about environment-improving projects. First, other types of nonenvironmental performance may impact approval and allocation decisions. A great deal of research has emphasized the importance of good governance in achieving aid outcomes and has found that donors tend to allocate more financing to recipients with good governance (Cline and Sargen 1975; Neumayer 2003; Hicks et al. 2008). While broad measures of governance quality do not contain information about recipient performance in bank projects, staff at development banks may nonetheless use these kinds of global and highly visible assessments. Thus, I use the World Bank Institute's Government Effectiveness index (*GOVERNMENT EFFECTIVENESS*) to control for general governance quality. In addition, when coding environmental performance as described above, we also collected the overall outcome rating given to each bank project by the evaluators. I control for overall project outcomes using the proportional variable *OVERALL SUCCESS*, which is the proportion of successful outcomes a borrowing country achieved during the preceding five years.[10]

In terms of environment-improving projects, more projects and greater allocation amounts are likely to be directed to recipients with greater environmental damages or the need to demonstrate international action. In the case of clean-energy projects, there is much greater pressure internationally for countries with high emissions levels, such as China and India, to manage greenhouse gas emissions. Both because large borrowers face international pressure to demonstrate action and because multilateral development banks must increase clean-energy lending because of donor country pressures, borrowing countries with high carbon emissions levels (*CO2 GT*) might receive more projects and greater allocation amounts.[11] Likewise, more urban environment projects might be directed to recipients with higher levels of urban environmental degradation. Thus, I take the air pollution damage as a proportion of GDP for each borrowing country, as recorded in the World Bank's Adjusted Net Savings data (*AIR POLLUTION BURDEN*).

There are a number of broad programs and trends that might influence decisions about clean-energy projects and activities. First, bank-wide decisions to emphasize certain sectors, oftentimes operationalized through the adoption of new policies or strategies, can alter allocation patterns (Nielson and Tierney 2003). Thus, I code a binary variable (*CLEAN ENERGY INITIATIVE*) for any year after the conclusion of the Kyoto Protocol for the World Bank and any year after the initiation of the Energy Efficiency Initiative for the Asian Development Bank in 2005. In no cases did these variables increase model fit, and thus I have removed them from the regressions that I report below.

There also might be important differences in allocation decisions for countries that have access to highly concessional loans as compared to countries that borrow from the multilateral development banks at market rates. In general, low-income countries that have very low per capita income, high external debt levels, and low capacity to implement projects receive highly concessional financing, consisting mainly of loans with interest rates as low as 0.75% and grants. For the multilateral development banks considered here, these funds come from the World Bank's International Development Association (IDA), the Asian Development

Bank's Asian Development Fund (ASDF), and the African Development Bank's African Development Fund (AFDF). Each recipient that borrows concessional financing receives a set allocation each year, leaving limited room to increase or decrease financing based on performance, unless other sectors are deemphasized. In contrast, middle-income countries that have higher per capita income and lower external debt tend to borrow from the multilateral development banks at market rates, through the World Bank's International Bank for Reconstruction and Development (IBRD), the Asian Development Bank's Ordinary Capital Reserves (OCR), and the African Development Bank's Ordinary Capital Reserves. There is no set cap on the amount of financing that can be borrowed from these sources, and since borrowing takes place at market rates, the projects that are financed tend to be very demand-driven and much larger. Thus, owing to income effects and the amount of financing that can be approved from the market lending window, countries that borrow at market rates are more likely to receive both clean-energy and urban environment projects. Thus, I create a variable (*CONCESSIONAL*) that represents the proportion of concessional lending as part of the total lending amount approved for each country in a given year.

Researchers have also found that "recipient size" is a determinate of multilateral aid allocation. In operational terms, this has meant either population or size of the economy (Dowling and Hiemenz 1985; Neumayer 2003). In terms of approval and allocation decisions, I expect borrowers that have a greater number of project in the previous five years (*NO. PROJECTS IN PREV 5 YRS*) or a greater portfolio size in a particular year (*COUNTRY PORTFOLIO SIZE*) to receive more projects and higher allocation amounts.

Subsetting the Panel

For each of the models presented below, I use the same predictor variables for two subsets of the data. The first subset includes in the sample all years when a borrowing country received at least one project ("allocation" models). Because aggregate or total allocation decisions are made prior to project approval decisions, it would bias estimates to include country-years in the approval panel when the borrowing country did not receive any projects because of higher-level decisions. The second subset includes all country-years when a project evaluation was completed during the previous five years ("allocation & evaluation" models). Because projects are not assigned randomly to evaluation and because I cannot rule out missing evaluations during the early years of the panel, model estimates might be biased by the selection of certain types of countries into project evaluation. To the extent that model estimates are similar across these two subsets, the results should not be driven by selection into evaluation.

MODEL RESULTS

For clean-energy projects and activities at the World Bank, I find that evaluations indicating the successful achievement of clean-energy goals have no impact on future lending (table 6.2). This result is consistent when the outcome variable includes only projects with primary clean-energy purposes and for projects with any purpose and clean-energy activities. In the project evaluations that our team coded for this research, there is only one instance where clean-energy goals were not

TABLE 6.2

APPROVAL OF CLEAN ENERGY PROJECTS AND ACTIVITIES
AT THE WORLD BANK

Model	1a	1b	1c	1d
Outcome variable	Project	Project	Activity	Activity
NO. CLEAN ENERGY SUCCESSFUL	−0.05 (0.60)	−0.25 (0.65)	−0.66 (0.43)	−0.60 (0.43)
NO. CLEAN ENERGY UNSUCCESSFUL				
CO_2 (GT)	0.43** (0.24)	0.26 (0.33)	0.18** (0.10)	0.17* (0.11)
OVERALL SUCCESS (PROPORTION)	0.40 (0.38)	−0.36 (0.62)	0.24 (0.19)	−0.14 (0.26)
GOVERNMENT EFFECTIVENESS	0.12 (0.42)	0.91 (0.81)	0.08 (0.13)	0.13 (0.26)
CONCESSIONAL	−0.16 (0.51)	0.01 (0.70)	−0.08 (0.15)	−0.12 (0.24)
NO. PROJECTS IN PREV 5 YRS	0.03** (0.01)	0.03 (0.03)	0.02** (0.01)	0.00 (0.01)
Random intercept variance	2.38	1.59	0.06	0.00
Data subset	Allocation	Allocation & evaluation	Allocation	Allocation & evaluation
Observations (countries)	1,411 (131)	348 (74)	1,411 (131)	347 (74)
Residual deviance	154.9	76.5	627.9	218.7
Null deviance	166.1	80.3	654.9	226.9

Note: All models are random-effects probit specification. Null Deviance is calculated using country random intercept as only predictor.

Statistical significance levels for one-tailed tests: ** $p < .05$, * $p < .1$.

successful, making it impossible to specify models that include this variable.[12] For models that include the full panel of country-years with any lending, the amount of greenhouse gas emissions is associated with more clean-energy projects and activities, as predicted (Models 1a/1c). This result is more tenuous for the subset of country-years that are covered by a project evaluation during the previous five years (Models 1b/1d). In all cases, the amount of greenhouse gas emissions is collinear with the number of projects approved in a country for the past five years. This is not surprising, as larger countries have both more emissions and larger lending portfolios. If the number of previous projects is dropped from the regression, the amount of emissions becomes significant in all cases. Thus, the results are consistent with larger countries receiving more clean-energy lending, though the exact mechanism cannot be identified.

For clean-energy projects and activities at the Asian Development Bank, I find that the content of evaluations has no impact on future lending (table 6.3). An initial examination of the data shows that successful achievement of clean-energy goals, as recorded in project evaluations, increases the probability of receiving future projects with a clean-energy focus. Upon a closer look, this effect is also found for countries with project evaluations indicating unsuccessful clean-energy outcomes. It does not seem to matter what evaluations say; the result of bargaining between Asian Development Bank staff and borrowing country officials tends to produce more clean-energy projects when past clean-energy activities have been the subject of an evaluation. Like the World Bank, the amount of emissions for each borrowing country does not have a clear relationship with the amount of clean-energy financing, since this variable is collinear with the number of projects received by each country. Larger countries receive more clean-energy projects and activities. It is possible that a larger sample size would help to clarify these results. As a robustness check, I estimated the same model using the ADB's own listing of clean-energy projects, which includes many large hydropower projects and efficient fossil-fuel power generation projects. In this case, borrowers with high emission levels and low environmental performance are most likely to receive clean-energy projects, indicating an response that is opposite to selectivity.

For urban environmental projects and activities, both the World Bank and Asian Development Bank allocate more projects to countries that are found to be successful in evaluations of similar activities. I model both projects with a primary purpose to improve urban environmental conditions and projects with relevant activities, because the multilateral development banks might accomplish selectivity by changing either allocation decisions about stand-alone projects or environmental components in response to information about performance. For the World Bank,

TABLE 6.3

APPROVAL OF CLEAN ENERGY PROJECTS AND ACTIVITIES AT THE ASIAN
DEVELOPMENT BANK

Model	2a	2b	2c	2d
Outcome variable	Project	Project	Activity	Activity
NO. CLEAN ENERGY SUCCESSFUL	0.72** (0.36)	0.64* (0.36)	0.19 (0.33)	0.15 (0.33)
NO. CLEAN ENERGY UNSUCCESSFUL	0.67* (0.34)	0.64* (0.35)	0.42 (0.29)	0.39 (0.29)
CO_2 (GT)	0.61 (0.50)	0.50 (0.57)	0.89* (0.47)	0.59 (0.52)
OVERALL SUCCESS (PROPORTION)	−1.36** (0.63)	−1.41* (0.75)	−0.13 (0.37)	0.06 (0.47)
GOVERNMENT EFFECTIVENESS	−1.21** (0.52)	−0.86 (0.75)	−0.36 (0.31)	0.09 (0.40)
CONCESSIONAL	−0.59 (0.39)	−0.67 (0.60)	−0.14 (0.29)	−0.22 (0.38)
NO. PROJECTS IN PREV 5 YRS	0.01** (0.00)	0.01** (0.00)	0.01** (0.00)	0.01** (0.00)
Random intercept variance	0.00	0.00	0.00	0.00
Data subset	Allocation	Allocation & evaluation	Allocation	Allocation & evaluation
Observations (countries)	282 (37)	192 (27)	282 (37)	192 (27)
Residual deviance	113.8	80.4	162.8	119.8
Null deviance	144.2	104.9	190.2	144.2

Note: All models are random-effects probit specification. Null deviance is calculated using country random intercept as only predictor.

Statistical significance levels for one-tailed tests: ** $p < .05$, * $p < .1$.

borrowing countries with more evaluations that report satisfactory results related to urban environmental goals receive more urban environmental projects in future periods (table 6.4, Models 3a–3b). This result is consistent across both the full panel and the subset of country-years that have an evaluation during the past five years, indicating that selection into evaluation does not account for these results. For the World Bank, the number of evaluations with satisfactory findings about urban environmental goals does not predict the borrowers will receive a project with an urban environment activities (table 6.4, Models 3c–3d). This is likely due to the long

TABLE 6.4

APPROVAL OF URBAN ENVIRONMENTAL PROJECTS AND ACTIVITIES
AT THE WORLD BANK

Model	3a	3b	3c	3d
Outcome variable	Project	Project	Activity	Activity
NO. UEI SUCCESSFUL	**0.59**** (0.23)	**0.57**** (0.22)	0.14 (0.19)	0.19 (0.19)
NO. UEI UNSUCCESSFUL	−0.18 (0.21)	−0.27 (0.23)	0.12 (0.16)	0.13 (0.18)
AIR POLLUTION BURDEN	−0.01 (0.14)	−0.45 (0.39)	0.09 (0.09)	−0.14 (0.26)
OVERALL SUCCESS (PROPORTION)	0.08 (0.20)	−0.14 (0.30)	**0.29*** (0.15)	0.30 (0.23)
GOVERNMENT EFFECTIVENESS	0.06 (0.13)	−0.11 (0.27)	−0.01 (0.10)	−0.12 (0.21)
CONCESSIONAL	**−0.88**** (0.16)	**−0.90**** (0.28)	−0.46 (0.11)	**−0.57**** (0.22)
NO. PROJECTS IN PREV 5 YRS	**0.03**** (0.01)	**0.02**** (0.01)	**0.02**** (0.00)	**0.02**** (0.01)
Random intercept variance	0.14	0.13	0.05	0.06
Data subset	Allocation	Allocation & evaluation	Allocation	Allocation & evaluation
Observations (countries)	1,371 (126)	340 (72)	1,371 (126)	340 (72)
Residual deviance	682.7	225.5	1211.8	351.1
Null deviance	747.4	254.1	1,265.5	371.0

Note: Null Deviance is calculated using country random intercept as only predictor
Statistical significance levels: ** $p < .05$, * $p < 0.1$.

history of "mainstreaming" of environmental activities into many projects across
the World Bank, leaving little room to find additional opportunities to pursue environmental components based on success (Ekbom and Bojo 1997).

At the Asian Development Bank, evaluations that report satisfactory performance implementing urban environmental goals are associated with more lending
that includes urban environmental activities (table 6.5, Models 4c–4d). Unlike
the at the World Bank, the number of evaluations reporting the achievement
of urban environmental goals does not significantly predict that a borrowing

country will receive more projects with an urban environmental purpose (table 6.5, Models 4a–4b). As compared to the World Bank portfolio (174/5,805), the Asian Development Bank portfolio (43/6,245) has a lower proportion of projects that have as a primary purpose to improve environmental conditions in urban areas. At the World Bank, the proportion of projects with urban environmental activities (393/5,805) is also significantly higher than for the Asian Development Bank (121/6,245). Because the Asian Development Bank has not integrated urban

TABLE 6.5

APPROVAL OF URBAN ENVIRONMENTAL PROJECTS AND ACTIVITIES
AT THE ASIAN DEVELOPMENT BANK

Model	4a	4b	4c	4d
Outcome variable	Project	Project	Activity	Activity
NO. UEI SUCCESSFUL	0.27 (0.22)	0.25 (0.22)	0.60** (0.29)	0.56** (0.28)
NO. UEI UNSUCCESSFUL	0.00 (0.22)	0.06 (0.23)	0.13 (0.22)	0.17 (0.22)
AIR POLLUTION BURDEN	−0.10 (0.33)	−0.09 (0.37)	−0.20 (0.35)	−0.26 (0.38)
OVERALL SUCCESS (PROPORTION)	−0.09 (0.38)	0.32 (0.51)	0.25 (0.38)	0.33 (0.49)
GOVERNMENT EFFECTIVENESS	0.56* (0.33)	0.47 (0.44)	0.16 (0.36)	0.42 (0.44)
CONCESSIONAL	−0.45 (0.33)	−0.81* (0.43)	−0.48 (0.34)	−0.77* (0.41)
NO. PROJECTS IN PREV 5 YRS	0.01** (0.00)	0.01* (0.00)	0.01** (0.00)	0.01** (0.00)
Random intercept variance	0.08	0.07	0.16	0.10
Data subset	Allocation	Allocation & Evaluation	Allocation	Allocation & Evaluation
Observations (countries)	254 (29)	184 (23)	254 (29)	184 (23)
Residual deviance	154.5	120.4	169.1	137.6
Null deviance	173.0	136.7	187.8	156.1

Note: All models have binary dependent variable with a probit link function. Null deviance is calculated using country random intercept as only predictor.

Statistical significance levels of one-tailed tests for stated directional hypotheses: ** p < .05, * p < .1.

environmental activities as widely into its portfolio, it has more opportunities to pursue this "mainstreaming" process in response to information about performance. The World Bank, having widely integrated urban environmental activities into its portfolio, exhibits selectivity by pursuing more focused, stand-alone environmental projects in successful countries.

To aid substantive interpretation of the statistical results in this chapter, figure 6.2 shows the predicted probabilities of receiving projects with different types of purposes and activities at the World Bank and Asian Development Bank. It uses predictions from the models that consider the full panel of country-years. It compares, using the uncertainty in the estimated effect for information in evaluations, the probability of receiving projects with different purposes and activities when up to two evaluations contain negative or positive information about the achievement of goals in the past. In these figures, selectivity would be represented by an increase in allocation after positive evaluations and a decrease in allocation after negative evaluations, as compared to the situation where no evaluations document performance.

When two evaluations at the World Bank contain positive information about the achievement of urban environmental goals, the probability of receiving an urban environmental project increases from 4% to 24%, though a similar effect is not found for evaluations containing negative information. At the Asian Development Bank, this finding is similar for projects with urban environmental activities, with positive evaluations raising the probability of receiving such a project from around 3% to 35%. Unlike for urban environmental projects and activities, there is no clear pattern between evaluations and the allocation of clean-energy projects and activities that are consistent with selectivity at either the World Bank or Asian Development Bank.

Allocation Amounts for Environmental Projects

It may be the case that performance information is reflected not only in *whether* to approve an environmental project, but also in *how much financing* to allocate for environmental projects once the decision has been made to move forward with projects, with more successful countries allocated larger projects because of both lending supply pressures and borrower demand. In order to examine this dynamic, I respecified the models presented above with the amount of financing allocated to a particular purpose as the outcome variable, conditional on a country having received any clean-energy or urban environment financing during the relevant time period.

However, in no case across the multilateral development banks considered here did I find that past environmental performance predicted the size of

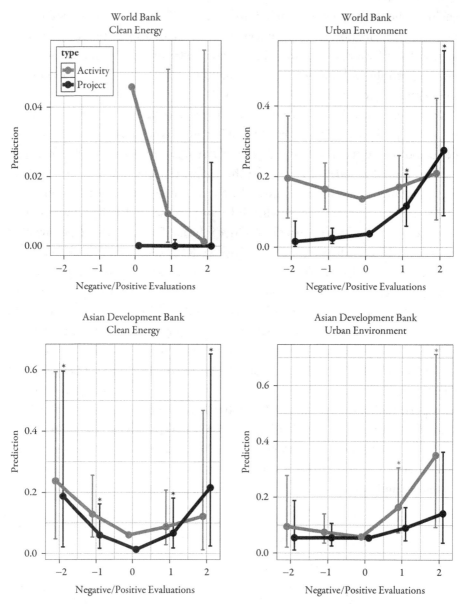

FIGURE 6.2 Number of positive and negative project evaluations and predictions about the allocation of environment-improving projects and activities

Note: The point estimates show the predicted probability of receiving at least one clean-energy or urban environment project as a function of the number of negative or positive evaluations for that project type. The error bars show the 95% confidence interval, with stars indicating a difference from the baseline condition of no positive or negative evaluations.

environment-improving projects, conditional on having received a project. For the World Bank, the overall portfolio size of a particular borrowing country during a given year was the only significant predictor of project size for both clean-energy and urban environment projects. However, countries with larger portfolio sizes receive less environment-improving financing as a proportion of their total portfolio allocation, indicating that increasing borrowing does not fundamentally alter development priorities among middle-income countries. For the Asian Development Bank, there are no significant predictors of environment-improving project size.

What the combined results of the approval and allocation models show is that high-performing countries *do* receive more environment-improving financing in certain circumstances (see approval models), but that this effect is primarily observed in "go or no go" decisions about these projects. This result reflects how decisions are made about projects. Several operational staff that I spoke with indicated that project size decisions are made in reference to project goals, rather than past performance.

STAFF INTERVIEWS ABOUT ENVIRONMENT-IMPROVING LENDING

The interviews that I conducted confirmed the general conclusion that it is difficult for multilateral development banks to practice selectivity by responding to environmental performance information contained in project evaluations. For all three multilateral development banks that complete project evaluations, the formal procedures to respond to environmental performance are weak or nonexistent. At all three of the multilateral development banks, evaluation staff reported that the most significant way that they influenced decisions about projects was through interdepartmental comment periods during project design. Over the last decade, it has become standard practice to circulate project information and appraisal documents to relevant departments for comment. Evaluators frequently use this process to bring up lessons from past projects, especially when there are environmental targets in the projects or operations being considered. Evaluators reported that project designs will often be altered in response to comments. While such comments might provide evaluators more influence, they rarely affect decisions about which projects to pursue.

This raises the possibility that evaluations influence projects in ways that are difficult to capture in the kind of data used in the statistical analysis above. It is possible that evaluations alter the designs of projects, rather than shift allocation between different types of projects. This is an important question, but more difficult to explore systematically across the portfolios of the multilateral development banks. For instance, both the World Bank and the African Development Bank have quality assurance groups that conduct desk reviews that consider whether project designs account for the lessons contained in evaluations, among other tasks. However, staff members in quality assurance readily admit that there is nothing systematic about the review of past lessons. To the extent that the multilateral development banks produce hundreds of assessments and evaluations each year, all with multiple lessons and recommendations, operational staff are likely to pick up on a few recommendations that are relatively easy to reconcile with the project being designed. Operational management across the multilateral development banks indicated that it is primarily the responsibility of the relevant task leader to complete a search of past lessons when designing new operations, with little in the way of formal procedure. One exception is the Management Action Record tracking system of the Asian Development Bank, which is used to track responses to recommendations in evaluations. In the future, this system might be used to examine responses to evaluations that are not well measured by decisions about allocation.

The general consensus about the formal process for using evaluations leaves open the possibility that evaluations exert influence in less formal ways as part of ongoing dialogue between staff at the multilateral banks and their counterparts in borrowing countries. But even less formal types of influence are likely to be limited by formal constraints on lending practices. In the case of concessional lending, the overall portfolio size for a borrowing country is largely fixed. This can leave little room to expand environment-improving lending even when past projects have had good results, unless the borrowing country is willing to forgo other development priorities. For example, an operational staff member at the African Development Bank indicated that even after a very successful first-round sewerage project in the Gambia, the government was unwilling to expand urban environment investments at the expense of other priorities. This is a likely reason why borrowing countries with concessional lending are significantly less likely to receive environment-improving projects of all types in the models reported in this chapter.

Furthermore, evaluations with clear information about performance might not result in more selectivity when operational staff are being pushed to increase the amount of environment-improving lending generally. Staff at the management level across the multilateral banks reported significant pressure from donor country executive directors to address environmental issues of all types in their projects. Asian Development Bank energy staff report that this is one area of the portfolio where investments are still primarily "donor driven," with pressure to demonstrate the "do something" approach to donors as part of the replenishment of concessional lending resources. Under this pressure, negative evaluations are unlikely to prompt selectivity by causing these organizations to withdraw from unsuccessful project areas, as is reflected in all of the models reported above.

It is also very difficult for project evaluations to set the tone for high-level strategic decisions. Indeed, it is uncommon for the board or the subset of the board that deals with development effectiveness (e.g., World Bank Committee on Development Effectiveness) to consider individual project evaluations. An executive director at the Asian Development Bank reported that only project evaluations dealing with very high-profile operations are considered at the board level. This means that there is not a significant audience among donors for the kinds of detailed information in project evaluations. This issue is further compounded by the fact that only the African Development Bank has a standardized score for environmental performance within its project evaluations. None of the multilateral development banks use a consistent set of environmental performance indicators, which has been recognized as an impediment to responding to environmental performance (Independent Evaluation Group 2008). In addition, because membership in the World Bank's CODE has significant turnover, there is little opportunity for CODE members to accumulate knowledge that is necessary to synthesize information in particular countries over time. Senior management and board members report having greater ability to respond to high-level, synthesizing, or thematic evaluations. Indeed, when I asked operational staff about influential evaluations, they often reported high-level, thematic evaluations.

In addition, several operational staff reported that project evaluations do not frequently contain information that is relevant for current decisions. In many countries, lending priorities shift. Indeed, many mid- and low-level operational staff across the different banks could not point to a project evaluation they had read that subsequently influenced their decision-making, especially as related to approval and allocation decisions. Senior operational staff at both the World Bank and African Development Bank reported that their primary purpose is to lend money and that they are evaluated on their ability to shepherd loans through the pipeline process. An Asian Development Bank staff member called this the "path of least resistance" logic to approval and allocation decisions. Considering old lessons is not a priority under these pressures.

Additionally, several operational staff reported that the culture inside the multilateral development banks tends to view poor performance, especially as related to environmental targets, as a capacity issue. The solution to poor performance may in some cases be to approve more environment-improving projects, or at least more technical assistance related to environmental management. This is apparently the norm, especially at the Asian Development Bank. In addition, many operational staff see development finance as a long-term process that might be harmed by strict selectivity. For example, one operational staff member reported that energy investments in Pakistan have been planned as part of a 10-year strategy, first building up the policy environment through traditional investments, with a goal of eventually pursuing clean-energy projects.

Despite these reservations, the models in the previous section do show significant evidence of a positive relationship between information about environment-improving targets and the allocation of projects with environmental targets that have clear local benefits. This follows from the hypothesis that for projects primarily driven by the demand of the borrower, but with uncertain outcomes, information about the results of previous projects can reduce uncertainty. When the borrowing country, together with the project team at the World Bank, finds that a new and uncertain approach can be successful, they are more likely to choose additional projects in that area. Consistent with the cases of water supply and sanitation in Indonesia, the model results in this chapter suggest that this pattern of decreased uncertainty and increased demand is a systematic part of decision-making at the multilateral development banks.

Staff members at the multilateral development banks whom I interviewed agreed that the interaction between information on results, uncertainty, and borrower demand can produce this pattern of allocation. Operations that address local environmental issues, especially as they relate to sanitation and sewerage, are not driven by pressures from donor countries. Instead, countries that are facing significant pollution often turn to the multilateral development banks for assistance because it can be difficult to borrow for environment-improving projects from other sources. When the borrowing country is invested in the success of the project, it often seeks new projects after success with projects in the same sector. For example, the Asian Development Bank has supported a string of small-scale water resource management projects in Bangladesh that have proved very successful.[13] Evaluation helps overcome uncertainty about the types of projects that can be scaled up most effectively.

In addition, for local environment-improving projects, specifically those that relate to the urban environment, there is likely to be a correlation between the demand and capacity for implementation as countries move from low to middle income. It is often countries undergoing rapid industrialization that have the greatest need for urban environment projects, but also the resources to achieve better environmental management (Bai and Imura 2000). In addition, middle-income countries also borrow from commercially competitive financing sources, leaving them room to expand borrowing for urban environment projects when they achieve successful outcomes. Indeed, staff in the water supply and sanitation sector report that large middle-income countries are the easiest to convince about taking on water quality projects following successful operations.

CONCLUSIONS

The models, case studies, and interview data presented in this chapter cast doubt that project evaluations are capable of prompting selectivity, except when they overcome uncertainty that limits demand for environment-improving projects and activities. Because previous work has shown environmental projects must align with the priorities of recipients in order to be successful (Connolly 1996), focusing evaluations on solving information problems for borrowers should be a clear priority. As a practical matter, this might mean focusing evaluation efforts on the types of projects that both meet local environmental needs and are relatively new parts of a country's borrowing portfolio.

Under pressure from the largest member countries to increase environmental lending that contributes to global environmental goods, there is little chance for the development banks to practice selectivity. The results of the analysis presented in this chapter suggest that development banks face incentives that detract from their impact and effectiveness. Indeed, it is somewhat puzzling that donor countries continue to push for a rapid expansion of clean-energy lending, when pressure to lend without regard for performance has been the root of so many problems at the multilateral development banks.

Recent research has explored how emerging economies have maintained a unified bargaining position on climate change in order to increase financing from donor countries (Kasa, Gullberg, and Heggelund 2008). To the extent that large emitters are able to maintain this coalition, donor countries may have no choice but to continue financing large emitters without regard for performance. The results presented here suggest that the multilateral development banks are not in a strong position to facilitate the production of global environmental goods in cost-effective ways, given their positioning between donor and recipient governments and the international politics of climate change.

In response to the findings in this chapter, interviewees suggested that I examine the effect of country program evaluations. These evaluations are written to feed directly into the process of planning country portfolios, and because they are considered by high-level decision-makers and state representatives, they may have more of an effect on allocation. Thus, in the next chapter I turn to the question of whether the provisioning of performance information into a formal decision process that involves state shareholders can promote selectivity in allocation.

7

Strategic Planning

INTEGRATING EVALUATION INTO HIGH-LEVEL

DECISION-MAKING

STRATEGIC PLANNING—THE PROCESS an organization undertakes to align its future actions with its goals in light of its environment—is the last pathway to selectivity that I assess in this book. Many types of organizations engage in strategic planning for many reasons. It may be the case that the environment where the organization operates has changed in a way that requires a new direction. New strategies might be necessary to deal with the changing actions of other organizations, new public policies, or changing market environments. It is often equally important to assess whether past actions have successfully achieved the goals of the organization, especially if the goals of the organization remain the same. In a way, strategic planning is the most obvious setting for evaluations to influence decision-making in organizations. Strategic planning typically involves decision-makers that have authority to change the plans of an organization in light of assessments about past performance and new information about the strategic environment.

Despite the natural pairing of strategic planning and evaluation, there are barriers to the incorporation of evaluation results into future plans. As discussed in the previous chapter, decision-makers might be skeptical about the findings or recommendations in evaluations, especially if the evaluators lack direct operational experience. Actions that led to poor results might have been recognized and corrected in real time and thus be moot by the time they are discussed in an evaluation. Evaluators might make recommendations that are not operationally viable, given their analytical training and relative lack of operational experience. There are both strong positive and negative reasons to expect that evaluation will have an influence on strategic planning and thus the actions of organizations that undertake strategic planning. Indeed, past research on the role of evaluation in strategic planning has yielded mixed results (Pearce, Freeman, and Robinson 1987; Mintzberg 1994; Berry and Wechsler 1995; Bryson 2010).

In light of these mixed results, I seek to delineate and test the conditions that allow high-level, thematic evaluations to impact lending plans and thus future decisions about allocation at the multilateral development banks. Doing so will help explain when and why strategic planning with high-level decision-makers can be used to overcome performance problems at international organizations. I extend the core argument of this book that the multilateral development banks will respond to past performance and recommendations when doing so helps them to approve new projects expeditiously. The question is then whether the results of past projects come to light in a way that empowers states and other powerful stakeholders to effectively demand changes to lending or helps operational staff overcome uncertainty that limits demand from borrowing countries. Since strategic planning takes place at all types of international organizations, the results speak to more general questions about the mechanisms of state control over international organizations. At its best, strategic planning is a process that empowers decision-makers to use information about past performance to align decision-making with desired results.

For the multilateral development banks, the creation of multiyear country assistance strategies brings together information about performance and a setting where donor countries have significant influence over future decisions. States that oversee the multilateral development banks are most directly involved in setting strategies and policies that transcend individual projects. The question is then whether information provided about the performance of the entire lending portfolio of a country can help to steer future lending toward high-performing projects and away from low-performing projects.

The participation of states in decision-making about country assistance strategies is important for overcoming the problems with project evaluations that were highlighted in previous chapters. During the interviews that I conducted at the headquarters of the multilateral development banks, evaluation staff were skeptical that individual project evaluations directly influenced lending decisions. Project evaluations are often completed several years after the close of projects, limiting their relevance to future operations. If the only function of project evaluation, as one country manager argued, is to tell operational staff "what they already know," then tens of millions of dollars might be redirected toward providing information that is more relevant to approval and allocation decisions.

A focused examination of strategic planning and evaluation thus offers an important window into managing discretion at large and complex organizations like the multilateral development banks because it focuses on information that reaches influential decision-makers. One of the primary challenges for states is that they are unable to monitor the myriad decisions made by international organizations on a regular basis (Dai 2007; Hawkins et al. 2006b). Even more important, they are unable to intervene and micromanage the frontline actions of organizations because they lack technical expertise and are thwarted by simple logistical challenges (Weaver 2008). Under these circumstances, member states created opportunities to influence high-level decisions and directions, potentially gaining indirect influence over the multitude of small decisions that are beyond their reach. Jupille (2004) describes how states seek to exert control over high-level procedures and rules to expand their influence and power in international organizations, recognizing the limitations they face in directly controlling the actions of frontline international bureaucrats. Evaluations that aggregate performance information might be an important way to overcome challenges of technical expertise and complexity.

The limits of project evaluation have not gone unnoticed by evaluation departments themselves. Beginning in the mid-1990s, the leadership of evaluation departments at the multilateral development banks recognized that they needed to prioritize new types of evaluations that were more relevant to the formulation of assistance strategies and sensitive to the timing of decisions about allocation. Since their establishment, the multilateral development banks have all planned assistance strategies for individual countries on a multiyear basis. According to Robert Picciotto, director-general of operations evaluation at the World Bank from 1992 to 2002, evaluation activities shifted during the mid-1990s in recognition that the most important lending decisions were being made in the context of multiyear country planning:

> The first of the strategic objectives—move to a higher plane—was driven by the comprehensive development agenda adopted by the Bank. It paralleled the shift of the Bank's privileged unit of account from the project to the country assistance strategy. The move to the higher plane called for systematic evaluation of country assistance strategies and for feeding evaluation findings into the Bank's sector strategy papers. (Picciotto 2003, 66)

In 1995, the Operations Evaluation Department at the World Bank completed the first in a series of these "new style" evaluations, which reviewed "the relevance and efficacy of the Bank's overall country assistance strategy and the effectiveness of various lending and nonlending instruments of Bank assistance" (Operations Evaluation Department 1995, memorandum). This new style of evaluation was "a performance audit report on the Bank's total assistance program" (7). Whereas project evaluations were narrowly focused on single operations, *country program evaluations* assessed the performance of whole sectors and types of projects within a borrowing country's portfolio over multiple years and made recommendations about future lending. This offered the opportunity to aggregate findings and provide more useful recommendations to high-level decision-makers.

Country program evaluations are different from project evaluations because they are directly integrated into the process of designing strategies for country lending. Every three to five years, the multilateral development banks plan a multiyear lending strategy for each borrowing country. As part of this process, management of the multilateral banks and borrowing country ministries discuss the sectors and types of projects that will best address development needs, accounting for emerging priorities and past lessons. Country program evaluations are often produced prior to these negotiations and are intended to make new assistance strategies response to past results. Each country program evaluation contains recommendations for the new country assistance strategy. The MDB management must respond to these recommendations at board and sub-board meetings, where donor countries exert considerable influence (World Bank 2009a).[1] In the words of the inaugural Asian Development Bank country program evaluation for China in 1998, "The objective is to draw lessons from past experience and to suggest ways of improving country assistance plans" (Operations Evaluation Department 1998a, iv).

In this chapter, I test whether high-level evaluations that are built into the process of designing lending strategies prompt the selective allocation of environmental projects based on recommendations and past performance. Since these evaluations are designed to solve information problems facing state representatives and managers at multilateral banks, they offer a way to examine whether the lack of information in a usable form is the fundamental constraint limiting selectivity. To the extent that future lending decisions are responsive to recommendations made in country program evaluations, integrating evaluations into core decision-making processes would be an important way to promote better oversight of international organizations. To the extent that future lending decisions are unresponsive to recommendations made in country program evaluations, this indicates that information problems are not a primary reason why the multilateral development banks fail to practice selectivity.

AUDIENCE, PROCESS, AND INFORMATION AGGREGATION
EFFECTS: HYPOTHESES FROM INTERVIEWS

High-level evaluations and strategic planning are common across large organizations. Corporations regularly create organization-wide strategic plans, and these
plans can have positive effects on performance and coordination across units, even
when significant autonomy, flexibility, and discretion are maintained by managers
(Andersen 2000). Bureaucratic agencies have substantially increased their effort
devoted to strategic planning and have developed management systems that can put
plans into action (Poister 2010). Likewise, international organizations hold regular meetings with member states to review progress on collective goals and set new
directions. The multilateral development banks are no exception, with management holding regular consultations with shareholder countries, often to review past
achievements and chart new directions.

Strategic planning can be an effective way to manage discretion at large organizations because it prompts decision-makers to step back and assess the cumulative
outcomes of many small decisions. When aided by evaluation, this process offers an
opportunity to correct decisions that have not led to good results and capitalize on
decisions that have led to good results, potentially leading to selectivity. By aggregating information and creating common understanding about performance between
principals and agents, this process can also raise expectations for accountability
by revealing whether the agent acted in ways that are aligned with the principal's
preferences. Aggregate evaluations are also likely to reduce uncertainty about what
programs are likely to work and why by looking across the strategic environment.
At the multilateral development banks in particular, strategic planning might make
member states aware of big-picture issues that lead to the poor outcomes in particular countries and prompt them to adjust lending portfolios.

Indeed, operational and evaluation staff at World Bank, the Asian Development
Bank, the Inter-American Development Bank, and the African Development
Bank reported that country program evaluation should have the most direct
impact on lending decisions among the different types of evaluations for several reasons. First, recommendations contained in country program evaluations
are likely to be more influential because of an *audience effect*, which is created
by significant involvement of donor states in assessing past performance. Second,
unlike project evaluations, country program evaluations are directly integrated
into the process of designing country strategies, likely making them more influential because of a *process effect*. Third, performance information about lending
outcomes is scattered among a variety of different reports and evaluation prod-
ucts, especially environmental performance that is often a subcomponent of larger

project evaluations. Country program evaluations synthesize dispersed information, making conclusions about performance more accessible, which I call the *information aggregation effect*.

Anecdotal evidence suggests that the combination of these effects gives country program evaluations the potential to shape lending decisions. A recent example is the *Country Assistance Program Evaluation for Pakistan* that the Asian Development Bank completed in 2007. This evaluation chronicled the achievements of lending and technical assistance projects in the country since 1985. This was the first "whole-program" evaluation for Pakistan, and it sought to examine whether decisions about portfolio composition were properly aligned with development targets. The findings and recommendations indicated that decisions about allocation were not being made effectively:

> ADB has too many loans in its Pakistan portfolio, spread across too many sectors and subsectors . . . since resources are unlikely to increase significantly, the number of loans must be reduced. . . . ADB should reduce the number of sectors and subsectors in which it is involved. (Operations Evaluation Department 2007d, vii)

Particular to environment-improving lending, the same evaluation found that investments in water supply, sanitation, and waste management were largely unsuccessful (Operations Evaluation Department 2007d, v). In its conclusion, the evaluation recommended that the future portfolio should focus on other sectors:

> Under this [proposed] scenario, ADB would move out of the health, water supply and sanitation, and urban development sectors . . . urban development, which has a prominent place in the pipeline portfolio, does not feature under the scenario because of past poor performance in this area . . . clear evidence would be needed that the approach proposed, and/or changed context, would increase significantly the chances of success [in this sector]. (41)

Following this evaluation, the ADB management developed a new country assistance strategy that focused on only four sectors. From January 2007 to August 2008, the number of active loans was reduced from 80 to 58 (Asian Development Bank 2009). The country assistance strategy mentions that this process was driven by "major attention" to the findings of the country program evaluation (Asian Development Bank 2009, para. 41). This process showed the potential for *country program evaluations* to influence portfolio composition decisions in ways that are not possible with individual project evaluations, which are limited to single operations. Before proceeding, it is worth explaining how this might have occurred in greater detail.

Audience Effect

State shareholders of the multilateral development banks are involved primarily in high-level and strategic decisions that structure a broad range of day-to-day operational practices. Given the size and complexity of operations at the multilateral banks, member states have a very limited ability to monitor project-level decisions and outcomes, unless they are forced into the spotlight through the inspection process (see chapter 5). Explaining the source of slack between state preferences and World Bank behavior, Ascher comments that "the proliferation and increasing complexity of projects has reduced the capacity of the Executive Board to oversee the Bank's operations with any mastery" (1983, 422). More broadly, the inability of states to monitor day-to-day operations at international organizations has been cited as a key source of slack between state preferences and the actions of international organizations (Lyne, Nielson, and Tierney 2006).

Both operational and evaluation staff at the multilateral development banks reported that country program evaluations are likely to have a larger influence on allocation decisions than project evaluations because they appeal directly to an audience of donor states, which at the World Bank and Asian Development Bank have a majority on the board. Donor countries have stated an increasing interest in promoting accountability for results. In addition, donor countries have typically been interested in increasing the supply of environment-improving lending. Recommendations to emphasize environment-improving operations in country program evaluations might help donors' push for environment-improving lending. One operational staff member at the World Bank commented that the country planning process is "where the action takes place" in terms of donor country influence on allocation.[2] Thus, country program evaluations benefit from an engaged audience that is capable of steering allocation decisions.

In practice, state shareholders most directly engage country program evaluations as part of sub-board development effectiveness committees that oversee the performance of bank operations. At both the World Bank and Asian Development Bank, the Development Effectiveness Committee meets to discuss all country program evaluations and is tasked with ensuring that recommendations are properly addressed before a final country assistance strategy comes to the full board for approval. For each country program evaluation, high-level meetings are held between state representatives to the committee, vice-presidential-level operational staff, and evaluation directors to discuss and address evaluation findings.

At the Inter-American Development Bank the similar sub-board committee is the Policy and Evaluation Committee. Thus, unlike project evaluations, state shareholders are well apprised of the content and recommendations in country program evaluations. A World Bank assessment found that state representatives most often look at the recommendations in country program evaluations and management's plan to address them in preparation for board meetings where country assistance strategies are discussed and approved (Operations Evaluation Department 2005a).[3]

Other studies of evaluations have found that appealing to authoritative decision-makers is key to influence. Scientific reports and evaluations that are influential at the international level almost always have the attention of key decision-makers (Bamberger 2000). Mitchell and colleagues (2006) find that the influence of global environmental assessments must be understood in "relational" terms, that is the extent to which they are relevant, timely, and credible to a particular decision-making audience, rather than the specific content contained within assessments. For the International Monetary Fund, Weaver (2010) finds that higher-level, cross-cutting evaluations often have the greatest influence on the organization because they feed into decisions made at the board level. Selin (2006, 178) examined scientific assessments related to persistent organic pollutants and found that assessments that were pushed into "higher-level political agendas" were the most influential. Thus, because country program evaluations more effectively engage state shareholders with recommendations about performance, they might have an important influence on decisions about allocation.

Process Effect

Country program evaluations are also likely to have a more direct influence on allocation decisions than project evaluations because they are formally integrated into the process of designing new country assistance strategies, which in turn steer lending decisions (see Picciotto 2002, 10). At several points in this process, the findings and recommendations in country program evaluations are considered by both member states and operational staff. In contrast, when I spoke with evaluation staff at the multilateral development banks, they could not identify a specific process that required bank management or state shareholders to actively address the recommendations in project evaluations. The common components of the country assistance strategy process across the multilateral development banks are these:

1. Evaluation department drafts a country program evaluation.
2. Operational staff comment on the country program evaluation draft.
3. Evaluation department finalizes the country program evaluation.

4. Management issues a response to the recommendations in the country program evaluation.

5. Evaluation department, sub-board Development Effectiveness Committee, and senior operational management meet to discuss the country program evaluation and management responses.

6. Country team drafts a concept note for country assistance strategy.

7. Evaluation department provides interdepartmental comment on the concept note.

8. Country team drafts a country assistance strategy.

9. Evaluation department provides interdepartmental comment on the draft strategy.

10. Board members provide comments on the draft strategy.

11. Country team prepares a final country assistance strategy.

12. Board considers the final country assistance strategy for approval.

Importantly, this process requires both the board and operational staff to deal with the findings and recommendations of country program evaluations at several points. The country teams that are responsible for writing country assistance strategies pass drafts around to relevant technical and evaluation departments for comment, both when the strategy is in a concept phase and when a full draft of the country assistance strategy is available. When evaluators comment on draft country assistance strategies, they highlight the findings and recommendations in country program evaluations. One evaluator at the ADB reported that these comments are taken seriously by the team drafting the country assistance strategy, because delays can result if interdepartmental comments are not addressed properly in the opinion of board members or senior operational management. In addition, operational managers must justify their response to the recommendations in country program evaluations to board members. The degree to which they properly address such recommendations are often critical parts of board discussions about country assistance strategies.[4] To the extent that recommendations are incorporated into the strategy, they have a high likelihood of impacting lending decisions, since new projects must reference how they support the overall country assistance strategy.[5]

Institutional processes constrain the ways that information is used within organizations. Accordingly, most research on the utilization of evaluations more generally has found that the integration of evaluations into decision-making processes is more important than evaluation content. For instance, Clark and colleagues (2006, 14) find that global environmental assessments become influential not by containing certain types of content, but rather by being well integrated into "the social process of assessment." Information in the form of assessments, analysis, and evaluation is often most influential when it has a clear and institutionalized role in some specific decision (Hansson 2006). Patton (2008), a pioneer in utilization focused evaluation, argues that useful recommendations must be formulated in ways that directly address the context of decision-making. Thus, influential evaluations must focus not only on the credibility and validity of findings, but must be designed for the decisions and settings they intend to influence. This argument echoes much of the evaluation literature that has thought of influential evaluations as a collaborative process between decision-makers and evaluators (Mathison 1994; Torres and Preskill 2001; Weiss 1998).

Information Aggregation Effect

Decision-makers at large organizations must often search through dispersed sources of information when making strategic decisions; designing a country assistance strategy is no exception. Research on strategic decision-making has found that the accessibility of synthesized information is critical in complex settings (O'Reilly 1982; Hardy 1982). Indeed, one of the primary challenges is not so much the lack of information, but the organization of information in ways that are usable to decision-makers. As one evaluator at the World Bank stated, country program evaluations have the advantages of driving operational changes because they address issues that cut across multiple projects.

This point has not gone unnoticed by scholars who are interested in the utilization of evaluations within organizations. As Feinstein (2002, 436) writes, "Evaluation use capacity involves a capacity to search for relevant information." Even if state shareholders wanted to seek out information about environmental performance when considering country assistance strategies, they would face extremely high transaction costs in processing diverse streams of performance information from the multilateral development banks. Indeed, Weaver (2008, 70) is skeptical that the board can provide oversight for the multilateral development banks because "supervision of policies and programs requires extensive time and expert resources." Thus, to the extent that country program evaluations aggregate performance information and utilize more macro-level measures of performance (Gutner and Thompson 2010), they solve information problems for the principals of the multilateral development banks in ways that project evaluations cannot. Indeed, scholars have argued that the primary reason donor countries have pushed to establish independent evaluation at international organizations is "to reduce information asymmetries to enable donors to better hold Fund staff and management to account for process and outcome performance" (Weaver 2010, 378). Many operational staff that I spoke with at the multilateral development banks thought that thematic evaluations are more influential because they are able to synthesize highly dispersed information about performance across programs.

It is not only by aggregating information for donor countries that evaluations are likely to be more influential. Evaluation offices also view management and staff of the development banks as important stakeholders who must also search out diverse sources of dispersed information when making decisions about allocating projects. Thus, country program evaluations might also help MDB staff to organize information about performance in ways that can lead to better decisions. A recent OED assessment found influential evaluations tend to aggregate findings across projects (Operations Evaluation Department 2004). A similar review at the Asian Development Bank also found that aggregate evaluations were most influential (Operations Evaluation Department 2007e, sec. 7). A review of the IMF Independent Evaluation Office found that senior staff found synthesizing reports most useful for making decisions about broad strategic issues (Lissakers, Husain, and Woods 2006, 23). Thus, country program evaluations may be useful to state shareholders that face significant challenges of processing information about performance in achieving mandated outcomes.

Hypotheses

The MDB staff whom I interviewed believed that the findings and recommendations contained in country program evaluations should be more likely to have a direct effect on lending decisions than the findings contained in project evaluations. Given the audience, process, and information aggregation effects that should be driven by country program evaluations, I test whether the findings and recommendations contained in country program evaluations drive selectivity. In particular, I expect that donor state representatives will use recommendations that suggest a focus on environment-improving projects and activities to steer future allocation decisions in that direction:

> **Hypothesis 1:** Borrowing countries that receive a recommendation to focus on clean-energy operations will receive more projects with a primary clean-energy purpose and more clean-energy activities in all projects.

> **Hypothesis 2:** Borrowing countries that receive a recommendation to focus on urban environmental operations will receive more projects with a primary urban environment purpose and more urban environment activities in all projects.

The findings in country program evaluations might also promote selectivity, by indicating that certain types of projects are successful or unsuccessful on average.

Although representatives from member states do not report spending a great deal of time sifting through the details of country program evaluations (see below), it might be the case that statements about the performance of environment-improving activities and projects will strengthen the position of successful operations in the country assistance strategy and reduce the presence of unsuccessful operations:

Hypothesis 3: Borrowing countries with a country program evaluation that indicates environment-improving operations are successful (unsuccessful) will be more (less) likely to receive environment-improving projects and activities in the future.

COUNTRY PROGRAM EVALUATIONS AT THE MULTILATERAL DEVELOPMENT BANKS

The World Bank Operations Evaluation Department completed the first country program evaluation for Ghana in 1995.[6] The Asian Development Bank soon followed suit, completing its first country program evaluation for China in 1998. In 2001, the African Development Bank and Inter-American Development Bank evaluation departments completed their first country program evaluations (figure 7.1). However, since that time, the country program evaluation has grown into being a primary product of each of the evaluation offices, rising in number each period, with the exception of the World Bank Independent Evaluation Group.[7]

Country program evaluations consider a wide variety of sectors for general operational lessons. Information about environmental performance does not enjoy any special emphasis. Thus, the inclusion of information about environmental

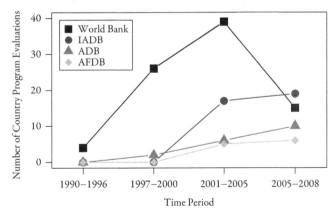

FIGURE 7.1 Number of country program evaluations at the multilateral development banks, 1990–2008

performance in country program evaluations is dependent on how important eval-uators believe it is to achieving broad, country-level development targets. Indeed, across the different multilateral development banks, there is substantial variation in the extent to which environmental performance information appears in evaluations.

The country program evaluations themselves are thick documents filled with micro-level detail and analysis. As such, they are not specifically intended to be read by representatives of the member states. Indeed, surveys of these representatives indicate that the member states scan them for overall findings and assess whether the management is taking findings seriously in its response (Operations Evaluation Department 2005a).

To examine whether findings and recommendations in country program evalu-ations influence lending decisions, I assembled a team to code whether 21 binary items related to environmental performance appear in each of the country eval-uations that have been completed since 1990 by four multilateral development banks. Rather than attempting to code performance on an ordinal scale, as with project evaluations, we found it more reliable to code whether specific pieces of information were present in the different sections of the country program evalu-ations. The coding procedure (described in greater detail in appendix 1) focuses on four main sections of the country program evaluations. First, the executive summary often receives the most attention by higher-level decision-makers. Thus, we coded whether the country evaluation recognized environmental programs as a priority within a particular borrowing country and whether information indi-cating the achievement of environmental goals was contained in the executive summary. Second, we noted whether evaluators considered environmental issues to be a priority development issue for a particular borrower. We coded a variety of items on whether background information identified environmental degra-dation as a development constraint. Third, we coded any documentation about the achievement of environmental objectives from the analytical sections of the country program evaluations. Finally, we coded whether final recommendations emphasized the desirability of environmental projects in future periods. Table 7.1 contains descriptive information for some of the coded items used in the analysis below. The percentages show the proportion of evaluations that were positive on a particular coding item.[8]

Evaluations at the World Bank and the Asian Development Bank more often deal with environmental outcomes and produce more recommendations related to the environment than the Inter-American and African Development banks. This reflects prevailing wisdom that the IADB and AFDB have placed less emphasis on environmental operations because borrowing countries enjoy majorities on their boards. One of the other striking findings in the descriptive data is despite focus

TABLE 7.1

DESCRIPTIVE DATA ON SELECTED ITEMS CODED FROM COUNTRY
PROGRAM EVALUATIONS, 1990–2008

	World Bank	IADB	ADB	AFDB
Total country evaluations	84	36	18	11
Executive Summary				
Environment identified as programmatic priority	14%	24%	33%	0%
Background section				
Concern over degradation of global environmental resources	8%	9%	28%	0%
Concern over environmental degradation for local well-being	42%	28%	61%	27%
Performance assessment section(s)				
Specific evaluation section dealing with environmental performance	40%	25%	78%	45%
Unsatisfactory environmental outcomes	40%	41%	72%	9%
Unsatisfactory borrower environmental implementation	24%	19%	44%	0%
Satisfactory environmental outcomes	45%	38%	61%	45%
Satisfactory borrower environmental implementation	15%	0%	5%	0%
Conclusions and recommendations				
Emphasize any environmental goals in future lending	20%	8%	33%	9%
Emphasize clean-energy goals in future lending	4%	0%	11%	0%
Emphasize urban environment goals in future lending	6%	3%	17%	0%

Note: Percentage is calculated by dividing the number of evaluations where information is present by the total number of evaluations where the relevant section is present.

by the IADB on environmental performance in country program evaluations, recommendations about future environment-improving operations are almost never made. Because the IADB and AFDB do not make many recommendations based on environmental performance, there is not an opportunity to be more selective about allocation because of recommendations.

CASE STUDY: COUNTRY-LEVEL PLANNING FOR BANGLADESH
AT THE ASIAN DEVELOPMENT BANK

To illustrate how country program evaluations can contribute to greater selectivity at the multilateral development banks, I turn to Bangladesh and the Asian Development Bank. As of the time of writing, Bangladesh is one of the only countries that has been through multiple cycles of country program evaluation and the planning of new country assistance strategies. Because the country program evaluations in Bangladesh called for greater selectivity in the portfolio, it offers an illustration of the logic behind the idea that selectivity can be promoted by solving the information needs of decision-makers in authority. In response to a series of country program evaluations that indicated poor performance, the portfolio became more focused and the results of development assistance to Bangladesh improved.

The Asian Development Bank began lending to Bangladesh in 1973, shortly after it achieved independence. Much like its lending portfolio to other countries at the time, the Asian Development Bank pursued a broad and multisector lending portfolio without clear sector or thematic priorities. While the 1993 Country Operation Strategy by the Asian Development Bank shifted toward poverty reduction from economic growth, by this time a wide-ranging lending portfolio had become entrenched. The broad approach did not yield good results, as operational management itself later recognized. According to the 2000 country assistance plan for the period 2001–2003, of the projects in the lending portfolio that had been evaluated, only 37% were classified as "generally successful," compared to the average rate of 54% across the organization (Asian Development Bank 2000). As a consequence, the assistance plan advocated halving the number of sectors in the portfolio by postponing new investments in sectors like water resource management and forestry where there was not clear evidence of government commitment.

In 2003, the evaluation group at the Asian Development Bank completed an evaluation of the progress made under this country assistance plan. The evaluation indicated that limited progress had been made toward a more focused lending portfolio. The evaluation criticized continued involvement in sectors where there was limited evidence of government commitment and a poor record, such as railway projects. The evaluation also highlighted that the lack of performance goals in operations limited the degree to which management at the Asian Development Bank could practice evidence-based selectivity. This evaluation also raised concerns about the divergent preferences of management with respect to the directives for greater selectivity laid out in the 2001–2003 assistance plan:

Despite the gradual transformation of ADB from a lending institution to a broad-based development institution, it is not yet clear whether this has been reflected in a general change in the pattern of ADB's interventions or the institutional priorities that determine them. In particular, the country program still appears to be unduly influenced by the urge to meet minimum targets for loan approvals and/or disbursements during a given period of time. Consequently, loans that involve a relatively low level of funding relative to the time and resources required to prepare and administer them are less favored even if their developmental impact and demonstration effect might be significant over the long term. (Operations Evaluation Department 2003, 52)

As an example, the country program evaluation highlighted that there had been no follow-up to the successful Small and Cottage Industries Project, which extended financial access to smaller private firms. The evaluation argued that future lending strategies should be formulated on the basis of past results. In other words, future lending strategies should be more selective, a goal that was not being achieved because of misaligned incentives. The evaluation further cautioned that additional lending should not be pursued for reform efforts related to capital markets and railways until Bangladeshi authorities demonstrated more commitment.

The next country assistance strategy, formulated in 2005 for the 2006–2010 period, took these recommendations into consideration. Progress was already being made toward a more selective portfolio. Management noted that $138 million in loans to Bangladesh had either been restructured or canceled between 2001 and 2005. This was not a token amount, considering that Bangladesh received about $300 million annually during this period. But this assistance strategy also showed evidence of a direct response to recommendations contained in the 2003 country program evaluation and a commitment to modify lending in response to the evaluation. For example, the country assistance strategy stated that "consistent with the [country program evaluation] recommendations, ADB will provide capacity building for capital market development, and only provide major support when the Government is prepared to proceed with key reforms" (Asian Development Bank 2005).

In 2009, the Independent Evaluation Group completed a second country program evaluation for Bangladesh and noted improvements in performance, with 79% of completed projects since the previous country program evaluation rated as successful. This evaluation also noted that investments had become more focused, with programming declining from five sectors in 2004 to three sectors in 2008. A similar pattern is reported for technical assistance activities, though technical assistance covered roughly twice as many sectors. Despite increasing success in achieving outcomes, the evaluation noted that new projects were approved in sectors that were not recommended, particularly related to rural livelihood development. The evaluation noted that development lending had actually broadened in some areas, such as law and economic management. The evaluation also noted that while management had adopted performance benchmarks, less than a third had been met, and most were very broad and not under the realistic control of the development programs financed by the bank. Despite these concerns, this new evaluation noted that both the strategy and the lending program shifted to support fewer sectors.

In 2011, a new country assistance strategy was adopted, and again this strategy contained a great deal of information about how the upcoming lending program would respond to recommendations in the 2009 country program evaluation. In particular, management agreed that a stronger and more specific results framework would be developed and modified annually, with the goal of ensuring that ongoing decisions about lending and project implementation are made in light of the outcomes of programs. At the time of writing, the measures of program accomplishments are tracked and made publicly available, along with information about the latest project effectiveness ratings for active projects. In the future, it will be useful to examine whether this new strategy has improved the management and selection of projects that are part of the Bangladesh lending portfolio.

While this sequence of evaluations and strategies demonstrates direct connections between recommendations and lending strategies, it also shows the slow and sometimes cumbersome path to selectivity. Since management at the Asian Development Bank were under strong pressures to meet lending goals, early recommendations were not always implemented immediately. Nonetheless, the move toward a narrower lending program and a focus on measuring results for accountability appear to be the direct result of country program evaluations, as stated in subsequent strategies.

MODELING THE INFLUENCE OF COUNTRY PROGRAM EVALUATION RECOMMENDATIONS

Systematic data compiled from country program evaluations can be used to test whether findings and recommendations influence later decisions about lending more generally, both for stand-alone clean-energy and urban environment projects and for projects that have activities in these areas. The main variables used in the analysis below are indicators of information about performance from the analysis sections of country program evaluations and recommendations about future lending.

For findings about performance, I introduce several new variables that were coded from country program evaluations as described above. *POOR ENV.*

PERFORMANCE and *GOOD ENV. PERFORMANCE* are positive when unsatisfactory or satisfactory achievement of environmental goals are noted to be the results of borrowing country actions in the last five years. At some of the multilateral development banks, particularly the Asian Development Bank, attributing poor performance to the borrowing country is not a norm, thus only satisfactory environmental outcomes (*GOOD ENV. OUTCOME*) and unsatisfactory environmental outcomes (*POOR ENV. OUTCOME*) are used in models, again for the previous five years. This information is coded from the body of the evaluation.

Internal studies on the use of country program evaluations indicate that board members infrequently use information from the body of evaluation texts in their discussions of country strategies, focusing instead on recommendations, which may heighten the audience effect (Operations Evaluation Department 2005a, annexes C–D). I split recommendations that appear in country program evaluations into three variables. First, *ENV. RECOMMENDATION* indicates that a recommendation was made to increase lending emphasis for environment-improving targets. By contrast, *CLEAN ENERGY RECOMMENDATION* and *UEI RECOMMENDATION* are subsets that indicate a recommendation was made specifically to emphasize clean-energy or urban environment-improving lending in subsequent years. The projects and activities approved following these recommendations are the primary outcomes of interest in this analysis. In all cases, the binary variables from the country program evaluations become positive beginning the year after the evaluation is completed and remain so for five years, roughly the cycle of country assistance strategies.

In all of the models reported below, I employed a random-intercept probit model. The unit of analysis is the country-year. In most cases, I examine the effect of evaluation findings and recommendations on both the full panel and within the subset of years covered by a country program evaluation, to account for selection into evaluation.

Clean-Energy Projects and Project Components

Table 7.2 displays regression results for the approval of clean-energy projects by the World Bank. The Inter-American Development Bank had only one clean-energy project approved during a year covered by a country program evaluation, and the African Development Bank does not have a portfolio of clean-energy projects. This makes statistical modeling for these cases impossible. For the Asian Development Bank, no country receives a clean-energy project in a year that is covered by a recommendation for clean-energy lending or by a country program evaluation more generally, making it impossible to model this relationship empirically. Results from these banks are omitted for these reasons.

TABLE 7.2

COUNTRY PROGRAM EVALUATIONS AND APPROVAL DECISIONS ABOUT
CLEAN-ENERGY PROJECTS AT THE WORLD BANK

Model	1a	1b	1c	1d
MDB	World	World	World	World
CLEAN ENERGY RECOMMENDATION	1.89 (1.48)		−0.36 (1.49)	
ENV. RECOMMENDATION		0.43 (0.63)		−0.05 (0.50)
POOR ENV. PERFORMANCE	−0.30 (0.67)	−0.55 (0.77)	−0.64 (0.58)	−0.62 (0.58)
GOOD ENV. PERFORMANCE	1.01* (0.67)	1.07* (0.67)	0.31 (0.52)	0.34 (0.52)
CO_2 GT	−0.21 (0.42)	0.12 (0.29)	0.23 (0.30)	0.17 (0.16)
CONCESSIONAL	−0.28 (0.46)	−0.27 (0.47)	−0.34 (0.41)	−0.33 (0.41)
NO. PROJECT PREV 5 YRS	0.02** (0.01)	0.04** (0.02)	0.02 (0.02)	0.02 (0.02)
YEAR (COUNT)	0.03 (0.03)	0.03 (0.03)	0.05 (0.07)	0.05 (0.07)
Random intercept variance	2.38	2.56	0.00	0.00
Data subset	Full panel	Full panel	Covered by country evaluation	Covered by country evaluation
Observations (countries)	1,443 (135)	1,443 (135)	311 (68)	311 (68)
Residual deviance	149.2	150.7	55.9	55.9
Null deviance	166.2	371.9	58.5	58.5

Note: All models are random-intercept probit estimated by Laplace approximation.
Statistical significance of one-tailed hypothesis test: * $p < .1$, ** $p < .05$.

For the World Bank, it was possible to examine both the effect of clean-energy recommendations and general environmental recommendations. For stand-alone clean-energy projects, in no model did a specific or general environmental recommendation increase the probability of receiving clean-energy projects in future years. For the World Bank, there was no discernible effect of clean-energy recommendations on clean-energy lending (table 7.2, Models 1a, 1c). Likewise, recommendations to emphasize any environmental targets have no discernible effect on subsequent clean-energy lending (table 7.2, Models 1b, 1d). These results indicate that clean-energy recommendations do not influence future lending decisions.

I find limited evidence that the environmental performance reported in country program evaluations influences lending decisions about clean-energy projects. In the models based on the full panel data set (Models 1a–1b), information about good environmental performance is associated with a clean-energy project being allocated in subsequent years. This effect is not present in years covered by a country program evaluation, making it difficult to assess whether the effect reflects countries with better performance being evaluated more often. As expected, countries that received a larger total number of projects are more likely to receive clean-energy projects in the full panel, but this effect is not present for the subset of country-years covered by country program evaluations.

It may be the case that recommendations to pursue environmental or clean-energy goals in future lending do not influence the allocation of stand-alone projects, but rather whether clean-energy activities are incorporated into other types of projects. Indeed, "environmental mainstreaming" has been one of the primary ways that the multilateral development banks have increased their focus on the environment (Hicks et al. 2008). In order to identify which projects have clean-energy activities, I utilized activity codes from AidData and included any project with renewable energy activities and/or energy conservation activities (Tierney et al. 2011).

Similar to the results reported above, the evidence does not show that recommendations about either clean-energy projects or general environmental recommendations make it more likely that countries will receive projects with clean-energy activities in subsequent years (table 7.3, Models 2a–3b). Instead, the level of carbon emissions from a particular borrowing country is a strong predictor of whether the multilateral development banks approve projects with clean-energy components. The only case where carbon emissions are not a statistically significant predictor (Model 2b) occurs because having a clean-energy recommendation is collinear with carbon emissions. For purposes of consistent exposition, both variables are included in table 7.3.

For the World Bank (Models 2a–2b), there is evidence of an association between the results of environmental activities reported in country program evaluations and the future approval of projects with clean-energy activities. This association holds both for the full panel of country-years and for only those country-years that are covered by a country program evaluation, indicating results in these evaluations may be more likely to drive selectivity, a result that was not present with project evaluations (see chapter 6). In terms of control variables, the allocation of projects with clean-energy activities is less common for countries with larger portfolios and more common in later years of the period under consideration.

TABLE 7.3

COUNTRY PROGRAM EVALUATIONS AND APPROVAL DECISIONS ABOUT
PROJECTS WITH CLEAN-ENERGY ACTIVITIES

Model	2a	2b	3a	3b
MDB	World	World	Asian	Asian
CLEAN ENERGY RECOMMENDATION	−1.08 (0.81)	−0.55 (1.38)		
POOR ENV. PERFORMANCE	−0.77** (0.32)	−0.63** (0.35)		
GOOD ENV. PERFORMANCE	0.81** (0.32)	0.86** (0.33)		
ENV. RECOMMENDATION			0.93 (0.80)	2.47 (2.47)
POOR ENV. OUTCOME			−0.77 (0.65)	−1.64 (2.17)
GOOD ENV. OUTCOME			−1.09 (0.79)	−2.20 (2.13)
CO_2 GT	0.20* (0.15)	0.14 (0.27)	2.02** (0.71)	3.07* (2.11)
CONCESSIONAL	−0.16 (0.13)	0.11 (0.27)	−0.09 (0.28)	−0.21 (2.69)
NO. PROJECT PREV 5 YRS	0.02** (0.01)	0.02 (0.01)	0.01** (0.00)	0.02 (0.02)
YEAR (COUNT)	0.05** (0.01)	0.04 (0.04)	0.04* (0.03)	0.00 (0.22)
Random intercept variance	0.08	0.00	0.00	0.00
Data subset	Full panel	Covered by country evaluation	Full panel	Covered by country evaluation
Observations (countries)	1,443 (135)	311 (68)	285 (38)	44 (12)
Residual Deviance	634.2	151.6	159.1	19.3
Null deviance	680.0	167.3	190.7	35.3

Note: All models are random-intercept probit estimated by Laplace approximation.

Statistical significance of one-tailed hypothesis test: * $p < .1$, ** $p < .05$.

For the Inter-American Development Bank, in no case was a project with a clean-energy component approved following a recommendation to emphasize environmental targets in future assistance strategies. This descriptive finding offers further support that the content of country program evaluations is not driving lending decisions related to clean energy. Taken together, the results in this section do not support the proposition that recommendations in country program evaluations influence lending decisions related to clean energy. In many cases, recommendations related to clean energy are not available, and when they are, they do not exert a discernible influence on project approval decisions. There is some evidence that the results reported in country program evaluations influence future lending at the World Bank, which contrasts with the lack of such evidence in the previous chapter. This result is suggestive that country program evaluations offer an effective way to aggregate performance information that project evaluations cannot achieve.

Urban Environment Projects and Project Components

Urban environment-improving goals are likely to be in higher demand by borrowing countries; thus recommendations about future projects might help solve information problems for borrowing countries themselves. More country program evaluations made recommendations about urban environment-improving goals than about clean-energy goals. This may provide a more powerful statistical test for the influence that recommendations have on future lending. However, as displayed in table 7.4, recommendations about urban environment projects did not have a discernible influence on urban environmental projects at any of the development banks (Models 5a–7b). At the Inter-American Development Bank, no recommendations specifically deal with urban environmental activities, and only two recommendations exist about environmental operations generally, making modeling impossible. Likewise for the African Development Bank, an urban environment project was approved in only one year covered by a country program evaluation, making modeling impossible. These results fail to produce any evidence that recommendations about lending are changing future lending decisions.

Confirming what I found in the previous chapter, World Bank borrowing countries with noted problems achieving environmental objectives will receive fewer urban environment projects in future years, while borrowing countries with good performance receive more of these projects (Models 4a–4b). For both the World Bank and Asian Development Bank, more urban environment projects are approved for middle-income countries that have access to market-rate lending (Models 4a–5a).

As above, it is possible that environmental recommendations in country program evaluations primarily cause the "mainstreaming" of urban environment project

TABLE 7.4

COUNTRY PROGRAM EVALUATIONS AND APPROVAL DECISIONS ABOUT URBAN
ENVIRONMENT-IMPROVING PROJECTS

Model	4a	4b	5a	5b	6a	6b
MDB	World	World	Asian	Asian	IADB	IADB
UEI RECOMMENDATION	−0.12 (0.50)	0.00 (0.46)				
POOR ENV. PERFORMANCE	−0.44* (0.30)	−0.53** (0.30)				
GOOD ENV. PERFORMANCE	0.75** (0.32)	0.85** (0.30)				
ENV. RECOMMENDATION			0.04 (0.68)	1.89 (2.10)		
POOR ENV. OUTCOME			0.09 (0.52)	−1.07 (1.36)	0.48 (0.54)	0.85 (0.74)
GOOD ENV. OUTCOME			0.41 (0.56)	−0.13 (0.90)	0.33 (0.58)	0.70 (0.71)
POLLUTION DAMAGE	−0.06 (0.14)	−0.13 (0.28)	−0.24 (0.34)	1.59 (1.77)	−0.05 (0.22)	1.17 (1.06)
CONCESSIONAL[a]	−0.87** (0.15)	−0.48** (0.24)	−0.65** (0.32)	−1.56 (2.01)	0.22 (0.23)	−0.02 (0.68)
NO. PROJECT PREV 5 YRS	0.03** (0.01)	0.04** (0.01)	0.01** (0.00)	0.02* (0.01)	0.03** (0.01)	0.01 (0.02)
YEAR (COUNT)	−0.00 (0.01)	−0.03 (0.04)	−0.00 (0.03)	0.05 (0.15)	−0.07 (0.03)	0.24 (0.26)
Random intercept variance	0.14	0.00	0.06	0.00	0.00	0.00
Data subset[b]	Full	Eval	Full	Eval	Full	Eval
Observations (countries)	1,382 (127)	303 (67)	254 (29)	44 (12)	350 (25)	59 (20)
Residual deviance	685.6	162.6	157.9	23.9	197.5	32.3
Null deviance	748.3	196.6	173.0	34.1	223.3	38.8

Note: All models are random-intercept probit estimated by Laplace approximation.

[a] Systematic data about project-level concessional lending are not available for the IADB. Instead, I use the IADB classification for "Fund for Special Operations" countries in these models.

[b] Full: full panel; Eval: years covered by country evaluation.

Statistical significance for one-tailed hypothesis tests: * $p < .1$, ** $p < .05$.

components into traditional projects, such as including a sewerage component in a water supply project. Thus, I used AidData activity codes to identify all projects with urban environment components, including all activity codes related to waste management, sewerage, and urban pollution abatement. Thus, the dependent variable becomes a project with any component in these areas.

As displayed in table 7.5, both general environment recommendations and recommendations specific to urban environmental project fail to have a discernible influence on decisions to include environmental components in urban projects (Models 8a–9b). This again indicates that recommendations in country program evaluations do not have a direct impact on lending decisions despite their audience, process, and information aggregation advantages. In contrast, for the World Bank both poor performance and good performance at meeting environmental objectives seem to drive selectivity (Models 7a–7b). For the Asian Development Bank, the recognition of good environmental outcomes in a country program evaluation is associated with increased probability of receiving a project with an environmental component in future years (Models 8a–8b). All of these results hold up both in the full panel of country-years and the subset of observations covered by a relevant country program evaluation. For the Inter-American Development Bank, borrowing countries that do not achieve environmental outcomes are not less likely to receive projects with urban environment components in future periods, and borrowing countries that achieve good outcomes are not more likely to receive such projects (Models 9a–9b).

For the African Development Bank, countries that received projects with urban environment components were never identified as having the environment as a bank priority or poor environmental outcomes, making modeling impossible. Taken together, the results of these models do not support hypotheses about how recommendations in country program evaluations influence decisions about lending. Instead, the results confirm that clean-energy projects mainly respond to the global importance of borrower countries as emitters and that the urban environmental project decisions respond to past outcomes rather than recommendations. A possible explanation of these findings is offered below.

SELECTIVITY IS NOT SOLELY AN INFORMATION PROBLEM

In the models presented above, I find no positive evidence that the recommendations present in country evaluations influence lending decisions about environment-improving projects. Only past environmental performance affects lending decisions in some models, a result that I also observed in the previous chapters. Thus, I continue to find that donors' lending pressures and recipients' borrowing demands are better predictors of whether particular countries receive clean-energy or urban

TABLE 7.5

APPROVAL DECISIONS ABOUT PROJECTS WITH URBAN ENVIRONMENT-IMPROVING ACTIVITIES

Model	7a	7b	8a	8b	9a	9b
MDB	World	World	Asian	Asian	IADB	IADB
UEI RECOMMENDATION	0.11 (0.40)	0.06 (0.40)				
POOR ENV. PERFORMANCE	−0.37* (0.23)	−0.58** (0.25)				
GOOD ENV. PERFORMANCE	0.53** (0.27)	0.53** (0.28)				
ENV. RECOMMENDATION			−0.59 (0.64)	0.07 (0.91)		
POOR ENV. OUTCOME			−0.05 (0.46)	−0.89 (0.83)	−0.15 (0.49)	−0.16 (0.50)
GOOD ENV. OUTCOME			1.32** (0.49)	1.22** (0.70)	0.22 (0.54)	0.29 (0.54)
POLLUTION DAMAGE	0.04 (0.09)	−0.22 (0.22)	−0.50 (0.35)	−0.55 (1.21)	0.17 (0.22)	0.23 (0.69)
CONCESSIONAL[a]	−0.43** (0.10)	−0.21 (0.19)	−0.71** (0.30)	−1.15 (1.13)	0.24 (0.23)	0.12 (0.48)
No. PROJECT PREV 5 YRS.	0.03** (0.00)	0.04** (0.01)	0.01** (0.00)	0.02** (0.01)	0.03** (0.01)	0.03** (0.01)
YEAR (COUNT)	−0.01 (0.01)	0.01 (0.03)	−0.01 (0.03)	−0.20 (0.17)	−0.06 (0.02)	−0.04 (0.18)
Random intercept variance	0.05	0.00	0.00	0.00	0.07	0.00
Data subset[b]	Full	Eval	Full	Eval	Full	Eval
Observations (countries)	1,382 (127)	303 (67)	254 (29)	44 (12)	350 (25)	59 (20)
Residual deviance	1223	273.7	167.1	28.5	348.1	51.7
Null Deviance	1275	304.6	187.8	40.5	365.0	56.8

Note: All models are random-intercept probit estimated by Laplace approximation.

[a] Systematic data about project-level concessional lending are not available for the IADB. Instead, I use the IADB classification for "Fund for Special Operations" countries in these models.

[b] Full: full panel; Eval: years covered by country evaluation.

Statistical significance for one-tailed hypothesis tests: * $p < .1$, ** $p < .05$.

environment projects. This result suggests that information problems are not the only obstacles to selectivity, since the formalized process of creating country assistance strategies has not resulted in more selectivity in either the positive or negative direction.

This is a surprising result, given that operational staff expected country program evaluations to be the most influential type of evaluation. I explore two further reasons that recommendations in country program evaluations might not have an influence on future lending. First, although the country program evaluations are formally considered in the process of country strategy planning, the systems in place to monitor the *implementation* of recommendations are weak in many cases. Second, the ability of operational staff to follow the recommendations coming out of country program evaluations, especially those advocating greater focus on environmental activities, is constrained by the lack of borrowing country demand for increased environment-improving investments. These constraints point out the need to ensure that selectivity is encouraged through incentives that apply at the project level.

Lack of Processes to Ensure Implementation of Recommendations

Even though the multilateral development banks have formal procedures to consider the recommendations that are made in country program evaluations, they mostly lack management systems to ensure that recommendations are carried out. At each of the four multilateral development banks considered here, the management must provide a response to the recommendations in country program evaluations. This "management response" provides an operational perspective on the recommendations and includes a set of operational steps that will be taken in response to the recommendations. However, absent pressure for selectivity from donor or borrower countries, as discussed in previous chapters, there are few systems in place to ensure that management commitments are implemented. Given the wide range of mandates facing management at the multilateral development banks, there is little capacity to follow up on the literally dozens or hundreds of recommendations that come out of evaluations absent strong incentives to do so.

At the World Bank, for example, although country program evaluations are discussed at the sub-board level within the Committee on Development Effectiveness, the planning of a country strategy still very much rests with the country director and the country team. One country director that I spoke with indicated that evaluators who are part of producing a country program evaluation rarely have knowledge of the country at a level similar to operational staff's knowledge. Thus, this country director viewed the process of responding to country program evaluations as a chance to "give the Independent Evaluation Group actual facts." Although a country program evaluation is considered in the process of designing a country strategy (if available), other forms of analysis often take precedent. In particular, country planning teams often assemble both internal and external sector experts to analyze the conditions that are likely to foster an effective lending program going forward. Furthermore, once the country strategy is adopted, implementation realities mean that recommendations from evaluations are not priorities, unless they receive considerable attention and oversight at the board level and are thus made a priority at the divisional level, which is rare given the myriad of projects and strategies that come up for consideration at the board level each year. Furthermore, in many cases through the 1990s and early 2000s, country program evaluations were completed after initial drafts of country strategies at the World Bank, further limiting their influence.

At the IADB, operational staff whom I interviewed were skeptical that the *country strategy* process had much of an effect on eventual lending decisions. Unlike their counterparts at the World Bank, operational staff at the IADB reported following a more borrower-driven, "practical" approach to lending decisions that allows the borrower country to change the projects that are being prepared in the pipeline on a year-to-year basis. Staff reported great variation in the degree to which country strategies drive lending at the country level, with one evaluation staff member going so far as saying they "have no influence on lending." In specific country program evaluations, this is known as the "improvisation rate," and indicates the degree to which approved projects are not those envisioned in the country assistance strategy.[9] Thus, given the weak nature of the country planning process, there is little opportunity for country program evaluations that are one step further removed to influence lending decisions about environment-improving projects. Furthermore, evaluation staff express reservations about being "completely out of the process" in terms of project-level lending decisions, and are skeptical that their findings have much influence under prevailing organizational policy. Because there is no tracking system for evaluation recommendations, evaluation staff were unable to report whether operational managers were following their recommendations.

Similarly at the African Development Bank: there is no formal process to track whether management follows through on recommendations made in country program evaluations. Given that the first AFDB country program evaluation was not completed until 2001, there were no repeated evaluations at the time of writing that examine whether past recommendations have been followed. Evaluators, however, are pessimistic about the prospects of having direct influence over lending decisions. Evaluators highlighted that operational management is pulled in many directions, particularly by borrowing and donor country demands. These pressures may make responding to past performance a lower priority. As at the other multilateral development banks, management must issue a formal response to country program evaluations, but that is the final formal step to be followed in the country program evaluation process, effectively closing off that evaluation.

The Asian Development Bank is the only MDB considered here that has a formal way to track the implementation of recommendations made in evaluations. Since 1982, the evaluation office has been tracking the implementation of recommendations. In 2008, the board approved an electronic tracking system to improve oversight of the follow-up to recommendations. Furthermore, responses to recommendations made in country program evaluations must be formally included in new country strategies, making the Asian Development Bank an important test case for the importance of high-level evaluations in future research. An initial evaluation of this system indicates that it is producing significant responsiveness from operational management (Independent Evaluation Department 2009). However, despite the institutional pressures to follow recommendations, functioning of the Management Tracking System depends entirely on the self-reporting of operational staff, and evaluators indicated that they have very limited means to undertake independent monitoring of implementation. Furthermore, when the ADB evaluation department comments on future operational documents by evaluating whether findings and recommendations are taken into account, they "check what the plan says," rather than check implementation. One operational staff member whom I spoke with indicated that unless a recommendation received attention from high-level management (vice presidents or directors general), there was little systematic responsiveness to recommendations prior to the establishment of the Management Tracking System.

Implementation of Recommendations Constrained by Borrower Demand

As was introduced in previous chapters, borrowing countries have tended to give less priority to stand-alone environmental projects, especially those countries that have a set window of concessional lending available. Both evaluators and operational staff across the multilateral development banks reported that the lack of borrower demand constrains their ability to implement recommendations coming out of country program evaluations. Although evaluators have tried in recent years to broaden their audience to include government ministries of borrowing countries, evaluation departments still report to the boards and thus produce evaluations for country representatives to the board (Operations Evaluation Department 2005a). Country program evaluations infrequently are written to borrowers as a primary audience, which is likely to decrease their influence when borrowers' demands are the barrier to more environment-improving lending.

At the country level, operational staff are often able to distinguish between borrowing countries that are interested in environment-improving financing and those that are not. For example, operational staff members at the Inter-American Development Bank reported that while Brazil and Peru have generally been interested in "green" portfolios, environment-improving lending has not been a priority for Argentina. Even when recommendations might exists, through country program evaluations or country environmental assessments, the country director in question must work within the limits set by the borrowing government. This may mean "mainstreaming" environmental components into traditional development projects or finding grant resources to address environmental issues. Some countries show much more willingness to pursue such negotiations than others.

The larger the size of the borrowing country and the greater the development level, the more constrained the multilateral development banks will be in pursuing recommendations that do not have borrowers' support. At the Inter-American Development Bank, the majority of lending is directed to just four countries. At the Asian Development Bank, the majority of lending is directed to just six countries. These large countries often have specific ideas about how their portfolios should be managed. For example, one operational staff reported that China generally approaches the ADB with projects that are almost fully designed, leaving little room for evaluations to influence the selection of projects. In recent years across the multilateral development banks, more emphasis has been placed on having countries develop their own development strategies that frame lending negotiations. As the lending process becomes more borrower-driven, there may be less room for recommendations in country evaluations that serve the information needs of donor countries to shape lending.

Perhaps the one clear area of responsiveness to country program evaluations reported by MDB staff has been the drive toward greater sector selectivity at the Asian Development Bank. In recent years, country program evaluations for Pakistan, Cambodia, and Laos have all recommended greater sector selectivity and a lending portfolio that focuses on at most two or three sectors within the country.[10] Operational staff have reported that these evaluations have caused many underperforming projects to be closed (47 in Pakistan) and subsequent country strategies to have greater focus (Asian Development Bank 2009). Furthermore, recommendations about sector selectivity fed into the development of Strategy 2020, which set ADB priorities for the following 10 years. This example shows that even when evaluations are influential, they have an influence on organizational processes and priorities, rather than specific lending decisions.

Given that the implementation of recommendations coming out of country program evaluations are constrained by borrower country demand, it will make sense in future periods for evaluators to expand their sense of audience to include borrowing country stakeholders. While this has happened in some evaluations, with recommendations directed at borrowing countries, this has not been a priority and will likely constrain the direct influence of country program evaluations in future periods.

CONCLUSIONS AND IMPLICATIONS

I do not find positive evidence in models that strategic planning at the country level creates sufficient incentives for operational staff to respond to recommendations about environment-improving operations. This is an important finding in the context of the larger question considered in this book, indicating that evaluations are unlikely to have a *direct* effect on lending decisions by providing information to donor countries. If information produced by evaluation drove lending decisions, we would see that result most clearly in the context of recommendations from country program evaluations. This result confirms that the most important obstacles to selectivity is finding a party with influence over programming decisions, incentives to be selective, and the information to act on those incentives. Information alone is insufficient.

For research in international relations about the relationships between states and international organizations, the results of this chapter show that many times principal-agent problems are not significant drivers of allocation patterns that lead to poor results. Member states do not simply have information problems; in many cases they may benefit from aid allocation to certain sectors regardless of performance. This result points to the need to identify when preferences are aligned, since poor results from a development point of view can be obtained without divergent preferences. It also points to the possibility that the control mechanisms that are removed from day-to-day decisions may not solve delegation problems, given chains of delegation. It appears that control mechanisms that operate at the level of staff decisions, together with incentives for selectivity by states, are more effective in prompting selective allocation for better results.

This suggests a need in the future to examine other ways that thematic evaluations influence large organizations. For example, several evaluation staff members reported that one of the primary effects of evaluations at the multilateral development banks is to induce more candid self-evaluations (e.g., completion reports) that are completed for every project by operational staff, since operational staff know that such reports might come up for independent evaluation. Other evaluators reported that carrying out diligent evaluations gave them credibility to engage in conversations about performance with both MDB management and member states through the board, thus widening the review *process* when approving new operations. Operational management reported that the opportunity to respond to evaluations prompts reflection about performance that might not otherwise occur among operational staff.

Similar avenues of evaluation influence are well documented and even emphasized within the evaluation literature (Kirkhart 2000). This chapter suggests that future work that seeks to understand the influence of evaluations must look deeper into how it affects the process of decision-making within organizations. Indeed, the literature on evaluation emphasizes the importance of the indirect effects of evaluations, rather than instrumental effects. This line of reasoning runs counter to the corpus of program evaluation research that focuses on reaching better and more robust conclusions. Indeed, the findings presented here confirm a more pessimistic view that, without supporting incentives, evaluations are seldom used in direct, instrumental ways within complex organizations (Torres and Preskill 2001).

The models presented in this chapter also support the findings of previous chapters with new data. For clean-energy projects, borrowing countries that are globally important to climate change continue to receive the bulk of clean-energy activities. For urban environment projects, I confirmed that the World Bank's approvals reflect past borrower performance, likely because of reduced uncertainty for borrowing countries. This result also extends to the Asian Development Bank and Inter-American Development Bank in relation to urban environmental activities. Operational policies that incentivize the use of evaluation and borrower-driven lending continue to be the primary ways to induce selectivity in allocation decisions based on performance.

8

Conclusions and Implications

STUCK WITH THE APPROVAL IMPERATIVE

Can the allocation of aid be made compatible with achieving good development and environmental outcomes? To this day, international aid remains largely stuck in a system that focuses on the approval of projects and the disbursement of funds. Donor countries demonstrate their commitment to international development by delivering aid, and multilateral donors gain additional resources by mobilizing their existing resources. As a result, the annual cycle of donor meetings focuses on *how much* financing should be mobilized, with side discussions about administering aid effectively. There is even less focus on updating allocation practices to learn from past performance. We need only look at recent international negotiations to see the overwhelming emphasis on approval amounts. Take, for instance, the 2009 United Nations meeting in Copenhagen that aimed to mitigate climate change. Donor countries pledged to mobilize an additional $100 billion annually for climate change mitigation and adaptation in less-developed countries. This pledge was made without a plan for implementation and has become a set of lofty goals that are nearly impossible to achieve given the current budget situations in many donor countries (Bloomberg New Energy Finance 2011).

This $100 billion annual pledge has anchored international negotiations about climate change following the Copenhagen meeting. Negotiations do not focus on achieving maximum impacts with scarce climate financing, but rather on finding ways to reach financing targets. While it is undeniable that more financing, if allocated well, could have greater impacts, it is surprising how little discussion has focused on maximizing the returns to climate change investments. For example, a 2010 forum on aid effectiveness, where recipients of climate finance in the Pacific met with several multilateral development organizations, focused only on establishing better administrative structures for coordinating and managing climate-related financing, rather than a system of accountability and performance-based allocation that is selective based on results (Thornton 2010).

This cycle of grandiose pledges of aid and subsequent wrangling over unmet pledges is not unique to environmental finance. Whenever donor countries are under pressure to address poverty, public health crises, or the aftermath of civil conflicts, the approval imperative emerges. Take for instance pledges of aid that were made during the first part of the 21st century. In 2002, political leaders from donor countries assembled in Monterrey, Mexico, to address calls from UN Secretary General Kofi Annan and civil society groups to double official development assistance to $100 billion annually (Cornwell 2002). At the 2005 G8 meeting in Edinburgh, Scotland, G8 leaders signed a pledge to supply an additional $50 billion annually in aid to poor countries by 2010, after coming under pressure for failing to meet the Monterrey targets (Blustein 2005). Speaking about those same pledges at the 2009 G8 meeting in L'Aquila, Italy, the Italian prime minister, Silvio Berlusconi, remarked, "It's true: we haven't kept our promises on Africa" (Seith 2009). This cycle of ever increasing aid pledges and disappointing disbursement amounts continues to play out year after year and robs the development community of a chance to discuss instead the types of programs that are highly successful at alleviating poverty and the ways that those programs might be scaled up. Perhaps even more importantly, little discussion focuses on scaling down development programs that are ineffective.

No single party is responsible for perpetuating the approval imperative. For their part, donor countries are under considerable internal and external pressure to live up to aid pledges. Domestically, citizen groups have little capacity to assess the effectiveness of foreign aid (Van Heerde and Hudson 2010). This means that citizens in donor countries assess the generosity of their country's programs not by what they accomplish, but by how much money they give (see Noël and Thérien 1995). Donor countries face pressures from international organizations like the United Nations to live up to aid disbursement targets. For example, the United Nations produces a number of reports that assess whether or not donor countries have lived up to their pledges to allocate 0.7% of GDP to international aid, a target that was established alongside the Millennium Development Goals (MDG Gap Task Force 2009). These types of reports carry the implicit assumption that if donor countries were just able to spend more money on aid, many important problems could be solved.

Donor countries even compete with each other to give more development and environmental aid. For example, the host country of G8 meetings is generally under pressure to secure greater aid commitments from their counterparts, in order to secure the legacy of the meeting they host. This same dynamic of competition among states for symbolic leadership is a driving force of policymaking in other transnational arenas, most importantly the European Union (Schreurs and Tiberghien 2007). Immediately prior to the G8 meetings in Scotland during 2005, UK Prime Minister Tony Blair flew to Washington, D.C., to pressure President George W. Bush to double aid to Africa and proposed financing for international climate change programs (Hartley-Brewer 2005). Diplomacy focuses on aid amounts, likely because it is difficult to make aid effectiveness a salient public issue.

Civil society groups also play a role in maintaining a focus on disbursing ever more aid, despite research showing that rapid increases in aid may actually harm the long-term development and institutional reform in recipient countries (Birdsall 2007; Devarajan, Dollar, and Holmgren 2001). For the 2005 G8 meetings in Scotland hosted by Prime Minister Blair, a group of prominent international civil society groups and celebrities, most notably Bono, came together to ratchet up pressure on donor countries to make greater aid pledges. Live 8, which became the name for this civil society gathering, suggested that world poverty could be eliminated if only donor countries were more generous. For example, Bono gave a speech to a meeting of UK Labour Party leaders in 2004 leading up to the G8 meetings, saying:

> We are the first generation that can look extreme and stupid poverty in the eye, look across the water to Africa and elsewhere and say this and mean it: we have the cash, we have the drugs, we have the science—but do we have the will? Do we have the will to make poverty history? Some say we can't afford to. I say we can't afford not to.[1]

Even following the G8 meetings, the Live 8 groups kept up the pressure, publishing guides about how donor countries failed to live up to their aid promises (Elliott 2006). The popular pressure employed by such antipoverty coalitions tends to focus only on the lack of donor generosity, not the institutional weakness and corruption problems that plague many poor countries.

Aid recipients hide behind these pressures. Although aid recipients rarely criticize donor countries openly for their lack of generosity, many have been slow to implement reforms that would increase the impacts of foreign aid. It is not in their interest to do so in many cases. Research suggests that aid can help authoritarian governments stay in power and allow recipient leaders to reward their most important political constituencies (Morrison 2009; Wright 2010). In 2005, both donor and recipient countries agreed to the Paris Declaration on Aid Effectiveness, which aimed to make aid flows more transparent and accountable for results. An evaluation of the implementation of the Paris Declaration found that recipient countries had not established as many aid transparency and accountability reforms as intended (Working Party on Aid Effectiveness 2008). Despite commitments, most aid recipients have been slow to adopt domestic processes that measure the performance of aid projects implemented within their borders (Organization for Economic Cooperation and Development 2011). These shortcomings notwithstanding, less-developed countries continue to push for higher amounts of assistance related to both environmental and development issues (Torello and Williams 2009).[2]

International organizations like the multilateral development banks find themselves caught in the middle of this approval imperative. On the one hand, donor countries demand that the multilateral development banks achieve good and transparently measured results. On the other hand, donor countries look to the multilateral development banks as conduits to meet lofty aid pledges. The multilateral development banks, through capital increases and replenishments, are under pressure to allocate ever increasing amounts of development and environmental assistance. Recipient countries, many of which are exerting more influence over the multilateral development banks, are insisting that approval procedures be streamlined so that they can receive more projects with fewer preparation costs (Asian Development Bank 2009). Under these conditions, the multilateral development banks are stuck between allocating ever higher amounts of financing and achieving effective results. These goals are not always compatible.

As a result of these pressures, staff at the multilateral development banks continue to focus on steering new projects through the pipeline to board approval. At the departmental level, the ability to hire new staff and gain control of additional administrative and lending resources likewise depends on securing new lending. Thus, the imperative to approve new lending has become the logic of organizational survival and expansion, even when there are contradictory pressures to achieve effectiveness by being selective about allocation. Whenever the multilateral development banks prioritize new lending over effective lending, the outcomes of their operations are likely to suffer. This is a significant issue given that the multilateral development banks are expected to manage a large share of international climate financing in the coming years.

The approval imperative is a core source of ineffective aid and development assistance delivery worldwide. The approval imperative often prevents donors from withholding aid for poor performance (Collier et al. 1997; Svensson 2000). Given that aid is often disbursed despite poor performance of the host country, aid can even undermine the development of functioning institutions (Birdsall 2007; Knack 2001). Likewise, foreign political leaders that are not accountable for the effective use of aid can better engage in rent-seeking and politically motivated aid disbursements that subtract from effectiveness (Knack 2001). Many of the challenges to aid effectiveness originate from the approval imperative. It is essential to find ways to either change this system or restrain it in ways that promote effectiveness.

ADDRESSING THE APPROVAL IMPERATIVE

In this book, I examined whether the approval imperative at multilateral development banks can be addressed through a combination of monitoring and evaluation, administrative policies, and external pressures. Evaluation might overcome the problem of performance at the multilateral development banks by providing information to the right parties. The provision of independent performance information from evaluation offices and Inspection Panels might allow shareholder countries to press the multilateral development banks for greater selectivity in allocation and thereby overcome the difficulty that shareholder countries have in monitoring day-to-day project decisions and outcomes. In addition, better information about results that decreases uncertainty might allow staff at the multilateral development banks and their counterparts in recipient countries to make more informed decisions that help them pursue projects that are likely to be successful.

I have shown that better information alone is not sufficient to alter allocation practices at the multilateral development banks. There is not a uniform response to information about results across the types of projects considered in this book. Instead, I have shown that incentives to be selective from donor countries, civil society groups, and recipient countries can change allocation decisions when they make it easier or harder for the multilateral development banks to approve new projects. Since prevailing allocation arrangements have remained relatively stable at the multilateral development banks, promoting selectivity depends on making it difficult to approve projects that are not likely to achieve satisfactory results within individual country portfolios. Because member states on the board of executive directors very rarely make it difficult to approve projects by casting negative votes, selectivity hinges on finding administrative policies, preparation requirements, and external pressures that can change the costs of approving projects in line with past performance. This book shows that when parties with incentives to be selective are armed with the right information, they can make projects with a record of poor performance harder to approve or projects with a record of good performance easier to approve. This makes it possible to maintain the benefits of the discretion granted to the multilateral development banks without the problems of performance generated by the approval imperative.

The Power of Administrative Policies

When operational policies and administrative requirements change the costs of approving new projects in line with past performance, the multilateral development banks practice selectivity while maintaining discretion about allocation. Safeguard policies, for example, have created strong incentives for staff to respond to past performance because they make it difficult to approve environmentally risky projects in countries that implement safeguard requirements poorly. These policies work so well to manage discretion precisely because the approval imperative places staff under tremendous pressure to get new projects approved. At both the World Bank and Asian Development Bank, special safeguard units exist to ensure safeguard requirements are met prior to board approval, which decreases the ability of operational staff to shirk these requirements. Operational policies and institutional design combine to constrain the approval imperative in ways that favor allocation decisions that align with performance.

In the future, creating incentives for selectivity at the multilateral development banks and other international donors will hinge on establishing policies and practices that make it more difficult to approve new projects when similar projects have been ineffective in the past. To do so, the pipeline process at the multilateral development banks needs to require more intensive planning in countries that performed poorly in the past. In addition, specialized offices might be required to certify that future lending plans account for past lessons. These types of institutional "checks," where different parts of organizations have opposing priorities, have been recognized as an important way that principals can manage the activities of bureaucratic agencies (Kiewiet and McCubbins 1991). Executive agencies can be audited by specialized units whose sole responsibility is to monitor performance, a way of delegating oversight (Norton and Smith 2008). In addition, principals can mandate certain administrative practices that make it easier to verify that agencies are acting in desired ways (McCubbins, Noll, and Weingast 1987).

This same logic extends to international organizations, where donor countries can mandate internal oversight and administrative procedures as part of the project approval process. These checks can provide the "hard incentives" needed to overcome the approval imperative. Pollack and Hafner-Burton (2010) found, for example, that environmental considerations were not effectively mainstreamed into the European Commission through informal socialization, but rather through administrative procedures that universally required "impact assessments" prior to new operations. Such administrative procedures have the advantage of being easy to monitor.

Similar procedures could be put in place for a wide variety of sectors at the multilateral development banks. Whereas current project appraisal documents at the multilateral development banks require a one- or two-paragraph account of how a project responds to past lessons, a more complete performance assessment could be automatically required for particular countries when past operations in the same sector did not achieve satisfactory results. This extra preparation requirement, combined with an additional review of operational plans, would incentivize staff to choose projects that have been successful in the past.

This type of incentive might also be created in the opposite way. Both the World Bank and Asian Development Bank are certifying that domestic procedures to safeguard the environment in certain high-performing countries are equivalent to bank policies.[3] By allowing "country systems" to move forward, the multilateral development banks decrease the design and administrative costs of environmentally risky projects in high-performing countries. This might have the additional effect of creating incentives for poor-performing countries to be more diligent about the implementation of safeguard procedures, so that they can gain access to streamlined administrative processes in the future.

It should be possible to extend streamlined processes for project approval to other types of projects in high-performing countries. For example, bank staff still must write up project proposals and information documents according to a standardized bank format. It may be possible to have high-performing borrowing countries take the lead on producing such documents according to domestic planning systems, in order to decrease the time and resources involved with producing duplicative documentation. These duplicative requirements can drain scarce administrative resources from recipient country ministries (Leandro, Schafer, and Frontini 1999). In countries with proven records of performance, the multilateral development banks could allow recipients to move forward entirely with their own planning processes, since effectiveness is no longer dependent on meeting donor requirements for preparation. Regardless of the way these incentives are created, the implication of this research is that approval processes at the multilateral development banks must be designed carefully and deliberately to constrain the approval imperative and incentivize selectivity by changing the cost of project approval in line with past performance.

There are worrisome indications, however, that the multilateral development banks are moving in the opposite direction. In 2009, the Asian Development Bank approved a strategy that seeks to halve the time that projects spend in preparation (Asian Development Bank 2009). Borrowing countries, which are increasingly making their voices heard at the board level of the multilateral development banks, describe current preparation requirements as onerous and often seek alternative forms of financing when they are likely to face significant delays during project preparation. In 2015, China proposed the Asian Infrastructure Investment Bank, which some observers are calling a response to the costly and time-consuming procedures of the multilateral development banks considered in this book.[4] The initial official stance against this new infrastructure bank by the United States is based on concerns about environmental and social safeguards (Talley 2015). Until the organization and its management procedures are formalized, it is not clear if and how administrative procedures will be used to check the approval imperative.

Both the trend to more streamlined procedures at the existing development banks and potentially weaker administrative procedures at the Asian Infrastructure Investment Bank raise doubts about the future ability of the multilateral development banks to manage discretion through administrative procedures. They might simply relax procedures in response to this new competition because of an incentive to approve projects and to maintain influence and market share. However, it is not clear why the multilateral development banks should compete with these new sources of finance, especially if safeguards create real value by improving the outcomes of projects and decreasing the negative impacts of projects (see Independent Evaluation Group 2010b). As one staff member I interviewed put it, safeguard policies are what make the multilateral development banks "different from Citibank." If borrowing countries have such good policy and economic environments that they no longer need the multilateral development banks, they should be graduated from borrowing from these organizations. Doing so would allow the multilateral development banks to refocus their efforts on implementing programs in places where strong planning requirements are needed to implement programs well.

The Exercise of Accountability by Civil Society

Civil society opposition can also change the costs of approving and implementing environmentally risky projects, an important result that reveals overlooked capabilities of nonstate actors in international politics. For domestic groups that are impacted by global decision-making processes beyond their reach, accountability at the international level is often considered to be weak. Recent decades have seen a surge of protest from civil society groups around the world against decisions taken at the international level. Prominent examples include protests over economic globalization (Roberts 2008), the environmental impacts of multilateral development projects (Khagram 2004), and the imposition of macroeconomic policies of austerity and restructuring (Almeida 2007). Civil society groups have been able to extend their reach by forming international networks based on information exchange, but their ability to directly influence decisions made at the international level still depends crucially on gaining access to powerful states that are sympathetic to their interests (Keck and Sikkink 1998).

More specifically, civil society groups have had few effective mechanisms for sanctioning international organizations in the absence of appealing to powerful states. Accordingly, Grant and Keohane argue that "sanctions remain the weak point in global accountability since they can only be implemented by the powerful—for example, by powerful states over multilateral organizations" (2005, 41). This notion reflects the standard model of a delegation relationship between states and international organizations (Nielson and Tierney 2003). Existing outside of this delegation relationship, civil society groups must rely on "peer" and "public reputational" forms of accountability and use informational strategies to highlight how international organizations fail to live up to standards of performance set by powerful states (Grant and Keohane 2005). They argue that incentives of staff at international organizations result in discretion being misused. Following this line of reasoning, most existing research highlights how nonstate actors can play a role in inducing good performance at international organizations by acting as low-cost monitors for states (Raustiala 1997; Lake and McCubbins 2006; Dai 2007).

The establishment of accountability mechanisms at the multilateral development banks is a novel and important attempt to promote accountability at international organizations. Civil society groups in less-developed countries may face the difficult task of gaining access to international advocacy networks to exercise even weak forms of accountability (Keck and Sikkink; Kravchenko 2009). The accountability mechanisms provide civil society groups a high-level platform for the expression of grievances that receive automatic attention by professional auditors, without requiring active approval from member states. In turn, these auditors are authorized to recommend costly remedial actions. Poor environmental practices are the most common grievance lodged by civil society groups at the Inspection Panels, reflecting the advantage civil society groups have in monitoring performance of this type. With the advent of communication technologies, it is easier to monitor and disseminate information about the environmental consequences of MDB projects that are implemented in even remote locations. This raises the possibility that civil society groups can play an important role in prompting selectivity at the multilateral development banks by exerting claims for accountability and providing information that they uniquely possess.

I have shown that civil society groups can substantially influence the lending practices of the multilateral development banks in different ways. First, both the World Bank and Asian Development Bank favor environmentally risky projects in recipient countries with lower levels of political rights. Second, after matching on relevant variables, the World Bank is less likely to approve an environmentally risky project for a country that has experienced an inspection investigation during the previous five years. Taken together, these results indicate that civil society groups can drive lending decisions in ways that favor responsiveness to past performance. Of course, the establishment of the Inspection Panels required support from powerful member states, in this case the United States (Shihata 2000). However, the decentralization of accountability through the Inspection Panels has had impacts far beyond the temporary alignment between the interests of strong states and civil society groups. It steers the discretionary decisions of multilateral bank staff away from projects that are likely to raise problems.

This approach to accountability has its drawbacks, however, since civil society monitoring and advocacy is not uniformly available across recipient countries. Even though inspection investigations decrease the approval of environmentally risky projects in the future, requests for inspection at the World Bank are submitted primarily from countries will high levels of political rights and active environmental civil societies. In the data that I collected, these countries show no particular tendency for poor performance at implementing environmental safeguards as compared to countries without active civil societies. Civil society monitoring and advocacy is based on availability, rather than underlying performance. This means that civil society monitoring and advocacy cannot substitute for more systematic, internal processes for monitoring and evaluation.

There are also risks for civil society groups when they advocate against certain types of projects at the multilateral development banks. For example, civil society groups have been so vehemently opposed to hydroelectric projects in southeast Asia that the multilateral development banks have almost entirely exited from the sector (Khagram 2004). In response to persistent civil society criticism, the World Bank and Asian Development Bank jointly financed the Nam Theun II project in Laos, with best-practice environmental safeguards and resettlement procedures. The project has taken years to plan and implement in a responsible manner.[5] When I spoke with Asian Development Bank staff about the project, they indicated that there is little willingness from either the multilateral development banks or borrowing countries to pursue similar projects in the future, owing to the persistent delays caused by civil society monitoring and opposition.

At the same time, China has financed hundreds of dams throughout Southeast Asia without stringent environmental safeguards. Civil society groups are unable to effectively target Chinese hydropower companies or Southeast Asian governments for better environmental practices in the numerous projects that are currently being constructed (Hirsch 2011). With these outcomes in mind, it seems that civil society groups may have won one battle, but lost the broader war against poor environmental consequences. The multilateral development banks are a convenient target for monitoring and advocacy, owing to their centralized administrative structure and their relation to donor countries that are sympathetic to the claims of civil society groups (Keck and Sikkink 1998). By pushing these organizations out of sectors like hydropower, civil society groups may have actually caused outcomes that are worse than would be the case if the multilateral development banks were still engaged.

Civil society groups would do well to think about the broader impacts they have on decisions made under discretion. While focusing on individual projects may be an effective fundraising and advocacy strategy, it does not ensure that the multilateral development banks are more responsible to environmental performance across all countries. Higher-stakes decisions are often made at the policy and strategy level. It is unclear whether local civil society groups are able to participate effectively in such decisions. Recent reforms at the multilateral development banks make it more possible for civil society groups to consult on draft policies, but their influence over policy outcomes remains unclear.[6]

Recent policies have also made it possible for civil society groups to play a greater consultative role in the design of individual projects.[7] Civil society groups are now routinely consulted about new projects that affect them and given the opportunity to provide feedback about the design of projects. Still, we have very little knowledge about how far decision-makers at the multilateral development banks go to accommodate the preferences expressed by civil society groups. As I have argued, this will depend on whether civil society groups can make certain decisions more costly. At a minimum, projects must avoid noncompliance with operational policies that could send the project to the Inspection Panel. But above this bar, there is no systematic evidence that civil society groups influence decisions about allocation. Part of the problem is that civil society groups get to consult on projects that are already worked out, without the ability to block or delay projects that do not meet their interests. In the future, the decisions about the allocation of projects at the multilateral development banks would be drastically altered if civil society groups could more easily affect the design of projects. For example, the inspection process might be made more accessible to civil society groups during project design, which would significantly increase the incentives of decision-makers to avoid harming their interests.

One interesting possibility that might be explored in the future is whether independent evaluation is an avenue for greater civil society participation in decision-making. Civil society groups have seized on the findings of independent evaluations to press their own agendas. Indeed, civil society groups may not have sufficient information about many activities at international donors, and publicly available evaluations may allow them to connect their local issues to broader performance problems at the multilateral development banks. Currently, evaluation practices do not include debriefing sessions with civil society groups and do not draw from data that civil society groups might provide. Perhaps a civil society working group could ensure that the results of evaluations are better disseminated within advocacy networks. The consequences of doing so might be to more closely align allocation practices with effectiveness, by creating the conditions for civil society groups to more effectively monitor performance and subsequently oppose poor practices.

Increasing Borrowing Demand by Reducing Uncertainty

Selectivity can also come about when high-performing borrowers select the types of projects that they have previously implemented with success. This suggests that the audience for whom project evaluations are written needs to shift. Information in evaluations can help to overcome uncertainty about the programs and projects that work well, steering discretionary decisions toward projects with greater chances of success when they have strong local benefits. The problem is that donor countries have pushed for programs that address global environmental concerns in all recipient countries without clear buy-in and an emphasis on local benefits. They have done this largely to demonstrate commitment to transboundary environmental issues without incurring high costs domestically. It is often much cheaper for donor countries to finance clean-energy projects in foreign countries than to adopt regulations domestically that increase the costs of power generation (Pizer 2006). This creates a situation where borrowing countries have lower incentives to implement donor-driven projects well.

At the multilateral development banks, it is very uncommon for donor countries to be critical of increased financing of environment-improving projects, despite the comparatively poor performance of these projects (Operations Evaluation Department 2005b). Donor countries have set targets for amounts of environmental lending, which places multilateral development bank staff under considerable pressure to demonstrate that they are doing something about this mandate.[8] In the case of large emitters, donor pressures to lend are high owing to the cartel-like influence large emitters have on climate change outcomes (Darst 2001). Under these pressures, staff at banks have incentives to approve environment-improving projects and integrate environmental activities into standard development projects regardless of past performance.

One consequence of these incentives is that there is no discernible difference in the allocation of climate and clean-energy projects between large emitters with records of good or poor environmental performance. Staff report that these types of projects are among the most "donor-driven" in the portfolio. Donor countries may be diverting existing development assistance resources to climate change and biodiversity conservation programs, often to the chagrin of less-developed countries that prefer programs with more local benefits (Brown, Cantore, and Willem et Velde 2010). It is quite clear that if prevailing allocation practices continue, a great deal of resources that could otherwise be directed toward global environmental concerns will be wasted. Donor countries can actually create incentives that countervail the practice of selectivity by demanding certain types of lending.

On the other hand, I show that high-performing borrowers are much more likely than low-performing borrowers to receive projects that address local environmental issues. Staff at the multilateral banks report that high-performing countries that face significant environmental problems select projects to address the problems. It may be possible, therefore, to make additional environmental financing available to high-performing countries and allow them to select their own projects. Low-performing countries tend to avoid environment-improving projects. It is likely better for the multilateral development banks to focus on projects that are higher priorities for these borrowers, especially when benefits are global in nature.

These findings echo current consensus in the development community about the need to move to recipient-driven development. Donor countries must recognize the overwhelming evidence that "donor push" is likely to lead to ineffective outcomes in the delivery of development assistance. There is evidence to support this argument across many sectors, including environment, democracy promotion, economic adjustment, and civil society promotion (Knack 2004; Easterly 2005; Goldsmith 2008). While the goals of such projects might be desirable, the research presented here confirms experiences elsewhere that show scarce financing will be wasted in pursuing donor-driven projects. In effect, these pressures limit the discretion of staff and recipient governments to be selective about projects that do not have strong local demand.

Donor countries themselves have recognized the need to move toward demand-driven development that aligns with priorities identified by recipient countries. This principle was most clearly enshrined in the 2005 Paris Declaration on Aid Effectiveness, which stated the goal of "increasing alignment of aid with partner countries' priorities, systems and procedures." Despite this call, a recent evaluation of progress in implementing the Paris Declaration found that improving "country ownership" in the delivery of development assistance continues to be weak (Organization for Economic Cooperation and Development 2011). Even recipient countries have collectively called for greater ownership over their aid programs. A recent declaration of African countries prepared for the Fourth High Level Forum on Aid Effectiveness in Busan, Korea, emphasized "the ultimate and indispensable need for the Continent to take full responsibility for its own development, through effective utilization of both internal and external resources."[9] Future progress on aligning allocation practices with effectiveness will require such a shift. It will also require that evaluations be written to solve the information problems of broader audiences.

Limits to Strategic Planning

This research also shows that top-down planning and high-level thematic evaluations do not produce selective allocation of environment-improving projects. Country program planning rarely changes the incentives surrounding discretionary decisions in line with past performance. Indeed, staff are mostly responsible for ensuring that environmental priorities, codified in organization-wide policies, are successfully integrated into future lending portfolios. At every multilateral development bank considered in this book, environmental programming is mandated across the lending portfolio. This precludes the multilateral development banks from being more selective about the countries where they engage in substantial environment-improving lending. Indeed, I found no country program evaluation across any of the four banks that called for greater selectivity in environment-improving operations. So long as country planning is an exercise in aligning allocation decisions with the approval imperative as related to the environment, insufficient incentives exist to promote selectivity. Furthermore, since country program evaluations can only make recommendations based on past operations, evaluators have little room to make recommendations about expanding environment-improving programs in countries with few or no projects in this area.

Despite the fact that country program evaluations are directly connected to allocation decisions within the multilateral development banks, I find no evidence that recommendations about clean-energy, urban environment, and natural resource management projects influence lending decisions. In terms of the behavior of international organizations, this result suggests that information about performance does not create sufficient incentives to be selective about allocation. Instead, as found in previous chapters, internal "hard incentives" to meet lending goals must align with incentives to fund high-performing projects.

An issue that will be important future studies about the performance of international organizations is how the rising tide of borrower-driven lending will interact with evaluation. To this point, evaluation departments see their primary audience as the boards of the multilateral development banks, which are largely dominated by donor countries. However, recent organizational reforms at the multilateral development banks have placed a higher burden on borrowing countries to develop their own poverty alleviation strategies, project requests, and project implementation systems. As lending processes move toward a partnership model, it will be important to reassess whether evaluation departments are focused on the right audiences.

As allocation and design decisions are driven more and more by borrower demand, evaluations will need to shift in that direction. From a practical perspective, joint evaluations with national authorities might be a useful way to improve domestic evaluation capacity.

More generally, the results about country program evaluations speak to the tension between top-down and bottom-up planning for the allocation of development assistance. As Easterly writes, "All the hoopla about having the right plan is itself a symptom of the misdirected approach to foreign aid taken by so many in the past and so many still today. The right plan is to have no plan" (2006, 5). Easterly argues that top-down planning has a poor record of identifying programs that are successful and have a large impact in the recipient country. Evaluation might offer systematic learning about what works, but only if it is aimed at the right audiences. To reduce repeated failures, policies need to exist that change incentives around individual projects, prompting staff to practice selectivity at the level of decisions about portfolio composition for individual countries.

RETHINKING SELECTIVITY

Selectivity can seem at odds with the desire to address environment and development needs in countries that are poor, have low governance capacity, and are politically or economically unstable. The tension involved with selectivity is the fundamental paradox of development assistance: the countries that need aid the most are also the countries that are least likely to benefit from aid, since they are unable to use it effectively. Although the multilateral development banks supervise grant and lending projects, borrowing countries are still responsible for implementation. Thus, if the multilateral development banks only allocated infrastructure projects or environment-improving projects to borrowing countries with strong performance records or high governance capacity, it is likely that they would be working almost exclusively in middle-income countries. These middle-income countries often have access to commercial lending markets and less need for assistance from development donors. Indeed, several MDB staff that I interviewed suggested that selectivity runs counter to their role as "lender of last resort" to countries that have nowhere else to turn.

Despite the sentiment that borrowing country *need* should drive decisions about allocation at the multilateral development banks, waste is still waste, no matter where it occurs. Projects that fail to reach their objectives or are not likely to have a beneficial impact have no defensible place in the project portfolios of development organizations. Failing projects decrease public support for development assistance in donor countries, which may have long-term impacts on the availability of development assistance (Diven and Constantelos 2009; Paxton and Knack 2008). In addition, there is evidence that aid can actually harm institutional development in countries that are unable to use it effectively (Easterly 2006). Financing for international environmental and development concerns is well below international target levels. Given the magnitude of needs around the world, little good is served by allocating scarce development assistance to places where it is likely to be wasted.

However, shifting focus from selectivity practiced at the level of countries to selectivity practiced within the portfolios of countries offers a way to reconcile the paradox of development assistance. Development assistance is an exceptionally broad umbrella term for financing that can be delivered through different modalities, directed to a wide variety of sectors, and implemented by a number of different actors. Portfolios can be structured to emphasize projects or multitranche program lending, to target infrastructure or institutional capacity building, and even to give implementation responsibility to governments or NGOs. The multilateral development banks in particular have the advantage of exceptionally broad mandates and wide discretion, which allows them to structure lending portfolios in unique ways for individual borrowing countries.

In recent years, all of the multilateral development banks considered in this book have used increasingly sophisticated formulas for allocating their concessional resources to countries. These formulas take numerous institutional and project performance ratings, cut them up into small pieces, and add them together in a way that makes little intuitive sense to external observers.

Take, for example, the formula used to allocate concessional lending at the World Bank, which is made up approximately 20 indicators aggregated in seemingly arbitrary ways (Andersen, Hansen, and Markussen 2006). While this formula grants more concession lending on average to countries with better governance and higher project ratings, it is unresponsive to the possibility of mixed performance across different sectors in the portfolios of individual countries. Indeed, a 2006 review of the allocation process found that governance and performance ratings used to determine allocations are volatile and inconsistent over short time periods (Andersen, Hansen, and Markussen 2006, 13). Thus, while ever more emphasis has been placed on refining allocation formulas for countries, the more important task is to ensure that recipient countries pursue the projects that are likely to succeed.

Whereas the institutionalized performance-based allocation frameworks at the multilateral development banks deal with aggregate lending amounts, there is substantial leeway for the banks to customize portfolios in even the poorest countries in ways that respond to past performance. This often involves being more selective and focused on the types of projects that can be implemented well, rather than trying to address all needs in all countries. Based on evaluations, for example, the regional development banks have attempted to focus their portfolios in a limited number of sectors where they have comparative advantages in managing successful projects (see Operations Evaluation Department 2007d; Asian Development Bank 2009). This performance-based allocation is practiced through decisions about portfolio composition and a commitment to selectivity *within* a country portfolio, and should be prioritized by donor organizations.

The ability to practice selectivity hinges on staff having discretion to shift allocation between sectors and types of projects. Indeed, in practicing selectivity within countries, discretion contributes to success (Honig 2014). Take, for example, programs to reduce greenhouse gas emissions. For this goal, it does not matter where in the world emissions reductions occur, just that they actually occur. In this case, it makes very little sense to send clean-energy projects to all large emitters. To achieve the largest reductions possible with scarce financing, clean-energy projects should be allocated to the borrowing countries that can successfully implement such projects and to countries where the catalytic effect on the private sector is highest (Buntaine and Pizer 2015). Thus, instead of requiring climate change activities to be implemented across all countries, as is presently required by MDB climate strategies, a certain amount of financing should be allocated according to performance-based eligibility criteria. If donor countries are trying to induce specific outcomes, then allocation systems need to reward success.

On the other hand, if financing is intended to solve the most pressing development problems where it can be most useful, then selectivity allocation can be accomplished through flexibility and managed discretion within individual countries. The multilateral development banks should receive incentives to move in and out of sectors as performance dictates. One of the obstacles to this type of flexibility is that staffing creates inertia for certain programs based on the present mix of expertise. Thus, to truly use their discretion to practice selectivity, the multilateral development banks might need to adopt more flexible staffing policies and continue their reliance on contractors where technical expertise is required.

There is something to be said, however, for building the capacity of a borrowing country over time in a particular sector. Operational staff I spoke with at the Asian Development Bank, for example, described a series of technical assistance and traditional energy projects that are being implemented in Pakistan to build capacity for future clean-energy investments. While this is certainly a part of MDB mandates, when borrowing countries perform poorly on initial projects in a capacity-building series, this calls into question the likelihood of success in building capacity over time in that sector. Many operational staff state that they begin with "easy" projects and then scale up size and complexity as particular borrowing countries gain more capacity. If borrowing countries fail to implement these easy projects well, then it is difficult to imagine that they will be able to progress to more difficult operations. This situation calls for either choosing a different way to build capacity or focusing on sectors where the multilateral development banks can be successful.

In addition, it is clear from this research that when development banks have organizational policies to pursue certain types of projects in all countries, results will be at best mixed and financing will be wasted. When donor countries in essence want to purchase certain results, they should do just that. Indeed, the future of financing for global environmental goods is not likely to be as effective as possible under prevailing allocation practices.

FUTURE DIRECTIONS IN INTERNATIONAL ENVIRONMENTAL ASSISTANCE

We enter the 21st century facing transboundary environmental problems of growing scale and urgency. Yet no clear solutions are in sight. States are still struggling to establish cooperative mechanisms that effectively address climate change, deforestation, and a host of domestic environmental problems. Many of the most severe environmental problems occur in less-developed countries. For the last two decades, international attempts to address environmental problems have revolved around financing mechanisms. Beginning with Agenda 21 and the 1992 Rio Earth Summit, donor countries pledged $2 billion and established the Global Environment Facility to finance environmental programs in less-developed countries.

International environmental finance will arguably be the most dynamic area of development assistance over the coming decades. Current climate negotiations have centered around drastically increasing the availability of environmental financing in order to secure global environmental goods. At the 15th Conference of the Parties to the United Nations Convention on Climate Change in Copenhagen during 2009, Secretary of State Hillary Clinton announced that the United States aimed to mobilize $100 billion of climate financing annually to be used to address mitigation and adaptation in less-developed countries. At present, several new international financing mechanisms are being established to manage the initial resources that have been pledged toward this commitment, including the Climate Investment Funds and the Green Climate Fund, both of which are slated to be administered by multilateral development banks. In addition, the divisions of the multilateral development banks that lend to the private sector have scaled up climate-related financing more than any other type of investment.

The approval imperative has important implications for the future of international environmental finance. Negotiations over the Green Climate Fund, for example, have focused on the relative role of public sector versus private sector financing. Donor countries have argued that the private sector can be mobilized to provide a large portion of the pledged amount for climate change mitigation and adaptation. Less-developed countries, on the other hand, have emphasized the need for new and additional public sector financing as the basis for future international environmental financing (*Africa News* 2010). This position is not surprising given how recipient countries benefit from the approval imperative. Private sector actors have a clear profit motive and are likely to invest in countries that can provide clear property rights and functioning institutions that are conducive to business (Busse and Hefeker 2007). As a consequence, private sector financing does not offer the same lack of accountability and rent-seeking potential to political leaders as does public financing. Under these circumstances, it is understandable why recipient countries prefer climate financing to be allocated according to the status quo—they are likely to face little accountability for performance and receive big increases in financing. They also get to have a much more direct influence on which countries receive financing, rather than allowing the private sector to sort out the question based on risk and return calculations.

What is clear from this book is that international environmental finance needs to turn away from an allocation system built on the approval imperative. Lending driven by disbursement targets results in waste through poor outcomes and rewards large countries regardless of their past performance. I have shown that the multilateral development banks show little propensity toward allocating climate financing in ways that reward good performance in past projects without supporting pressures from member countries. This suggests several lessons for the future of international environmental assistance and finance.

First, and perhaps most important, financing mechanisms for climate change must avoid being driven solely by donor supply preferences. Given that most of the recent negotiations about climate change financing have centered around drastically increasing the *supply* of climate financing, the results here suggest that unless mechanisms are put in place to direct the bulk of this financing to high-performing countries, a great deal of resources will be wasted owing to poor performance. In my interviews, MDB staff often commented that projects related to climate change continue to be one of the most "donor driven" areas of development assistance. As was seen in models of the allocation of clean-energy projects, the bulk of climate financing tends to be directed toward large emitters, without reference to past performance. This suggests that increasing the *supply* of climate-related financing and managing it as traditional public-sector project lending will be inefficient.

At the very least, allocation mechanisms should be put in place that create incentives for donor organizations to direct financing to high-performing countries, since donor countries are essentially contracted to secure global environmental goods. Two possibilities immediately follow from this suggestion. Recipient countries must be incentivized to implement climate mitigation projects well. Climate mitigation financing institutions like the Clean Development Mechanism incentivize such performance because only verified emissions reductions are eventually purchased (Streck 2004). Likewise, a recent proposal for "cash on delivery" development financing would provide recipient countries incentives to achieve certain outcomes (Birdsall et al. 2011). Related to this approach, recent climate negotiations have included the possibility that less-developed countries would undertake specific mitigation commitments in exchange for financing to meet such goals. All of these mechanisms would provide host countries the incentives necessary to actually reduce climate emissions and allow those countries that could not produce successful outcomes to opt for other types of development financing.

Likewise, incentivizing private sector actors to invest in clean-energy technologies in less-developed countries will be key to addressing climate mitigation targets internationally. Already, a significant portion of MDB private sector lending is directed toward clean-energy investments. In related work, I find that private sector operations are very responsive to the past performance record of borrowing countries.[10] This suggests that ramping up private sector investment in mitigation activities would offer a way to spend scarce financing efficiently.

On the other hand, climate adaptation financing, which is used to prepare less-developed countries for the changes associated with climate change, might fruitfully be managed as standard public sector project financing. As I demonstrate in this book, when an environment-improving project is primarily intended to meet domestic environmental needs and does not face strong donor supply pressures, high-performing countries with strong needs for better environmental management tend to pursue available financing. When they face lower uncertainty about the benefits of projects, they are even more likely to pursue environment-improving projects. This suggests evaluators need to pivot to new audiences. While the multilateral development banks might be wise to build up the expertise necessary to administer climate adaptation projects and have the availability of financing on hand for these directives, borrower requests should drive lending in these areas. Given that climate change mitigation is a long-term process, it may be several years or decades before such demand fully materializes. However, because the spatial effects of climate change are expected to be highly heterogeneous (Intergovernmental Panel on Climate Change 1998), climate adaptation has the potential to be substantially borrower-driven and thus more effective.

Regardless, approval-driven lending will result in waste. And to the heart of the theoretical concern in this book, it is a waste of the discretion that is necessary to take advantage of the capacities of multilateral organizations. Donors need to play the role of screening projects based on past performance, with projects designed and proposed by borrowing countries. This would transform the multilateral development banks into grant-making organizations, an orientation that would be more responsive to past performance. As the international community presses forward with attempts to address a number of entrenched environmental problems, it will be necessary to design effective mechanisms for financing environmental improvements. I have shown that monitoring and evaluation do not provide a silver bullet for the problem of performance at the multilateral development banks. Instead, member states and civil society groups must use information to restrain the approval imperative and promote selectivity to achieve better developmental and environmental results.

DATA COLLECTION PROCEDURES

CODING PROCEDURE FOR PROJECT EVALUATIONS

Our team coded several items from project evaluations completed by the World Bank, Asian Development Bank, and African Development Bank from 1990 to 2008 (figure A.1). I first recruited and trained research assistants on the coding items. Based on initial practice coding sets, I iteratively revised the coding criteria to increase intercoder reliability. Following the adoption of final coding criteria, all research assistants were required to pass a 20-evaluation practice set at 90% coding reliability before they were allowed to move onto the final coding stage that produced the data for this book.

Two research assistants independently coded each project evaluation in the sample. In all cases, the research assistants made note of the evaluation section and/or page numbers that they used to determine their coding. When the two coding results matched, the coded value was entered into the final data set without further review. When the two coded values were different, I examined the sections that the research assistants noted in their coding sheets and made a decision about the final coding value. Our team coded all project evaluations before I specified any of the models contained in this book.

Item 1. Environmental Target Performance. The purpose of this item is to assess the quality of implementation for environmental *targets*. Environmental targets are any project goals that attempt to make some environmental condition *better* than it was before the project. In other words, environmental targets are project components that are designed to "do good," rather than "do no harm" (which is safeguard performance, item 2). Environmental targets measure an attempt to improve the *quality or extent* of some environmental resource (e.g., water, forest, land, soil, etc.).

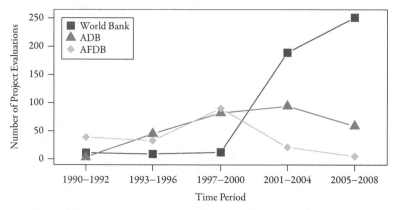

Number of Project Evaluations — ■ World Bank, ▲ ADB, ◆ AFDB — Time Period: 1990–1992, 1993–1996, 1997–2000, 2001–2004, 2005–2008

FIGURE A.1 Total number of project evaluations per time period, 1990–2008

Environmental targets do not have to be the primary purpose of the project to be coded. If several environment targets are the primary purpose of the project, an aggregate summary of their achievement is coded according to the criteria below. There must be some information about outcomes or indication of performance to code this item. The intention to address environmental issues is not sufficient. Targets to improve an environment-related institutions or to improve management/policy related to environment resources are considered to be environmental targets if the implied goal is improved environmental management.

Both information about the achievement of targets generally and the borrower's performance at achieving targets specifically are coded. If the project evaluation specifically mentions that the lack of achievement of environmental targets was the result of bank actions (design, monitoring, etc.), that information is noted in coding item about design problems (item 3). Both the environmental target item and the design item (item 3) can be coded for the same evaluation.

Items related to *water supply/quantity* are coded as an environmental target only if they related to (1) more efficient use of water resources; (2) improved management of water extraction; (3) decreased extraction of water resources from surface or groundwater. Flood control is not an environmental target, unless it involves improved natural resource management or the restoration of wetlands. Agriculture targets are not considered environmental targets unless they involve improvement to some environmental resource, such as through decreasing soil erosion, improving water use efficiency, or restoring upper watershed areas. For projects that have multiple environmental targets, the score is the aggregate of all components that best meets the criteria in table A.1.

Item 1b: Environmental Target Sector. If the achievement of an environmental target is coded, the sector to which the target applies is also coded as follows:

1: Climate change, clean energy, climate adaptation projects (excluding dams)
2: Conservation: biodiversity, forestry conservation, forestry management
3: Rural sector: sustainable agriculture, water management, erosion control, soil conservation, community resource management
4: Local/urban environmental issues: water pollution, sanitation, sewerage, and urban improvement

TABLE A.I

CODING CRITERIA FOR ENVIRONMENTAL TARGET PERFORMANCE

Coding	Meaning	Criteria
4	Highly satisfactory	Exceeds environmental goals or targets; specifically mentioned for outstanding environmental performance; efforts significantly improve environmental outcomes as compared to preapproval expectations; fairly detailed description of excellent performance with no room for improvement.
3	Satisfactory	Meets all environmental goals or with only minor exceptions observed; **summary statement of performance is positive**; any negatives are minor and easy to fix; summary statement of satisfactory performance without detail outlining strengths or weaknesses.
2	Partly satisfactory	Meets some environmental goals or conditions with significant deficiencies observed; **summary statement of performance is negative.**
I	Unsatisfactory	Does not meet most environmental goals or targets with major deficiencies observed in most areas; nonachievement of targets and mentions of failure and unsatisfactory performance.
NA	Not available	Project has no environmental aspects *or* insufficient information is available in evaluation report to assess environmental target implementation performance.

Item 2. Environmental Safeguard Performance. Each of the development banks has adopted environmental safeguard procedures to ensure projects "do no harm" to the environment. In most cases, evaluations will contain information about the implementation of safeguards for projects with substantial physical components, such as dams, large infrastructure, roads, and urban improvements. As opposed to environmental targets, environmental safeguards attempt to maintain environmental quality as it existed before the project. Words that are associated with safeguard performance include "loan covenants," "safeguards," "environmental compliance," "environmental impact," and so on.

Items related to *water supply/quantity* are coded as performance related to environmental safeguards if they deal with (1) depletion of surface or groundwater sources; (2) conversion of wetlands to other uses; (3) extraction of water from natural areas.

Safeguard performance must relate to *project activities*, rather than general environmental issues surrounding a project. Unsatisfactory outcomes related to safeguards that are the result of bank actions or decisions about design, if they are specifically mentioned, are indicated in the Design category (item 3). How a borrowing countries responds to unexpected safeguard

TABLE A.2

CODING CRITERIA FOR ENVIRONMENTAL SAFEGUARD PERFORMANCE

Coding	Meaning	Criteria
4	Highly satisfactory	Exceeds environmental conditions in terms of monitoring plans and mitigation activities; specifically mentioned for outstanding remediation efforts; environment is maintained in high quality despite risks posed by project design.
3	Satisfactory	Meets all environmental safeguards and conditions with only minor exceptions observed; summary statement of performance is positive.
2	Partly satisfactory	Meets some safeguard goals met with significant deficiencies observed; does not meet monitoring or evaluation standards in projects with no discernible environmental impacts; **does not meet safeguard standards with no discernible environmental impacts;** summary statement of performance is negative or indicates that major improvements are required.
1	Unsatisfactory	Does not meet most environmental goals or conditions with major deficiencies observed in most areas; outright noncompliance with environmental loan conditions; failure to address the project environmental impacts during implementation.
NA	Not available	Project has no environmental aspects *or* insufficient information is available in evaluation report to assess recipient performance.

issues is recorded as part of safeguard performance. For projects that have multiple safeguards or subprojects, the score is the aggregate of all components that most closely meets the coding criteria in table A.2.

Item 3. Design Issues Decrease Environmental Performance. For many early projects in the sample, a full consideration of the environmental issues was not part of project preparation. Some evaluations state that environmental performance was low because environmental issues were not fully appraised, which is the intended content for this coding item. If a borrowing country fails to conduct monitoring or planning as agreed, the performance is coded in the performance item above (item 2). In order to code this item, environmental outcomes of the project need to be less satisfactory than they would have been if environmental issues had been considered at the design phase of the project. In the case that the project or borrower failed to respond to unexpected challenges, the appropriate performance rating is coded in either item 1 or 2. The design issue is coded as follows:

1: No environmental planning was considered by the bank; failed to anticipate environmental problems; failed to anticipate factors that affect environmental performance.

0: None of the above issues apply and no design issues are mentioned in an evaluation that contains some information about the environmental aspects of a project

NA: The evaluation contains no information about the environment.

Item 4: Environmental Targets Mentioned in Lessons/Recommendations. For both item 4 and item 5, information is only be coded from the final, forward-looking sections of the project evaluation, not from recommendations that come up in the body of the evaluation. Different development banks have various names for these sections, including "Conclusions," "Lessons," "Recommendations," "Key Issues," "Follow-up Actions," and so on. This item is coded if either the recommendation section or the lessons section contain information about the achievement of *environmental targets*, as defined in item 1. Having a coding for item 1 does not mean that this item will necessarily be coded and vice versa.

1: The lessons/recommendations sections contains a statement about the achievement of *environmental targets* in either the current or future project.

0: There is no mention of *environmental targets* in the lessons/recommendation section.

Item 5: Environmental Safeguards Mentioned in Lessons/Recommendations. This item is coded if either the recommendation section or lessons section contain information about the achievement of *environmental safeguards*, as defined in item 2. Having a coding for item 2 does not necessarily imply that this item will be coded and vice versa.

1: The lessons/recommendations sections contain a statement about the achievement of *environmental safeguards* in either the current or future project.

0: There is no mention of *environmental safeguards* in the lessons/recommendation section.

Additional items compiled from project evaluations. In addition to producing the original coded data described in this section, our team also compiled performance ratings that were already assigned by evaluators in the project evaluations. All project evaluation assign an *overall performance rating* to each project, which we compiled. In addition, project evaluations often included a rating for *borrower performance*, which we also compiled.

CODING PROCEDURE FOR COUNTRY PROGRAM EVALUATIONS

Our team coded 21 binary items from every available country program evaluation completed by the World Bank, Asian Development Bank, Inter-American Development Bank, and African Development Bank from 1990 to 2008. As in the coding procedure for the project evaluations, I recruited and trained research assistants on the items described below. I first worked with a group of research assistants to revise the coding items for reliability. I assigned research assistants to pairs and had them independently code five-evaluation practice sets. In an iterative fashion, we closely scrutinized any item that was coded differently between the coders to arrive at final coding definitions. Once we finalized the coding criteria, research assistants were assigned to five-evaluation practice sets, which they had to code at 90% reliability before they were allowed to move onto the final coding stage to produce the data used in this book.

Two research assistants independently coded every country program evaluation in the sample. In all cases, the research assistants made note of the evaluation section that they used to determine their coding. When the two coding results matched, the coded value was entered into the final data set without further review. When the two coding results were different, I referenced the sections that the research assistants noted in their coding sheets and made a decision about the final coding value. All of the coding was completed before I specified any of the models contained in this book. We coded the following items according to the rules listed below.

Executive Summary Item 1. *Is the environment (sustainability, degradation, sanitation, deforestation, etc.) mentioned as a bank priority/area for emphasis?* In the case that there is no executive summary, a memorandum to the board can be used for this and all executive summary items. All executive summary items can only be coded from an executive summary or memorandum to the board.

Executive Summary Item 2. *Are the general (not project related) environmental practices or lack of appropriate environmental management in the recipient country mentioned as a concern?* This item is coded if environmental problems are identified and either environmental practices are noted as deficient or if there is no mention of any actions taken to address the problems.

Executive Summary Item 3. *Are improvements to the general (not project related) environmental practices (policy, monitoring, implementation) of the recipient country during the period under evaluation mentioned?* This item is coded if there is any mention of government actions that positively address environmental problems that are unrelated to the MDB's projects and programs. This item is coded unless the environmental practices are mentioned as being specifically tied to a project/program. This item is not mutually exclusive with ES2.

Executive Summary Item 4. *Are environmental safeguard issues in any of the projects that are evaluated mentioned as a concern?* For a definition of environmental safeguard issues, see project evaluation coding item 2 above.

Executive Summary Item 5. *Is the implementation of environment-improving activities in the evaluated projects mentioned as less than satisfactory?* For a definition of environment-improving activities, see project evaluation coding item 1 above.

Executive Summary Item 6. *Is the implementation of environment-improving activities in the evaluated projects mentioned as satisfactory?*

Executive Summary Item 7. *Is there an unsatisfactory summary assessment of bank programs?* Keywords used to make this determination include major/many problems; poor execution/implementation; not been effective; fallen short of expectations; shortcomings; below par/average; systematic shortcomings; fraught with challenges; persistent problems; disappointing; ineffectual. The summary assessment is the success of the *entire* bank lending program, including projects that are unrelated to the environment. This coding item uses performance information over the entire period being evaluated. When overall performance has been mixed, neither ES7 nor ES8 is coded.

Executive Summary Item 8. *Is there a satisfactory summary assessment of bank programs?* Keywords used to make this determination include effective; successful; positive outcome; highly favorable; good level of performance; significant gains; above average. If the overall performance is qualified by numerous shortcomings, this item is not be coded.

Background Item 1. *Are global environmental resources (i.e., biodiversity, tropical forests, deforestation, climate, global fisheries) in the recipient country described as having notable importance/abundance?* All background coding items are related to general, nonproject conditions and practices that are in place in the country (all other sections relate to bank activities). Items in this section capture the context in which the MDB operates. Background items are coded primarily from the background section of country program evaluations, but are allowed to be coded from other relevant areas, including the executive summary. Global environmental resources concern environmental resources that cross international borders and are often subject of international treaties.

Background Item 2. *Is the degradation of global environmental resources without a link to local well-being listed as a concern?* This item is coded if the degradation of environmental resources is not linked to human well-being, but rather for the existence value (e.g., biodiversity preservation). This item is only coded when a specific environmental issue is listed or at least two sentences about general environmental concerns are present.

Background Item 3. *Is the degradation of the environmental resources described and also linked to development and human well-being in the borrowing country?* This item is only coded when a specific environmental issue is listed or at least two sentences about general environmental concerns are present.

Background Item 4. *Are the general (not project related) environmental practices or lack of appropriate environmental management in the borrowing country mentioned as a concern?* This item relates to the institutional and policy response of the borrowing government. This item is coded positively if significant environmental problems are identified and are not being addressed, or are getting worse despite being addressed. This item is only coded when a specific environmental management concern is listed or at least two sentences about general environmental concerns are present.

Background Item 5. *Are improvements to the general (not project related) environmental practices (e.g., policy, monitoring, implementation) of the borrowing country during the period under evaluation mentioned?* This item relates to the institutional and policy response of the borrowing government. This item is coded if there is any mention of government actions unrelated to bank *projects* that positively address environmental problems. This item is coded positively if improvements are being made to general environmental conditions, even if problems remain. Policy changes that are influenced by dialogue with the MDB, but that do not result from a specific project or program, are coded for this item.

Project Performance Item 1. *Is there a subsection (at least one paragraph) that deals primarily with environmental performance during project implementation?* All project performance items relate to the implementation of specific MDB projects. Information from any section of the country program evaluation is coded, so long as it refers to the performance of specific MDB projects or programs.

Project Performance Item 2. *Are the environmental impacts of development projects (aka "safeguards") during the period under evaluation mentioned as a concern?* This item is coded only when a specific environmental mitigation concern is listed or at least two sentences about general environmental mitigation concerns are present.

Project Performance Item 3. *Are the goals or targets of MDB development projects said to be at risk because of general (not project specific) environmental concerns?* This item is coded if environmental degradation negatively impacts other development goals. This item is only coded

when a specific environmental concern is listed or at least two sentences about general environmental concerns related to development goals are present.

    Project Performance Item 4. *Are concerns mentioned about the achievement of environmental
goals or targets in bank projects?* This item is coded only when a specific project performance concern is listed or at least two sentences about general project performance concerns are present.

    Project Performance Item 5. *Are unsatisfactory borrowing country environmental practices
(e.g., policy, monitoring, implementation, ownership) listed as a reason for unsatisfactory achievement of environmental goals or targets in bank projects?* This item is coded only when PP4 is positive and the evaluation attributes concerns about environmental targets in bank projects to the
borrowing country. PP4 and PP5 are not mutually exclusive with PP6 and PP7, and both can be
coded when mixed performance is noted in the evaluation.

    Project Performance Item 6. *Is the satisfactory achievement of environmental goals or targets
in bank projects noted?* This item is coded only when an achievement of environmental goals in
specific bank project(s) is noted or at least two sentences about general environmental performance in bank projects are present.

    Project Performance Item 7. *Are good borrowing country environmental practices (e.g., policy,
monitoring, implementation, ownership) listed as a reason for the achievement of environmental
goals or targets in bank projects?* This item is coded only when PP6 is positive and the evaluation
attributes the achievement of environmental targets performance in bank projects to actions of
the borrowing country.

    Recommendations Item 1. *Is mitigating the negative environmental impacts (aka "safe-
guards") that result from bank projects recommended?* All items in the recommendations section
are coded only from the recommendations section at the end of the country program evaluation
or from the concluding recommendations list that is set aside from other parts of the evaluation.
If a recommendations section only exists as part of the executive summary, these items can be
coded from that section.

    Recommendations Item 2. *Is future action on environmental goals or targets recommended?*
This item is coded for project activities that directly and tangibly improve environmental
resources. For a definition of environment-improving operations, see project evaluation coding
item 1.

    Recommendations Item 3. *Is a focus on environmental capacity building recommended?*
This item is coded for actions to improve institutions related to environmental management
in future periods, without directly and tangibly improving the condition of environmental
resources.

SEMI-STRUCTURED INTERVIEW TEMPLATE

From 2008 to 2010, I conducted semistructured interviews with 54 staff at the MDBs considered in this book. In general, I sought to interview the widest possible range of operational and
evaluation staff in order to capture the full variation in observations about how different information mechanisms influenced lending decisions. My interviews were often based on "snow-
ball sampling," with interviewees suggesting additional contacts to capture a wider variation
in observations (Goldstein 2002). In each interview, I utilized a semistructured interview template and asked about incentives among operational staff and responses to different kinds of

information. I guaranteed all interviewees anonymity in order to generate candid responses. I used the following basic template to guide interviews:

Background on interviewee
Organization:
Position:
Roles relevant to evaluation and allocation decisions:

Observations about use of performance information and evaluation

- Have you observed performance information being used in operations and decisions about the allocation of projects? Examples?
  - What type of information? How as it produced? How was it disseminated?
- At what stage of decision-making (project screening, project design, etc.) have you observed performance information being used?
- Have you observed evaluations being used in decision-making? Examples?

Factors framing responses to performance (use examples provided above to guide interview)

- What are the external conditions (donors, civil society pressure, press, etc.) that promote/impede use of performance information to adjust allocation decisions? Examples?
- Project types (i.e., involving safeguards, easily measurable targets, focus areas)? Examples?
- Internal processes (i.e., incentives for implementing staff, relationship between departments)? Examples?

Appendix 2

A BRIEF HISTORY OF EVALUATION AT THE MULTILATERAL
DEVELOPMENT BANKS

Like many other types of organizations, the World Bank and the regional development banks have all greatly increased their capacity to conduct evaluations in recent decades, with the intention of contributing to future decisions about lending.[1] Whereas evaluations in the early 1990s rarely looked beyond the administrative and budgetary practices of MDB programs, since that time evaluation departments have expanded their activities to measure outcomes and impacts.

World Bank. The evaluation function at the World Bank was created during McNamara's presidency (Grasso, Wasty, and Weaving 2003, annex C). Initially, the evaluation unit was staffed with five professionals, who were tasked with conducting evaluations of World Bank operations in Colombia and electricity sector investments. These pilot evaluations were considered successful by donor countries, and by 1973 the evaluation office was elevated to the Operations Evaluation Department, with responsibilities for broad evaluations and audits of individual projects following their completion. By 1974, the Operations Evaluation Department reported directly to the Board of Executive Directors, for the stated purpose of avoiding conflicts of interest with World Bank management.

The World Bank entered the 1990s with a need to improve performance, given both internal and external indications that the performance of bank projects was poor, which generated strident external criticism (Picciotto 2002). In 1992, member states discussed the now famous "Wapenhans report," which chronicled deteriorating World Bank performance (Wapenhans 1992). This event spawned a renewed interest in increasing the World Bank's capacity for evaluating its own programs, and, in response, the World Bank increased both staff and resources for evaluation. At this stage, the World Bank evaluation office emphasized defining indicators of performance, measuring baseline data to which outcomes could be compared, monitoring results, and reporting findings in ways that both satisfied methodological concerns and also generated results useful for decision-making within the bank (Kusek and Rist 2004).

Asian Development Bank. The ADB evaluation unit has changed its position within the organization and increased in importance with several formal upgrades in status over the last several decades. In 1978, the Post-Evaluation Office was established and tasked with evaluating the results of bank projects. To reflect a broadening mandate, the Post-Evaluation Office was renamed the Operations Evaluation Office in 1999. The ADB elevated its evaluation body to the departmental level, naming it the Operations Evaluation Department (OED) in 2001. This placed the head of the department on equal organizational status with the heads of the operational departments. The ADB also established its own Development Effectiveness Committee during 2001, which became the formal mechanism through which OED reported to the board of executive directors, thereby enhancing its accountability function (Asian Development Bank 2003). Further reforms were carried out to make the OED more autonomous and independent in subsequent years, and as of 2004 the department reported directly to the board of directors rather than the ADB president. Currently, the OED has a broad mandate to evaluate projects, policies, and bank-wide strategies. The OED was renamed the Independent Evaluation Department in 2009.

Inter-American Development Bank. At the behest of the United States, the Group of Controllers of the Review and Evaluation System was created in 1968. This group was charge with conducting high-level audits of bank programs and reporting them to the member states through the board of executive directors (Comptroller General 1974). At the time, only six technical staff were assigned to audit the whole of bank operations. Over the next decade, the audit and evaluation function grew considerably. By the 1980s, evaluation was split between the Operations Evaluation Office and the Office of External Review and Evaluation. The former office reported directly to the IADB president and was responsible for "evaluating the economic and social impact of the Bank's operations" (Inter-American Development Bank 1985, 23). The later reported directly to member states through the board of executive directors and assessed performance in "problem areas and sectors" (Inter-American Development Bank 1985, 12). Like the World Bank and Asian Development Bank, greater resources were directed to evaluation in the early 1990s, as reports of declining portfolio performance rippled across the different multilateral development banks (Inter-American Development Bank 1993). During 1999, the Office of Evaluation and Oversight was elevated to a more independent status that reported directly to member states through the board of executive directors.[2] Since that time, its work plan has emphasize broad, strategic level evaluations that are aimed at addressing decisions made at the board level.[3]

African Development Bank. Evaluation at the African Development Bank was established later than the other multilateral development banks. In 1980, the Evaluation Division was created within the Department of Planning and Research. While this division began the work of evaluating completed operations, it was unable to control staffing and administrative resources, as it reported to bank management, rather than to the board of executive directors from donor countries. As a result, donor states were unable to learn about or to raise concerns about the independence and objectivity of the Evaluation Division (General Accounting Office 1986). Reflecting these concerns, the Evaluation Division was promoted to the Operations Evaluation Office. Member states altered the organizational hierarchy further so that the Evaluation Division reported directly to the president beginning in 1987 and then to the board of executive directors (representatives of member states) in 1993. In 1995, the board committed additional resources to evaluation and upgraded the unit to the Operations Evaluation Department (OPEV).[4] Since that time, OPEV has been involved in project evaluations and higher-level consideration of themes, targets, and goals of development.

NOTES

⌒——————————————————————————————————————

CHAPTER 1

1. See Thomas 1991.

2. Full text of the hearing available at http://www.archive.org/stream/worldbankdisclosoounit/worldbankdisclosoounit_djvu.txt (accessed July 2012).

3. See, for example, http://www.heritage.org/research/commentary/2011/10/time-to-rein-in-the-bloated-unaccountable-united-nations (accessed June 2015).

4. The World Bank project database is available at http://go.worldbank.org/KPMUDAVVT0 (accessed May 2011).

5. For information on the components of this project, see the project information website at http://www.adb.org/projects/41435-013/main (accessed October 2015).

6. For a general treatment of the subject, see Gibson 2005; Martens 2005; Martens et al. 2002; and van Ufford et al. 1988.

CHAPTER 2

1. See http://www.unep.org/champions/ (accessed August 2014).

2. Bermeo (2010) argues that bilateral donors increasingly view economic development in recipient countries as a strategic priority, suggesting that strategic and development goals are not always misaligned.

3. See the 2011 USAID evaluation policy at http://www.usaid.gov/evaluation/ (accessed November 2011).

4. Milner presents a different logic for delegation, namely that delegation helps governments meet public demands for development activity that is not driven, at least directly, by geostrategic interests.

5. The International Bank for Reconstruction and Development (IBRD) is the lending arm of the World Bank that makes market-rate loans to middle-income countries with low external debt burdens.

6. Similar constraints have been found for the International Monetary Fund, which cannot credibly commit to punishing states that are closely aligned economically or militarily with the United States. See Stone 2011.

7. A copy of the speech is available at http://www.mof.go.jp/english/international_policy/mdbs/adb/2010st.pdf (accessed October 2015).

8. See the news release "New ADB Policy Targets Secure, Clean Energy for Asia," available at http://www.adb.org/Media/Articles/2009/12917-asian-clean-energies-policies/ (accessed May 2011).

9. I adopt this generic term for ease of use and consistency through the book. In reality, each MDB has its own name for these strategies. The World Bank uses "country assistance strategy"; the Asian Development Bank uses "country partnership strategy"; the Inter-American Development Bank uses "country strategy"; and the African Development Bank uses "country strategy paper."

10. Information calculated using the World Bank project database, available at http://go.worldbank.org/YLPQAHBY40 (accessed May 2011).

11. The Rio Declaration on Environment and Development is available at http://www.un.org/documents/ga/conf151/aconf15126-1annex1.htm (accessed May 2011).

12. The initial surge of green aid largely abated by the late 1990s, however. See Hicks et al. 2008 for more details.

13. These data are collected from the LexisNexis Congressional Database. For example, see "Beyond the Earth Summit: Developing an Energy-Efficient World," Senate Committee of Governmental Affairs Hearing 102-973, May 21, 1992.

14. For information on the 1991 *Environmental Assessment Sourcebook* and later updates, see http://go.worldbank.org/LLF3CMS1I0 (accessed November 2011).

CHAPTER 3

1. To this day, states continue to rely on the multilateral development banks for these functions. In 2008, for example, states that are donors to the Asian Development Bank agreed to replenish the concessional lending resources with $11.3 billion (Asian Development Bank 2008a). In 2009, the same donor countries chose to triple the general capital resources available for lending at the Asian Development Bank to $165 billion. In 2009, the World Bank Group had more than 10,000 staff, lent more than $50 billion, and had an administrative budget of more than $1 billion annually (World Bank 2009a).

2. The IADB and AFDB have articles of agreement that require borrowing countries to maintain a majority of the capital stock and voting power at the board of executive directors. For information on the Inter-American Development Bank, see http://www.iadb.org/en/about-us/capital-stock-and-voting-power,1352.html (accessed June 2011). For information on the African Development Bank, see http://www.afdb.org/fileadmin/uploads/afdb/Documents/Boards-Documents/2011-vp-eng-may.pdf (accessed June 2011).

3. For example, the World Bank suspended lending to Zimbabwe in 2000 after it failed to repay existing loans, following a period of violent political repression and undeclared war spending (Nyahti 2000).

CHAPTER 4

1. This search was performed using the AidData online database, purpose code Energy Generation and activity code Hydropower Plant. See http://www.aiddata.org/ (accessed July 2015).

2. The 1993 Environmental Assessment Guidelines are summarized by the Canadian International Development Agency, available at http://www.acdi-cida.gc.ca/inet/images.nsf/vLUImages/ea%20summaries/$file/AsDB.pdf (accessed October 2015). The 1995 Bank Policy of Forestry is available at https://openaccess.adb.org/bitstream/handle/11540/4861/The%20Bank's%20Policy%20on%20Forestry-March%201995.pdf?sequence=1 (accessed October 2015). The 1995 Inspection Policy is available at many academic libraries (Asian Development Bank 1995).

3. The Environment Policy is available at http://www.adb.org/sites/default/files/institutional-document/33343/files/environment-policy.pdf (accessed October 2015).

4. This calculation was made according to an environmental risk category database that was supplied to the author during a visit to the African Development Bank headquarters in Tunis, Tunisia, during June 2010.

5. According to interviewees, this funding pattern is especially likely for mid-income countries like India and China, which have access to competitive, commercial financing to pursue the most environmentally risky parts of transportation projects.

6. This figure is in constant 2005 USD according to the World Bank's World Development Indicators.

7. The press release is available at http://www.worldbank.org/en/news/press-release/2005/03/31/lao-pdr-one-of-the-poorest-countries-in-east-asia-receives-support-for-the-long-term.

8. Environmentally risky projects that have an AidData purpose code within "General Environmental Protection" are excluded, given that environmental projects with physical components often require environmental assessment, even though the goal is to achieve positive environmental outcomes.

9. While this chapter does not deal with how aggregated evaluations impact lending decisions, it is worth noting that the evaluation departments have spent considerable effort evaluating the safeguard performance of program staff and borrowing countries. Like project evaluations, these thematic evaluations have highlighted mixed safeguard implementation performance. Building upon project-level findings, the ADB evaluation office completed a 1998 *Special Evaluation Study on Environmental Mitigation Measures in Selected ADB-Financed Projects*, which found variable success and recommended that increased attention be paid to the management capacity and performance of borrowing countries and contractors in carrying out safeguard procedures during project implementation. A follow-up study examined the implementation of ADB safeguard policies in selected hydropower projects (Asia Development Bank 1999). This evaluation recommended better implementation of safeguards in complex, environmentally risky projects. Accumulating lessons on safeguard implementation, the OED conducted a broad review of the ADB safeguard policy in 2006 and recommended focusing less on procedural compliance and more on achieving good environmental outcomes (Operations Evaluation Department 2006). This is all to say that OED has been closely involved with evaluating the environmental outcomes of ADB projects during the study period considered here. Given the bank-wide emphasis placed on environmental safeguard policies and the immediate

involvement that evaluation has played in monitoring the implementation of environmental policies over time, the ADB offers an excellent opportunity to examine how environmental performance information impacts financing decisions about environmentally risky projects. The World Bank Independent Evaluation Group also completed a broad study of safeguard policies as part of an update to its safeguard procedures in 2010 (Independent Evaluation Group 2010b).

10. The evaluation department at the Inter-American Development Bank does not conduct project evaluations.

11. The rates of intercoder reliability within one point on the ordinal coding scale before adjudication by lead author are World Bank 76.3%; Asian Development Bank 74.2%; African Development Bank 78.2%.

12. In some cases, the source data for *FEWER POLITICAL RIGHTS* were available only biannually or for limited portions of the panel within a particular country. Since all of the control variables have most of their variation in the cross-section between countries, rather than over time within countries, I included the linear interpolation for all points between available observations and extrapolated the exact endpoint value up to three years beyond the available variable dates where applicable. These decisions are based on the judgment that casewise deletion based on missing data of slow-changing variables would introduce more problems for inference than interpolation/extrapolation, where applicable.

13. For robustness checks, I also use other control variables. Past research has found that multilateral development banks allocate more financing to borrowing countries that have good governance and a good record in implementing previous projects. In fact, recent reforms at the multilateral development banks have made these factors part of a formula that determines a country's access to concessional lending. Thus, I calculate *OVERALL REPUTATION* from the final project ratings in evaluations during the previous five years and use the World Bank Institute's rating of governmental effectiveness (*GOVERNMENT EFFECTIVENESS*) to control for project performance and governance of each borrowing country.

14. This is equivalent to estimating a nonparametric event history model, with a hazard function that is not based on distributional assumptions (Box-Steffensmeier and Jones 2004).

15. I observe differences in estimate of the effects of different measures of poor safeguard implementation for the World Bank and the Asian Development Bank. For the Asian Development Bank, environmental safeguard performance is a standard component of all project evaluations and is available for 180 of 283 project evaluations completed between 1995 and 2008. In contrast, environmental safeguard performance is not a standard component of project evaluations for the World Bank and is only available for 125 of 472 project evaluations completed between 1995 and 2008 (see also figure 4.2). As a consequence, project evaluations at the Asian Development Bank that document failed safeguard outcomes cover a much larger proportion of the total panel (74/280 country-years) than is the case for the World Bank (63/1450 country-years). For the Asian Development Bank, therefore, the number of project evaluations documenting safeguard failures regardless of preproject design flaws fails to achieve statistical significance at conventional levels, while excluding safeguard failures associated with design flaws proves to be a more discriminating test (this variable is used in Models 2a–2b). For the World Bank, because safeguard performance is not a standard component of project evaluations, failing to mitigate environmental damages tends to be associated with implementation problems, regardless of whether design problems are also noted, so all safeguard data regardless of design are used for the analysis.

16. As a robustness check, I examine the influence of environmental reputation on the approval of no-risk projects for each borrower. I find that safeguard implementation performance does not influence whether no-risk projects are approved. While these regression estimates are omitted for brevity, the only significant variables excluding fixed effects were portfolio characteristics, such as the number of projects and size of the portfolio.

17. Low political rights uses the Freedom House score of 6, while high political use the Freedom House score of 2 for the political rights index. The other model variable are set to the following levels: *NO. EVALS W/SAFEGUARD SUCCESS* (1); *CONCESSIONAL* (0); *NO. PROJECTS* (panel median); *TIME DUMMIES* (project approved in the previous year).

18. Unlike the other multilateral development banks, which have systematically applied their safeguard policies and classified each of their projects according to environmental risk, the African Development Bank has had weak systems in place to handle environmentally risky projects. Indeed, in the project-level environmental classification data that I obtained directly from the AFDB, only 869 of 1,746 project approved between 2000 and 2009 had been assigned to an environmental risk category. Within the projects that are not assigned an environmental risk, I find numerous examples of projects that are likely to be environmentally risky, including large hydropower, fossil fuel-based energy generation, and large-scale water projects. Thus, it is possible that high-performing countries simply avoid having their projects processed through the safeguards policy.

19. As introduced above, this requirement has been standardized across the MDBs because of the "Pelosi amendment" in the 1989 US International Development and Finance Act.

20. See the project information at http://www.adb.org/projects/36330-023/main (accessed October 2015).

21. For example, see how safeguard issues figure prominently in the background paper that was prepared for meetings with donor countries about the 12th African Development Fund replenishment (African Development Fund 2010).

22. This may even be a concern for low-income countries as nontraditional sources of financing, like Chinese development assistance, becomes available for environmentally risky projects. This shift has already occurred for the financing of large hydropower projects in Southeast Asia.

CHAPTER 5

1. For a more complete history of the establishment of the World Bank Inspection Panel, see Shihata 2000 and Clark et al. 2003.

2. Across the three multilateral development banks considered here, claimants must show that they have experienced material damages because MDB policies were not carried out, must have attempted to resolve the issue with bank management, and must file their claim while a project is active. For more specific rules on eligibility, see Clark 2003.

3. For example, US congressional leaders have commissioned independent Government Accountability Office (formerly called the General Accounting Office) reports on the environmental and social practices as part of replenishment discussions. See General Accounting Office 1998.

4. A related example is the establishment of the Ombudsman's Office at the World Bank International Financial Corporation. For more information, see http://www.cao-ombudsman.org/ (accessed April 2011).

5. See McGill 2001 for a discussion of institutional differences of the ADB panel. See Miller 2001 for a discussion of institutional differences of the IADB panel.

6. For example, on June 18, 2008, several environmental NGOs testified before the US House of Representatives Committee on Financial Services, urging that new environmental and accountability policies be adopted at the World Bank. These groups argued that the United States should use its leverage over IDA replenishment to push for these reforms. See the statement of Lori Udall, available at http://archives.financialservices.house.gov/hearing110/udall061808.pdf (accessed July 2012).

7. See the resolution establishing the World Bank Inspection Panel, at http://siteresources.worldbank.org/EXTINSPECTIONPANEL/Resources/ResolutionMarch2005.pdf (accessed March 2011).

8. For an excellent definition of risk aversion in international relations theory, see O'Neill 2001.

9. For example, Khagram (2004) documents a decline in the number of dam projects financed by the multilateral development banks over the last several decades. While the multilateral development banks are no longer actively involved in this area, many new dams are now financed by the Chinese and other bilateral donors that do not require any social or environmental safeguards. For an NGO perspective on this process, see the International River Networks' "Dams Built by China" page at http://www.internationalrivers.org/taxonomy/term/736 (accessed March 2011).

10. For example, inspection cases that were filed relating to the Yacyreta Dam Project, which was jointly financed by the World Bank and Inter-American Development Bank, became a major part of a hearing on US appropriations to multilateral development banks in 1997. See minutes for appropriations hearing, US House Subcommittee on Foreign Operations, Export Financing, and Related Programs on February 12, 1997, available at http://www.gpo.gov/fdsys/pkg/CHRG-105hhrg41767/html/CHRG-105hhrg41767.htm (accessed March 2011).

11. The IBRD did undertake a general capital increase in 2010, in order to have the resources to respond effectively to the global financial crisis.

12. See the Nepal Power Development Project (P043311) abstract at http://www.worldbank.org/projects/P043311/nepal-power-development-project (accessed September 2013).

13. Some of the independent variables are missing on an intermittent basis. Thus, I interpolate data values where possible and apply the latest value for up to three years when data is missing.

14. For another example of the approach taken here and a discussion of addressing selection effects with selection models and matching techniques, see Simmons and Hopkins 2005.

15. As King and Zeng (2007) argue, model dependence and biased estimation are more likely with extrapolation than with interpolation. An intuitive explanation of common support in two dimensions would be to stretch a rubber band around the tacks on a tackboard. If this process were completed for the two-dimensional values of any treatment group, control observations that do not fall within this area would be discarded and vice versa. This concept generalizes to multiple dimensions. This test is built into the R package MatchIt, which is described in Ho et al. 2008.

16. Genetic matching uses a weighted Mahalanobis distance to determine the optimal weight that each variable should have in determining the distance between any two observations. Unlike standard Mahalanobis distance, where each variables is weighted equally in determining

the distance between two vectors, a weighted Mahalanobis distance allows the importance of each variable for the distance measure to vary so long as it improves balance in the matched sample. The algorithm iteratively searches through a population of different matching solutions using evolutionary heuristics to minimize the maximum balance discrepancy between the treatment and control groups on any included matching variable. With genetic matching, a weight matrix with nonzero values on the diagonal is the object on which the evolutionary heuristics operate. A population of matched samples is created using different weight matrices and the loss function is the smallest p-value between the treatment and control groups on a single included matching variable as computed by Kolmogorov-Smirnov tests and paired t-tests for difference of means. Matching solutions that decrease the maximum discrepancy between the treatment and control groups are passed on to the following generation. Other cross-over and mutation observations are also passed along to ensure that the algorithm searches the full space of possible matched samples (Mebane and Sekhon 1998; Sekhon and Grieve 2008; see Diamond and Sekhon 2008). This process is completed using the R package "Matching" (Sekhon 2007).

17. All other continuous variables in the model are held at their mean, and discrete variables are held at their median.

18. For more information on the Integrated Coastal Zone Management and Clean-Up Project case see http://web.worldbank.org/WBSITE/EXTERNAL/EXTINSPECTIONPANEL/0,,,contentMDK:22512600~pagePK:64129751~piPK:64128378~theSitePK:380794,00.html (accessed April 2011).

19. This is reflected, for example, in the World Bank's preference for funding electricity transmission projects over electricity generation projects in many countries.

20. A copy of the rules and procedures used by the World Bank in preparing environmental impact assessments, for example, is available at http://www.env.go.jp/earth/coop/coop/document/10-eiae/10-eiae-7.pdf (accessed March 2011).

21. A copy of the rules and procedures used by the Asian Development Bank in preparing environmental impact assessments, as well as the operational "checklists," is available at http://www.adb.org/sites/default/files/institutional-document/32635/files/environmental-assessment-guidelines.pdf (accessed October 2015).

22. One exception might be the recent emphasis and reengagement in hydropower, given international goals to increase power generation while decreasing greenhouse gas emissions. For example, see the recent *Directions in Hydropower: Scaling Up for Development* (World Bank 2009b).

23. For information on IDA's performance-based allocation system, see International Development Association 2010.

CHAPTER 6

1. See the open letter, entitled "Dear Future World Bank President" at http://www.bicusa.org/en/Article.12616.aspx (accessed November 2012).

2. For example, the Asian Development Bank approved "Strategy 2020" in April 2008, which lists "environment" as one of the five main operational and lending areas during the following decade. The World Bank adopted an organization-wide Environment Strategy in 2001, which prioritized environmental management throughout the lending portfolio.

3. This figure is based on calculations using the GEF project database as of November 2012. See http://www.thegef.org/gef/gef_projects_funding (accessed November 2012).

4. The Secretary's speech to the World Bank/IMF 2011 Annual Meeting is available at http://www.imf.org/external/am/2011/speeches/pr31e.pdf (accessed November 2012).

5. For Inspection Panel cases, see "Summary of Inspection Panel Cases," available at http://siteresources.worldbank.org/EXTINSPECTIONPANEL/Resources/Panel_Cases_2010_Nov_8.pdf (accessed February 2011).

6. Independent evaluation departments were established at different times, but were all pushed by donor shareholders as a way to increase accountability. The World Bank Operations Evaluation Department (currently the Independent Evaluation Group) was established in 1975 and reported simultaneously to the board of directors and the president of the World Bank Group (see Grasso, Wasty, and Weaving 2003). In 2001, the Asian Development Bank upgraded its evaluation office to become the Operations Evaluation Department, placing it on an organizational level equal to other departments. The African Development Bank Operations Evaluation Department began reporting directly to the board of directors as of 1995.

7. Statement of Minister of Finance Koji OMI, May 6, 2007, available at http://www.mof.go.jp/english/international_policy/mdbs/adb/2007st.pdf (accessed October 2015).

8. These data are derived from a search for African Development Bank and World Bank agriculture projects in Senegal using the AidData database. Available at www.aiddata.org (accessed February 2014).

9. In the case of rural environmental projects, it is often much more difficult to consistently classify whether a project has an environmental purpose. For example, it is unclear whether agricultural projects that involve soil management should be considered stand-alone environment projects.

10. This proportional variable for overall success generally has low correlation with the relevant environmental performance variables. In all cases, statistically significant results are robust to dropping the overall performance variable. The highest correlations for World Bank / Asian Development Bank across all the models reported in the main text are proportion clean energy success (0.20/0.11); and proportion urban environment success (0.26/0.12).

11. I use the compiled emissions data from Carbon Dioxide Information Analysis Center, available at http://cdiac.ornl.gov/trends/emis/meth_reg.html (accessed April 2011).

12. The evaluation indicating unsuccessful clean energy activities was for the Household Energy Project in Mali, completed in 2003.

13. For more information, see the Asian Development Bank project database for Bangladesh water projects, available at http://wcm.adb.org/projects/search/country/ban/sectors/wus (accessed October 2015).

CHAPTER 7

1. Project evaluations, which were the focus of previous chapters, are weak with respect to audience in several ways. State shareholders acting through the MDB boards are rarely in a position to formally review individual project evaluations, unless a project has become high-profile because of poor performance that is highly publicized. In general, the board is responsible for setting higher-level, strategic directions for the multilateral development banks, and given the breadth of operations that come before the board, the shareholder states do not have the capacity to process implementation issues that come up in the context of individual projects. Because

performance outcomes in the context of single-country programs are often variable, project evaluations do not give state shareholders the ability to separate noise from more systematic performance issues that can be dealt with by higher-level policy and strategy decisions, such as when adopting a new country assistance strategy.

2. For example, see the World Bank's Operational Manual, sec. BP 2.11 for a description of the board's involvement in the development of a country assistance strategy.

3. The development effectiveness committees are composed of a subset of executive directors that are tasked with considering evaluations and improving practices that contribute to development effectiveness. For more information about the formal structuring of the sub-board committees at the World Bank Group, see "Boards at World," available at http://go.worldbank. org/R39ZLBTU10 (accessed April 2011).

4. Many country program evaluations contain a "management response," in which the management formally indicates how it will act on recommendations contained in country program evaluations. An analysis of the use of country program evaluations indicates that this management response often figures prominently in board discussion of country assistance strategies (Operations Evaluation Department 2005a).

5. Operational staff at the Inter-American Development Bank have been less constrained by planning documents, according to my interviews, which often leads to a higher "improvisation rate." This is the proportion of projects that were not planned in the country strategy but are eventually approved.

6. The World Bank has conducted very similar evaluations since 1990 that were not officially designated country program evaluations, but are included in its own database of country program evaluation documents. Those prior evaluations are included in the analysis presented here.

7. In recent years, the Independent Evaluation work program has focused on special evaluation studies of particular importance to the board of executive directors.

8. These environmental performance variables are not mutually exclusive.

9. For example, see the recent country program evaluation of the Dominican Republic, which indicates that 33% of operations were never programmed. Available at http://www.iadb. org/ove/Documents/uploads/cache/35398366.pdf (accessed April 2011).

10. Asian Development Bank country program evaluations are available at http://www.adb. org/Evaluation/resources-list.asp?type=5&p=evalcape (accessed April 2011).

CHAPTER 8

1. Transcript of Bono remarks to Labour Party Conference, September 29, 2004, available at http://www.atu2.com/news/transcript-of-bonos-speech-at-labour-party-conference.html (accessed November 2011).

2. See also the "pledging conferences" held by the African Union, where African leaders engage in proactive fundraising: http://www.au.int/pages/savinglives/events/pledging-conference-horn-africa-2011 (accessed November 2011).

3. For example, see "Strengthening and Effectively Implementing Country Safeguard Systems," Asian Development Bank, at http://www.adb.org/Safeguards/country-safeguards. asp (accessed December 2011).

4. For an interesting discussion of these dynamics, see http://foreignpolicyblogs.com/2015/04/06/will-chinas-new-bank-undermine-the-world-bank/ (accessed May 2015).

5. For example, see the frequently asked questions about the project at http://go.worldbank.org/NXRZK3DX20 (accessed June 2011).

6. For example, while designing a new environmental strategy in 2009, the World Bank visited 126 countries and met with a wide range of stakeholders. See "Environment Strategy Consultations": http://go.worldbank.org/RZIS61oMJo (accessed November 2011).

7. For example, recent guidelines for staff at the Asian Development Bank not only highlight that staff must consult relevant civil society organizations during project preparation, but also encourage the involvement of civil society organizations in the design of country assistance strategies. See Asian Development Bank 2009.

8. For example, the Asian Development Bank Energy Policy adopted in 2009 set an explicit target to increase clean energy financing from $1 billion in 2008 to $2 billion by 2013. See Asian Development Bank 2009.

9. The "African Consensus and Position on Development Effectiveness" (2011) is available at http://www.nepad.org/system/files/AFRICAN_CONSENSUS__POSITION_ON_DEVELOPMENT_EFFECTIVENESS_final.pdf (accessed November 2011).

10. Projects allocated to private sector actors by the World Bank's Carbon Finance Unit tend to be directed to countries that have strong environmental performance records, as revealed in evaluations.

APPENDIX 2

1. The academic field of program evaluation has grown substantially and has produced a vigorous and extensive literature on different ways to collect, analyze, and use evaluation data within organizations (for recent broad reviews, see, e.g., Schwartz and Mayne 2005; McDavid and Hawthorn 2006). As a scholarly discipline, program evaluation has primarily been methods-driven and has focused on ways to produce valid and reliable inference. Program evaluation is routinely applied in a variety of contexts, including conservation biology (Stem et al. 2005; Ferraro and Pattanayak 2006), international development projects (Woolcock 2009), and loan programs for pollution abatement (Akihisa 2008).

2. Information about the recent history of the Office of Evaluation and Oversight is available at http://www.iadb.org/en/office-of-evaluation-and-oversight/about-ove,1556.html (accessed May 2011).

3. As of 2003, however, OVE has conducted postproject validations of every completion report produced by operational departments.

4. Information about the recent history of the Operations Evaluation Department is available at http://www.afdb.org/en/operations-evaluation/history/ (accessed May 2011).

REFERENCES

Abbott, Kenneth W., and Duncan Snidal. 1998. Why States Act through Formal International Organizations. *Journal of Conflict Resolution* 42 (1): 3–32.

Abramson, Rudy. 1992. Rio Negotiators Search for Finance Plan: Summit: Accord Is Sought for a Long-Term Global Environmental Agenda. Resolution of the Issue Is Not Expected Quickly. *Los Angeles Times*, June 5.

Acharya, Arnab, Ana Teresa Fuzzo de Lima, and Mick Moore. 2006. Proliferation and Fragmentation: Transactions Costs and the Value of Aid. *Journal of Development Studies* 42 (1): 1–21.

Ackerman, John. 2004. Co-governance for Accountability: Beyond "Exit" and "Voice." *World Development* 32 (3): 447–63.

Acuña, Carlos H., and Maria Fernanda Tuozzo. 2000. Civil Society Participation in World Bank and Inter-American Development Bank Programs: The Case of Argentina. *Global Governance* 6: 433–56.

Adams, Chris. 1988. U.S. Lags on Payments to World Groups; Policy Disputes, Budget Deficit Blamed; Agencies Respond by Reducing Services. *Washington Post*, August 17, A16.

Africa News. 2010. The Africa Progress Panel Says World Leaders Must Honour Pledge to Provide Additional Annual U.S.$100 Billion in Climate Finance by 2020. June 30.

Africa News. 2011. Oversight over MGT of Oil Revenue Accounts Weak. December 7.

African Development Bank. 2001. Environmental and Social Assessment Procedures for African Development Bank's Public Sector Operations. African Development Bank.

African Development Bank. 2002. Strategic Plan 2003–2007. African Development Bank.

African Development Bank and African Development Fund. 2004. African Development Bank Group's Policy on the Environment. African Development Bank.

African Development Fund. 2000. Appraisal Report: Livestock Support Project—Phase II. Republic of Senegal. Tunis: African Development Bank.

African Development Fund. 2010. Update on Institutional Capacity and Business Process Reforms: Background Paper. Abidjan, Cote d'Ivoire: African Development Bank.

AidData. 2010. PLAID 1.9.1 Codebook and User's Guide.

Akihisa, Mori. 2008. Environmental Soft Loan Program in Asian Countries: Industrial Pollution Control or Mal-use of Foreign Aid Resources? *Journal of Cleaner Production* 16 (5): 612–21.

Alesina, Alberto, and David Dollar. 2000. Who Gives Foreign Aid to Whom and Why? *Journal of Economic Growth* 5 (1): 33–63.

Alesina, Alberto, and Beatrice Weder. 2002. Do Corrupt Governments Receive Less Foreign Aid? *American Economic Review* 92 (4): 1126–37.

Almeida, Paul D. 2007. Defensive Mobilization: Popular Movements against Economic Adjustment Policies in Latin America. *Latin American Perspectives* 34 (3): 123–39.

Alter, Karen J. 2006. Delegation to International Courts and the Limits of Re-contracting Political Power. In *Delegation and Agency in International Organizations*, edited by D. G. Hawkins, D. A. Lake, D. L. Nielson, and M. J. Tierney. Cambridge: Cambridge University Press.

Andersen, Thomas Barnebeck, Henrik Hansen, and Thomas Markussen. 2006. US Politics and World Bank IDA-Lending. *Journal of Development Studies* 42 (5): 772–94.

Andersen, Torben Juul. 2000. Strategic Planning, Autonomous Actions and Corporate Performance. *Long Range Planning* 33 (2): 184–200.

Andrews, Matthew. 2013. *The Limits of Institutional Reform in Development*. Cambridge: Cambridge University Press.

Arun Concerned Group. 1994. Request for Inspection. Washington, D.C.: World Bank Inspection Panel.

Ascher, William. 1983. New Development Approaches and the Adaptability of International Agencies: The Case of the World Bank. *International Organization* 37 (3): 415–39.

Asian Development Bank. 1992. Project Performance Audit Report: Bali Irrigation Sector Project in Indonesia. Manila: Asian Development Bank.

Asian Development Bank. 1994. Report of the Task Force on Improving Project Quality. Manila: Asian Development Bank.

Asian Development Bank. 1997a. Project Performance Audit Report on the Fisheries Infrastructure (Sector) Project. Manila: Asian Development Bank.

Asian Development Bank. 1997b. Proposed Loans to the Republic of Indonesia for the Coastal Community Development and Fisheries Resource Management Project. In *Report and Recommendation of the President to the Board of Directors*. Manila: Asian Development Bank.

Asian Development Bank. 1999. Social and Environmental Impacts of Selected Hydropower Projects. In *Special Evaluation Study*. Manila: Asian Development Bank.

Asian Development Bank. 2000. Country Assistance Plan (2001–2003): Bangladesh. Manila: Asian Development Bank.

Asian Development Bank. 2001. Reorganization of the Asian Development Bank. Manila: Asian Development Bank.

Asian Development Bank. 2002. Environmental Policy of the Asian Development Bank. Manila: Asian Development Bank.

Asian Development Bank. 2003. Enhancing the Independence and Effectiveness of the Operations Evaluation Department. Manila: Asian Development Bank.

Asian Development Bank. 2004. Country Assistance Program Evaluation for Cambodia. Manila: Asian Development Bank.

Asian Development Bank. 2005. Country Strategy and Program 2006–2010: Bangladesh. Manila: Asian Development Bank.

Asian Development Bank. 2008a. Asian Development Fund X Donors' Report: Towards an Asia and Pacific Region Free of Poverty. Manila: Asian Development Bank.

Asian Development Bank. 2008b. Strategy 2020: The Long-Term Strategic Framework of the Asian Development Bank, 2008–2020. Manila: Asian Development Bank.

Asian Development Bank. 2009. Learning for Change in ADB. Manila: Asian Development Bank.

Baber, William R. 1983. Toward Understanding the Role of Auditing in the Public Sector. *Journal of Accounting and Economics* 5: 213–27.

Bai, Xuemei, and Hidefumi Imura. 2000. A Comparative Study of Urban Environment in East Asia: Stage Model of Urban Environmental Evolution. *International Review for Environmental Strategies* 1 (1): 135–58.

Bailey, John. 1997. Environmental Impact Assessment and Management: An Underexplored Relationship. *Environmental Management* 21 (3): 317–27.

Balmford, Andrew, and Tony Whitten. 2003. Who Should Pay for Tropical Conservation, and How Could the Costs Be Met? *Oryx* 37 (2): 238–50.

Balogh, T. 1967. Multilateral v. Bilateral Aid. *Oxford Economic Papers* 19 (3): 328–44.

Bamberger, Michael. 2000. The Evaluation of International Development Programs: A View from the Front. *American Journal of Evaluation* 21 (1): 95–102.

Bardhan, Pranab. 1997. Corruption and Development: A Review of Issues. *Journal of Economic Literature* 35 (3): 1320–46.

Barnes, James H. 1984. Cognitive Biases and Their Impact on Strategic Planning. *Strategic Management Journal* 5 (2): 129–37.

Barnett, Michael N., and Martha Finnemore. 1999. The Politics, Power, and Pathologies of International Organizations. *International Organization* 53 (4): 699–732.

Barnett, Michael N., and Martha Finnemore. 2004. *Rules for the World: International Organizations in Global Politics.* Ithaca, N.Y.: Cornell University Press.

Barnett, Michael N., and Martha Finnemore. 2005. The Power of Liberal International Organizations. In *Power in Global Governance*, edited by M. Barnett and R. Duvall. Cambridge: Cambridge University Press.

Barrett, Christopher B., and Peter Arcese. 1995. Are Integrated Conservation-Development Projects (ICDPs) Sustainable? On the Conservation of Large Mammals in Sub-Saharan Africa. *World Development* 23 (7): 1073–84.

Barzelay, Michael. 1997. Central Audit Institutions and Performance Auditing: A Comparative Analysis of Organizational Strategies in the OECD. *Governance* 10 (3): 235–60.

Bauer, Michael W. 2012. Tolerant, If Personal Goals Remain Unharmed: Explaining Supranational Bureaucrats' Attitudes to Organizational Change. *Governance* 25 (3): 485–510.

Bawn, Kathleen. 1995. Political Control versus Expertise: Congressional Choices about Administrative Procedures. *American Political Science Review* 89 (1): 62–73.

Bawn, Kathleen. 1997. Choosing Strategies to Control the Bureaucracy: Statutory Constraints, Oversight, and the Committee System. *Journal of Law, Economics, and Organization* 13 (1): 101–26.

Beck, Nathaniel, Jonathan N. Katz, and Richard Tucker. 1998. Taking Time Seriously: Time-Series-Cross-Section Analysis with a Binary Dependent Variable. *American Journal of Political Science* 42 (4): 1260–88.

Bemelmans-Videc, Marie-Louise, Jeremy Lonsdale, and Burt Perrin, eds. 2007. *Making Accountability Work: Dilemmas for Evaluation and for Audit.* New Brunswick, N.J.: Transaction Publishers.

Bermeo, Sarah Blodgett. 2010. Development and Strategy: Aid Allocation in an Interdependent World. Duke University.

Bernauer, Thomas, and Carola Betzold. 2012. Civil Society in Global Environmental Governance. *Journal of Environment and Development* 21 (1): 62–66.

Berry, Frances Stokes, and Barton Wechsler. 1995. State Agencies' Experience with Strategic Planning: Findings from a National Survey. *Public Administration Review* 55 (2): 159–68.

Bhattarai, Binod. 1994. Nepal: Dam May Be Major Election Issue. Inter Press Service, July 14.

Biggs, Stephen, and Sally Smith. 2003. A Paradox of Learning in Project Cycle Management and the Role of Organizational Culture. *World Development* 31 (10): 1743–57.

Birdsall, Nancy. 2007. Do No Harm: Aid, Weak Institutions and the Missing Middle in Africa. *Development Policy Review* 25 (5): 575–98.

Birdsall, Nancy, Stijn Claessens, and Ishac Diwan. 2003. Policy Selectivity Forgone: Debt and Donor Behavior in Africa. *World Bank Economic Review* 17 (3): 409–35.

Birdsall, Nancy, William D. Savedoff, Ayah Mahgoub, and Katherine Vyborny. 2011. *Cash on Delivery: A New Approach to Foreign Aid.* Washington, D.C.: Center for Global Development.

Birol, Ekin, and Sukanya Das. 2012. Valuing the Environment in Developing Countries: Modelling the Impact of Distrust in Public Authorities' Ability to Deliver Public Services on the Citizens' Willingness to Pay for Improved Environmental Quality. *Urban Water Journal* 9 (4): 249–58.

Bloomberg New Energy Finance. 2011. The Past, and Future, of Development Bank Finance to Clean Energy Projects. In *Clean Energy: Research Note.* New York: Bloomberg New Energy Finance.

Blustein, Paul. 2005. After G-8 Aid Pledges, Doubts on "Doing It." *Washington Post*, July 10.

Board of Governors. 1994. Report on the Eighth General Increase in the Resources of the Inter-American Development Bank. Washington, D.C.: Inter-American Development Bank.

Boone, Peter. 1996. Politics and the Effectiveness of Foreign Aid. *European Economic Review* 40 (2): 289–29.

Bourguignon, Francois, and Mark Sundberg. 2007. Aid Effectiveness: Opening the Black Box. *American Economic Review* 97 (2): 316–21.

Bowles, Ian A., and Cyril F. Kormos. 1999. The American Campaign for Environmental Reforms at the World Bank. *Fletcher Forum of World Affairs* 23 (1): 211–24.

Box-Steffensmeier, Janet M., and Bradford S. Jones. 2004. *Event History Modeling: A Guide for Social Scientists.* Cambridge: Cambridge University Press.

Brech, Viktor, and Niklas Potrafke. 2014. Donor Ideology and Types of Foreign Aid. *Journal of Comparative Economics* 42 (1): 61–75.

Bretton Woods Project. 2010. Fuelling Contradictions: The World Bank's Energy Lending and Climate Change. London: Bretton Woods Project.

Brown, Jessica, Nicola Cantore, and Dirk Willem et Velde. 2010. Climate Financing and Development: Friends or Foes? In *Research Reports and Studies*. London: Overseas Development Institute.

Brummer, Alex. 1992. Industrial Countries Agree to Lend $18 Billion to Poor. *Guardian*, December 16, 13.

Bryson, John M. 2010. The Future of Public and Nonprofit Strategic Planning in the United States. *Public Administration Review* 70: s255–s267.

Bryson, John M., Barbara C. Crosby, and John K. Bryson. 2009. Understanding Strategic Planning and the Formulation and Implementation of Strategic Plans as a Way of Knowing: The Contributions of Actor-Network Theory. *International Public Management Journal* 12 (2): 172–207.

Buntaine, Mark T. 2011. Does the Asian Development Bank Respond to Past Environmental Performance When Allocating Environmentally Risky Financing? *World Development* 39 (3): 336–50.

Buntaine, Mark T., and Bradley C. Parks. 2013. When Do Environmentally-Focused Assistance Projects Achieve Their Objectives? Evidence from World Bank Post-project Evaluations. *Global Environmental Politics* 13 (2): 65–88.

Buntaine, Mark T., and William A. Pizer. 2015. Encouraging Clean Energy Investment in Developing Countries: What Role for Aid? *Climate Policy* 15 (5): 543–64.

Burnside, Craig, and David Dollar. 2000. Aid, Policies, and Growth. *American Economic Review* 90 (4): 847–68.

Burnside, Craig, and David Dollar. 2004. Aid, Policies, and Growth: Reply. *American Economic Review* 94 (3): 781–84.

Buss, Terry F. 2008. *Haiti in the Balance: Why Foreign Aid Has Failed and What We Can Do about It*. Washington, D.C.: Brookings Institution Press.

Busse, Matthias, and Carsten Hefeker. 2007. Political Risk, Institutions and Foreign Direct Investment. *European Journal of Political Economy* 23 (2): 397–415.

Böhmelt, Tobias. 2012. A Closer Look at the Information Provision Rationale: Civil Society Participation in States' Delegations at the UNFCCC. *Review of International Organizations* 8 (1): 1–26.

Carlsson, Ingvar, Sung-Joo Han, and Rufus M. Kupolati. 1999. Independent Inquiry in the Actions of the United Nations during the 1994 Genocide in Rwanda. United Nations.

Carpenter, Daniel P. 2001. *The Forging of Bureaucratic Autonomy: Reputations, Networks, and Policy Innovation in Executive Agencies, 1862–1928*. Princeton, N.J.: Princeton University Press.

Chamberlain, Gethin. 2007. Afghan Leaders Steal Half of All Aid, Says US Military: Needy Fail to Get Goods Meant to Woo Them from the Taliban. *Sunday Telegraph*, January 28.

Chhotray, Vasudha, and David Hulme. 2009. Contrasting Visions for Aid and Governance in the 21st Century: The White House Millennium Challenge Account and DFID's Drivers of Change. *World Development* 37 (1): 36–49.

Cingranelli, D. L., and T. E. Pasquarello. 1985. Human Rights Practices and the Distribution of US Foreign Aid to Latin American Countries. *American Journal of Political Science* 29 (3): 539–63.

Clark, Ann Marie, Elisabeth J. Friedman, and Kathryn Hochstetler. 1998. The Sovereign Limits of Global Civil Society: A Comparison of NGO Participation in UN World Conferences on the Environment, Human Rights, and Women. *World Politics* 51 (1): 1–35. M3—10.1017/S0043887100007772.

Clark, Dana. 2003. Understanding the World Bank Inspection Panel. In *Demanding Accountability: Civil Society Claims and the World Bank Inspection Panel*, edited by D. Clark, J. A. Fox, and K. Treakle. Lanham, Md.: Rowman & Littlefield.

Clark, Dana, Jonathan A. Fox, and Kay Treakle, eds. 2003. *Demanding Accountability: Civil Society Claims and the World Bank Inspection Panel*. Lanham, Md.: Rowman & Littlefield.

Clark, William C., Ronald B. Mitchell, and David W. Cash. 2006. Evaluating the Influence of Global Environmental Assessments. In *Global Environmental Assessments: Information and Influence*, edited by R. B. Mitchell, W. C. Clark, D. W. Cash, and N. M. Dickson. Cambridge, Mass.: MIT Press.

Cline, William R., and Nicholas P. Sargen. 1975. Performance Criteria and Multilateral Aid Allocation. *World Development* 3 (6): 383–91.

Clist, Paul, Alessia Isopi, and Oliver Morrissey. 2012. Selectivity on Aid Modality: Determinants of Budget Support from Multilateral Donors. *Review of International Organizations* 7 (3): 267–84.

Collier, Paul, Patrick Guillaumont, Sylvaine Guillaumont, and Jan Willem Gunning. 1997. Redesigning Conditionality. *World Development* 25 (9): 1399–407.

Comptroller General. 1974. Effectiveness of Independent and Comprehensive Audits of Inter-American Development Bank. Edited by Department of Treasury. Washington, D.C.

Connolly, Barbara. 1996. Increments for the Earth: The Politics of Environmental Aid. In *Institutions for Environmental Aid: Pitfalls and Promise*, edited by R. O. Keohane and M. A. Levy. Cambridge, Mass.: MIT Press.

Copelovitch, Mark S. 2010. Master or Servant? Common Agency and the Political Economy of IMF Lending. *International Studies Quarterly* 54 (1): 49–77.

Cornwell, Rupert. 2002. Monterrey Aid Pledges Fail to Hit UN Target. *Independent*, March 22.

Corson, Catherine. 2010. Shifting Environmental Governance in a Neoliberal World: US AID for Conservation. *Antipode* 42 (3): 576–602.

Cortell, Andrew P., and Susan Peterson. 2006. Dutiful Agents, Rogue Actors, or Both? Staffing, Voting Rules, and Slack in the WHO and WTO. In *Delegation and Agency in International Organizations*, edited by D. G. Hawkins, D. A. Lake, D. L. Nielson, and M. J. Tierney. Cambridge: Cambridge University Press.

Cotton, A. P., and R. W. A. Franceys. 1988. Urban Infrastructure: Trends, Needs and the Role of Aid. *Habitat International* 12 (3): 139–47.

Cousins, J. B., S. C. Goh, C. Elliott, T. Aubry, and N. Gilbert. 2014. Government and Voluntary Sector Differences in Organizational Capacity to Do and Use Evaluation. *Evaluation and Program Planning* 44: 1–13.

Crane, Barbara B., and Jennifer Dusenberry. 2004. Power and Politics in International Funding for Reproductive Health: The US Global Gag Rule. *Reproductive Health Matters* 12 (24): 128–37.

Crawford, H. 1988. Fiji Goes to Top of Forum Agenda. *Herald*, September 16.

Cronbach, Lee J., S. R. Ambron, S. M. Dornbusch, R. D. Hess, R. C. Hornik, D. C. Phillips, D. F. Walker, and S. S. Weiner. 1980. *Towards Reform of Program Evaluation*. San Francisco: Jossey-Bass.

Crossette, Barbara. 1989. Water, Water Everywhere? Many Now Say "No!" *New York Times*, October 7.

Crossette, Barbara. 1992. Movement Builds to Fight Harmful Projects in Poor Nations. *New York Times*, June 23, 4.

Dahl, Robert A. 1999. Can International Organizations Be Democratic? A Skeptic's View. In *Democracy's Edges*, edited by I. Shapiro and C. Hacker-Cordón. Cambridge: Cambridge University Press.

Dai, Xinyuan. 2007. *International Institutions and National Policies*. Cambridge: Cambridge University Press.

Darst, Robert G. 2001. *Smokestack Diplomacy: Cooperation and Conflict in East-West Environmental Politics*. Cambridge, Mass.: MIT Press.

David B. Spence. 1999. Managing Delegation Ex Ante: Using Law to Steer Administrative Agencies. *Journal of Legal Studies* 28 (2): 413–59.

Davis, Kevin E., and Sarah Dadush. 2009. Getting Climate-Related Conditionality Right. In *Climate Finance: Regulatory and Funding Strategies for Climate Change and Global Development*, edited by R. B. Stewart, B. Kingsbury, and B. Rudyk. New York: New York University Press.

Deininger, Klaus, Lyn Squire, and Swati Basu. 1998. Does Economic Analysis Improve the Quality of Foreign Assistance? *World Bank Economic Review* 12 (3): 385–418.

Dejong, Douglas V., Robert Forsythe, and Russell J. Lundholm. 1985. Ripoffs, Lemons, and Reputation Formation in Agency Relationships: A Laboratory Market Study. *Journal of Finance* 40 (3): 809–20.

Devarajan, Shantayanan, David Dollar, and Torgny Holmgren. 2001. Overview. In *Aid and Reform in Africa: Lessons from Ten Case Studies*, edited by S. Devarajan, D. Dollar, and T. Holmgren. Washington, D.C.: World Bank.

Diamond, Alexis, and Jasjeet S. Sekhon. 2008. Genetic Matching for Estimating Causal Effects: A General Multivariate Matching Method for Achieving Balance in Observational Studies. University of California, Berkeley.

Dietrich, Simone. 2011. The Politics of Public Health Aid: Why Corrupt Governments Have Incentives to Implement Aid Effectively. *World Development* 39 (1): 55–63.

Dietrich, Simone. 2013. Bypass or Engage? Explaining Donor Delivery Tactics in Foreign Aid Allocation. *International Studies Quarterly* 57 (4): 698–712.

Diven, Polly J., and John Constantelos. 2009. Explaining Generosity: A Comparison of US and European Public Opinion on Foreign Aid. *Journal of Transatlantic Studies* 7 (2): 118–32.

Dollar, David, and Victoria Levin. 2005. Sowing and Reaping: Institutional Quality and Project Outcomes in Developing Countries. World Bank Policy Research Working Paper 3524.

Dollar, David, and Victoria Levin. 2006. The Increasing Selectivity of Foreign Aid, 1984–2003. *World Development* 34 (12): 2034–46.

Dorotinsky, Bill, and Rob Floyd. 2004. Public Expenditure Accountability in Africa: Progress, Lessons, and Challenges. In *Building State Capacity in Africa: New Approaches, Emerging Lessons*, edited by B. Levy and S. Kpundeh. Washington, D.C.: World Bank Institute.

Dowling, J. M., and Ulrich Hiemenz. 1985. Biases in the Allocation of Foreign Aid: Some New Evidence. *World Development* 13 (4): 535–41.

Downs, George W., and David M. Rocke. 1994. Conflict, Agency, and Gambling for Resurrection: The Principal-Agent Problem Goes to War. *American Journal of Political Science* 38 (2): 362–80.

Drezner, Daniel W. 2003. The Hidden Hand of Economic Coercion. *International Organization* 50 (3): 379–406.

Dudley, Leonard, and Claude Montmarquette. 1976. A Model of the Supply of Bilateral Foreign Aid. *American Economic Review* 66 (1): 132–42.

Duke Center for International Development. 2011. Some Cross-Cutting Lessons. In *Doing a Better Dam: The Lao People's Democratic Republic and the Story of Nam Theun 2*, edited by I. C. Porter and J. Shivakumar. Washington, D.C.: International Bank for Reconstruction and Development / World Bank.

Easterly, William. 2002. The Cartel of Good Intentions: The Problem of Bureaucracy in Foreign Aid. *Journal of Policy Reform* 5 (4): 223–50.

Easterly, William. 2003. Can Foreign Aid Buy Growth? *Journal of Economic Perspectives* 17 (3): 23–48.

Easterly, William. 2005. What Did Structural Adjustment Adjust? The Association of Policies and Growth with Repeated IMF and World Bank Adjustment Loans. *Journal of Development Economics* 76 (1): 1–22.

Easterly, William. 2006. *White Man's Burden: Why the West's Efforts to Aid the Rest Have Done So Much Ill and So Little Good.* New York: Penguin.

Easterly, William. 2007. Are Aid Agencies Improving? *Economic Policy* 22 (52): 633–78.

Easterly, William, and Tobias Pfutze. 2008. Where Does the Money Go? Best and Worst Practices in Foreign Aid. *Journal of Economic Perspectives* 22 (2): 29–52.

Ebrahim, Alnoor. 2003. Accountability in Practice: Mechanisms for NGOs. *World Development* 31 (5): 813–29.

Economy, Elizabeth C. 2004. *The River Runs Black: The Environmental Challenge to China's Future.* Ithaca, N.Y.: Cornell University Press.

Eisenhardt, Kathleen M. 1989. Agency Theory: An Assessment and Review. *Academy of Management Review* 14 (1): 57–74.

Ekbom, Anders, and Jan Bojo. 1997. Mainstreaming Environment in Country Assistance Strategies. Washington, D.C.: World Bank.

Elgie, Robert. 2002. The Politics of the European Central Bank: Principal-Agent Theory and the Democratic Deficit. *Journal of European Public Policy* 9 (2): 186–200.

Ellerman, David P. 1999. Global Institutions: Transforming International Development Agencies into Learning Organizations. *Academy of Management Executive (1993–2005)* 13 (1): 25–35.

Elliott, Larry. 2006. G8 Progress Report: A Year after Live 8, Rich Countries Have Failed to Keep Their Promise. *Guardian*, June 30, 13.

Elsig, Manfred. 2010. The World Trade Organization at Work: Performance in a Member-Driven Milieu. *Review of International Organizations* 5 (3): 345–63.

Elsig, Manfred. 2014. Agency Theory and the WTO: Complex Agency and "Missing Delegation"? In *Political Economy of International Organizations.* Princeton, N.J.: Princeton University Press.

Engberg-Pedersen, Lars. 2014. Bringing Aid Management Closer to Reality: The Experience of Danish Bilateral Development Cooperation. *Development Policy Review* 32 (1): 113–31.

Environment Division. 1995. Environmental Considerations in Program Lending: A Review of the Bank's Experience. Manila: Asian Development Bank.

Environment Sector Board. 1998. Environment Matters: Annual Review 1998. Washington, D.C.: World Bank.

Epstein, David, and Sharyn O'Halloran. 1994. Administrative Procedures, Information, and Agency Discretion. *American Journal of Political Science* 38 (3): 697–722.

Eriksson, John. 2001. The Drive to Partnership: Aid Coordination and the World Bank. Washington, D.C.: World Bank.

Fairman, David, and Michael Ross. 1996. Old Fads, New Lessons: Learning from Economic Development Assistance. In *Institutions for Environmental Aid: Pitfalls and Promise*, edited by R. O. Keohane and M. A. Levy. Cambridge, Mass.: MIT Press.

Farmer, Paul, Mary C. Smith Fawzi, and Patrice Nevil. 2003. Unjust Embargo of Aid for Haiti. *Lancet* 361: 420–23.

Feeny, Simon, and Mark McGillivray. 2009. Aid Allocation to Fragile States: Absorptive Capacity Constraints. *Journal of International Development* 21 (5): 618–32.

Feinstein, Osvald N. 2002. Use of Evaluations and the Evaluation of Their Use. *Evaluation* 8 (4): 433–39.

Ferraro, Paul J., and Subhrendu K. Pattanayak. 2006. Money for Nothing? A Call for Empirical Evaluation of Biodiversity Conservation Investments. *PLOS Biology* 4 (4): 482–89.

Feyzioglu, Tarhan, Vinaya Swaroop, and Min Zhu. 1998. A Panel Data Analysis of the Fungibility of Foreign Aid. *World Bank Economic Review* 12 (1): 29–58.

Fiji Times. Education Ministry Misuse Aid Fund. 2008. October 16, 2.

Financial Times. 1996. Nepal Invites Power Bids. February 15.

Findley, Michael G., Darren Hawkins, Robert L. Hicks, Daniel L. Nielson, Bradley C. Parks, Ryan M. Powers, J. Timmons Roberts, Michael J. Tierney, and Sven Wilson. 2009. AidData: Tracking Development Finance.

Flanders, Stephanie. 1997. Truce Called in Battle of the Dams: Environmentalists, Public Agencies and Private Companies Agree They Must Try to Avoid the Pitfalls of the Past. *Financial Times*, April 16, 62.

Fleck, Robert K., and Christopher Kilby. 2006. World Bank Independence: A Model and Statistical Analysis of US Influence. *Review of Development Economics* 10 (2): 224–40.

Forss, Kim, Basil Cracknell, and Knut Samset. 1994. Can Evaluation Help an Organization Learn? *Evaluation Review* 18 (5): 574–91.

Forss, Kim, and Knut Samset. 1999. Square Pegs and Round Holes: Evaluation, Uncertainty and Risk Management. *Evaluation* 5 (4): 407–21.

Fortmann, Louise. 1990. The Role of Professional Norms and Beliefs in the Agency-Client Relations of Natural Resource Bureaucracies. *Natural Resources Journal* 30: 361–80.

Fox, Jonathan A. 2000. The World Bank Inspection Panel: Lessons from the First Five Years. *Global Governance* 6: 279–318.

Fox, Jonathan A., and L. David Brown. 1998. Assessing the Impact of NGO Advocacy Campaigns on World Bank Projects and Policies. In *The Struggle for Accountability: The World Bank, NGOs, and Grassroots Movements*, edited by J. A. Fox and L. D. Brown. Cambridge, Mass.: MIT Press.

Fox, Jonathan A., and Kay Treakle. 2003. Concluding Propositions. In *Demanding Accountability: Civil Society Claims and the World Bank Inspection Panel*, edited by D. Clark, J. A. Fox, and K. Treakle. Lanham, Md.: Rowman & Littlefield.

Freeman, Peter N. 2009. Ten Years of World Bank Action in Transportation: Evaluation. *Journal of Infrastructure Systems* 15 (4): 297–304.

Frey, Bruno S., Henrik Horn, Torsten Persson, and Friedrich Schneider. 1985. A Formulation and Test of a Simple Model of World Bank Behavior. *Weltwirtschaftliches Archiv* 121 (3): 438–47.

Frey, Bruno S., and Alois Stutzer. 2006. Strengthening the Citizens' Role in International Organizations. *Review of International Organizations* 1 (1): 27–43.

Gadd, Michelle E. 2005. Conservation outside of Parks: Attitudes of Local People in Laikipia, Kenya. *Environmental Conservation* 32 (1): 50–63.

Gailmard, Sean. 2009. Multiple Principals and Oversight of Bureaucratic Policy-Making. *Journal of Theoretical Politics* 21 (2): 161–86.

Gelman, Andrew, and Jennifer Hill. 2007. *Data Analysis Using Regression and Multilevel/Hierarchical Models*. Cambridge: Cambridge University Press.

General Accounting Office. 1986. African Development Bank: A More Independent Evaluation System Is Needed. Washington, D.C.: General Accounting Office.

General Accounting Office. 1996. World Bank: U.S. Interests Supported, but Oversight Needed to Help Ensure Improved Performance. Washington, D.C.: General Accounting Office.

General Accounting Office. 1998. Multilateral Development Banks: Public Consultation on Environmental Assessments. Washington, D.C.: General Accounting Office.

Gerlak, Andrea K. 2004. One Basin at a Time: The Global Environment Facility and Governance of Transboundary Waters. *Global Environmental Politics* 4 (4): 108–41.

Ghosh, Arunabha, and Ngaire Woods. 2009. Governing Climate Change: Lessons from Other Governance Regimes. In *The Economics and Politics of Climate Change*, edited by D. Helm and C. Hepburn. Oxford: Oxford University Press.

Gibson, Clark C., Krister Andersson, Elinor Ostrom, and Sujai Shivakumar. 2005. *The Samaritan's Dilemma: The Political Economy of Development Aid*. Oxford: Oxford University Press.

Gilbert, Christopher, Andrew Powell, and David Vines. 1999. Positioning the World Bank. *Economic Journal* 109 (459): 598–633.

Globe and Mail. 1991. World Bank Moves to Protect Forests. July 19.

Goetz, Anne Marie, and Rob Jenkins. 2001. Hybrid Forms of Accountability: Citizen Engagement in Institutions of Public-Sector Oversight in India. *Public Management Review* 3 (3): 363–83.

Goldsmith, Arthur A. 2008. Making the World Safe for Partial Democracy? Questioning the Premises of Democracy Promotion. *International Security* 33 (2): 120–47.

Goldstein, Kenneth. 2002. Getting in the Door: Sampling and Completing Elite Interviews. *Political Science and Politics* 35 (4): 669–72.

Gopalakrishnan, Raju. 2009. ADB under Pressure on Policy as It Seeks Funds. Reuters India, February 5.

Grant, Ruth W., and Robert O. Keohane. 2005. Accountability and Abuses of Power in World Politics. *American Political Science Review* 99 (1): 29–43.

Grasso, Patrick G., Sulaiman S. Wasty, and Rachel V. Weaving, eds. 2003. *World Bank Operations Evaluation Department: The First 30 Years*. Washington, D.C.: World Bank.

Grigorescu, Alexandru. 2007. Transparency of Intergovernmental Organizations: The Roles of Member States, International Bureaucracies and Nongovernmental Organizations. *International Studies Quarterly* 51 (3): 625–48.

Grigorescu, Alexandru. 2010. The Spread of Bureaucratic Oversight Mechanisms across Intergovernmental Organizations. *International Studies Quarterly* 54 (3): 871–86.

Guillaumont, Patrick, and Lisa Chauvet. 2001. Aid and Performance: A Reassessment. *Journal of Development Studies* 37 (6): 66–92.

Gutner, Tamar. 2002. *Banking on the Environment: Multilateral Development Banks and Their Performance in Central and Eastern Europe*. Cambridge, Mass.: MIT Press.

Gutner, Tamar. 2005. Explaining the Gaps between Mandate and Performance: Agency Theory and World Bank Environmental Reform. *Global Environmental Politics* 5 (2): 10–37.

Gutner, Tamar, and Alexander Thompson. 2010. The Politics of IO Performance: A Framework. *Review of International Organizations* 5 (3): 227–48.

Haas, Peter M., Robert O. Keohane, and Marc A. Levy, eds. 1993. *Institutions for the Earth: Sources of Effective International Environmental Protection*. Cambridge, Mass.: MIT Press.

Haftel, Yoram Z., and Alexander Thompson. 2006. The Independence of International Organizations: Concept and Applications. *Journal of Conflict Resolution* 50 (2): 253–75.

Hambrick, Donald C., Marta A. Geletkanycz, and James W. Fredrickson. 1993. Top Executive Commitment to the Status Quo: Some Tests of Its Determinants. *Strategic Management Journal* 14 (6): 401–18.

Hansen, Henrik, and Finn Tarp. 2000. Policy Arena Aid Effectiveness Disputed. *Journal of International Development* 12: 375–98.

Hansson, Finn. 2006. Organizational Use of Evaluations. *Evaluation* 12 (2): 159–78.

Hardy, Andrew P. 1982. The Selection of Channels When Seeking Information: Cost/Benefit vs Least-Effort. *Information Processing and Management* 18 (6): 289–93.

Harrigan, Jane, Chenggang Wang, and Hamed El-Said. 2006. The Economic and Political Determinants of IMF and World Bank Lending in the Middle East and North Africa. *World Development* 34 (2): 247–70.

Hartley-Brewer, Julia. 2005. Blair to Put Pressure on Bush to Aid Africa Aid; as Sir Bob Geldof Launches His Latest Crusade to Save Lives, the PM Vows to Win More Support from America. *Sunday Express*, June 5, 11.

Hawkins, Darren G., David A. Lake, Daniel L. Nielson, and Michael J. Tierney, eds. 2006a. *Delegation and Agency in International Organizations: Political Economy of Institutions and Decisions*. Cambridge: Cambridge University Press.

Hawkins, Darren G., David A. Lake, Daniel L. Nielson, and Michael J. Tierney. 2006b. Delegation under Anarchy: States, International Organizations, and Principal-Agent Theory. In *Delegation and Agency in International Organizations*, edited by D. G. Hawkins, D. A. Lake, D. L. Nielson, and M. J. Tierney. Cambridge: Cambridge University Press.

Hendry, John. 2002. The Principal's Other Problems: Honest Incompetence and the Specification of Objectives. *Academy of Management Review* 27 (1): 98–113.

Hicks, Robert L., Bradley C. Parks, J. Timmons Roberts, and Michael J. Tierney. 2008. *Greening Aid? Understanding the Environmental Impact of Development Assistance*. Oxford: Oxford University Press.

Hirsch, Philip. 2011. China and the Geopolitics of Lower Mekong Dams. *Asia-Pacific Journal* 9 (20): 1–4.

Ho, Daniel E., Kosuke Imai, Gary King, and Elizabeth A. Stuart. 2007. Matching as Nonparametric Preprocessing for Reducing Model Dependence in Parametric Causal Inference. *Political Analysis* 15 (3): 199–236.

Ho, Daniel E., Kosuke Imai, Gary King, and Elizabeth A. Stuart. 2008. MatchIt: Nonparametric Preprocessing for Parametric Causal Inference. *Journal of Statistical Software* 171: 481–502.

Ho, Peter. 2001. Greening without Conflict? Environmentalism, NGOs and Civil Society in China. *Development and Change* 32 (5): 893–921.

Hoeffler, Anke, and Verity Outram. 2011. Need, Merit, or Self-Interest: What Determines the Allocation of Aid? *Review of Development Economics* 15 (2): 237–50.

Honig, Dan. 2014. Navigation by Judgement: Organizational Autonomy in the Delivery of Foreign Aid. Harvard University.

Horta, Korinna, Samuel Nguiffo, and Delphine Djiraibe. 1999. The Chad Cameroon Oil and Pipeline Project: Putting People and the Environment at Risk. Washington, D.C.: Environmental Defense Fund.

Hostland, Doug. 2009. Low-Income Countries' Access to Private Debt Markets. Policy Research Working Paper. Washington, D.C.: World Bank.

House of Commons. 2012. EU Development Assistance: Sixteenth Report of Session 2010-12. Report HC 1680. London: The Stationery Office Limited.

Hout, Wil. 2002. Good Governance and Aid: Selectivity Criteria in Development Assistance. *Development and Change* 33 (3): 511–27.

Hout, Wil. 2007. *The Politics of Aid Selectivity: Good Governance Criteria in World Bank, US and Dutch Development Assistance.* London: Routledge.

Huber, John D., and Charles R. Shipan. 2000. The Costs of Control: Legislators, Agencies, and Transaction Costs. *Legislative Studies Quarterly* 25 (1): 25–52.

Huber, John D., and Charles R. Shipan. 2002. *Deliberate Discretion? The Institutional Foundations of Bureaucratic Autonomy.* New York: Cambridge University Press.

Independent Evaluation Department. 2009. 2009 Annual Report on Acting on Recommendations. Manila: Asian Development Bank.

Independent Evaluation Group. 2007. Environmental Technical Assistance Project. In *Project Performance Assessment Report.* Washington, D.C.: World Bank.

Independent Evaluation Group. 2008. Environmental Sustainability: An Evaluation of World Bank Group Support. Washington, D.C.: World Bank.

Independent Evaluation Group. 2010a. Phase II: The Challenge of Low-Carbon Development. In *Climate Change and the World Bank Group.* Washington, D.C.: World Bank.

Independent Evaluation Group. 2010b. Safeguards and Sustainability Policies in a Changing World: An Independent Evaluation of the World Bank Group Experience. Washington, D.C.: World Bank.

Independent Evaluation Group. 2012. The Matrix System at Work: An Evaluation of the World Bank's Organizational Effectiveness. Washington, D.C.: World Bank.

Inspection Panel. 2002. The Inspection Panel Investigation Report Chad-Cameroon Petroleum and Pipeline Project (Loan No. 4558-CD); Petroleum Sector Management Capacity Building Project (Credit No. 3373-CD); and Management of Petroleum Economy (Credit No. 3316-CD). Washington, DC: World Bank.

Inter-American Development Bank. 1985. Organization and Management of the IDB. In *Basic Training Courses.* Washington, D.C.: Inter-American Development Bank.

Inter-American Development Bank. 1993. Managing for Effective Development. Washington, D.C.: Task Force on Portfolio Management.

Inter-American Development Bank. 1996. Annual Report on the Environment and Natural Resources. Washington, D.C.: Environment Committee of the IDB.

Inter-American Development Bank. 2006. Environment and Safeguards Compliance Policy. Washington, D.C.: Inter-American Development Bank.

Intergovernmental Panel on Climate Change. 1998. *The Regional Impacts of Climate Change: An Assessment of Vulnerability*. Cambridge: Cambridge University Press.

International Bank for Reconstruction and Development and International Development Association. 2002. Management Report and Recommendation in Response to the Inspection Panel Investigation Report, Chad: Chad-Cameroon Petroleum Development and Pipeline Project. Washington, D.C.: World Bank.

International Development Association. 2010. IDA's Performance Based Allocation Systems: Review of the Current System and Key Issues for IDA16. Washington, D.C.: International Development Association.

International Development Committee. 2012. EU Development Assistance: Sixteenth Report of Session 2010–12. London: Stationary Office Limited.

International Institute for Sustainable Development. 2004. Costa Rica Case Study: Analysis of National Strategies for Sustainable Development. In *National Strategies for Sustainable Development*. IISD.

International Water Power and Dam Construction. 2002. Pressing Ahead with Nepalese Hydro. January 9.

Jacobs, Alex. 2010. Creating the Missing Feedback Loop. *IDS Bulletin* 41 (6): 56–64.

Johns, Leslie. 2007. Communication and the Selection of International Bureaucrats. *International Organization* 61: 245–75.

Johnson, Tana. 2013. Institutional Design and Bureaucrats' Impact on Political Control. *Journal of Politics* 75 (1): 183–97.

Jones, Bryan D., Saadia R Greenberg, Clifford Kaufman, and Joseph Drew. 1977. Bureaucratic Response to Citizen-Initiated Contacts: Environmental Enforcement in Detroit. *American Political Science Review* 71 (1): 148–65.

Jupille, Joseph Henri. 2004. *Procedural Politics: Issues, Influence, and Institutional Choice in the European Union*. Cambridge: Cambridge University Press.

Jupille, Joseph, and Duncan Snidal. 2006. The Choice of International Institutions: Cooperation, Alternatives and Strategies. University of Colorado at Boulder and University of Chicago.

Kaja, Ashwin, and Eric Werker. 2010. Corporate Governance at the World Bank and the Dilemma of Global Governance. *World Bank Economic Review* 24 (2): 171–98.

Kalbe, Peter. 2001. The Award of Contracts and the Enforcement of Claims in the Context of EC External Aid and Development Cooperation. *Common Market Law Review* 38 (5): 1217–67.

Kasa, Sjur, Anne Gullberg, and Gørild Heggelund. 2008. The Group of 77 in the International Climate Negotiations: Recent Developments and Future Directions. *International Environmental Agreements: Politics, Law and Economics* 8 (2): 113–27.

Keck, Margaret E., and Kathryn Sikkink. 1998. *Activists beyond Borders: Advocacy Networks in International Politics*. Ithaca, N.Y.: Cornell University Press.

Keefer, Philip, and Stuti Khemani. 2005. Democracy, Public Expenditures, and the Poor: Understanding Political Incentives for Providing Public Services. *World Bank Research Observer* 20 (1): 1–27.

Kelly, Josie. 2003. The Audit Commission: Guiding, Steering and Regulating Local Government. *Public Administration* 81 (3): 459–76.

Kenna, Kathleen. 1999. U.N. Failed Rwanda, Inquiry Charges Blood of Nation's 800,000 on Its Hands. *Toronto Star*, December 17.

Kennedy, William V. 1999. EIA and Multi-lateral Financial Institutions. In *OECD Conference on FDI and the Environment*. The Hague: European Bank for Reconstruction and Development.

Keohane, Robert O. 1988. International Institutions: Two Approaches. *International Studies Quarterly* 32 (4): 379–96.

Keohane, Robert O., Peter M. Haas, and Marc A. Levy. 1993. The Effectiveness of International Environmental Institutions. In *Institutions for the Earth: Sources of Effective International Environmental Protection*, edited by P. M. Hass, R. O. Keohane, and M. A. Levy. Cambridge, Mass.: MIT Press.

Khagram, Sanjeev. 2004. *Dams and Development: Transnational Struggles for Water and Power*. Ithaca, N.Y.: Cornell University Press.

Khawaja, Afshan. 2001. Influencing Project Design through Participation: Pakistan Ghazi-Barotha Hydropower Project. In *Social Development Notes*. Washington, D.C.: Environmentally and Socially Sustainable Development Network.

Kiewiet, D. Roderick, and Mathew D. McCubbins. 1991. *The Logic of Delegation: Congressional Parties and the Appropriations Process*. Chicago: University of Chicago Press.

Kilby, Christopher. 2009. The Political Economy of Conditionality: An Empirical Analysis of World Bank Loan Disbursements. *Journal of Development Economics* 89 (1): 51–61.

Kilby, Christopher. 2011. Informal Influence in the Asian Development Bank. *Review of International Organizations* 6 (3): 223–57.

Killick, Tony. 1997. Principals, Agents and the Failings of Conditionality. *Journal of International Development* 9 (4): 483–95.

King, Gary, and Langche Zeng. 2001. Explaining Rare Events in International Relations. *International Organization* 55 (3): 693–715.

King, Gary, and Langche Zeng. 2007. When Can History Be Our Guide? The Pitfalls of Counterfactual Inference. *International Studies Quarterly* 51 (1): 183–210.

Kirkhart, Karen E. 2000. Reconceptualizing Evaluation Use: An Integrated Theory of Influence. *New Directions for Evaluation* 2000 (88): 5–23.

Knack, Stephen. 2001. Aid Dependence and the Quality of Governance: Cross-Country Empirical Tests. *Southern Economic Journal* 68 (2): 310–29.

Knack, Stephen. 2004. Does Foreign Aid Promote Democracy? *International Studies Quarterly* 48 (1): 251–66.

Knack, Stephen, and Aminur Rahman. 2007. Donor Fragmentation and Bureaucratic Quality in Aid Recipients. *Journal of Development Economics* 83: 176–97.

Knox, David A. 1994. The Quest for Quality: Report of the Task Force on Project Quality for the African Development Bank. Oxford: Nuffield College.

Koremenos, Barbara, Charles Lipson, and Duncan Snidal. 2001. The Rational Design of International Institutions. *International Organization* 55 (4): 761–99.

Kravchenko, Svitlana. 2009. The Myth of Public Participation in a World of Poverty. *Tulane Environmental Law Journal* 32 (1): 33–55.

Kumar, Nalini, Naresh Saxena, Yoginder Alagh, and Kinsuk Mitra. 2000. India: Alleviating Poverty through Forest Development. In *Evaluation Country Case Study Series*. Washington, D.C.: World Bank.

Kusek, Jody Zall, and Ray C. Rist. 2004. *Ten Steps to a Results-Based Monitoring and Evaluation System*. Washington, D.C.: World Bank.

Lake, David A. 1996. Anarchy, Hierarchy, and the Variety of International Relations. *International Organization* 50 (1): 1–33.

Lake, David A., and Mathew D. McCubbins. 2006. The Logic of Delegation to International Organizations. In *Delegation and Agency in International Organizations*, edited by D. G. Hawkins, D. A. Lake, D. L. Nielson, and M. J. Tierney. Cambridge: Cambridge University Press.

Landau, Martin, and Russell Stout Jr. 1979. To Manage Is Not to Control: Or the Folly of Type II Errors. *Public Administration Review* 39 (2): 148–56.

Lanig, Thomas. 1995. 50 years of FAO: Fighting Hunger and Budget Deficits. *Deutsche Presse-Agentur*, October 13.

Large, William R., ed. 2005. *An Enduring Partnership for Development: Central America and the IDB since 1990*. Washington, D.C.: Inter-American Development Bank.

Lavelle, Kathryn C. 2011. *Legislating International Organization: The US Congress, the IMF, and the World Bank*. New York: Oxford University Press.

Leandro, Jose E., Hartwig Schafer, and Gaspar Frontini. 1999. Towards a More Effective Conditionality: An Operational Framework. *World Development* 27 (2): 285–300.

Leviton, Laura C. 2003. Evaluation Use: Advance, Challenges and Applications. *American Journal of Evaluation* 24 (4): 525–35.

Lewis, Paul. 1988. U.S. Plans Big Cut in Funds to U.N. Food Agency. *New York Times*, February 23, A14.

Lewis, Paul. 1992. The Earth Summit. *New York Times*, June 5.

Lewis, Paul. 1994. Rich Nations Plan $2 Billion for Environment. *New York Times*, March 17, 7.

Lewis, Tammy L. 2000. Transnational Conservation Movement Organizations: Shaping the Protected Area Systems of Less Developed Nations. *Mobilization* 5 (1): 105–23.

Lewis, Tammy L. 2003. Environmental Aid: Driven by Recipient Need or Donor Interests? *Social Science Quarterly* 84 (1): 144–61.

Linaweaver, Stephen. 2003. Catching the Boomerang: EM, the World Bank, and Excess Accountability: A Case Study of the Bujagali Falls Hydropower Project Uganda. *International Journal of Sustainable Development and World Ecology* 10 (4): 283–301.

Lipsky, Michael. 2010. *Street-Level Bureaucracy: Dilemmas of the Individual in Public Service*. 30th Anniversary ed. New York: Russell Sage Foundation.

Lipson, Michael. 2010. Performance under Ambiguity: International Organization Performance in UN Peacekeeping. *Review of International Organizations* 5 (3): 249–84.

Lissakers, Karin, Ishrat Husain, and Ngaire Woods. 2006. Report of the External Evaluation of the Independent Evaluation Office. Washington, D.C.: International Monetary Fund.

Lohani, Bindu N., J. Warren Evans, Robert R. Everitt, Harvey Ludwig, Richard A. Carpenter, and Shih-Liang Tu. 1997. Environment Impact Assessment for Developing Countries in Asia. Asian Development Bank.

Lundsgaarde, Erik, Christian Breunig, and Aseem Prakash. 2007. Trade versus Aid: Donor Generosity in an Era of Globalization. *Policy Sciences* 40: 157–79.

Lynch, Suzanne. 2012. Parliament to Discuss Report on Diverted Aid. *Irish Times*, November 9.

Lyne, Mona M., Daniel L. Nielson, and Michael J. Tierney. 2006. Who Delegates? Alternative Models of Principals in Development Aid. In *Delegation and Agency in International*

Organizations, edited by D. G. Hawkins, D. A. Lake, D. L. Nielson, and M. J. Tierney. Cambridge: Cambridge University Press.

Lyne, Mona M., Daniel L. Nielson, and Michael J. Tierney. 2009. Controlling Coalitions: Social Lending at the Multilateral Development Banks. *Review of International Organizations* 4 (4): 407–33.

Maizels, Alfred, and Machiko K. Nissanke. 1984. Motivations for Aid to Developing Countries. *World Development* 12 (9): 879–900.

Marra, Mita. 2007. How Does Evaluation Foster Accountability for Performance? Tracing Accountability Lines and Evaluation Impact within the World Bank and the Italian Local Health-Care Providers. In *Making Accountability Work: Dilemmas for Evaluation and for Audit*, edited by M.-L. Bemelmans-Videc, J. Lonsdale, and B. Perrin. New Brunswick, N.J.: Transaction Publishers.

Martens, Bertin. 2005. Why Do Aid Agencies Exist? *Development Policy Review* 23 (6): 643–63.

Martens, Bertin, Uwe Mummert, Peter Murrell, and Paul Seabright. 2002. *The Institutional Economics of Foreign Aid*. Cambridge: Cambridge University Press.

Mathews, Jessica T. 1997. Power Shift. *Foreign Affairs* 76 (1): 50–66.

Mathison, Sandra. 1994. Rethinking the Evaluator Role: Partnerships between Organizations and Evaluators. *Evaluation and Program Planning* 17 (3): 299–304.

Mbaku, John M. 1991. Military Expenditures and Bureaucratic Competition for Rents. *Public Choice* 71 (1): 19–31.

McCubbins, Mathew D. 1985. The Legislative Design of Regulatory Structure. *American Journal of Political Science* 29 (4): 721–48.

McCubbins, Mathew D., Roger G. Noll, and Barry R. Weingast. 1987. Administrative Procedures as Instruments of Political Control. *Journal of Law, Economics, and Organization* 3 (2): 243–77.

McCubbins, Mathew D., and Talbot Page. 1987. A Theory of Congressional Delegation. In *Congress: Structure and Policy*, edited by M. D. McCubbins and T. Sullivan. New York: Cambridge University Press.

McCubbins, Mathew D., and T. Schwartz. 1984. Congressional Oversight Overlooked: Police Patrols versus Fire Alarms. *American Journal of Political Science* 28 (1): 165–79.

McDavid, James C., and Laura R. L. Hawthorn. 2006. *Program Evaluation and Performance Measurement: An Introduction to Practice*. Thousand Oaks, Calif.: Sage.

McGill, Eugenia. 2001. The Inspection Policy of the Asian Development Bank. In *The Inspection Panel of the World Bank: A Different Complaints Procedure*, edited by G. Alfredsson and R. Ring. The Hague: Martinus Nijhoff.

McKinley, R.D., and R. Little. 1979. The US Aid Relationship: A Test of the Recipient Need and the Donor Interest Models. *Political Studies* 27 (2): 236–50.

MDG Gap Task Force. 2009. Strengthening the Global Partnership for Development in a Time of Crisis. New York: United Nations.

Mebane, Walter R., and Jasjeet S. Sekhon. 1998. Genetic Optimization Using Derivatives. *Political Analysis* 7 (1): 187–210.

Meier, Kenneth J., and Laurence J. O'Toole Jr. 2006. Political Control versus Bureaucratic Values: Reframing the Debate. *Public Administration Review* 66 (2): 177–92.

Michaelowa, Katharina, and Axel Borrmann. 2006. Evaluation Bias and Incentive Structures in Bi- and Multilateral Aid Agencies. *Review of Development Economics* 10 (2): 313–29.

Miller, C. C., and L. B. Cardinal. 1994. Strategic Planning and Firm Performance: A Synthesis of More Than Two Decades of Research. *Academy of Management Journal* 37 (6): 1649–65.

Miller, Daniel C., Arun Agrawal, and J. Timmons Roberts. 2013. Biodiversity, Governance, and the Allocation of International Aid for Conservation. *Conservation Letters* 6 (1): 12–20.

Miller, Gay Davis. 2001. The Independent Investigation Mechanism of the Inter-American Development Bank. In *The Inspection Panel of the World Bank: A Different Complaints Procedure*, edited by G. Alfredsson and R. Ring. The Hague: Martinus Nijhoff.

Miller, Judith. 2005. Report from Panel Shows Lapses in U.N.'s Oil-for-Food Program. *New York Times*, January 10.

Miller, Marian A. L. 1995. *The Third World in Global Environmental Politics*. Boulder, Colo.: Lynne Rienner.

Milner, Helen V. 2006. Why Multilateralism? Foreign Aid and Domestic Principal-Agent Problems. In *Delegation and Agency in International Organizations*, edited by D. G. Hawkins, D. A. Lake, D. L. Nielson, and M. J. Tierney. Cambridge: Cambridge University Press.

Milner, Helen V., and Dustin Tingley. 2013. The Choice for Multilateralism: Foreign Aid and American Foreign Policy. *Review of International Organizations* 8: 313–41.

Mintzberg, Henry. 1994. *The Rise and Fall of Strategic Planning*. New York: Free Press.

Mitchell, Ronald B., William C. Clark, David W. Cash, and Nancy M. Dickson, eds. 2006. *Global Environmental Assessments: Information and Influence*. Cambridge, Mass.: MIT Press.

Morgenthau, Hans. 1962. A Political Theory of Foreign Aid. *American Political Science Review* 56 (2): 301–9.

Morrison, Kevin M. 2009. Oil, Nontax Revenue, and the Redistributional Foundations of Regime Stability. *International Organization* 63 (1): 107–38.

Morrison, Kevin M. 2011. As the World Bank Turns: Determinants of IDA Lending in the Cold War and After. *Business and Politics* 13 (2).

Morse, Bradford, and Thomas R. Berger. 1992. Sardar Sarovar: Report of the Independent Review. Ottawa: World Bank.

Nelson, Paul J. 1996. Internationalising Economic and Environmental Policy: Transnational NGO Networks and the World Bank's Expanding Influence. *Millennium* 25 (3): 605–33.

Nelson, Paul J. 2001. Transparency Mechanisms at the Multilateral Development Banks. *World Development* 29 (11): 1835–47.

Ness, Gayl D., and Steven R. Brechin. 1988. Bridging the Gap: International Organizations as Organizations. *International Organization* 42 (2): 245–73.

Neumayer, Eric. 2003. The Determinants of Aid Allocation by Regional Multilateral Development Banks and United Nations Agencies. *International Studies Quarterly* 47: 101–22.

Nielsen, Richard A. 2013. Rewarding Human Rights? Selective Aid Sanctions against Repressive States. *International Studies Quarterly* 57 (4): 791–803.

Nielsen, Richard A., Michael G. Findley, Zachary S. Davis, Tara Candland, and Daniel L. Nielson. 2011. Foreign Aid Shocks as a Cause of Violent Armed Conflict. *American Journal of Political Science* 55 (2): 219–32.

Nielson, Daniel L., and Michael J. Tierney. 2003. Delegation to International Organizations: Agency Theory and World Bank Environmental Reforms. *International Organization* 57: 241–76.

Nilakant, V., and Hayagreeva Rao. 1994. Agency Theory and Uncertainty in Organizations: An Evaluation. *Organization Studies* 15 (5): 649–72.

Noël, Alain, and Jean-Philippe Thérien. 1995. From Domestic to International Justice: The Welfare State and Foreign Aid. *International Organization* 49 (3): 523–53.

Norton, Simon D., and L. Murphy Smith. 2008. Contrast and Foundation of the Public Oversight Roles of the U.S. Government Accountability Office and the U.K. National Audit Office. *Public Administration Review* 68 (5): 921–31.

Nunnenkamp, Peter, and Rainer Thiele. 2006. Targeting Aid to the Needy and Deserving: Nothing but Promises? *World Economy* 29 (9): 1177–201.

Nyahti, Nqobile. 2000. Zimbabwe Fails to Repay WB Loan. *Financial Gazette*, May 18.

Nye, Joseph S. 2001. Globalization's Democratic Deficit: How to Make International Institutions More Accountable. *Foreign Affairs* 80 (4): 2–6.

O'Reilly, Charles A., III. 1982. Variations in Decision Makers' Use of Information Sources: The Impact of Quality and Accessibility of Information. *Academy of Management Journal* 25 (4): 756–71.

Office of Evaluation and Oversight. 2009. Country Program Evaluation: Guatemala (2004–2007). Washington, D.C.: Inter-American Development Bank.

Operations Evaluation Department. 1995. Ghana: Country Assistance Review. Washington, D.C.: World Bank.

Operations Evaluation Department. 1998a. Country Assistance Program Evaluation for the People's Republic of China. Manila: Asian Development Bank.

Operations Evaluation Department. 1998b. Project Performance Evaluation Report: Bush Fire Control and Reafforestation Project in the North Eastern Region. Tunis: African Development Bank Group.

Operations Evaluation Department. 2000. Nigeria: Bauchi Township Water Supply Project, Project Performance Evaluation Report. African Development Bank.

Operations Evaluation Department. 2001a. OED Review of the Bank's Performance on the Environment. Washington, D.C.: World Bank.

Operations Evaluation Department. 2001b. Performance Audit Report: Indonesia, Second Jabotabek Urban Development Project (Loan 3219-IND), Semarang-Surakarta Urban Development Project (Loan 3749-IND), Water Supply and Sanitation Project for Low-Income Communities (Loan 3629-IND). Washington, D.C.: World Bank.

Operations Evaluation Department. 2001c. Review of the Performance-Based Allocation System, IDA10-12. Washington, D.C.: World Bank.

Operations Evaluation Department. 2001d. Risk Aversion: Safeguard and Post-conflict Lending. In *Lessons and Practices No. 16*. Washington, D.C.: World Bank.

Operations Evaluation Department. 2003. Country Assistance Program Evaluation for Bangladesh. Manila: Asian Development Bank.

Operations Evaluation Department. 2004. Influential Evaluations: Evaluations That Improved Performance and Impacts of Development Programs. Washington, D.C.: World Bank.

Operations Evaluation Department. 2005a. Country Assistance Evaluation Retrospective: An OED Self-Evaluation. Washington, D.C.: World Bank.

Operations Evaluation Department. 2005b. Improving the World Bank's Development Effectiveness: What Does Evaluation Show? Washington, D.C.: World Bank.

Operations Evaluation Department. 2006. Special Evaluation Study of Environmental Safeguards. Manila: Asian Development Bank.

Operations Evaluation Department. 2007a. Asian Development Bank-Global Environment Facility Cofinanced Projects: Performance and Process Evaluations. Manila: Asian Development Bank.

Operations Evaluation Department. 2007b. Bangladesh: Khulna-Jessore Drainage Rehabilitation Project. *Project Performance Evaluation Report*. Manila: Asian Development Bank.

Operations Evaluation Department. 2007c. Country Assistance Program Evaluation for India. Manila: Asian Development Bank.

Operations Evaluation Department. 2007d. Country Assistant Program Evaluation for Pakistan. Manila: Asian Development Bank.

Operations Evaluation Department. 2007e. Independent Evaluation at the Asian Development Bank. Manila: Asian Development Bank.

Operations Evaluation Department. 2007f. Policy-Based Lending: Emerging Practices in Supporting Reforms in Developing Member Countries. In *Special Evaluation Study*. Manila: Asian Development Bank.

Operations Evaluation Department. 2007g. Special Evaluation Study on Energy Policy 2000 Review: Energy Efficiency for a Better Future. Manila: Asian Development Bank.

Operations Evaluation Department. 2008. Bangladesh: Sundarbans Biodiversity Conservation Project. In *Validation Report*. Manila: Asian Development Bank.

Operations Evaluation Department. 2010. Project Supervision at the African Development Bank 2001–2008: An Independent Evaluation. African Development Bank.

O'Neill, Barry. 2001. Risk Aversion in International Relations Theory. *International Studies Quarterly* 45 (4): 617–40.

Organization for Economic Cooperation and Development. 2011. Aid Effectiveness 2005–10: Progress in Implementing the Paris Declaration. Paris: OECD.

Pallas, Christopher L., and Johannes Urpelainen. 2012. NGO Monitoring and the Legitimacy of International Cooperation: A Strategic Analysis. *Review of International Organizations* 7 (1): 1–32.

Pallas, Christopher L., and Jonathan Wood. 2009. The World Bank's Use of Country Systems for Procurement: A Good Idea Gone Bad? *Development Policy Review* 27 (2): 215–30.

Palmer, Richard. 1990. Funding Halted to Help Preserve Forests. *Sunday Times*, September 30.

Park, Susan. 2005. Norm Diffusion within International Organizations: A Case Study of the World Bank. *Journal of International Relations and Development* 8: 111–41.

Patton, Michael Quinn. 2008. *Utilization-Focused Evaluation*. 4th ed. Los Angeles: Sage.

Paxton, Pamela, and Stephen Knack. 2008. Individual and Country-Level Factors Affecting Support for Foreign Aid. World Bank Policy Research Working Paper 4714.

Pearce, Fred. 1990. Dam in Distress: A Victory for Indian Peasants. *Guardian*, June 29.

Pearce, John A., Elizabeth B. Freeman, and Richard B. Robinson Jr. 1987. The Tenuous Link between Formal Strategic Planning and Financial Performance. *Academy of Management Review* 12 (4): 658–75.

Picciotto, Robert. 2002. Development Cooperation and Performance Evaluation: The Monterrey Challenge. Washington, D.C.: World Bank.

Picciotto, Robert. 2003. The Global Challenge of Development Evaluation. In *World Bank Operations Evaluation Department: The First 30 Years*, edited by P. G. Grasso, S. S. Wasty, and R. V. Weaving. Washington, D.C.: World Bank.

Pietrobelli, Carlo, and Carlo Scarpa. 1992. Inducing Efficiency in the Use of Foreign Aid: The Case for Incentive Mechanisms. *Journal of Development Studies* 29 (1): 72–92.

Pizer, William A. 2006. The Evolution of a Global Climate Change Agreement. *American Economic Review* 96 (2): 26–30.

Poister, Theodore H. 2010. The Future of Strategic Planning in the Public Sector: Linking Strategic Management and Performance. *Public Administration Review* 70: s246–s254.

Pollack, Mark A. 1997. Delegation, Agency, and Agenda Setting in the European Community. *International Organization* 51: 99–134.

Pollack, Mark A., and Emilie Hafner-Burton. 2010. Mainstreaming International Governance: The Environment, Gender, and IO Performance in the European Union. *Review of International Organizations* 5 (3): 285–313.

Potoski, Matthew. 1999. Managing Uncertainty through Bureaucratic Design: Administrative Procedures and State Air Pollution Control Agencies. *Journal of Public Administration Research and Theory* 9 (4): 623–40.

Princen, Thomas, and Matthias Finger. 1994. *Environmental NGOs in World Politics: Linking the Local and the Global.* London: Routledge.

Pritchett, Lant. 2002. It Pays to Be Ignorant: A Simple Political Economy of Rigorous Program Evaluation. *Journal of Policy Reform* 5 (4): 251–69.

Project on Government Oversight. 2009. Inspectors General: Accountability Is a Balancing Act. Washington, D.C.: Project on Government Oversight.

Pronk, Jan P. 2001. Aid as a Catalyst. *Development and Change* 32 (4): 611–29.

Raustiala, Kal. 1997. States, NGOs, and International Environmental Institutions. *International Studies Quarterly* 41: 719–40.

Redfern, Paul. 2000. World Bank to Back Away from Big Dams. *Nation*, November 23.

Reinalda, Bob, and Bertjan Verbeek. 2004. The Issue of Decision Making within International Organizations. In *Decision Making within International Organizations*, edited by B. Reinalda and B. Verbeek. London: Routledge.

Reinisch, August. 2001. Securing the Accountability of International Organizations. *Global Governance* 7: 131–49.

Resh, William G., and David W. Pitts. 2013. No Solutions, Only Trade-Offs? Evidence about Goal Conflict in Street-Level Bureaucracies. *Public Administration Review* 73 (1): 132–42.

Rice, Xan. 2010. Ethiopia's Rush to Build Mega Dams Sparks Protests. *Guardian*, March 25.

Rich, Bruce. 1990. The Emperor's New Clothes: The World Bank and Environmental Reform. *World Policy Journal* 7 (2): 305–29.

Rich, Bruce. 1994. *Mortgaging the Earth: The World Bank, Environmental Impoverishment, and the Crisis of Development.* Boston: Beacon Press.

Rich, Bruce. 2013. *Foreclosing the Future: The World Bank and the Politics of Environmental Destruction.* Washington, D.C.: Island Press.

Riger, Stephanie, and Susan L. Staggs. 2011. A Nationwide Survey of State-Mandated Evaluation Practices for Domestic Violence Agencies. *Journal of Interpersonal Violence* 26 (1): 50–70.

Ringquist, Evan J. 1995. Political Control and Policy Impact in EPA's Office of Water Quality. *American Journal of Political Science* 39 (2): 336–63.

Roberts, Kenneth M. 2008. The Mobilization of Opposition to Economic Liberalization. *Annual Review of Political Science* 11 (1): 327–49.

Rothman, Franklin Daniel, and Pamela E. Oliver. 1999. From Local to Global: The Anti-dam Movement in Southern Brazil, 1979–1992. *Mobilization* 4 (1): 41–57.

Rowat, Colin, and Paul Seabright. 2006. Intermediation by Aid Agencies. *Journal of Development Economics* 79 (2): 469–91.

Rubin, Donald B. 1973. Matching to Remove Bias in Observational Studies. *Biometrics* 29 (1): 159–83.

Rubin, Donald B. 1973. The Use of Matched Sampling and Regression Adjustment to Remove Bias in Observational Studies. *Biometrics* 29 (1): 185–203.

Rubin, Donald B. 1979. Using Multivariate Matched Sampling and Regression Adjustment to Control Bias in Observational Studies. *Journal of the American Statistical Association* 74 (366): 318–28.

Rubin, Donald B., and Neal Thomas. 1996. Matching Using Estimated Propensity Scores: Relating Theory to Practice. *Biometrics* 52 (1): 249–64.

Sabatier, Paul A., and John Loomis. 1995. Hierarchical Controls, Professional Norms, Local Constituencies, and Budget Maximization: An Analysis of U.S. Forest Service Planning Decisions. *American Journal of Political Science* 39 (1): 204–42.

US House of Representatives. 1989. Subcommittee on Natural Resources, Agriculture Research and Environment Committee on Science, Space, and Technology *Sardar Sarovar Dam Project*. October 24.

SARI/Energy, Nexant. 2002. Regional Hydro-Power Resources: Status of Development and Barriers. Prepared for USAID-SARI/Energy Program.

Schelling, Thomas C. 1955. Review: American Foreign Assistance. *World Politics* 7 (4): 606–26.

Schneider, Christina J., and Jennifer L. Tobin. 2013. Interest Coalitions and Multilateral Aid Allocation in the European Union. *International Studies Quarterly* 57 (1): 103–14.

Schraeder, Peter J., Steven W. Hook, and Bruce Taylor. 1998. Clarifying the Foreign Aid Puzzle: A Comparison of American, Japanese, French, and Swedish Aid Flows. *World Politics* 50 (2): 294–323.

Schreurs, Miranda A., and Yves Tiberghien. 2007. Multi-level Reinforcement: Explaining European Union Leadership in Climate Change Mitigation. *Global Environmental Politics* 7 (4): 19–46.

Schwartz, Robert, and John Mayne. 2005. Assuring the Quality of Evaluation Information: Theory and Practice. *Evaluation and Program Planning* 28 (1): 1–14.

Schwartzman, S. 1985. Bankrolling Disasters: International Development Banks and the Global Environment: A Citizen's Guide to the Multilateral Development Bank. Washington, D.C.: Sierra Club.

Seawright, Jason, and John Gerring. 2008. Case Selection Techniques in Case Study Research a Menu of Qualitative and Quantitative Options. *Political Research Quarterly* 61 (2): 294–308.

Seith, Anne. 2009. G-8 Summit in the Rubble. *Spiegel Online*.

Sekhon, Jasjeet S. 2007. Multivariate and Propensity Score Matching Software With Automated Balance Optimization: The Matching Package for R. *Journal of Statistical Software* 42 (7): 1–52.

Sekhon, Jasjeet S., and Richard Grieve. 2008. A New Non-parametric Matching Method for Bias Adjustment with Applications to Economic Evaluations. University of California, Berkeley.

Selden, Thomas M., and Daqing Song. 1994. Environmental Quality and Development: Is There a Kuznets Curve for Air Pollution Emissions? *Journal of Environmental Economics and Management* 27: 147–62.

Selin, Noelle Eckley. 2006. From Regional to Global Information: Assessment of Persistent Organic Pollutants. In *Global Environmental Assessments: Information and Influence*, edited by R. B. Mitchell, W. C. Clark, D. W. Cash, and N. M. Dickson. Cambridge, Mass.: MIT Press.

Sell, Susan. 1996. North-South Environmental Bargaining: Ozone, Climate Change, and Biodiversity. *Global Governance* 2: 97–118.

Serra, Teresa, Mark Segal, and Ram Chopra. 2011. The Project Is Prepared. In *Doing a Dam Better: The Lao People's Democratic Republic and the Story of Nam Theun 2*, edited by I. C. Porter and J. Shivakumar. Washington, D.C.: International Bank for Reconstruction and Development / World Bank.

Sexton, Jennifer. 1996a. Massive Power Project in Laos Becomes Dam-Site Complicated. *Australian Financial Review*, June 25, 10.

Sexton, Jennifer. 1996b. Thai Authority Jeopardises $1.52bn Transfield Dam. *Australian Financial Review*, October 2.

Shabecoff, Philip. 1990. U.S. Backs World Bank Environment Unit. *New York Times*, November 30, 2.

Shihata, Ibrahim F. I. 2000. *The World Bank Inspection Panel: In Practice*. Oxford: Oxford University Press.

Simmons, Beth A., and Daniel J. Hopkins. 2005. The Constraining Power of International Treaties: Theory and Methods. *American Political Science Review* 99 (4): 623–31.

Simmons, P. J. 1998. Learning to Live with NGOs. *Foreign Policy* 112: 82–96.

Steelman, Toddi A. 1999. The Public Comment Process: What Do Citizens Contribute to National Forest Management? *Journal of Forestry* 97 (1): 22–26.

Steffek, Jens, and Maria Paola Ferretti. 2009. Accountability or "Good Decisions"? The Competing Goals of Civil Society Participation in International Governance. *Global Society* 23 (1): 37–57.

Stem, Caroline, Richard Margoluis, Nick Salafsky, and Marcia Brown. 2005. Monitoring and Evaluation in Conservation: A Review of Trends and Approaches. *Conservation Biology* 19 (2): 295–309.

Stone, Randall W. 2011. *Controlling Institutions: International Organizations and the Global Economy*. Cambridge: Cambridge University Press.

Storey, John, and Elizabeth Barnett. 2000. Knowledge Management Initiatives: Learning from Failure. *Journal of Knowledge Management* 4 (2): 145–56.

Streck, Charlotte. 2004. New Partnerships in Global Environmental Policy: The Clean Development Mechanism. *Journal of Environment and Development* 13 (3): 295–322.

Stutzer, Alois, and Bruno S. Frey. 2005. Making International Organizations More Democratic. *Review of Law and Economics* 1 (3): 305–30.

Sustainable Development Department. 2002. *Facing the Challenges of Sustainable Development: The IDB and the Environment, 1992–2002*. Washington, D.C.: Inter-American Development Bank.

Svensson, Jakob. 2000. When Is Foreign Aid Policy Credible? Aid Dependence and Conditionality. *Journal of Development Economics* 61: 61–84.

Svensson, Jakob. 2003. Why Conditional Aid Does Not Work and What Can Be Done about It. *Journal of Development Economics* 70: 381–402.

Talley, Ian. 2015. Obama: We're All for the Asian Infrastructure Development Bank. *Wall Street Journal*, April 28.

Teddlie, Charles, and Fen Yu. 2007. Mixed Methods Sampling a Typology with Examples. *Journal of Mixed Methods Research* 1 (1): 77–100.

Teodoro, Manuel P. 2011. *Bureaucratic Ambition: Careers, Motives, and the Innovative Administrator*. Baltimore: Johns Hopkins University Press.

Thiele, Rainer, Peter Nunnenkamp, and Axel Dreher. 2007. Do Donors Target Aid in Line with the Millennium Development Goals? A Sector Perspective of Aid Allocation. *Review of World Economics* 143 (4): 596–630.

Thomas, Christopher. 1991. Peasants March to Halt Gujarat Dam. *Times*, January 9.

Thornton, Nigel. 2010. Realising Development Effectiveness: Making the Most of Climate Change Finance in Asia and the Pacific. Asia Pacific Climate Change Finance and Aid Effectiveness Dialogue, Capacity Development for Development Effectiveness Facility.

Tierney, Michael J., Daniel L. Nielson, Darren G. Hawkins, J. Timmons Roberts, Michael G. Findley, Ryan M. Powers, Bradley Parks, Sven E. Wilson, and Robert L. Hicks. 2011. More Dollars Than Sense: Refining Our Knowledge of Development Finance Using AidData. *World Development* 39 (11): 1891–906.

Torello, Alessandro, and Selina Williams. 2009. Developing Nations Call for Rich to Aid Emissions Cuts. *Wall Street Journal*, December 9.

Torode, Greg. 1996. Bank under Pressure to Back Controversial Dam. *South China Morning Post*, November 18, 13.

Torras, Mariano, and James K. Boyce. 1998. Income, Inequality, and Pollution: A Reassessment of the Environmental Kuznets Curve. *Ecological Economics* 25 (2): 147–60.

Torres, Rosalie T., and Hallie Preskill. 2001. Evaluation and Organizational Learning: Past, Present, and Future. *American Journal of Evaluation* 22 (3): 387–95.

Treakle, Kay, Jonathan A. Fox, and Dana Clark. 2003. Lessons Learned. In *Demanding Accountability: Civil Society Claims and the World Bank Inspection Panel*, edited by D. Clark, J. A. Fox, and K. Treakle. Lanham, Md.: Rowman & Littlefield.

Turmbull, William N., and Howard J. Wall. 1994. Estimating Aid-Allocation Criteria with Panel Data. *Economic Journal* 104: 876–82.

Turnham, David. 1991. Multilateral Development Banks and Environmental Management. *Public Administration and Development* 11: 363–79.

Udall, Lori. 1995. Arun III Hydroelectric Project in Nepal: Another World Bank Debacle? International Rivers Network.

Uphoff, Norman. 1992. Monitoring and Evaluating Popular Participation in World Bank-Assisted Projects. In *Participatory Development and the World Bank: Potential Directions for Change*, edited by B. Bhatnagar and A. C. Williams. Washington, D.C.: World Bank.

US Department of State. 2010. *U.S. Climate Action Report*. Washington, D.C.: Global Publishing Service.

US House of Representatives. 1984. Subcommittee on International Development Institutions and Finance Committee on Banking, Finance and Urban Affairs. U.S. Participation in the International Development Association: Seventh Replenishment. 2nd Session.

US Senate, Foreign Operations Subcommittee, Senate Appropriations Committee. 1990. World Bank Fiscal Year 1991 Appropriations.

van der Knaap, Peter. 2007. Results-Oriented Budgeting and Policy Evaluation: Accountable for Learning. In *Making Accountability Work: Dilemmas for Evaluation and for Audit*, edited by M.-L. Bemelmans-Videc, J. Lonsdale, and B. Perrin. New Brunswick, N.J.: Transaction Publishers.

Van Heerde, Jennifer, and David Hudson. 2010. "The Righteous Considereth the Cause of the Poor"? Public Attitudes towards Poverty in Developing Countries. *Political Studies* 58 (3): 389–409.

van Ufford, Philip Quarles, Dirk Kruijt, and Theodore E. Downing, eds. 1988. *The Hidden Crisis in Development: Development Bureaucracies*. Tokyo: United Nations University.

Vanlandingham, G. R. 2011. Escaping the Dusty Shelf: Legislative Evaluation Offices' Efforts to Promote Utilization. *American Journal of Evaluation* 32 (1): 85–97.

Vaubel, Roland. 1996. Bureaucracy at the IMF and the World Bank: A Comparison of the Evidence. *World Economy* 19 (2): 195–210.

Vaubel, Roland. 2006. Principal-Agent Problems in International Organizations. *Review of International Organizations* 1 (2): 125–38.

Vaubel, Roland, Axel Dreher, and Uğurlu Soylu. 2007. Staff Growth in International Organizations: A Principal-Agent Problem? An Empirical Analysis. *Public Choice* 133 (3-4): 275–95.

Vengroff, Richard, and Alan Johnston. 1989. *Decentralization and the Implementation of Rural Development in Senegal: The View from Below*. Lewiston, N.Y.: Edwin Mellen Press.

Villadsen, Anders R. 2012. New Executives from Inside or Outside? The Effect of Executive Replacement on Organizational Change. *Public Administration Review* 72 (5): 731–40.

Vreeland, James. 2006. IMF Program Compliance: Aggregate Index versus Policy Specific Research Strategies. *Review of International Organizations* 1 (4): 359–78.

Wade, Robert. 1997. Greening the Bank: The Struggle over the Environment, 1970–1995. In *The World Bank: Its First Half Century*, vol. 2: *Perspectives*, edited by D. Kapur, J. P. Lewis, and R. Wedd. Washington, D.C.: Brookings Institution.

Wapenhans, W. 1992. Effective Implementation: Key to Development Impact. Washington, D.C.: World Bank.

Waterman, Richard W., and Kenneth J. Meier. 1998. Principal-Agent Models: An Expansion? *Journal of Public Administration Research and Theory* 8 (2): 173–202.

Water Power and Dam Construction. 1998. EGAT Postpones Hydro Power Purchases from Laos. December 22, 8.

Weaver, Catherine. 2007. The World's Bank and the Bank's World. *Global Governance* 13: 493–512.

Weaver, Catherine. 2008. *Hypocrisy Trap: The World Bank and the Poverty of Reform*. Princeton, N.J.: Princeton University Press.

Weaver, Catherine. 2010. The Politics of Performance Evaluation: Independent Evaluation at the International Monetary Fund. *Review of International Organizations* 5 (3): 365–85.

Weaver, Catherine, and Ralf J. Leteritz. 2005. "Our Poverty Is a World Full of Dreams": Reforming the World Bank. *Global Governance* 11: 369–88.

Weingast, Barry R., and Mark J. Moran. 1983. Bureaucratic Discretion or Congressional Control? Regulatory Policymaking by the Federal Trade Commission. *Journal of Political Economy* 91 (5): 765–800.

Weiss, Carol H. 1973. Where Politics and Evaluation Meet. *Evaluation* 1 (3): 37–45.

Weiss, Carol H. 1988. Evaluation for Decisions: Is Anybody There? Does Anybody Care? *Evaluation Practice* 9 (1): 5–19.

Weiss, Carol H. 1998. Have We Learned Anything New about the Use of Evaluation? *American Journal of Evaluation* 19 (1): 21–33.

Wenar, Leif. 2006. Accountability in International Development Aid. *Ethics and International Affairs* 20 (1): 1–23.

Werksman, Jacob. 2009. From Coercive Conditionality to Agreed Conditions: The Only Future for Future Climate Finance. In *Climate Finance: Regulatory and Funding Strategies for Climate Change and Global Development*, edited by R. B. Stewart, B. Kingsbury, and B. Rudyk. New York: New York University Press.

Wilks, Stephen. 2005. Agency Escape: Decentralization or Dominance of the European Commission in the Modernization of Competition Policy? *Governance* 18 (3): 431–52.

Williams, Marc. 2005. The Third World and Global Environmental Negotiations: Interests, Institutions, and Ideas. *Global Environmental Politics* 5 (3): 48–69.

Wilson, Sven E. 2011. Chasing Success: Health Sector Aid and Mortality. *World Development* 39 (11): 2032–43.

Winters, Matthew S. 2014. Targeting, Accountability and Capture in Development Projects. *International Studies Quarterly* 58 (2): 393–404.

Wood, C. Tyler. 1959. Problems of Foreign Aid Viewed from the Inside. *American Economic Review* 49 (2): 203–15.

Woods, Ngaire. 2001. Making the IMF and the World Bank More Accountable. *International Affairs* 77 (1): 83–100.

Woods, Ngaire, and Amrita Narlikar. 2001. Governance and the Limits of Accountability: The WTO, the IMF, and the World Bank. *International Social Science Journal* 53 (170): 569–83.

Woolcock, Michael. 2009. Toward a Plurality of Methods in Project Evaluation: A Contextualized Approach to Understanding Impact Trajectories and Efficacy. *Journal of Development Effectiveness* 1 (1): 1–14.

Working Party on Aid Effectiveness. 2008. Aid Effectiveness: A Progress Report on Implementing the Paris Declaration. Accra, Ghana: 3rd High Level Forum on Aid Effectiveness.

World Bank. 1989. Staff Appraisal Report: Arun III Access Road Project. Washington, D.C.: World Bank.

World Bank. 1991. Environmental Assessment Sourcebook. World Bank Technical Paper 0253-7494. Washington, D.C.: World Bank.

World Bank. 1992. World Development Report 1992: Development and the Environment. Washington, D.C.: World Bank.

World Bank. 1993a. Annual Review of Environmental Assessment 1992. Washington, D.C.: World Bank.

World Bank. 1993b. Environmental Assessment Sourcebook Update. Washington, D.C.: World Bank.

World Bank. 1993c. Staff Appraisal Report: Water Supply and Sanitation for Low Income Communities Project. Washington, D.C.: World Bank.

World Bank. 1996. Memorandum of the President of the International Development Association to the Executive Directors on a Country Assistance Strategy of the World Bank Group for Nepal. Washington, D.C.: World Bank.

World Bank. 1997. The Impact of Environmental Assessment. Washington, D.C.: World Bank.

World Bank. 1999. *Environmental Assessment Sourcebook*. Washington, D.C.: World Bank.

World Bank. 2000. Implementation Completion Report: Water Supply and Sanitation for Low Income Communities Project. Washington, D.C.: World Bank.

World Bank. 2001. Cost of Doing Business: Fiduciary and Safeguard Policies and Compliance. Washington, D.C.: World Bank.

World Bank. 2003a. Project Appraisal Document: Nepal Power Development Project. Washington, D.C.: World Bank.

World Bank. 2003b. Water Resources Sector Strategy: Strategic Directions for World Bank Engagement. Washington, D.C.: World Bank.

World Bank. 2005. Lao PDR, One of the Poorest Countries in East Asia, Receives Support for the Long Term. Washington, D.C.: World Bank.

World Bank. 2007a. Environment Matters at the World Bank: 2007 Annual Report. Washington, D.C.: World Bank.

World Bank. 2007b. Global Public Goods: A Framework for the Role of the World Bank. Washington, D.C.: World Bank.

World Bank. 2009a. Country Assistance Strategies: Retrospective and Future Directions. Washington, D.C.: World Bank.

World Bank. 2009b. Directions in Hydropower: Scaling Up for Development. In *Water Working Notes*. Washington, D.C.: World Bank.

World Bank. 2010. IDA at Work: Environment and Natural Resources Management. Washington, D.C.: World Bank.

World Bank. 2012. The World Bank's Approach to Public Sector Management 2011–2020: Better Results from Public Sector Institutions. Washington, D.C.: World Bank.

World Health Organization. 2012. Report of the External Auditor. World Health Organization.

Wright, Joseph. 2010. Aid Effectiveness and the Politics of Personalism. *Comparative Political Studies* 43 (6): 735–62.

Wright, Joseph, and Matthew Winters. 2010. The Politics of Effective Foreign Aid. *Annual Review of Political Science* 13: 61–80.

Wurfel, David. 1959. Foreign Aid and Social Reform in Political Development: A Philippine Case Study. *American Political Science Review* 53 (2): 456–82.

Young, Oran R., and Marc Levy. 1999. The Effectiveness of International Environmental Regimes. In *The Effectiveness of International Environmental Regimes: Causal Connections and Behavioral Mechanisms*, edited by O. R. Young. Cambridge, Mass.: MIT Press.

INDEX

Abdication hypothesis, 63

Accountability mechanisms, 22, 24, 110–41, 220–24; catalyst for, 111; defined, 61; importance of, 112; main reason for lack of, 114; organizational constraints imposed by, 118–19; principal-agent framework on, 60–61; sanctions and, 114, 221. *See also* Civil society groups; Inspection Panels

ADB. *See* Asian Development Bank

Administrative procedures, 2, 23–24, 68–109; controlling discretion with, 58, 76–77; impact of, 218–20; modeling of, 89–101; principal-agent framework on, 58–59; staff incentives and, 81–89

AFDB. *See* African Development Bank

Afghanistan, 52

Africa, 215, 225

African Development Bank (AFDB), 7, 43, 53, 127, 248n2; allocation decision process at, 39; approval imperative and, 18; Bauchi Township Water Supply Project, 69; Bushfire Control and Reafforestation project, 159–61; civil society groups and, 141; country program evaluations and, 186, 193, 193(figure), 194–95, 195(table), 199, 203, 205, 208–9, 239; Department of Planning and Research, 245;

Environmental Assessment Guidelines, 75; environmentally risky projects and, 69, 89, 90(figure), 251n18; environment-improving projects and, 159–61, 169, 177–80; Evaluation Division, 245–46; Gebay III Hydropower Project, 139; Inspection Panels and, 139; Livestock Support Project II, 160–61; Operations Evaluation Department, 246; Operations Evaluation Office, 246; Ordinary Capital Reserves, 169; project evaluations and, 143, 148, 149(figure), 164, 177–80, 235, 245–46; safeguard policies and, 72, 75, 82, 91, 94(figure), 99–100, 103–5; Safeguard Unit, 103

African Development Fund (AFDF), 169

Agency slack, 8

Agenda 21, 230

Agent shirking, 62, 106, 143

AidData database, 17, 73, 166–67, 201, 205

Air pollution, 168, 173(table), 174(table)

Albania, 136–37

Allocation: decision process and, 38–45, 39(figure); early research on, 28–30; of environmentally risky projects, 89–91, 95, 96, 100–101, 100(table), 131–33; of environment-improving projects,